THE LIFE AND SINS OF A CROFTER'S SON

North Highland Publishing Ltd
Craigmore
Reay
Caithness
KW14

www.northhighlandpublishing.com

North Highland Publishing

The True North

This paperback edition
1

First Published in Great Britain by
North Highland Publishing Ltd 2011

Available as a paper back from:
www.hughmatheson.co.uk

Cover design by Gillian Frampton

Hugh Matheson asserts the moral right to be identified as the author of this work

A catalogue record of this book is available from the British Library

ISBN: 978-1-908622-03-7

THE   LIFE AND SINS OF A CROFTER'S SON

By

HUGH   MACDONELL MATHESON

Wester Gruinards and Strathcarron

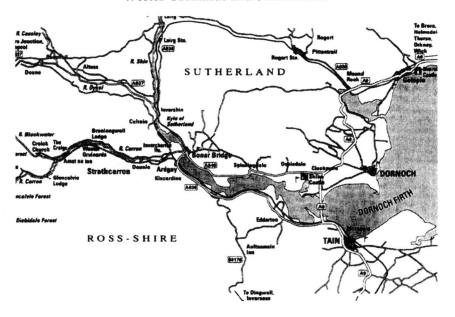

Dedication

To Marjory

Her scroll on the kitchen wall says

"When I married Mr Right I didn't know his first name was Always."

To Noel

A loyal and trusted brother.

To Eric Shepherd

He talked I listened but the very best.

To Andy

The life and soul of the party.

Table of Contents

Part Four – Coming Home

Annex 1 Colour images

ACKNOWLEDGEMENTS

My Mam and Dad taught me to always say please and thank you so I will first say thank you to both of them for bringing me into this world and perhaps somewhere up there this message will reach you.

To Marjory I say a big thank you for your tolerance in sticking with me for all those years and having to put up with my warped sense of humour, my so often ungratefulness and for being on another planet half the time. I have never been renowned for dishing out compliments but do not know the reason why, when within me I know I should. So for that failure please forgive me.

Over the years many visitors to Gruinard Estate suggested I should write a book on the history of my life but dismissed it immediately until Charlie McNeil, Achany, Lairg influenced me into doing so. To him for his doggedness in pushing me to get started I have to thank him, otherwise it probably would not have began.

The bulk of it has been written from my own memories but others who have helped in one way or another I must express my gratitude to them as well. They are Catriona, Fiona, my own family, the Shepherd family and in no particular order, Billy Dunbar, Bunty Gordon, Norman Macdonald, George and Elsie Ross, Ronnie Ross, Findlay Munro, David Henderson, Derek and Kate Matheson, Al and Elaine Munro, Russell Walker–Smith and the wizard with a computer paint brush, Geordie Gunn. The List is endless and I could go on and on but for all of you not specifically mentioned my appreciation is extended to you all as well, if only for the cups of tea or coffee I have enjoyed in your welcoming homes.

The writing of the transcript has been the easy bit and I have thought long and hard who I would choose to publish it. After much deliberation I kept returning to the Web Site for North Highland Publishing Ltd. To me it had the most appeal so I contacted Roy Kirk, and he set the ball rolling. With his good lady Elizabeth and his daughter Cara it gained momentum by the day. I cannot thank them all enough for their advice and guidance in the preparation and design of the finished article, which requires the professionalism that they gave.

No book would look right without a good and appealing cover and for this I have to thank Gillian Frampton for her expertise in this field.

FOREWORD

All who know and care for the Highlands will recognise the quality of Hugh Matheson's book, "The Life and Sins of a Crofter's Son".

It is a success at a number of levels. Firstly in accurately recording a way of life that has been very typical of the counties of Ross-shire and Sutherland – but is as completely different to life further south as it is possible to imagine.

Additionally this book gives a colourful account of a most interesting career both in and outside the Highlands. Perhaps it is the sheer breadth of Hugh Matheson's experience that has given him the special gift of being able to pick out some of the colours and contrasts that make up the fabric of this country.

Very possibly the use of the word "Sins" in the book's title is a first reference to the candour with which Hugh writes. Nevertheless that is exactly how life is: people come in all shapes and sizes – and not all are as kind and well behaved as they should be. Not that a suggestion of a lack of kindness could be laid at Hugh's literary door – for his candour is more than balanced by generosity. Readers will see this for themselves when they encounter characters that they themselves know, or have known.

Lastly this splendid book is a full and proper record of Hugh's deep and abiding knowledge of nature. If there were no other reasons (and there are!) then for this reason alone "The Life and Sins of a Crofter's Son" will be read and enjoyed for many years to come. It is a great achievement. Hugh has done the Highlands a great honour.

Jamie Stone, Columnist and former Member of the Scottish Parliament for Caithness, Sutherland and Easter Ross - 1999 to 2011

INTRODUCTION

It was never a dream of mine to write a book and not for one minute did I ever think I would end up doing so. My father was a born story teller and I think I must have inherited some of that trait. I would put my brother Noel in the same category and I often heard his two sons, John and Derek make the remark in a nice way, "Here is Dad with another of his mouldy old stories." What else was there to do with friends by the fireside on the long dark nights of winter.

Guests, who I was privileged to meet, coming to Gruinard to fish or shoot were very interested in my life story and many of them suggested I should write a book on it. One of them a Sheriff from the Central Belt of Scotland asked me where I came from. I said, "I was born in that old house behind you and then moved over there." In reply he said, "You have not travelled very far then." "No" I said. "But I may have probably seen more of the seedier side of life than you have."

About two years ago a friend brought the subject up several times and on each occasion asking if I had started it. After much prompting by him and others I said to my self, "Why not?" and began to put pen to paper. It may not be a master piece in the literary sense but in its non flamboyant down to earth way it should be easy, interesting and in some parts humourous reading, not only for family and friends but to a much wider readership.

I grew up as the second youngest of a family of eight with my parents who were far from well off, managing to scratch an honest living from the croft, the land and river. The opportunity to learn was there where teachings from the age of five were very much on a one to one basis. It was also available again through secondary schooling but I was not interested, instead longing for the day I would leave. Work in a remote glen was limited and I was gratefull to my father for employing me until I was eighteen years old but my horizons went beyond that. Hair brain schemes never materialised but the four years that followed took me to Germany, Holland, Belguim and Denmark, returning to the North East of Scotland where on demob I joined the local police force, serving at many stations. During this time I met and married Marjory who gave me two lovely daughters in every respect, and marrying into a family not that much different to my own.

Times of hardness financially forced us to take the huge step to the London Metropolis where we stayed and worked for fourteen and a half years but the yearning to return to Scotland was never far away. Unfortunately the untimely death of my brother Noel brought me back to my grass roots, a rural way of life where combined with my job I was able to pursue the sporting activities I had learned and loved in earier years. Some may not have been with the blessing of the actual owners but there was always a way round it if only a nod and a wink from others in between. From the time we bought our first house, DIY was to take up much of my time but was always seen as an investment. To sum that part of my life up I could be described as a "Jack of all trades but a master of none." However, for my involvement in four houses that stand testament to my work it was nice sometimes to be referred to as the "Clerk of Works" and not just the labourer. My pointer and setter dogs took me to many grouse moors as far north as Melvick and south to the borders of England giving me the opportunity to view the landscapes well beyond the roadsides and to meet so many interesting fellow dog handlers and other people on the way.

Fortunately my five grandchildren live reasonably close by and in spite of all their after school activities are able to spend days or the odd weekend at Dalriada. No price can be put on the joy that I have had in watching them grow up but one cannot escape thinking of what lies ahead for them in this fast track world we live in. I can only pray that they will be blessed with a life as good as or even better than the one I have had. In the meantime continue to entertain us all with your mini concerts and so much more.

I invite you to read on and discover the life and times that brought so much joy and happiness to me and I hope a smile and understanding to you.

PART ONE

EARLY DAYS

CHAPTER 1

CHILDHOOD AND EARLY MEMORIES

Born the son of a crofter on 11th April, 1935 at Wester Gruinards, Strathcarron, Ardgay, Ross-shire, Scotland a somewhat insignificant address but only a few miles up the strath stands the highly renowned building of Croick Church, known throughout the world for its connection with the Highland Clearances. Little would be known of this was it not for the etchings on one of its windows stating that the people of Glencalvie during the Highland Clearances took shelter in the churchyard after their homes were burned down. Since then many books, articles and even a dissertation by my daughter Fiona have been written about it with historians and authors living off the backs of the peoples grief ever since. Highland folk still harp on about the clearances but my honest opinion, although I do not endorse the methods use, is that a lot of them because of their meagre existence would have died of starvation or poor health anyway. The spelling of gaelic words particularly place names have forever been changing and the "s" at the end of Gruinard as far as I know should only apply to Wester Gruinards as in Greenyards which was the way it has sometimes been spelt in the past. Later on I write about Sgodachail where we once lived but again the spelling is different from Scuitchal or Scuittechaell dating back to 1642. The pronounciation, as if it was spelt skootchall, is more in keeping with those two spellings as well, meaning small farm or part of one.

In my youthful years this church was our place of worship. Prior to my arrival into this world my sister Morag tells me that the family would travel up to Croick in one or other of the horse "spring carts" driven by my father and grandfather, Morag preferring grandfather's because of the better seating. Both my parents are buried there as are other members of my family. I don't know the reason for it but I was not christened as a baby at the church. Ernest, Anne and I were all christened on the same day in the house at Sgodachail. I remember it fine with Mr Craig the minister arriving and all three of us lined up in the living room come kitchen in awe of what was to take place. It has crossed my mind several times since but the finer details are long gone. Did the water come from the burn or did the Minister take it with him? What utensil was used? Sunday school classes were held weekly at Croick School with Nina Craig and John Ross (Pecka) as teachers. The Pecka had a little green van at the time and he would take up some of the Munro children with him. On week days each morning we had to recite an entry from the catechism book. When older we went to bible classes held at the Mission Hall up at The Craigs where Pilgrims came to teach Christianity and hand out free bibles. It was what our parents believed in and this indoctrination was so deep seated that it has remained with me ever since, not that I abide by all I was taught. Sunday was a day of rest and strictly adhered to with only the essentials being done. My father would sit by the fire and read the bible and sing hymns or psalms, his favourite being the Lord's My Shepherd. If we were not at church ourselves we were not allowed out to play, more so when other families were going to or from the church. If we saw the minister arriving at the house us kids would climb out through the little window of Mam and Dad's bedroom and keep out of sight until he went away. Changed times now though but for better or worse you can make up your own minds.

My earliest memory goes back to when I was only 2 years old. This was the day when we flitted out of Wester Gruinards across the river to Sgodachail on Braelangwell Estate. I distinctly remember my mother pushing the pram with Ernest, the baby lying in it and me sitting on the end of it next to her, with my sister Joan walking along beside us. I do not recall what my thoughts were at the time; only looking back at the home we had just left. My mother took the easier route via the footbridge over the river at Croick School. My father and older brothers took the horse and cart with our belongings and probably the few sticks of furniture we had up round Coneas Bridge where the road crossed the river Carron. In the evening the cows were driven through the river at the ford below our house to return to the croft for grazing each day. At such a tender age the move must have created a huge impression on my tiny brain for it to remain so vividly ever since. The same year I remember travelling down to Ardgay in a large vehicle owned by Amat Estate to the Coronation Celebrations for King George VI and coming home with a commemorative mug of the occasion.

Our two goats were left behind to look after themselves which they were more than capable of doing or as we thought. A few years later, "Blacky" the nanny whilst browsing for young shoots and leaves, unfortunately got hung up and died in a forked branch of a tree down by the riverside. The other one was a large white billy. He was a dirty smelly brute and got so dangerous that he had to be put down, probably shot. On one occasion my sister Anne and I were walking home from our granny's carrying a stone of oatmeal which my mother bought from the grocery van when the billy chased us to get at the meal. We climbed over some wooden fencing by the footbridge at the school to get away from him but we ended up feeding him most of the meal before he would leave us alone. For no reason at all, he would chase us indoors and then stay there boxing at the door with his huge horns. The only thing he was frightened of was the collie dogs. If you set them on him they would really get stuck into him and see him off, but he would always come back for more at some other time.

It was not just the goats they were good at sending off. Most crofters' collies did not like the tinkers, a term you do not often hear used today, and we would set the dogs on them as well. One crowd of them came down from Caithness and they were reckoned to be a bad lot. I think they were called McPhee's and they would steal anything they could lay their hands on. With my father working away from home a lot of the time my mother was terrified at the sight of them and would gather us bairns together and take off up the hill and hide until they went away. When I was older I came home just by chance to find some of them sitting in the lobby and demanding tea and food from my mother. Others were raking about outside to see what they could find to steal. Straight away I went to the stable and let about three or four collie dogs out and boy did the tinkers run for it. Today we would be charged with keeping dangerous dogs or with assault, but all they were doing was protecting us.

My mother, both at Wester Gruinards and Sgodachail, cooked on an open fire in the grate, soups and stews with tatties boiled in their skins. The skins, not eaten by us as they are today, but were mixed with oatmeal or flake maize and fed to either the hens or dogs. The scones, oatcakes and pancakes were baked on a girdle and I cannot remember her using scales to weigh anything, just a bit of this and a drop of that. The kettle was boiled by hanging it on a hook suspended from a crossbar up the chimney. The kettle was never very far off the boil in readiness for the cups of tea we often had throughout the day. Visitors, usually glen folk always sat down with us to tea and baking at the table. It was a time when news of the happenings in the locality or further afield was exchanged, gossip I suppose you could say. In the summer time if there was not much of a fire on Mam would nip into the little birch wood beside our house and gather up some birch twigs from the many dead branches lying about, place a couple of iron bars across the grate and have the kettle boiling in a jiffy. There was an oven at the side of the grate in which she would bake our cakes or make rice pudding in a white enamel dish that was used for that purpose only. No food was ever wasted and nobody said, "I don't like that." You just had to eat what was put in front of you or go without. The grate was common in houses of that erra and they were far from the most efficient available. The fuel just blazed away with most of the heat going up the chimney. Even in the winter months' birch logs were brought into the house with ice and snow still attached and you had to keep putting them on the fire as they sizzled, spitted and burned away so quickly.

Thinking about the oven, the door from the one left behind at Wester Gruinards now adorns the sitting room wall of a home in Hampshire. Although I have not seen it for a long time I'm sure it is well polished with the same type of black enamel my Mam and other mothers used on their stoves sometimes called a range and looked after with the same pride with the bare steel parts kept shiny with regular efforts of elbow grease and emery paper. Many years later at Gruinard Noel installed a solid fuel Raeburn stove which heated the water as well, all in all a far better piece of equipment.

Breakfast always began with porridge but sometimes I would have brose. I had to have sugar and cream on them though. The brose was made from oatmeal scalded with boiling water and mixed up with a pinch of salt in it. When I later joined the Royal Air Force you had no choice but to take the porridge made without salt and the tea with sugar in it. Because of so many complaints from the Scots they began to serve it up with or without to satisfy everyone. We could have toast when there was a good red glow of the burning coal, peat or wood. Even then it had to be done on the end of a very long fork. We had plenty of eggs, both hen and duck, boiled, fried or scrambled. The ducks, about eight of them, we would take them to a pond in the wood when at certain times of the year it would be alive with frogs. The fun for us was to choose a couple or so ducks and count the number of frogs they ate, some of them managing to down at least six. The odd thing about it was the way they swallowed them, always by catching them between the back legs, gobbling away at them until the legs were facing forward and down their throats they would go, still alive. The ducks had a habit of going away some distance to make their nests. Sometimes we would keep them in their shed until lunch time to get their eggs but even then we would have to follow some of the more determined ones from a distance to find their nests.

Mam took as many eggs as she could to the grocery vans to pay for things she bought, necessities like bread, tea, sugar, baking powders, rennet for making crowdie, salt and pepper, but never luxuries like candy or toffee which she made herself. There were only two types of bread came out on the vans, Plain or Pan loaves and I cannot recall seeing brown bread then. My favourite was Plain and still is to this day but because there is less demand for it the loaves tend to sit on the shelves longer and is not always fresh. The vans came out from the shops in Bonar Bridge and Ardgay. They carried just about anything you needed which was just as well because there was no public transport to get you to the village. One of the van drivers that I remember of was always referred to as "Jimmy the Van". He was fond of the dram and often would not arrive at our house until all hours of the night and my mother would have to stay up to get her messages in other words shopping. One night he arrived on foot having put the van in the ditch which was not an uncommon thing. When Dad went along to near Coneas Bridge to see if they could get it out it was on its side with a terrible mess inside. Crates of eggs all broken, bags of flour burst and bottles of this or that smashed. Rosy our horse would sometimes be used to get the van back on the road. In Ardgay alone at that time there were two general merchant shops, a painter and decorator business, a barber, a butcher, Post Office, private car hire firm, a hotel, two garage repair businesses with petrol pumps and a blacksmiths. Down at the Railway Station there was a bookstall and a thriving goods yard serving not only the local area but the North West as well. I am not sure but I think there was a bank next door to Fraser's shop on the corner. Coal wagons came in to empty in the yard. Animal feed fertilizers and just about everything else that was needed for agricultural, the shops and other businesses, arrived there. Livestock came and went from there as well. No fleet of lorries and delivery vans from a distance to be seen anywhere.

The hotel, The Balnagown Arms, caught fire one evening in an upstairs room and apart from the stone and lime walls was burned to the ground. One of the first people to see smoke coming out from the roof was Mary Macgregor from the bookstall down on one of the station platforms. She went up to the Post Office which at that time remained open at weekends until 8 or 9pm to serve customers from the glens and alerted Bunty Gordon the assistant. The alarm was raised and the fire brigade called. Also watching the excitement was Billy Dunbar. In the meantime Tom "White" (Ross) went up on the roof and with good intentions opened a hole by removing the slates to get at the fire but this only worsened the situation by giving vent to the flames. By the time the fire brigade arrived which I assume was from Tain the place was well ablaze. There was no public water supply in the village at the time so the firemen ran their hoses down to the Kyle for water but as the tide went out mud and other sludge was sucked into the pump and blocked up the system.

Balnagowan Arms Hotal, Ardgay 1943

In the midst of all this Billy tells me that a Wellington Bomber came low up over the Kyle and circled the village before returning the way it had come from the Morrich Mor Air Field at RAF Tain. Today it is an Air Weapons Range and is one of the most heavily used bombing ranges in the country. By coincidence when Billy was doing a welding course at R.A.F Weeton he met the very man who piloted the plane. He was a guy name Paul from Poland and was on a resettlement course, also doing welding, before immigrating to Australia and as people do were exchanging backgrounds. When Billy told him where he came from Paul said, "I know that place. I flew over it just after it was bombed."

Canadian troops from No.17 Forestry Corp who had their billets in Spinningdale and Mid Fearn were drinking in the bar and they set about to rescue what they could but in their stupidity they threw the furniture down from upstair windows supposedly for their colleagues on the ground to catch but most, if not all of it, smashed to pieces. Lord Conygham from Amat Estate who was a guest in the hotel at the time was up there with them throwing mattresses out of the windows with his good lady down on the ground calling to him, "Come out of there Freddie". Cartridges stored for shooting guests could be heard exploding, crates of whisky and other spirits were being carried out to the barn and other buildings.

Canadians did not go without their share of this and hid a lot of it in the stack-yard with the intention of going back for it at a later time. Evidence of this was found by locals when the corn-stacks came in for threshing. An assortment of bottles kept coming to light from where they had been stuffed into the sheaves.

Fergus McLeod the proprietor, or "Fergie" as he was better known, and his good lady were re-housed by a relative in neighbouring property, Ardgay House. "Fergie" then set up a temporary bar in part of the steading. I did not know him until years later but he was a very moody man. Sometimes we would try to get him to sell us a bottle of sherry or port before going to the dances but because we were under age he just chased us from the place. We would then resort to getting someone older who we knew to buy a bottle for us. "Fergie" knew that this went on but did not turn down a sale in this way. I ask you are things much different today? Part of the old steading still stands there but a new prefabricated Doran type structure named the Lady Ross was built to replace the hotel but sadly this lies almost empty today and one can only describe it as an eye sore. It has twice been damaged by fire since.

To make way for the building of the Lady Ross the ruins of the Balnagown Arms were completely demolished and carted away except for the Clach Eitach, a large quartz stone that previously in the early eighteen hundreds had been built into the gable of the original hotel. It is thought that the location of this stone determined where the Feil Eiteachan, a market for all domestic animals and poultry would change hands and for itinerant traders and hawkers to come from afar and set up their stalls to barter their wares. The stone now sits across the road at the top of the brae down to the Railway Station. The last that I can recall of this fair was my father coming home with a cow from it. I don't know if he had a dram in at the time he bid for it but it was not one of his better purchases. I remember Mr Brown the vet from Invergordon telling him to put mustard poultices on its back for whatever reason.

There were two pieces of cutlery that none of us as children wanted to eat with, one was a horn spoon and the other was a silver spoon which my mother gave us castor oil from, purgative stuff. It may have cured the sore tummies but the taste was about the worst I can think of. It was so bad my mother would give us a spoonful of sugar afterwards. Doctor Macrae from Bonar Bridge only prescribed two things, castor oil or black ointment but having said that he was there when needed at Wester Gruinards for the birth of all of us. Before 'phones were common place Willie MacDonald from Amat, would go to Bonar in the spring cart and bring the doctor up and take him home later. The nurse would cycle up and do whatever was necessary in the days after a birth. Before the National Health Service was introduced doctors had to be paid by the people but because many of them were so poor they often did not call or visit a doctor resulting in many premature deaths. Sometimes doctors would turn out through the goodness of their hearts knowing quite well that payment would not be forthcoming. If they were lucky they sometimes would be paid in kind with potatoes, fresh vegetables, mutton, pork or anything else that came off the croft or river.

There was not a resident dentist in Ardgay or Bonar and this was an additional aspect of Doctor MacKay's profession. I would have been about twelve or thirteen at the time and was having terrible toothache, the hell of all pains, in four of my back teeth. My whole system got run down and I kept coming out in boils. Noel and I cycled down to the surgery one evening and after I got injections for all four teeth Doctor MacKay set about to pull them. If it was possible the pain was worse than the toothache and each time I responded to it by pulling my head away and screaming out. He kept injecting me with more cocaine to the point that he ran out of the stuff and sent Noel with a prescription to the chemist for more. In the end I jumped out of the chair and would not get back into it. For about a week afterwards my head was extremely woozy but the toothache disappeared. Three months later I plucked up courage and went to a full time dentist, Mr Quinn from Tain, who rented a room once a month in the Caledonian Hotel and he took them out with no problem. To this day I still regard myself as a coward when it comes to the dentist and each of them are told in advance what they are dealing with and that an injection which I don't mind is a must before any drilling begins.

The Bath (Timespan, Helmsdale)   *Wash tub and Wash board*

For washing ourselves, we used the same basin as the dishes were washed in, all water having to be carried from the Sgodachail Burn and later on at Gruinard from a small stream that came down off the hill in front of the house. As it flowed over some rocks a piece of cast iron guttering was placed to catch the water from under the end of it. For drinking water, particularly in the summer, we went along the road a couple of hundred yards or so to a well at the Torroo. It was only a few steps down off the road and the water was very clear and cold. An enamel mug was left beside it to fill a bucket with and for people walking past to stop for a drink. To have a bath we used a specially shaped metal or tin tub. Several kettles and pans were boiled for it and we would each use the same water. Hand towels were pieces of hessian sacking but for washing our faces or having a bath we had proper ones.

In the summer months we washed or bathed down in the pool in the burn where my mother did the washing. As we got older we were allowed to bathe in the river and it was in the tail of the "Millers" pool and "Moral" where I first learned to swim, no trunks just trousers cut off above the knees. It was not until the late nineteen forties before we got our first proper toilet and bathroom. Before that we used a "po", I assume short for potty or a "chanty" both words coming from chamber pot, and when we were big enough we went out to the byre or the nearest clump of trees. There were certainly no toilet rolls and newspaper was not easy come by either. Outside it was hay without thistles or a bunch of dead grass or moss, not to mention the shirt tail, so you had to be selective where you did it. The female members used a dry or chemical toilet, a sort of "bucket and chuck it" affair.

The only reason my father could afford to install a bathroom at that time was the fact that Mr MacKenzie a plumber from Culrain was given board and lodgings by mother whilst he carried out a lot of work at Gruinard Lodge for Brigadier Flemming and family. My dad was working for the Brigadier at the same time and he rescued a lot of the second hand fittings including iron piping for a piped water supply. Mr McKenzie whose only mode of transport was an old fashioned bicycle and for his tools he had a specially made leather bag slung below the full length of the bar. He would cycle up on a Monday morning and go home on a Friday night. In those days it was almost all lead piping that required special skills to complete the joints etc. Copper and brass fittings did not come into common use until years later.

Geordie "Ma" (Ross) the mason was also working at the lodge and he installed the sceptic tank and drainage. Geordie's brother, Norman "Ma" ran the family croft at Syall and a joinery business from Lower Gledfield. The nick name "Ma" as I understand it was attributed to them by the fact that their father John D Ross qualified as a Master Builder and was the main building contractor for many houses in this area. Carbisdale Castle may be just one of them but I have it on record that a Mr MacTavish a builder from Inverness was responsible. When I was renovating Lower Hilton Cottage at Culrain Ross's name and business address was written in pencil on some of the old wooden timbers. Norman was the registrar for the Parish and on the birth of a child he got so many of the names wrong. He had his own idea how the name should be spelt and often with the parent, usually the father, just agreeing with him. He got my own middle name wrong. He insisted that my sister's name was Johan and not Joan and for another family there was no such name as Sheena. According to him it was Sheila but having looked at entries by other registrars they were not much better.

The Brigadier came from a farm on the Isle of Wight and brought with him Shire horses, large four wheeled carts and dairy cows. He also took with him lots of wooden tripods for coling the hay to dry on and boasted to Duncan Munro the farmer form Invercharron that they used them in England where they made better hay. In response Duncan said, "That's funny we have better cattle in Scotland", a claim that still stands to this day. Duncan was proud of his cattle and liked nothing better than giving you a tour of the byres and telling you the history of each one.

Gruinard Lodge and Tradesmen, 1896. Willie "Floor" Senior, Extreme Right with His Horse

The Lodge More Recently

My dad worked for Mr Flemming for a time until they fell out over a fence the Brigadier erected on the common grazings for a herd of highland cattle he bought, to the exclusion of the crofters' sheep. The controversy over this fence went on for

23

many years until Derek, my nephew, through Mr Milligan the factor, had everything reinstated and the fence allowed to fall into complete disrepair.

The Brigadier at first did not have access to farming Gruinard Farm. This was rented from the Estate by two brothers, Davie and Christen "Gidd" (Ross) with their sister Mrs Walker who lived next door keeping house for them. When some of the locals were helping out one day and went into the house for their dinner a row got up at the table between the two of them over who had eaten more tatties than the other. Christen then asked the sister if there were more and when she said there were plenty more in the pot he told her to get them on the table and that they were no good there. George Ross was in for his dinner with them one day and Davie sat at one end of the table and Christen at the other. The sister put a dinner plate in front of each of them and emptied a big black pot of tatties on to Davie and Christen's one. There was not enough room on the two plates so they spilled over on to the table. George was sitting at one side of the table and was not sure which plate he should take them from or just take those on the table. The tatties still had the skins on them and Christen was picking them up with each hand and stuffing them whole into his mouth, the skins he managed to remove in the process and throw down on the table. George could not recall any meat or anything else to eat with them. At one stage Christen announced that he had already eaten fourteen but was going to have more. Tatties appeared to be their main diet. Noel, for pocket money helped at the harvest and after there was no sign of payment for it he was told that his work would be in lieu of getting the services of a tup for a cheviot ewe he was given as a pet lamb.

I don't remember who Christen was talking to about his long term lover, Teeny Fraser from Tivady, Kincardine Hill, but he was telling him how he had cycled back and fore to see her for over twenty years and the conversation ended with him saying, "And I haven't seen the tops of her stockings yet." The courtship continued for some time after that but they eventually married, with Tommy Ross, Gledfield, as best man. For as long and as well as Tommy and Christen knew each other there was no mention of marriage until one day he just said, "Can you spend five minutes in Tain with me."

To get extra ground to farm up at the lodge the Brigadier set about what I can only describe as an act of vandalism. He brought in a squad of Italian prisoners of war who were billeted at Kildary near Tain and ripped out all the shrubbery and exotic trees that had grown there from the time the lodge was built. It was laid out in a similar way that you find in city public parks. Everything at first was cut down, tree stumps and roots blasted out of the ground with gelignite to be burned, and the site levelled with a bulldozer, all for a few more acres of arable. The tennis courts were used to keep dogs in. The prisoners' to get some extra money or cigarettes made ashtrays and photo frames from bully beef tins. They made moulds in turnips and melted down old lead into them for ornaments.

I think also it was sacrilege of Brigadier Fleming to demolish and remove any trace of the private burial site of Hannah Coupland, wife of Richard Thomas Coupland, joint owners of Gruinard Estate, who died on 26th July, 1896, the same year as the building of their lodge of that name was completed. Up until then there was no lodge at Gruinard, the proprietors coming from Gledfield House as and when necessary.

The burial took place on the small knoll on the top side of the road above the main gates to the lodge. A stone wall with black and gold painted metal railings on top and square sandstone pillars for the ornate gate was placed around it. Surrounding that was a mixture of rhododendron shrubs and an appropriate foot path leading up through the birches from the gate opposite the letter box. Subsequently, Jim Gilmour was given the stones that formed the gate pillars to use likewise for his house at Cornhill.

Two years after the burial the ground was consecrated by the Bishop of Moray and Ross, the Right Reverend James B.K. Kelly DD. In January 1904 the remains were reburied at St Georges Cemetary, Hanwell and at the time the red polished granite memorial stone was replaced on top of the empty grave. Having removed all the stone and railings for new dog kennels the Brigadier then buried the memorial stone on site where it remained hidden for the last sixty or more years until Jim Gilmour and Robert Sawyer were doing some digger work in the area for the current owners of the estate, Mr and Mrs Cluff, and lifted it to the surface for display. The original kennels along the riverside were partly dismantled for the stone and railings and the remainder converted to a cattle court. It has now been redeveloped into a small but smart fishing bothy.

The Coupland Memorial Stone

The Brigadier brought with him an old lorry type mobile home which my Dad used to drive after the original body was removed and it was converted for carrying general goods. He got his licence long before the driving tests became compulsory and I'm not sure but the lorry may have been his first vehicle to drive. In any case on his first outing coming home with a load of straw he knocked the ornamental tops off the gate posts as he entered the drive. On reaching the barn he knocked out the wooden gable end from it which now has a Lairg brick one in its place, one of Geordie "Ma's" many jobs he did there. Dad's driving career ended some time after he bought his first car. Coming home from the village after closing time he put the Morris in the ditch above the lodge, with it bellied on top of a culvert.

After a lot of engine revving and the bearings knackered it was towed home with the Fergie tractor.

The old body from the lorry was used for keeping poultry feed when the Kemmis's were there and one evening when I was watching Noel feeding the Muscovie ducks beside it I asked him if they ever took one to eat which he assured me they had not. I told him how we often had one when I ate in the bothy at Glencalvie and that they were very good. Without saying any more to him I used a garden rake and took a swipe at a nice young one knocking its head clean off. Noel panicked a bit and said, "You will get me the sack." After a quick clean up of the feathers the fowl was plucked and cleaned ready for the oven. Noel said, "That was good but don't you ever do it again." I know it is said that all game should be hung for a time before eating, but like rabbits I don't think duck improves any.

CHAPTER 2

THE ALDERSON MEMORIAL STONE

Another memorial stone known locally as the Alderson Stone which in a small way dominates the eastern hill-side of Gruinard Estate is in memory of Edmont K. Alderson, head keeper to the Duke of Wellington who was accidentally shot by his under keeper, John Ross, when out deer stalking.

Apparently John Ross had "Rushee" his dog on a rope tied round his waist and on raising his gun to fire at the deer the dog sprang forward setting off the weapon. The lament by John Ross is reproduced herein and is self explanatory. There was no lodge at Gruinard at that time and I understand the injured man was carried to Gledfield where he was seen by a doctor some sixteen hours later but could not be saved. One would assume that the only anaesthetic available in those days was whisky for what it was worth to numb the pain of a dying man. Rumours handed down over the years which I personally would not wish to believe had a slightly different but serious aside to events, alleging that Edmont was having an affair with John's wife and that it was no accident.

LAMENT for EDMONT ALDERSON killed on GRUINARD HILL by
JOHN ROSS Under Keeper.

It was the first month of the year.
It was severely frosty
That even deer to our homes came near
Although we feared to poach them.

Early Monday morning,
In imitation of the snow
That day they wore white clothing.
When Alderson called out his men

See them now climb up the snow clad hills
On the south side of Gruinard
With rapid stride, through snow they glide
Each step desires to grow keener.

They now approached some noble deer
With hope and fear he marks one
His gun he raised, and took his aim
And fired away so smartly.

His under- keeper was close behind
A dog beside him crouching
With gun in hand, he prepared to fire
But tried not to announce it.

The deed was done, alas
When John was in the act of firing,
Brave "Rushee" sprung and shook his hand,
No stag or hind low lieth.

The fatal bullet pierced not a deer,
But pierced the brave young Edmont.
In through the hair, out through the brain
See how he falls headlong.

Ye men of Gruinard off to the hills
Make haste and do not tarry,
To the nearest house, go find some means,
This dying man to carry.

For sixteen hours he feebly breathed
The vital spark still lingering,
But from the time he received his wound
He never moved a finger.

Thus died the young, the brave, the bold
The tall, the comely Edmont
The frank, the free, the liberal kind,

The happy smiling fellow.

He had such fine obliging ways,
Such pleasant ways of winning
His manly heart and noble mind,
Were free from guile and cunning.

Oh, who would envy the wicked man
Beneath who's hand now lieth
The widow's wail, the orphan's cry,
Must to his heart be galling.

If such a deed should happen me,
I would not stand my country,
I would rather pick up a burning brand
Than gun in hand to hunt with.

CHAPTER 3

BEFORE ELECTRICITY CAME UP THE GLEN

Lighting was by either candle or a paraffin lamp, the type with the tall glass chimneys and wicks that had to be trimmed every so often to get rid of the sooty ends. They came in different shapes and sizes, from the all glass smaller ones to big brass and chrome affairs. We had different lamps called lanterns for going outside to the byre or stable. It was a blessing when tilley lamps were invented. You had to heat them up first with a methylated spirit burner and then pump up pressure to force the paraffin through a jet into the mantle. The mantles after use, if touched, would disintegrate into powder. When the light started to fade someone had to pump it up again. We had a battery powered radio which was only put on for the news to hear what was happening in the War, Lord Haw-Haw with Germany Calling and the Scottish Dance Music, by Jimmy Shand or one of the other broadcasting bands, but never on Sundays. There were two batteries for it. One was on the radio whilst the other went on the grocer's van to the village garage for charging.

Brass Candlestick   *Iron*   *Lamp*

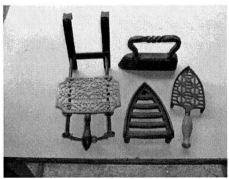

Tea Pot stand, Oatcake rack and Iron stands

30

As I said in my early years religion was very strict and Sunday was adhered to as a day of rest but as recent as 1984 we had a Free Church minister at Bonar who took religion to the extreme. Why he was up at Lower Hilton I do not know but he stopped his car and gave me a right lecture about working on a Sunday. Because I had travelled there from Gruinard he give me a further tonguing that only necessary journeys should be made on a Sunday and that was to church only. I often wonder was his journey really necessary that day because there was not a church in the vicinity. At funerals he insisted that the coffin and remains sat outside whilst the service went on indoors, taking the opportunity to lecture a full house on religion and their failings with little or nothing said about the deceased. On at least one instance a funeral service was moved to an alternative church when he flatly refused to have the coffin inside. In spite of his strict teachings I witnessed one of his regular worshipers on the way home from church stealing road chips from a pile belonging to the council. Plenty of people will have done the same thing but not on their way home from church and what difference were a few chips to fill the puddle by her door step going to make anyway.

Only the other day I was discussing religion with a good friend when I was told of a habit, a dirty one at that, when unmarried mothers entered the church on Sundays were spat on by the elders at the door. I thought I would have heard this talked about before at home but I was assured that it went on even at Croick Church where a Kate "Havvie" Ross was spat on by a David MacKay a local business man and elder of that time. I remember both parties very well but I don't think I ever heard my parents speak of it. I don't believe the practice was an act of God but was it to do with the death of the child soon after the birth. I promised my self that I would keep politics and religion out of this book so I will move on, or back in this case.

CHAPTER 4

SGODACHAIL DAYS

The reason for moving to Braelangwell Estate was that my father got a full time shepherds job with the Department of Agriculture who took a lease of Braelangwell Farm where they were to run a hirsel of Blackface Ewes. My brother Arthur was taken on as under shepherd. Hogs, year old sheep came home there as well. Because they were not hefted on that hill, they were hell bent on going down the strath. Every morning they would have to be dogged back up the road and driven out to the hills. A lot of the arable land, my father fenced and had it ploughed up for growing turnips and oats for winter feed and kale for the lambs to fatten up on before going off on the train to the sales at Dingwall. Apart from our own cows I don't recall commercial cattle on the farm until a farmer by the name of Mr Monk took it over.

At clippings or dippings or other big handling of the sheep, help was brought in on a reciprocal basis with local crofters and shepherds, who I got to, know well, looked up to and respected. Geordie Ross, Heatherlea, Jimmy MacGregor, Willie MacDonald and Davie Havvie (Ross) all crofters of Amat na Tua, Jimmy Moffat, manager, Hughie MacLeod and John MacRae, shepherds at Croick, who all I frequently remember with nostalgia, their characters and personalities played a significant role in my flush of youth. They were "one- offs" and a breed that is rarely encountered today.

Hugh, Ernest and Fan at Sgodachail

Today electric clippers are used instead of the old fashioned shears of bygone years. I would listen to the men talking about the makes and the different strengths. Some preferred weak ones, others stronger all depending on the grip of their hands, but whichever one they used they would go on all day and for weeks until all the clippings in the district were done and no complaint did I hear. Some sat astride the narrow end of a clipping stool with the sheep lying on the wider end in front of them. Others, particularly the younger men, used to fold a wool bag in half and clip on the ground. How their backs didn't give in by the end of it all I do not know. On sheep dipping days similar conversations took place between the men discussing the strength of the paste dip used and the incoming liquid and powder dips, with Cooper, MacDougal and Robertson being the main supplier of that time. At the end of each dipping session the sheepdogs with thumbs pressed over their closed eyes were dunked in it to kill off any fleas and mites they may have had on their bodies. Nowadays I understand it is no longer safe to continue with this practice.

Sgodachail Fanks with Glencalvie and Alladale Hills in the distance

Other big days in the fanks were for the marking of the lambs and the branding of the hogs horns with initials of the owner and a number to denote the year of birth and certain lug marks knotched out of the ear also for identification purposes. The marking of the lambs consisted of cutting the tail ends off the ewe lambs and removing the testicals of the wedder ones, usually referred to as cutting the lambs. For most at Sgodachail this involved three or more people for the day, one to catch the lamb and pass it to another person who would hold it in a sitting position on a face high shelf where my dad would cut off the end of the sack, squeeze out the testicles and draw them with his teeth. One of us boys would then put a keel mark on them before they were released. Today a rubber ring is slipped over the sack gripping it so tightly that the testicles drop off after a few weeks

My dad would cycle some distance to help out at clippings at Birchfield, Kincardine Hill and Badavoon. There was also a reciprocal agreement with all the local crofters. I don't recall him going to Mid Fearn but he may have done. I am not going to mention the name of the woman he and others went to clip for at Kincardine but she was far from clean in her person or hygienic about the house. When they were offered whisky some would tip it into a flower pot or get rid of it in some other way rather than drink it. The braver ones without putting the glass to their lips would toss it over their throats. It was common in those days for the women to wear fold over type aprons and her one was as black as the ace of spades and never washed. When the soup was dished up she would hold the loaf of bread against her breast and go round the table cutting a slice off for each of the men. Every alternative slice she would grip between her thumb and the blade and give it to one of the dogs in the house, the blade each time disappearing half way down the dog's throat in the process. Apparently before sitting down on a seat you first had to check that there was no cat shit on the cushions or the arm rests. The staff at the Balnagown Arms were quite used to her coming into the kitchen to see what "left overs" in the way of food she could get. It was not uncommon for her to scoop out with her dirty hands what was left in the porridge pot and put it down inside the top of her apron as a means of carrying it home. The place would not have been flooded with carrier bags then.

Dad, second from right, back row.
Slamp on his left and Fergus McLeod centre front.

The Badavoon shepherd for Fergus McLeod from the hotel was a Donald MacKenzie or "Slamp because of his fitness, as he was better known and previously worked under my father at Braelangwell. In fact the old cottage he used to live in was for many years afterwards known as "Slamp's." I understand he was the last person to be born in a very old settlement, the remains of which are still standing where the Balblair, Achenduich and Sleastry hill ground meet. He was fond of the dram and although he visited most of the establishments most of his earnings went back to his boss through the till. I did not really know the man to speak to but Billy Dunbar and I were in the Bridge Hotel and Billy asked him if he knew who I was. "Slamp" stared at me for a little while and then said, "Yes your sister "pished" on my lap." A funny reply but he went on to say that he had been in our house one day and was nursing Joy (Joan) at the time.

Another Clipping Day with Dad centre front and Fergus Mcleod on his Right

I have been told of two accounts when in his later years and living up at Dounie. The first one was well into the early morning when he was found drunk and asleep on the bank of the road. His clothing and hairs from his nostrils were white from the hard frost that night and after being put in the car for a lift the remainder of the way home he started to steam like a boiling kettle with the driver continually having to stop and clean the windscreen. The second occasion, and if the truth was known probably many more, again he was found in a similar inebriated state with his back trapping water that ran down the bank into the ditch. The water was coming over his shoulders and on to his front. When awakened he just stood up and shook the water from the lapels of his jacket and went on his way.

As children we had our jobs to do at the clippings, like buisting with keel the newly sheared sheep. Helping the men with the rolling and bagging of the wool which was hot and smelly work especially when we had to get inside the wool bags to tramp down the fleeces. We were always glad when the bags were nearly full and our heads were out in the fresh air again although not as bad as what the boy chimney sweeps had to do. Probably the best part of the day for us was when my mother would arrive mid- morning or afternoon with our usual wholesome home baking of girdle scones and pancakes laced with homemade jam from berries in our garden. Beer (screw tops) was available for the men and homemade ginger beer for us kids. There was always a pail of water from a nearby well. It was sprinkled with oatmeal to give it a better taste but as the day went on it needed a stir up to get the full benefit of the mealy tase. Dinner was always taken in the house about 1pm, broth to start with, followed by meat stew, or cold mutton from a sheep that dad would kill and butcher for the occasion. Sometimes Mam would roast a leg and have it either hot or sliced cold for them, ending with rice pudding or rhubarb and custard. There would be cups of tea as well with most of the men drinking from their saucers. We never had coffee and it was much later in life when I first tasted it and even then it was in liquid form from a bottle. In the lodges they ground down the coffee beans in special grinders. Supper was also served in the house before the men went home by foot or bicycle.

When I listed the helpers I deliberately omitted to mention Willie or Wull Renwick, a remarkably fit man with a dry sense of humour. He would walk over the hills several times in the week from his croft at Birchfield, Strathkyle, taking stray sheep with him. At the end of what was a hard day's work he would set off for home taking stray sheep from his own flock back over the hills to his own croft. Occasionally, on stormy nights he would borrow my father's bicycle and cycle home via Invercarron and Culrain, taking the bike back to Dad in the morning. Imagine men of today doing that. Well if they did it would be in the comfort of a 4X4, ATV or similar. I don't think many working men except Dan Campbell the trapper at that time had any form of motorised transport that was used regularly and if they did it would have been an old ex-army motor bike. Later on I remember the keeper in Dounie and Gruinard, Eric Campbell, using what was called an autocycle. It had a small petrol engine that drove the front wheel but going uphill you had to assist it by pedalling in the normal way. Geordie Heatherlea had an old Douglas motorcycle that lay idle in the barn. I never knew of it ever being used and eventually it was sold to a man they called Sydney the Post.

CHAPTER 5

THE WAY WE LIVED

Like the house at Wester Gruinards, Sgodachail was very similar in size with the same layout and room numbers. We were far from well off. None of us was born with a "silver spoon" in our mouths so to speak. We had to do with very little in the way of furnishings but perhaps more content than the children of today even with all the modern toys and equipment they have. We slept top and tail in the limited number of beds in the space available, the boys and girls in separate rooms with Mam and Dad always occupying a very small room behind the lobby and between the two down stair rooms'. I cannot recall seeing wardrobes or chests of drawers. There was no room for them anyway. For a time there, I was prone to sleep walking until one morning I was found sleeping on the top of bags of animal feed in the shed attached to the back of the house. After that the key to the door was hidden to keep me in the house at least. It was often said to put the door key in a pail of water but my parents never tried it. Another use for the key it was said was to put it on the back of your neck to stop nose bleeding. An old wife's tale and there were so many of them. I was and still am prone to this problem but it never worked on me. Nose bleeds I mean.

We did not have very much in the way of clothing. Dad would have two sets of working tweed plus- fours and a plain dark blue suit for church on Sundays and funerals. He always wore matching waistcoats and jackets. When dressed in the suit it was always with a white shirt and starched collar and a tie. In fact he was seldom without a tie. Across the waistcoat from a button hole to a pocket he wore a gold chain and pocket watch. Half way along the chain hung a cairngorm pendant mounted in gold. At work it was a silver pocket watch and chain. The last bowler hat he owned he wore it down to Ellon for our wedding but on the way home at Huntly it blew off his head and was never found. Next day Noel 'phoned the police there but it had not been handed in and it was thought that the local boys had made use of it as a football. My mother was a very efficient dress maker and made most of what we wore from cast off clothes from the gentry at the lodges, particularly Lord and Lady Conygham from Amat Estate. If anything had to be bought it was from a JD Williams catalogue and paid C.O.D. (Cash on delivery). However, we were regarded as the best dressed kids in the school but not taking any credit away from my Mam, what I can remember all the pupils were well dressed. One evening my sister Morag was asked why she was not going to the dance in the village that night and in reply she said, "I do not have a blouse to put on." Nothing was any trouble to my Mam so she immediately found a piece of material and cut out the pieces for a blouse. In no time at all she run it up on the sewing machine and Morag went off to the dance as proud as punch. It may not have been on that occasion but I recall her using the silk material from parachutes wherever she got that from.

My mother, as I said did all her own baking and a lot of that was required for a growing family. Flour and oatmeal was bought by the hundred-weight and stored in wooden kists, tall pine chests with a hinged lid on the top. Amongst the meal she would keep white and black puddings. The flour came in white linen type bags and after picking out the seams they would be washed several times with us having to tramp them in the tub we bathed in before they were put through the mangle to get wrung out and then hung over the whins and fences to bleach. I don't believe the wringer was invented by then. With her trusty pedal operated Singer sewing machine she would sew them up into sheets for our beds. Wool-bags that were not used at clipping time went through the same process until they were soft and when split open they fitted a double bed. For most there initial treatment was to tie them to a branch over hanging a stream in the burn and let them soak there for weeks. With two of them on the bed you were nice and cosy. I suppose the horse hair mattresses on our beds gave us a lot of warmth from below and had the other advantage of not having to be changed as often as the chaff filled ones that other people had to put up with. Rugs for the concrete floors were made from strips of rags woven into pieces of hessian sacks which the oats and flake maize came in. As time went on we were able to afford linoleum for the floors. We may have been cosy at night but coming down stairs on a frosty morning with the ice patterns still on the inside of the window glass it could be quite different. I cannot recall the children at school ever having head lice but at home we got the occasional flea off the dogs in spite of Dad putting them in the sheep dipper. Irritating little buggers they were and nigh impossible to catch. As soon as you tried to snatch one it would jump a mile.

Rosy our horse came with us to Braelangwell and with her, Dad ploughed up a piece of ground beside the house and grew our own potatoes. Always "Kerrs Pinks", a popular tattie to this day. Later on he planted Edzell Blues which were also favourites. For the winter months to keep the frost from them a pit or clamp was dug and then they were covered with dead bracken and a couple of layers of peat turf still with the heather on it. A special tool known as a flacter spade was used for cutting it. Dead bracken was also cut and gathered for bedding the cows and Rosy. In the spring when the ground temperature got warmer early potatoes would show signs of growing in the pit where they had been stored all winter. When the shaws got to reasonable size, as kids we would dig them up and boil the young tatties which were not much bigger than marbles, in syrup tins. Mam would give us butter to put on them and that made them nicer to eat. Indoors at meal times she would butter them and sprinkle oat meal and chives on them.

Today I know a lady who does gardening for others and she curses one owner who lifts the potatoes at this stage instead of leaving them to get bigger. I can sympathise with both parties. It was not uncommon for us boys to pull a swede turnip from the field, whack it over the top of a fence post and eat the best of it. There were many plants growing in the wild that we recognised as safe to eat either the leaves or the roots. We did not do this through hunger. It was something we just did like picking a berry from a bush or fruit from a tree. We learned from our parents what was good and not good to eat. Mushrooms growing in the wild were a definite no and even today I do not know the good from the bad. So much has been passed down from them that has stuck in our minds ever since.

Place names were also handed down and my father could name them all in Gaelic but with the younger generations coming up they were mostly lost, more modern versions taking over. Part of the croft at Gruinard was known as Croit na Caillich, the old wife's croft and the burn running through it took on the same name. Coming up Strath Carron just about every part of the road to Gruinard and beyond has a name to it, particularly the braes such as Gledfield Brae, Harry's Brae getting the name from a Game Keeper who lived in the house nearby. The Tup Park Brae and Skinners' were similarly named. Doll's Brae, which is a few hundred yards from the entrance to Gruinard Lodge probably got its name from the widow crofter, Dolina Ross whose home was nearby. There is little or no trace of her croft house but another possibility to that name was the fact that she was small and dainty and referred to as a doll. I can remember a story told about her when she was reaching down to the bottom of the meal kist she fell head first into it and could not get out. By good luck a neighbour called on her and came to her rescue. Another story was when the toffs were shooting rabbits close to her house and a wounded one ran round the end of the byre. The toff asked if she had seen where it went and she replied, "Yes up my spout hole." She did not explain that it was the hole for the wash to come out from the byre. American place names have always fascinated me. They have a certain ring to them.

I'm sure wherever you go in the Highlands you will find the same with place names as you will also find with other sayings that stuck with us from childhood like directions, up to Amat, Croick and Gencalvie down to Ardgay and Bonar but if you were in either of those villages you went over to the other. In to Tain or Inverness but down to Dornoch, up to Lairg or Wick and on and on it goes. I would like to think I am not superstitious but a couple of odd things I heard some people say that when a burial took place the head of the coffin should be towards where local running water comes from and the other that you should not move house on a Saturday. The saying was, "A Saturday flitting is a short sitting."

We had a very well stocked garden on the sunny slope at front of the house that provided us with all the vegetables and fruit we needed. Arthur kept bees for their honey. The best sections were sold to the lodges but there were always plenty for our selves. Every so often my Dad used to get a forty five gallon drum of treacle to put on the straw for cattle feed but we always had some of it in the house for ourselves to eat on our pieces. Mam would also use it for baking treacle scones or making treacle toffee and gingerbread. During rationing, because you kept bees you were seen as providing food and you got extra sugar so this went a long way in the jam making. Off the hill we unofficially got venison which my mother sometimes salted to make it keep longer and have it boiled but it was never as good as the boiled rib of beef we often have today. I have to say though it was more edible when minced. Venison liver fried along with onions bought from the "Onion Johnies" from Brittany in France, who cycled the countryside with their laden bikes, was a welcome change. For most we grew shallots in the garden and they were used in the stews.

My Uncle Danny at Gruinard also kept bees until his death and afterwards Noel took over the looking after of them. He increased the number of hives and sent for supplies of sections, frames and wax from a firm called Steele and Brodie down south. To introduce new queens to his hives he would send away for them as well, perhaps to the same firm. They would arrive in small boxes no bigger than match boxes sent through the normal postal service (GPO). When we were in London he sent down two sections of honey by post. He made a corresponding size of plywood box to put them in but getting knocked about in the parcel service they did not arrive intact. We got notice from the sorting office in Romford that there was a parcel to collect but we were unable to go for it for several days until our local posty told us that if we did not collect it soon there would not be much left of it. Because the honey was leaking from it the staff put it on a tray in the kitchen and all and sundry were helping themselves to it for their sandwiches. Unlike the salmon he sent down by British Rail we did salvage some of it. After several journeys to Euston Railway Station to collect the salmon off the next train I was told that it had been located at some "God forsaken" railway siding in the far north of England and that it would be sent on the next day. They were told to leave it where it was and to pay compensation in lieu which they did.

Each year we kept a pig to kill for pork or bacon. Most crofters and shepherds did likewise. When the pig was so fat that it was about to go off the legs only then would it be killed. No worries about the excess fat on the chops in those days and far fewer obese people about as well. The killing of the pig was a big event of the year. Humane or not it was the normal thing to do and no regulations to say otherwise. Often a neighbour would come to help. The pig was stunned by a blow to the forehead with a 14 pound hammer, its throat cut, strung up by the hind legs and with copious amounts of scalding hot water the bristles were shaved off with razor sharp knives. The blood was saved for making black puddings, meat from the head, particularly the cheeks, was made into brawn or potted head as it was more commonly known then. The shoulders were cut up for ready use, some of which was given to neighbours knowing that a piece would come in return when their pig reached the inevitable end to its lifetime. The remainder was cut into hams and loins and cured in half sherry or whisky barrels filled with salty brine, including spices, treacle, brown sugar and saltpetere which we got from the chemist. Because it is a property used in the making of explosives it has been taken off the market. Every couple of weeks or so the pieces were turned over and the bree rubbed into surfaces.

On the day of the killing we would salvage the bladder, wash it out in the burn and then blow it up with a bicycle pump to make a football out of. It had to be left to dry before we could use it and only then in the grass park because we never had a leather football case to put it into. It never lasted that long but it was fun whilst it did.

When ready after six to eight weeks the pork was taken out of the barrels and left to drip dry before being wrapped in muslin cloth and hung up on special hooks screwed into the rafters above the fireplace where a bit of birch and peat smoke got to them. The smaller pieces were usually boiled to have as ham with mashed potatoes, chives and white sauce, cauliflower and pickled beetroot. The hams were kept whole, for a good fry up of bacon and eggs and for most they would last throughout the year or at least until the next pig were killed. No fancy slicing machines then, only a good sharp knife which Dad would sharpen on the door step and which we were dared not to use. If at any time we were seen to put a knife into our mouths we got a telling off and told that if we cut our tongues we would bleed to death. I cannot remember when we first started to call it bacon and eggs but in my youth it was always referred to as ham and eggs and no white stuff left in the frying pan as you find for most nowadays from the water that is pumped into it in the curing process. The last time I can recall having a fry up like this was when Marjory and I were on our way to Blackpool in 1960 when we stopped at a roadside cafe at Shap.

CHAPTER 6

ONE FOR THE POT

From late April throughout the summer salmon was abundant in the River Carron. From the front of the house you could see them splashing with their backs out of the water as they struggled up stream over the shallow ford. If you were quick enough you could run down with a long handled gaff or pitch fork and have one out for the pot. Because there were no fridges or freezers, only an outside larder, there was little point in taking many more at any one time. There were few gamekeepers or river-watchers then. Most of them were called up for war service. When there was a keeper in residence one of the crofters would call on him for a ceilidh while the others went to the river for a bit of poaching, safely knowing where he was.

A ceilidh as I remember them, was when friends and neighbours called on one another for the evening and sat round the log or peat fire, telling stories or listening to the talented ones who could sing, play the fiddle, accordion, mouth organ or even the Jewish Harp or Jaw's Harp as it is sometimes called. By placing a piece of paper over a comb some could take a tune out of that. Some evenings we would listen to records played on the gramophone, the favourite ones played over and over again until past there sell by date because of the blunt needles we used. Today a ceilidh is held in a hall or hotel what we would once have called a concert. The first one that I can remember going to was in Ardgay to raise funds for the Invercarron Sheepdog Trials which was always followed by a dance to the music of the Bonar Bridge Ardgay Dance Band or BBA Band as it was more often referred to. Alec Ross, The Mill, band leader on drums Cathy Coul, accordionist George Peat, saxophone Willie Macdonald, fiddle and Jessie "The Library" on the piano. For the odd eightsome reel Sandy "Bobbin" would play the pipes. Then of course there was always the display of Irish tap dancing by Paddy McGinlay I must not forget the Master of Cermonies, Willie Bain who had a watchful eye for the lady who turned down a request to dance and then went on the floor with another man. He would politely usher them back to their seats. Singers who took to the stage at various functions were Duncan Ross, Davie "Stag" Ross and Argo Cameron.

My father, although not averse to taking one for the pot, so often rightly or wrongly referred to as a "Highland man's right" or "God's given right", could not be described as a poacher in the truest sense of the word. If rivers belonged to everyone it would be a free for all and what would the state of things be now or in years to come? Having said that he and a couple of other crofters from Amat na Tua, armed with big hooks tied together in trebles and weighted with lead, would cycle up to the Croick Falls on the Black Water River and get a salmon or two each. Before coming home they would call on the Moffats' at Croick for a game of cards, usually "catch the ten". Geordie Bruce, who you will read about later, told me that he used to get a lift up to Croick with a friend who was courting one of the daughters. He went to the same falls or the Glencalvie ones for a bag of salmon and the two of them would split the proceeds of the sale later.

Dad with His Gaff   *Marjory by the Black Water*

Catriona at Croick Falls   *Fiona at Moral*

Just along the road from Forrest Farm House was the manse occupied by Mr Craig and family but on their departure it was taken over for the two Alladale and Deanich Estate Stalkers, Donald and his father James Clark who each day would walk over the pony path to Alladale Lodge to carry out their daily tasks. Donald, describing one of his ghillies said about him, "A nice chap but oh how stupid." All about getting his bearings wrong on the hill but a bit contradictory I thought. Watt Clark was another member of the same family and he also was keeping at various estates in the north including Glencalvie. When living near Invercarron he called Mr Brown the vet out from Invergordon to look at a sick cow but the only advice he could gave Watt was to put it in a hole or a hol as it would have been said then. Needless to say Watt received a bill from the vet for his examination which was duly sent back to Invergordon with a letter telling Mr Brown to do likewise with it but not in such polite terms. When sending a salmon south he placed a rusty old pocket knife in its stomach resulting in a story appearing in a country magazine outlining the mystery of it all. When asked what he did with his pointer and setter dogs when they got too old for the grouse he replied, "I cut the legs off at the knees and make terriers of them."

I have visited Alladale many times but only on two or three occasions did I make it to Deanich. The first time I went up there Richard McCair was the proprietor who very kindly gave me the roofing slates from the old bothy which had been demolished as there was no further use for it, all deer carcases being taken directly to the modern larder at Alladale. I chugged up there with my old Leyland Tractor and took home two loads of slates to Strathkyle. I went back again to tidy up the broken stuff and put two stone lintels on top of the load which I had earmarked for use over the fireplaces in Ruie an Taoir. To put it mildly I was overawed by Deanich and its beautiful surroundings having heard my Dad relate so many experiences and the people he met there as a ghillie. It was so peaceful and over the two days the sun shone brightly and the hills were as as clear as you could wish them to be. High up near to the top of one the ridges pockets of dear were feeding peacefully until a golden eagle came over the ridge and spooked them. Hinds with calves at foot were most frightened and they scattered in panic with most of them coming down the hill to near the road. The eagle remained over them for about half an hour but made no serious attempt to go for a calf. My self and the tractor may just have been enough to ward him off.

For a good many years the summer grazings at Deanich were let to a Sandy McKay from Evanton and during the months when he had sheep there he would live and sleep in the bothy until one night he got such a fright, the cause he never made known to anyone, he left and never went back. Was it a ghost he saw? We will never know. Not long after that, along with his brother Kenny they built a bungalow on the croft he had at Amat na Tua but even there for a long time he would not stay overnight by himself. When I was at Gruinard Estate I often called on them and it was good to hear them get into arguments over Celtic and Rangers. To change the subject I would ask Sandy if he had any success at the sheepdog trials. From the newspapers I knew that he had not and Sandy would always blame the sheep, never the dogs. Kenny would get stuck into him then telling him his dogs were no damned good and that was why he had not been winning anything. Sandy was a very serious sort of person but Kenny liked a good laugh. I was not long at Gruinard and was doing work at the River bank when I met Kenny on the road and asked him what type of wire I should use for under water. Kenny replied with the question, "How long will you be hoping for it to last?" I said, "Until I leave Gruinard." Kenny then said, "In that case any wire will last a couple of years." At that he drove off and he never did give a better answer. I was working at the gates to the lodge another day when Kenny brought his Landrover to a screeching halt. From the open window he shouted, "You better get to hell out of there. There's a mad driver coming up the road. She just about put me in the ditch." Then without a smile on his face he quickly drove off. Who could this be I wondered? A few minutes later Marjory arrived and when I told her what he said, it transpired that she pulled into a passing place to let him overtake, but that was

Kenny. At the fencing he took a pride in being able to put stables into a post or dropper with one blow from the hammer. A "oner" he called it.

CHAPTER 7

SALT HERRING, COD AND FRESH TROUT

Another part of our diet was salt herring, which to this day I dislike only because of the amount of bones in them. The herring came from a fisher-wife who travelled down from Golspie by train and then walked up Strath Carron with a creel on her back to sell them. Her young daughter came with her and by coincidence when I was in the Police in Buckie I had occasion to call at a house in the Seatown area and there she was. We had a good chat about our younger days and the hard time her mother had to make a living. The houses in the Seatown area were occupied mainly by old fisher families and numbered as and when they were built and it was very difficult to find the one you wanted. Like other people I suppose, the fisherwomen left at home on their own, dreaded the knock on the door from a policeman fearing that something had happened at sea. This was brought home to me one day when an old lady answered the door and collapsed in my arms before I had time to speak to her and ask her for directions. At the top of the glen the herring was brought over by horse from Ullapool. I'm not sure where my mother got dried cod from but it was good. They were filleted, salted and dried as hard as boards and very difficult to cut up into pieces the size of one helping. When the pieces were soaked in cold water for a day or more to soften them and to remove some of the salt it was amazing how they swelled out to their normal shape. This was another welcome change served with mash and white sauce etc not unlike the "Boil in the Bag" you get today.

Many years later when I was patrolling the street near Bow Road Police Station, East London a lorry from Peterhead pulled up along side me. On the back was a lone barrel which the driver said he could not deliver because the bree was leaking from it. He thought my self and the rest of the guys at the station might like something different and in this case fillets of marinated herring. When he had no takers for it we dumped it in the skip the Mounted Branch used and he was more than happy just to get rid of it. At Peterhead one of the officers on night duty found a watchman almost on the point of death after he had fallen into the smouldering fire at a kippering yard. The owner of the company in a mark of appreciation requested the officer on that beat to pay a nightly visit and in return to pick up a few kippers for anyone who wanted them. This was never abused as not everyone liked them but it came to stop after the owner reported that boxes of them were disappearing and there was no account as to where they were going. Cycling home for breakfast one morning I saw boxes being loaded into the boot of a Jaguar and on investigating I found that the foremen was the culprit and both he and the Jaguar owner, a hotel keeper, were arrested. Any kippers we were given after that were not worth having.

Up until the 1960s there were plenty of trout in the burns and lochs. In Strathcarron the Sgodachail Burn was one of the best and any day after a spate of fresh water you could always come home with at least six to eight trout all of a good edible size. Mam would gut them, roll them in oatmeal and fry them in butter until the outer part was quite crisp. The trout from the loch above Sgodachail at Meal Dheirgidh, tended to be much bigger and pink fleshed, supposedly Loch Leven trout. We used to troll a fly behind the boat and it was quite easy to catch twelve to sixteen in an evening. Occasionally we would catch an escapee from the loch in the burn and this tended to add a bit of excitement as did the odd sea trout that could be caught as far up as the highest waterfall. After the fishing season closed and from October onwards it was quite common to see spawning salmon up the first few hundred yards of the burn. Because of the decline in stocks now it will be a rarity to see a salmon up any burn to spawn.

Another person who fished that loch successfuly was Willie Munro, Balnabruich, who along with other men were draining the hills near to it, often staying there overnight for several days and I would imagine that much of the food they ate was a good fry up of freshly caught trout. Willie for a time was ghillie to the Conyghams at Amat and to the Lamberts at Braelangwell and like my dad was not averse to having a salmon for the pot but preferred to catch them on the fly. He was renowned for his casting skills and when he took part in a fly casting competition in Ardgay at the Poplars Farm he came first, the prize for which was a box of salmon flies. Second prize was a salmon which should have gone to Eric Campbell the keeper from Dounie but he got the flies and Willie got the salmon. One can ask the question did he not get the flies so as not to encourage him in fishing without permission or was it because of his sizeable family he had to feed.

From October through to the end of March I could safely say that rabbit was our stable diet and perhaps now and again mutton from the flock on a Sunday. From the age of about six or seven I used to go out with my older brothers to ferret and snare them. Even on our way to and from school we had snares to check. The morning catch we would hang in a tree and take them home later. My mother would joint them, soak them in salty water for twenty four hours to get rid of the rabbity smell and then stew them slowly until the meat was just about falling off the bone. She would further season the juices and thicken it with flour for gravy. Some people preferred it stuffed and roasted but that did nothing for me. Oxo cubes but no Bisto then. Carrot, turnip and shallots would already be part of the stew. We never tired of it. In fact on a Sunday my mother might say, "There is a bit of rabbit left over from yesterday, would anyone like it?" Not that we did not have enough on our plates some of us would always be wanting it. From time to time one of our hens would come home with a clutch of chickens or sometimes my mother would deliberately set a broody hen. When the chickens got older the cockerals, usually Rhode Island Reds were kept separate and fattened off for killing. The same happened when there were too many drakes or ganders about.

On the odd occasion she would hatch out a turkey or two to bring on for Xmas but they were delicate things as chicks and often she lost them.

In the middle of the day if it was only us kids that were at home we often got just a bowl of mashed potatoes and milk or maybe other times a plate of skirly, fried oatmeal and onions with mashed potatoes and a glass of fresh milk to wash it down and then a proper meal at night when Dad came home. Today I'm not that keen on white mealy puddings and much prefer the home made stuff like skirly. As I said earlier the mutton we ate for most was from good wholesome carcases killed and butchered by my father. However, it was quite common then to eat Braxie mutton. This came from young sheep that died from a disease of the intestines. It was often cured like pig-meat and eaten as mutton-ham. In more modern times it was said to be rotten or putrid meat but that is just a fallacy. Even with the amount of myxamatosis that appears every year I still enjoy a casserole of rabbit but first I have to see it running about and check the liver, heart and kidneys for healthiness. I don't have it so often now, but very young rabbit fried, makes a tasty bite as well. When I was in digs at Cullen the Landlady there took in holiday makers on a weekly basis for dinner, bed and breakfast, and one afternoon she said to me its rabbit for dinner tonight so do'nt you say anything to the guests. The dish was made from cooked rabbit meat she had removed from the bone and compressed it with a seasoned jelly made from gelatine. I never before had it like that but thought it was excellent and so did the guests who were very complimentary about it and asking about the way she had done the chicken.

Kim Sawyer at Dounie is into smoking various meats and one day at a shoot he was dishing out smoked rabbit. I took a taste of it but to be honest I'm not very fond of smoked meat, fish yes but meat no. With us that day was a party of French guys and they could not get enough of it. Very impressed they were with Kim's talent. Ronnie Ross dabbled in smoking as well but I had to laugh when he showed me a haunch of red deer venison he had newly smoked. It had not been dressed after coming out of a chimney and its exterior was as black as the soot in the lum. Needless to say our colleagues all got a taste but I was given a miss. I'm sure Ronnie, it was just as good as Kim's rabbit. I don't remember us having it but Ronnie has told me that in their home deer haunches that were pickled like the pork were hung up in the same way for eating as and when required. I mentioned earlier that my Mam salted venison but perhaps she did it in a brine but I don't recall it being hung up like the hams.

When we lived at Wester Gruinards I was too young to remember it myself but apparently we often had meat from the goat kids to eat. Several people have told me that you would not know the difference from mutton and one ex butcher in London I was friendly with sold it in his city butcher shops as such. I will not miss the opportunity to try it should the occasion arise.

During the war years' food was scarce in places like London where some of my aunts and uncles lived and my mother would send them down eggs and rabbits. For this purpose there were special returnable boxes sectioned off to hold 2 dozen eggs. The rabbits, still in the fur, were coupled together and tied round the necks with a piece of string bearing a label with their destination, and sent through the post like that. Try that today! In return my aunts and uncles would send us hardware such as pots, pans, kettles and other metal goods that were near nigh impossible to get in the Highlands. Until they arrived we had to use pot menders to patch the holes. To keep us in a supply of matches they would stuff one of the items with them. My uncle, Ernest Scott had a road haulage business which was taken over for war time military use and latterly a motor repair and filling station business, aptly named Scott's Corner in Harlesden. On the black market he could just about get anything bar food.

Every summer the rich relations as we called them from London came up to stay with us in the summer time for two weeks holidays. I don't know how my mother slept everyone but she did. The highlight for us boys was the fishing. They were just as keen as us to go up the hill burns or to the loch for trout and with them they brought proper fishing line, cane rods and little brass reels and hooks that had gut already attached to them. Young as we were we acted as ghillies showing them the best pools to fish and to make sure the worm was dropped into the eddies where soapy suds gathered because you could rest assure a trout would be lurking there, also putting worms on their hooks and searching the heather behind them for trout that went flying off their hooks in the excitement. Peat I understand has a certain amount of paraffin in it and this softens the water causing the suds to gather in pools below waterfalls or other places in spate water. It is supposed to be a cure for warts and I understand a local doctor recommended it in the past. Peat still in the bog is certainly a preservative for metal and wood. When they went back to London they left behind for us an abundance of hooks and lines. More recently I fell heir to the old fashioned cane rods. They don't have any significant value other than happy childhood memories, something you cannot put a price on.

We were also assured of good Xmas presents from them as well. We hung up one of Dad's big knee stockings and got up early as children of today do. However, what a difference in the contents, perhaps a new pencil and rubber, some sweets, a pair of new stockings always navy blue with white stripes round the top, and a rosy red Canadian apple which made us just as excited. From London came new board games like ludo, snakes and ladders, dominoes, tiddly winks, and marbles and later in year's fountain pens and pocket knives with our initials or names engraved on them. On the dark winter nights under the light of the tilley lamp we would play the board games or take out the new pack of cards. Another hour or so would be passed hunting the thimble. With everyone out of the room each of us would take it in turn to hide it. I suppose there was a Xmas party at the school each year but I do not recall very much about them other than making paper decorations which we coloured. A hamper of goodies came up from London to Mam and Dad but we all benefitted from that. It usually contained chocolates and other sweets, tinned fruit and Princes's Ham, different kinds of biscuits, dates packed in wooden boxes and so many goodies that we never got at other times of the year. We did not often get sweets as "num nums" but Mam give us dried fruit like raisins and currents instead. Then of course every so often she would boil up a pan of candy or toffee for us. On occasions she would make two lots one of which would have treacle in it. We would have to help rolling or pulling it out like thin rope and then twist them both together to give it a different look and when set chop it up into sweet size pieces.

Coming north for their annual holidays took the same pattern each time leaving Harlesden together and heading for an overnight stay in a hotel in Stevenage not a great distance even in those days. Between them they had three cars.   Uncle Ernest and Aunt Anne travelling in one which was usually one of the higher horse power models. Alastair and my cousin Ellen until she died came together in Alastair's Hillman coupe. Aunt Morag drove up in her Baby Austin along with boyfriend Jack Brown. She did not mind the long journey but said she was frightened of meeting Noel on his motor bike on the Gruinard road. Their second stop was at Scotch Corner and a third one at Perth. On one of the journeys Alastair got gyp from his father for missing out Stevenage. Apart from his opinion that cars at that time were not up to continual driving over long periods they were not at the hotel when they arrived and because they had no way of making contact with him they thought something had happened to him and Ellen. Jack Brown always brought up a set of bag-pipes with him and most days he would try to play them but even as children we would recognise when he got the notes all wrong and he would give us hell for laughing and tell us to clear off.

CHAPTER 8

EARLY SCHOOLDAYS

At five years old I was off to walk the mile or so to Croick Public School with Anne, Noel and an older sister Joan or Joy as she has been called ever since. Noel unofficially had his named changed from Neil and pronounced Noil to distinguish him from my dad who was also Neil. Croick School closed during the Summer Holidays of 1979 with the last two pupils, David Campbell and Marcus Munro being taken by bus to Tain. From then on all pupils in the Strath went by school bus to Gledfield Primary School at Ardgay before going on to Tain Royal Academy for their secondary education. Only this week, Mrs Mary Bruce, the last person to teach at Croick School died at the age of 96 years. Gruinard Estate had a pre-emption right to buy the property from the Council and when they did it was first used as accommodation for fishing guests. Since then it has been sold twice and the current owners have extended and modernised it completely.

The teacher, a Miss Judge, put me in a double seat right in front of her desk with a girl called Roberta from down the Braelangwell Lodge way. We were given a jigsaw puzzle to do and I just sat there looking at it and made no attempt to put it together. Miss Judge came over to my desk and was showing me what to do. Then she told me to do the same. I said "Anne will do it" "No you do it" said the teacher. "I will not" said I. My reply was obviously the wrong thing to say and angered Miss Judge. In a very raised voice she said "I do not like little boys who say they will not" and in the same mouthful told an older girl, Helen Ross, who was sitting in the back row with my sister Joy, to get the strap from her desk. I was taken out onto the floor in front of everyone and got a good whack of the belt, the first of many to come.

My response was not to cry even if I was only five but to run for the door wetting my pants on the way and leaving a trail of piddle across the wooden floor. On reaching the door I turned round and shouted back at her that I was not coming to school again. Home I went but next morning with sandwiches in my bag I was off to school again as if nothing had happened. Although I fell out with Miss Judge within the first hour of my schooling I still remember her with fondness and to this day I think she was the best teacher I ever had. When I stood beside her at her desk to learn my reading I was attracted to a fairly large cairngorm brooch she wore on the lapel of her jacket and I would stop the reading every so often and play with it. She did not mind but told me to concentrate on the book and my reading instead.

I never see children with it now but when I was first taught to write we had books with all the letters and figures outlined by a series of dots and we had to join them up to form the letter and then started to write them without the dots. Joined up writing was taught in the same way. Tables up to twelve were learned off by heart. This stood the test of time and I'm not sure why some schools don't teach them. I got into an argument with a young man from London who was never taught them and he relied entirely on a pocket calculator to do arithmetic but could not tell if the answer was correct or otherwise. He did not have a clue how to work things out in the traditional way I was taught.

Although the Second World War had started by then I didn't really know at first what it meant. I remember ration books being issued for everyone and black coloured blinds being put on our living room window at night to blot out any light that could be seen from outside. My Dad had a carbide gas lamp for the front of his bicycle but he was not allowed to use it. I may still have the twin cell battery torches we had. One had a metal front to it instead of a lense with a slit across the middle that let out the minimum of light. The other had a metal hood that hinged down over the lense. They were khaki coloured so may have been military issue to the Home Guard of which my Dad was a member. We were issued with gasmasks and had to carry them back and fore to school. There were times when we had to practice getting them on and off. News bulletins and propaganda like "Germany Calling," were broadcast on the radio throughout the day and everyone listened to them.

Dad's bicycle carbide lamp   *Home guard hand torch*

A game we played at school was called French and English where the playground was divided into two with a line drawn across the middle. There were rules to it but the main theme was to take prisoners from the opposing team or get everyone from your team to the far off wall. At Croick it never changed to German and English although that would have been more appropriate for the time. Catriona has told me that they played the same game but called it "Bulldog."

Were the summers warmer then or not? I do not know but often we would walk home from school barefoot. The road on the Braelangwell side was tarmacadamed up as far as Coneas Bridge. Beyond that and up the Gruinard side it was a rough gravel track, often in places with heather or rushes growing in the middle, maintained by men like Davie Ross, Mid Gruinard and Charlie MacGregor from Amat who each looked after a few miles of it keeping the ditches and off lets clear and filling in the potholes with material they dug out with pick and shovel from small quarry holes along the way and barrowed the stuff to wherever it was needed. Scrub or tree branches were never allowed to encroach over the verges and each of those dedicated men took a pride in their work. Sadly Charlie was found some years later dead in the small burn that comes down off the hill above Urquhart's Croft house. Davie was a contractor in his own right and must have been involved in blasting rock because he had loads of surplus fuse which every so often we would go along and get from George Ross to flush out a sticking ferret from down a burrow. They did not like the obnoxious smell or the intense smoke that came off it when burned. Sometimes it found its way to the village where it would be set alight and not always at Halloween. The pool in the river behind the croft house at Mid Gruinard is named, The Contractors. After the Second World War broke out concrete gun emplacements were sited at strategic places along the roadsides throughout the country and up the Braelangwell side of Strathcarron. The milestones were buried so not to assist the enemy. On many main routes they have been replaced but the ones I remember of are still buried.

Home Guard Rifle and Shell Target

Some ferrets were notorious for lying up in the burrows after they had killed a rabbit and had a good feed. When you dug in to retrieve them they would be curled up in the fur and sound asleep. For most we carried with us a length of stout fence wire with one end flattened out to about twice its width. If the dead rabbit was not too far in we would push the wire to it and keep twisting it until it had a good grip of the rabbit's fur and then pull it out. We always did a dummy run with the wire first to check that it was not the ferret we were in contact with. This we could tell from the hair on the end of the wire. There were no electronic locaters in those days or proper muscles available then but we improvised with string to prevent them getting hold of and killing the rabbits down the holes. The string was first put across the ferret's mouth making sure the tongue was not trapped and both ends were tied under the bottom jaw with a single knot. The ends were then taken up over the bridge of the nose and tied with a single knot before being tied securely under the lower jaw. To stop the ferret from clawing it off with its feet we would tie it back to a collar made from the same string. A more callous and cruel method to stop them killing was to snap off the ends of their incisor teeth with pliers. I saw it done but never resorted to it myself.

It was a good feeling to walk bare-foot on the tarred road but on a hot sunny day when the tar softened and oozed out from between the chips the soles of our feet got rather sticky with it and Mam had to rub butter into the skin to dissolve it and get our feet clean but she never complained. We were living at Gruinard by the time they tarred the Gruinard side and only then as far as the gates to Gruinard Lodge. The proprietor at that time was Mrs Kemmis and it just so happened that she was a member of the District Council. With a bit of sarcasm, good for her everyone thought. When the next stretch of road was done the roadmen first laid out forty gallon drums of tar and heaps of chips from the quarry in readiness. Wicked as we were then, a few of us hit on the idea of testing our ex army jack knives which had a spike on them for piercing tins to see if we could hole the barrels in the same way. After we all had a go at this we then decided it would be fun to roll the barrels down the braes on the road and watch the tar spurting out as they went.

CHAPTER 9

THE CARRON IN SPATE

Not long after I started school there was a tremendous spate in the river. My father came to the school about lunch time and asked the teacher to get the pupils away home because of flooding. The water was flowing over the wooden cladding on the school footbridge and my father said we had to go up and cross Coneas Bridge and go home that way. Just to get some idea how high the river rose that August day Jim Gilmour and I measured the distance from the cladding on the bridge down to the water and for an average summer level we reckoned it would be eight metres. Further down the strath some of the wooden bridges across the road got washed away and coles and rucks of hay with rabbits on top of them floated either down the river or to the edges of the fields where fences stopped them from going further. When we got to Coneas Bridge we found that the river was out on the banks and flowing round the end of the stone parapets. We had to wait with Donald Urquhart and his wife at their croft until 7pm when the water had subsided enough for us to get across the bridge. When we got down near Sgodachail to the Millers Pool the river was across the road and up into the wood and we could not get anywhere near the road bridge over the Sgodachail Burn to get to our home. We took a route through the hill to a suitable crossing place in the burn and Arthur carried each of us across on his back. After that flood dead salmon and trout could be found out on the fields when the water level subsided and where they got trapped in hollows and ditches.

When I worked at Gruinard Estate the school bridge got into such a state of disrepair that it was under threat of closure or to be removed altogether. A dispute arose as to who was actually responsible for it, the Council saying it was the Education Authority and vice versa. They also tried to say it was the responsibility of the estates on either side of the river. I had a couple of meetings with Colonal Gilmour the local District Councillor and who got EEC funding for the replacement of Coneas Bridge. From a small fund that he administered I was successful in getting the road up to Lower Hilton surfaced with tar macadam and he arranged to have the cladding on the school bridge replaced. In my opinion to date he was the best Councillor we ever had and never slow to fight for a worthy cause. It always amused me when I heard one councillor describe to me about a colleague from this area who was pretty useless in the Chamber and was likened to the doggie in the back window of a car that shook and nodded its head but never spoke The paintwork on the steel structure of the bridge is now badly in need of restoration and I would like to think the Community Council for Ardgay and District would pursue this as a worth while project.

Although the bridge was built for foot passengers only it was used by cyclists both pedal and motor. Live stock, such as cows going to Braelangwell to the bull and our horse for whatever reason, was taken across it. If they were shy and reluctant to go over on it we would put our jacket over the head and it was amazing the difference that made. George Ross who rented the land that Renwick used to have at the top of Strathkyle put about 100 sheep there for grazing and several times a year for clipping or dipping along with Elsie he would drive them across the hills via Whale Cottage and over the footbridge.

The School Bridge and the Gorge

A good spate coming down the Gorge but well below the bridge cladding

The same flood, two worthies were standing on Bonar Bridge discussing the high water and watching the debris going past when a third approached them and asked what they were expecting to see. The reply was, "Marak" Eyre. Mary was an elderly lady who lived in an old cottage very close to the water edge of the Carron. I knew her quite well because she came up every evening to clean the school and reset the fire and if she was unable for any reason the teacher got me to do it for ten shillings a week. She was a bit eccentric and cycled everywhere on her old bike, always wearing several raincoats at the same time to keep the newer ones clean. Her son Alec, if you went into the house would stick his head in a recess in the gable end of the living room so that you could not see him. Well that is what he thought. If he was outside he would take off up the banks of the Altdoyne Burn and hide until you went away. I have spelt the name of the burn as it has been pronounced for as long as I can remember but it has a Gaelic title and when linked with Corvest the croft next to it, refers to a deep burn flowing through a gully known as the Monsters Corrie. Their house has been empty for many years but the last time I was in it the wooden box beds were still there.

Another eccentric, Donald Urquhart or just Urquhart as he was better known, had a great fancy for Nina Craig the local church minister's daughter but she would have nothing to do with him so he advertised for a wife and many women from the Inverness area came up to his croft but never stayed very long. Then the one he subsequently married arrived. After about a week she went home to Inverness only to return next day with her family which she never told him about. We got to know the kids and although they were younger than us we sometimes went to their house to play with them. We were sat down at the table with them for dinner one day and platefuls of broth was dished up with a meat pie in it for each of us. Another time we were all at the table having tea with Urquhart sitting at one end and his wife at the other. Urquhart asked his wife to pass the butter to him but she just ignored him. When he asked again she told him to get his own so and so butter. At that point he jumped from his chair and made for her. She ran out at the door. He followed, grabbing an axe on the way. That was time for us to run like hell for home and I think it was the last time we went there.

He wanted a sixpence in the shilling and his wife, before leaving him took every penny off him. On their wedding day he would have dropped her if Nina would just have said yes to him. Before the wedding he would be asking people if they were coming to it. No invitations were sent out to anyone. He would say, "Just follow the crowd." Before he married he used to come to our house on a Sunday for his dinner. One day we had a good laugh at him trying to sup custard and prunes with his fork until my dad suggested he used his spoon. He brought some washing for my mother to do and each time he would say, "Just the cuffs and the collar Mistress." He had two old horses which he tried to do the croft work with and one day he was ploughing a field with them opposite the Sgodachail fanks. He carried a pail of stones on the shaft of the plough to throw at the horses each time they stopped. I should have mentioned among other things he was quite deaf. My father and Willie MacDonald would be calling across the river for the horses to stop, which they were only too pleased to do, and after a stone was thrown they would set off again. This went on until the bucket was empty and in his temper at the horses he flung the empty bucket up between them.

He was a member of the local branch of the Home Guard and on training nights they had many a laugh at his expense. They were taking it in turn during rifle practice to fire at a rock some distance away. When it came to his turn he fired at a rock about twenty yards from where he was and could hardly do anything other than hit it. He rolled over on his back shouting, "I hit it, I hit it," whilst the others dived for cover at the sound of the bullet as it ricocheted over their heads. He worked on the crusher at Ardcronie quarry and wore his army issue of boots until the toes were out of them. Not being fit for training sessions he wore a pair of brown shoes on parade but still put on the ankle gaiters as well. It was not uncommon for him to stick the ends of birch saplings in the fire to burn and leave the long ends trailing across the floor and out at the door if they were that long. Archronie Quarry at that time employed thirty to forty men, some of them billeted on site. Now it is all done mechically and only one permanent person there.

In more recent years a retired shepherd came to live in Amat but he wanted something as well. He had a small flock of sheep he brought with him but when ordering feed for them it was in quantities more in keeping with numbers he looked after when in employment. He worked for a spell at Forest Farm where on top of every bit of hill he built a cairn of stones and got his nickname "The Curlew". At a sheep sale at Lairg by his way of it he would run up the price of a tup but this back-fired on him when the auctioneer knocked it down to him for a figure in the region of nine hundred pounds. A few days later another tup killed it. He was very popular at the lodges for entertainment as a kind of local jester who they had a good laugh at. He used to buy shepherds crooks for fifty pounds or more and kid people on that he made them. He would then sell them on to the fishing guests but for a lot less than what he paid for them and often going home with only a bottle of whisky for his troubles but having said all of that he was a character and well liked in the district.

CHAPTER 10

ILLICIT WHISKY

In the croft above Alec Eyre's one, lived two brothers at Corvost, Jimmy and John Ross the "Pecka". John was a very religious man attending church every Sunday, whilst Jimmy was the complete opposite. Jimmy did most of the work on the croft but in his younger days spent much of it distilling whisky in illicit stills up the Aldoyne burn side. On a Sunday he would come to see my father and I would sit there in awe listening to him about getting chased by the excisemen and the narrow escapes he had. He was grabbed once by the collar of his jacket but managed to riggle out of it leaving the jacket behind and ran and hid for days in the woods and gully above Corvost. The "Pecka", on his way home from the village one day stopped on Carron Bridge and got talking to one of the toffs who was fishing there. The river had been in spate but the level was falling fast and the toff remarked to Jimmy about how quickly it had fallen. In reply Jimmy said, "Yes it rises and falls as quick as a man's penis." The same toff asked which fly he should be fishing with and Jimmy replied, "A Green Highlander." The toff thinking he was taking the "Mickey" out of him departed very quickly without saying another word. The Green Highlander fly, although not so now, was a very popular one for catching salmon.

He talked about other worthies like Geordie Burke and Willie "Floor" Ross, senior who lived a little bit further down the strath from him. Not only were they salmon poachers but had their illicit stills as well. They used to shoot the salmon going up over the fords or send the collie dogs out for them. The excisemen arrived one day to search Geordie Burke's house but luckily they were seen coming by his wife who stuffed a cushion up below her dress to make out she was pregnant and then sat on the cask of whisky by the fireside with the dress down on the floor around her. When the excisemen arrived another time to arrest him Geordie armed with a shotgun and cartridges escaped into the wood. He fired a number of shots in their direction warning them not to come any nearer and Jimmy thought it was about a week he stayed in the wood before it was safe to come home. Hiding for long periods seem to be quite common and food would be put out for them at pre arranged places. Geordie was subsequently arrested and imprisoned at Tain. Sir Charles Ross of Balnagown Castle who also owned Braelangwell apparently advised him to plead insanity and secured his release. To stop the excisemen from finding one lot of illicit whisky he took the casks to Braelangwell Lodge and placed them amongst similar ones in the cellar, going back for it when things quietened down. I would say by the sound of it he was Sir Charles's supplier.

A market existed for the illicit whisky in Tain but the problem was getting it there by horse without being caught. George Ross's Great Grandfather Hugh was making such a journey when he got arrested by the excise men. On reaching Edderton he said he needed to relieve himself but instead took the opportunity to make a run for it and took off into the hills. He made his way to Carn Bhren which he was familiar with and not far from his home, where he hid for days because his house was being watched for his return. The search ended when he was seen above the house and the excise men set a dog after him. By some means or other he killed the dog and they did not bother him after that. Up on the flats where the peats were cut above my old home at Gruinard "The Pecka" was adamant that a flagon of whisky was hidden there but never found, not even by the person who put it there. Something else that was never found was a diamond engagement ring lost on the steepest part of the path after it leaves the fir wood above the lodge.

A Rutter Spade, Two Tuskers and a Flachter Spade (Sandy Chisholm)

A day on the hill cutting the peats was very much a job for all the family but the highlight of the day for the kids was the picnic. If it was new peat bank that was to be started, Dad would probe with a long stick, usually hazel, to establish sufficient depth and length of the bank so that cutting there could go on for several years. An old and well used bank was straight forward. Firstly the area to be cut, probably a strip up to two yards wide, would be marked off with a specially shaped spade known as a rutter. The pieces of heathery or deer grass turf would then be scaled off with another tool made for the purpose known as flachter spade to expose the suitable peat for cutting. Those pieces would be laid out in the bottom to cover over the previous year's peat cuttings and let the vegetation carry on growing. The actual peat required for burning was then cut with a knife known as a tusker made in the shape of the letter "L" with a long handle attached. With this tool they could be thrown out on to the clean ground for drying but sometimes a man or woman would stand down in the bottom and throw them out by hand. Several more visits to the site, normally referred to as "the moss", would be made to turn the peats as they dried, set them up on end and when completely dried to build them into stacks to wait being brought home.

The Moss

As I said John was very holy and gave plenty to the church and not just at Harvest Thanks Giving. He and Jimmy took week about to do the cooking and when a lot of men were there for the threshing of the oats it was Jimmy's turn. When they sat down to have dinner the men were very complimentary about the potatoes and other vegetables Jimmy had on the table. John not wanting Jimmy to get all the credit said, "I'll show you vegetables. Far better than what is on your plates." At that he went out into the front porch to find that Jimmy had used the vegetables he had ready for the church on Sunday. An enormous row then got up between them. Once a week Jimmy would walk up to the Post Office at The Craigs to collect his pension and when he did not return home after one such trip a search was made for him and he was found walking up the track towards Loubconich. It was thought that he had stopped to light his pipe, turned his back to the wind and set off again in that direction. John was into making hazel walking sticks of various designs. The practice was to select a straight sapling growing out from the side of a tree and cut out a block of wood along with it. It is then left to dry out or season to avoid it splitting. The carving of the head takes time and patience and a work of art when finished. The question is often asked, "When is the right time to cut it from the tree?" You will be told, "In the winter time when the sap has gone out of it." That may be correct but other good advice is to cut it when you see it otherwise someone else will get there before you. The same is often said about deer heads.

My brother Ernest was ploughing for them one spring in a very old Fordson tractor. He did not take a piece with him to eat thinking he would get his dinner or at least a cup of tea from them but to overcome his hunger he raided their henhouse and took several eggs which he tied into his handkerchief and hard boiled them in the radiator of the tractor which had a large oval shaped opening on the top and washed them down with a drink of water from the burn.

Regular army troops marched up and down past the school and we were allowed to sit in the windows and watch them go by and see some of them jumping in the puddles to splash their colleagues. They were camped just below our house at Schodachail and down at Braelangwell. Sometimes for night training they would do route marches across the hills to Strathkyle. Others would be driven round there during the day and would have to cross the hills in the opposite direction. One night, sometime after midnight, we were awakened by one of the soldiers who had to turn back off the hill and slightly lost his way in the dark resulting in him stumbling over a low wall down into the sheep fanks and breaking an ankle. They had big guns sited down near Braelangwell and practiced firing fifteen pound shells up on to the hills between Croick and Alladale, with the shepherds and keepers being warned for their own safety to stay off the hills when this went on.

CHAPTER 11

THE MINISTER'S DAUGHTER

As I said, that was the first of many whacks of the belt to come my way, both in primary and secondary, from teachers who wielded it with all their might on alternative hands until they thought they had a submission. One was a history teacher called Mr Dick at Tain Royal Academy. A very tall man and boy oh boy he knew how to hurt you. He first made you pull up your sleeves and if you tried in the slightest to move your hand for him to miss, he went for the wrist and forearm the next time, something like going for the jugular. He was renowned for the belt throughout the academy and many teachers sent us to him if they thought that was more appropriate punishment. A few of us who got it regularly would dare one another to pull our hands back or tilt them over just as the belt was coming down on it so that the teachers would get it down their legs.

The science teacher, "Sniffy" as he was known, was a very short man and many of the boys including myself were taller than him. We would deliberately provoke him, forcing him to get the belt out for the simple reason he had to stand on an upturned orange box to give it. He was not a bad sort and a long way short of the worst, a woman who we called "The Shark". In one term alone I got the belt from her every day for six weeks. It never bothered me other than the fact I was kept back until the next class, made up of sixth form pupils, came in. To any scholar reading this, the moral of this story is to learn your poetry verbatim even if it is, "How They Brought The Good News From Ghent To Aix". A story I was told recently about "The Shark" was that she was the victim of a road accident in Tain when she was knocked over by a car. Two of her ex pupils were discussing it and one said to the other, "I hope you just left her there". I wonder why but not much sympathy was extended to her by them either.

Returning to Croick School where I first started, Miss Judge left to take up another post, and as a temporary measure Miss Nina Craig, the Croick minister's daughter, stood in until the vacancy was filled by a Mrs Bruce who remained there until its closure. This took the best part of a year or maybe longer. She was a nice person but far too soft to be a teacher. She never got Miss Craig, simply Nina, nor did she get the respect she deserved and certainly not from me and other older boys. To put it mildly we just about ran riot and her having no control over us whatsoever.

Once a week, regular like clock work Bowie's bakery van would stop at the school for us to buy a penny square of iced ginger bread. No way was that van not going to stop but we insisted that all of us should go out to the roadside to wait for it. This went on for several weeks but somehow she managed to coax us into the class room to wait for it. This did not last very long and we started climbing up on the high window sills to watch for the van. The rule was for two pupils per window but like every other rule she made they were broken immediately and as many pupils as physically possible were up there. So much pushing, shoving and a sort of friendly squabbling went on that no lessons could be taught and poor Nina just had to sit there unable to do anything about it.

The rocks of the river or over in Whale Cottage Caledonian Pine Wood was more of a playground to us than within the bounds of the school. This part of the river up from the foot bridge is known as the gorge, steep cliff like rocks on either side with narrow but fast and deep running water below. When the river level was low enough and you had the nerve, at one point you could actually jump across from one side to the other. One slip or wrong move and I would not be writing this today. Some of our earlier goats drowned in that stretch, a horrifying thought but boys will be boys.

The whale cottage wood had been planted a hundred or more years previous by the proprietors of Braelangwell Estate in the shape of a whale, with a cairn of white quartz rocks built to form the eye. It remains today very much as it was built and can be found a little bit south and west of the old cottage which has lain empty for as long as I can remember and has now fallen into a complete state of disrepair. Whoever the men were that built the eye did not choose a level piece of ground. Instead they built it on a slope using very large rocks at the lower part and smaller ones around the higher ground to form what looks like a level plinth. The centre is built up about four or five feet higher. We as children got fun from following one another round and round on the base and I can recall my mother continuously telling us to be careful and not fall off it. There was a bit of a drop down the slope at the lower part. Men in those days must have taken a pride when building walls or other structures to use the biggest rocks or stones they could find and not always for the base.

When the mood took us at lunch time us boys would take off up the wood to guddle for trout in the burn. This was great fun but the mischief started when Nina tried to get us back to our classes at 2 o'clock. She would be out at the front of the school calling and blowing her whistle. We knew perfectly well what that meant, but for us it was time to give her the run around and she would end up over in the wood chasing after us. When she was up at the top by the cottage we would be down at the bottom or vice versa. This would go on for half an hour or more and then we would quietly run back to the school, sit at our desks like little angels, waiting for her return. She knew it was pointless talking to us and just got on with the other pupils lessons. We were out at 3 o'clock and away home anyway. The amazing thing about her was that she never once reported our bad behaviour to our respective parents. Heaven help us had she done so.

I for one was not going to forget the thrashing my father gave Ernest and me for walking back and fore over the parapet of Coneas Bridge. Jimmy MacGregor had been working in the fields when he saw his son Willie, Ernest and I on the parapets some twenty feet above rocks and the water so, nothing for it but to get on his bicycle and chase us home. As soon as he told Dad, we got for our own good our just deserts. Willie told us later that he got the same. Believe it or not, but that was the only spanking I can recall my father ever giving us. Some would say I never got enough of it, but then at home I was quite well behaved. Corporal punishment never did me any harm and I think it was wrong for the strap to be banned in the schools or home.

Local people reading this book where it refers to Coneas Bridge will I assume say it has been wrongly spelt. Over the years people have known it as Connies Bridge taking its name from some person but it was also said to me by Willie MacDonald that it was related to the willows in the wood nearby but I could never see the connection with that. At the same time if it did relate to a person named Connie, Willie would certainly have known about her. On researching gaelic place names I came across the word "eas" meaning a fall as in waterfall and with the word "con" meaning adjoining area. The two words put together I am convinced means the adjoining waterfalls and fits in perfectly with that particular crossing of the river so for that reason I am going to stick to the name Coneas.

Whale Cottage itself was built about the early eighteen hundreds for a river watcher but evidence of much older settlements are visible nearby. It was so high up on the hillside that he had a very good view up and down the river. Apparently there were very few trees on the banks then to interrupt his view but now the landscape has changed so much that from the cottage one can barely see the river. The last watcher, a man named John Ross, lived there with two unmarried sisters, Martha and Mary. I remember Willie MacDonald telling me that when he was at school he went up to get his lunch from them. I often heard my Dad talk about them and the big family there were of the Ross's and McKay's there. Most of them died around 1920 but a Robert MacKay who was married to Mary was accidentally shot on the 13th August, 1880. She herself died in 1919. The grouse shooting season had started the day before and I wondered if he had been out with a party when it happened but I could not find any information to establish that. The last of the occupants to die there was a Janet Ross and she passed away in July, 1924 and some years later Martha and Mary went to America for a holiday and asked my mother to look after the house and contents until they got back. The holiday turned out to be a rather extended one and eventually when they decided to come home they could not get their money out of the country so they decided to stay for good.

We visited the cottage regularly to check on things. Sometimes Mam would put a fire on to warm the place up or, for just to make a pot of tea. It was fun for us to be with her, a sort of magical feeling, not only in the house which had a distinct smell of moth balls but to the wood itself. Because of the dense canopy there was little or no vegetation just masses of pine needles, cones and plenty of deep hollows and rocks for hiding behind when playing hide and seek. A few yards out from the front door was a white quarts rock which was special to us. It stood only two to three feet high at the front and had a sloping back to it. Bearing in mind that we were still very much tiny tots then we would climb up on to it and jump off at the front. I think the red squirrels added to all of this good feel factor to the place but we did have to keep a look out for adders. Often they would be out in the day time curled up on a rock or other sunny place. From time to time our collies and sheep got bitten by them. Dad would use his pocket knife to lance the swelling, squeeze out the venom and then just let the wound bleed to get rid of any poison left in it. When fishing the Sgodachail burn one day we came across an adder with a huge swelling down its neck and after killing it we cut it open to find a half grown dead rat inside it. Noel, after carrying home a sack of coal from the fanks at Sgodachail dumped it down at the door and went into the house. Minutes later an adder came crawling along the passage and the frightening assumption was that it came from the sack and if so Noel was lucky that he did not get bitten on the back of his neck. Red squirrels were quite common up Strath Carron. You could see them in other woods I mention but also at Braelangwell Lodge and up at Amat Lodge where there appeared to be an abundance of them.

Mam, without fail, always had a basket of home baked goodies for our picnics at Whale Cottage and the same basket was used to take home gooseberries, black currents, rasps and apples from the garden. Some times before going home we would gather fir cones or "doorkins" as we called them. This was our make believe sheep, lambs, tups etc, depending on their size and make pens or other enclosures from twigs, nothing plastic, all biodegradable. Other times Mam would tie up little bundles of dry sticks for each of us to carry home for kindlers.

On a recent visit to Whale Cottage there was not a trace of a berry bush or apple tree of any kind. Gone also is the bridge made from tree trunks that you had to cross on your way up to the house. In fact the entire track is only now accessible by all terrain vehicles. Bracken and nettles grow right up to the house walls and gone is the grassy front where we had our picnics. Tranquillity of the place remains but the only living creature I encountered was a barn owl that flew silently from the east bedroom and disappeared over the burn into the more recently planted forest. Apart from that the only other signs of life was a few deer droppings amongst the dead bracken and where a fox had been and left his calling card at the skeleton of a dead sheep which probably died of starvation during the past winter snow storm. Back in the severe winters of 1941/42 I can recall seeing herds of red deer that took shelter in that same wood and the carcases of many that died from starvation. They were so desperate for food that they stripped the bark of mature pine trees. Like the deer the sheep had a very hard time as well and I can recall my Dad and Arthur probing with long poles in search of those buried in the deep drifts but many never survived their ordeal.

When my mother got the letter from Martha and Mary to say that they were not coming back, word of this went round the district very quickly and the cottage and shed kept getting broken into and things stolen. My mother was then instructed to take everything she wanted from Whale Cottage for her own use. Well that came as a godsend. We had real blankets and sheets, cutlery for everyone and so much more. Some of the larger items which we did not need were left there and the rusty old remains of the beds still lie under the rubble to this day. In recent years the roof fell in and the shed down by the burn has rotted away and there is not a trace left of it now. Even to this day family members and friends pay a visit to Whale Cottage, a sort of Pilgrimage one could say, but no place to be when the midges are out.

For a number of years the apple trees at Whale Cottage failed to bear fruit and I had learned from somewhere that if you hammered a rusty nail into the trunk just above ground level it could start them fruiting again. I was curious about this but sure enough fruit came on them the next season. I tried it again on a crab apple tree near the roadside below Heatherlea and Geordie said it was the first time he had ever seen apples on it. Years after that in the garden at Gruinard I did it successfully with other apple trees.

Our behaviour at school under Miss Craig got so bad that the local bobby was up at us twice. The first time when some boyish pranks got out of hand, the wooden panels in the lower half of the door got kicked in by boys on the outside trying to get in, after being shut out by others on the inside. The telling off from him had no effect either because only weeks later when we were up the riverside and came across rabbit gin traps set by a trapper we pulled about six of them out of the burrows and threw them into the river. At first it was thought that they were stolen but we admitted to the policeman what we had done. Because of our age he could do nothing more than tell us off for a second time. My father would have been well justified in giving us another thrashing but for some reason he did not perhaps because others were involved.

Every summer about hay time a tramp by the name, Bill Murray, came up the strath and would sleep in barns where he got work on the crofts. Tramps then as opposed to tinkers were referred to as "Milestone Inspectors" and in the cities today "The Homeless". One day he was walking up the road on the Braelangwell side from the school and the usual gang on our bikes cycled up past him calling him names about being a tramp. At first he was sitting on the bank of the road but chased after us saying he would get us. Stupidly we never thought about having to cycle past him again to get back to the school and we were forced to take a detour through the hill to avoid him. He was up at Amat another time cutting firewood at the riverside for Mrs MacGregor but to distinguish her from Jimmy MacGregors's wife she was always referred to as the widow and the croft took on the name, "The Widow's". She was a very nice person and allowed us to kill rabbits on her croft. She had three of a family all much older than me and I understand David was held prisoner for sometime by the Japanese. It was very frosty and we were messing about on our bikes and on seeing him, again we started shouting cheek at him. When we got fed up with that we went on to a frozen pond by the roadside near the old Free Church and were sliding about on it when Bill Murray suddenly appeared from nowhere and tried to get hold of one of us. Willie Macgregor and I made off on our bikes but Ernest got cut off and tried to run for it at the same time shouting, "It wasn't me." Bill gave up after a while and went back to the firewood. That was the last time we give cheek to him.

CHAPTER 12

OUR NEW TEACHER

A new teacher, Miss Molly Ellis, arrived which probably was just as well and she was a different kettle of fish. She put up with no nonsense or wickedness and I found myself at the other end of the belt on many occasions with her. About the time of her arrival the Whale Cottage wood, like two other woods on Braelangwell Estate, "The Clump and The Egg" were cut down by Canadian lumberjacks from the Forestry Corp who came over here during World War ll for a massive tree felling programme, similar to when the Americans came during the First World War. Miss Molly saw the limbs as an excellent source of firewood and was not long in making use of our excess energy in getting the firewood across the foot bridge. She also had us digging the garden, planting and weeding.

Mentioning the Clump Wood reminds me of two things. I do not know the reason why but my younger brother Ernest was frightened of passing along the road beside it if he was alone. Yet he would happily play in it as long as somebody else was with him. The other thing I am reminded of was an owl's nest in a disused rabbit hole under fir tree roots. She would fly off as you approached it. After the eggs satisfactorily hatched out we would watch the fluffy white chicks grow until they left the nest. Thinking back on it they must have been the best fed chicks in the area with the amount of young rabbits we provided them with. When the new-born rabbits started to run about we used to catch some of them up and keep them as pets in a netting run with a chicken coup as their shelter. They lived on a mixture of oatmeal and tea leaves but so that they had plenty fresh grass we moved the run every few days. They loved to nibble away at Dandelion leaves we collected and other greens from the vegetables in the garden. On the hillside above the clump was a holly tree rich with red berries. Every year Mam would get us to fetch twigs from it to add to our other Xmas decorations. Near the clump at the roadside were two rocks which we as little ones often played on. To us they had steep sloping faces and quite slippery when wet. We never went past them without trying to climb up and slide down them.

She did not remain Miss Molly for long and soon got her claws into the most eligible bachelor in the glen, Willie MacDonald from Amat na Tua, the upper township, and soon afterwards they got married. Because of the distinctiveness of their hair they were nicknamed the black cock and the grey hen. The marriage did not last. Willie went home to live on the croft with his mother and sister Lottie. Just beside their house stands the gable end only of a house once lived in by two of Willie's great aunts. Willie often spoke to me about it as a memorial to Sandy McGregor, Jimmy's father, who built it and how it stood the test of time. He thought a plaque with such details should have been put on it. Sandy also built foot or pony paths on the Gruinard hills, the last one from the Glen Burn up to the bottom of Carn Bhren which means Raven's Cairn but legend has it that Fingal's dog Bran entered a cairn there and was never seen again Willie told me that Sandy would set off every Monday with his horse and provisions for a week and work there until Friday, sleeping over night under a stack cover draped over fence posts. I came on the grassy spot just by chance when I found pieces of a cast iron kettle, fire clay jam pots and bits of other old crockery.

Sandy MacGregor more often than not was known as Sandy Harn. The spelling of Harn I use for pronunciation only and it is thought to come from the Gaelic word Chairn as in Loch a Chairn on Glencalvie Estate which means a cairn. It is possible that Sandy or his forbears were in service or worked as a stalker or in some other employment at the lodge there and took on the byname from that. It is more likely to be from a cairn near to their original home on the croft at Amat which was along by the burn and above the road. This cairn is actually on the west side of the burn and rises steeply from the roadside to form a sort of knoll with plenty of evidence at the top of it being a cairn of stones originating from some historical building. Jimmy MacGregor, his son, who I have also written about and worked the family croft was known by the same name and so was his son Ali but not any other members of the family, although collectively I used to hear them referred to as "The Harns". Disrespect was never the intention in using by-names. It was only to distinguish one person or family by the name of the place where they lived or the type of work they carried out so that they were not confused with others of the same name in the community. Willie MacDonald related a story to me that Sandy once told him of, where a fox hunter was killed by his own terriers. It was alleged to have happened about half way on the track going out from the west end of Amat to Sallachy. I have passed by the area several times but I could not see any cairn or indication that such a thing had ever happened.

Miss Molly regularly went home at weekends to the family croft at Knockfarrel, Dingwall, to look after her father and brother Dan and on retirement she went there to live permanently. She was good to my parents, calling on them weekly to make sure they were alright and to see if they needed shopping. My mother said she always took back a nice piece of fresh white fish for them. Stealing apples from her garden was not such a big sin in her eyes as throwing stones into the trees to get them down. She heard stones fall on the corrugated iron roof of her garage one day and tried to find out who was responsible but none of us would admit to doing it. Us boys always stuck together and would not tell tales on any one. She had us lined up and belted each of us in turn, going up and down the row several times, then told us we had until the next day to own up. The following morning Geordie Heatherlea came to the school and told the teacher that it was his son Robin who threw the stones on his way home for lunch and that we should never have been strapped for it. Robin, who was not punished by the teacher, had to apologise to us instead. The reason for this we always said was that he was regarded as the teacher's pet because she got her milk and eggs from his father. We had Robin's sister Sybil to thank for going home and telling her dad what had happened.

Geordie was to visit the school on another occasion and he was not a happy man. One windy day at lunch time we, the boys yet again, decided it would be fun to take the contents of five waste paper sacks, set the pieces alight at the class room fire and send them up the chimney. We took it in turn to sit on the play ground wall and watch the burning paper come out the top and blow across the heathery moor. Now Geordie or Geordie Heatherlea as he was always known because of the name of his croft was a very, very, tidy man and he was having none of that mess. He left Miss Molly in no uncertain terms that he wanted every piece of unburned paper gathered up. I went home that afternoon, not only with very sore hands, but with very wet feet as well. For some reason most bits of paper happened to land in one of the many peat bogs.

Miss Molly arranged with Willie to have the school sports day in a field up at Urquhart's Croft near Coneas Bridge which he was tenant of. It was the first and only one of its kind that I can remember. The usual games and races were held, but it was a bit of a disaster for me in as much that the special shorts my mother made for me fell apart at the seams and I had to be taken home to get them changed. They were made from black velvet instead of the more robust tweed I was used to, not the material to stand up to the rough and tumble I put them through. Willie MacDonald and his cousin Charlie MacGregor, took their fiddles to the field to provide the necessary music for the likes of The Grand Old Duke of York, musical chairs, pass the parcel and other games. As the afternoon wore on the games turned to dancing Eightsome Reels, Strip the Willow, the Gay Gordons' and many more, all of which we learned to do at school.

Somebody came up with the good idea that we should retire to Willie's barn at Urquhart's croft and continue the dancing there. My father and other parents cleared the few items in it and swept the concrete floor, shavings of candle grease, the next best thing available to slipperene, was sprinkled over it. My mother and some of the other ladies went home to make more food and brought it back for a tea that was planned for later in the evening. The last of the dancers I understand did not get home until the small hours of the morning, a very good night had by all. So good, it was to be the first of many in that barn, "Barn Dances" in the truest sense of the word. Long before my time my father told me that dances and dance classes were held in the barn at our croft at Gruinard. When the woodcutters were in the area boxing went on it with the locals.

The dances to follow were more organised and the empty house next door was used by the ladies for the preparation of the food before it was taken into the barn to be passed around to everyone. Some of the young and old were invited up from the village including Ken the bobby. He liked a good drink and as a tup that was lying beside the building ran away from him he was heard to say, "There's no need to run off, come in and enjoy yourself". He was the same bobby that was standing outside Bob Fraser's shop in Ardgay discussing the window that got broken. "And what is it like on the inside?" he asked. In the same shop he asked for an empty bag of sugar. Incidentally Bob Fraser like so many other people had a nickname and his was "Quality Bob". Everything he sold according to him was of the best quality and not the utility stuff more commonly sold during the war years. They took beer and whisky up with them and an old hen-house was adapted as the bar and Ken was supposedly the best customer. Popularity and numbers soon made it necessary for a new venue to be found and the butler from Amat Lodge arranged for the use of the disused laundry. This turned out to be the ideal place, a wooden floor, plenty seating and free beer and soft drinks, all free from the lodge. Singing and dancing went on there for many years and to this day the odd private party is held in it.

Even as primary pupils we were taught to knit for the Red Cross. We started off with squares to be sewn up into blankets or garters which were quick and easy to knit. Soldiers and country people who wore breeches used them to keep up their stockings and there was a big demand for them. I learned to knit socks, even the correct way to turn the heel. They were all plain but we had to put a purl stitch down the back as far as the heel. It was not thought to be sissy like. Plenty men, gamekeepers, shepherds and others who wore plus fours or breeches knitted their own stockings during the long dark evenings. One game keeper I knew made his own plus four trousers. He unpicked an old pair stitch by stitch and cut out the shape of each piece on brown paper to retain as a pattern and because times were hard then and tweed not easy to get he made some of them up from ex army blankets. Jackets were not so easy to make. My mother who knitted for all of us would cut off the feet of stockings with all the darned holes in them and then pick up the stitches and knit new feet for them and not always in matching wool. Another thing we had to do for the war effort was to gather lichen from the birch and rowan trees to be used as a sterile dressing for wounded soldiers. Spagnum moss and tin foil was also collected on behalf of the Red Cross. We were also asked to bring to the school 2lb syrup tins, sheep wool that we could find mostly on fences and any other material which collectively could be made into foot stools. We also made things from paper mashy.

In my age group at Croick School, in the same class were Sybil Ross, Sheila Moffat and Julia MacIvor. We were the first of the Croick pupils to go to Tain Royal Academy for secondary education. This coincided with the school leaving age going up to 15 years. We all went into a "B" class, a sort of the middle of the road grading. French was a compulsory subject which I disliked in a big way. Much against my mother's wishes she wrote the headmaster and asked for me to be down- graded to a "C" class to benefit more from wood and metal work. This was agreed to and I thoroughly enjoyed that subjects. The teacher was aptly named "Dry Rot". My 15th birthday coincided with the Easter holidays and again, against my mother's wishes, I never went back. It will come as no surprise that I left school without any certificates. I think Miss Judge once gave me a book for religious knowledge perhaps because I could recite the books of the bible and that of the New Testament. Was that why I liked her so much! I don't believe we had a dictionary at home and relied solely on my mother for spelling and the meanings of words.

CHAPTER 13

MY GRAND PARENTS

My granny and grandad, John Matheson, owned the croft house a mile and a half or so down the strath from the school and on Gruinard Estate. I never knew my Grandad. Coming home one night from the village, probably the worse of having had too many drams, and as he often did, left the horse to make its own way home with the result it cut the corner to come down the brae to the house and the spring-cart capsized and Grandad was thrown out and killed. My uncle Danny who was a gamekeeper on Cawder Estate and latterly Amat for Lord Conygham, came home to work the croft and to look after Granny who was in a wheel chair as a result of a broken hip that never healed properly.

My old home at Gruinards

Uncle Danny at Cawder

I can only remember granny vaguely. She sat by the fire in the wheel chair with a blanket over her knees and a shawl wrapped round her shoulders. My mother or one of my older sisters usually Morag would go over from Sgodachail on a daily basis to look after her and latterly Uncle Danny in his final years. I spent one whole day at the fireside beside granny. I was wrapped in a blanket when Morag stripped off all my clothes and footwear to wash and dry them before going home to Sgodachail in the evening. When I arrived at Granny's that morning I ran down the brae so fast that I went head first into the midden of cow and horse dung. With all the cow wash amongst it I got myself into a right smelly mess. Not long after that my Granny died and soon after that Uncle Danny died from tuberculosis. Looking back through old church records many people, some of them in their very early years, died from TB or consumption as it was often referred to.

That year, 1942, my dad gave up the job with The Department and moved us all to this croft house but only after it was thoroughly fumigated by burning sulphur in it, the doors, windows and chimney sealed for forty eight hours. Apparently it was the normal thing and no stigma attached to it.

Back row: Joan, Noel, Morag, Arthur, Mam, Dad
Front row: Ian, Fan, Hugh, Ann, Ernest

My Mam, Mary Elizabeth Wilhemina McDonell, was born at The Keepers Cottage, Balnaboth, Glen Prosen near Kirriemuir. On leaving school she went into service and came up to Gruinard Lodge as a cook and it was there that she met my dad. On the ninth day of March, 1923 they got married at the Queensgate Hotel in Inverness by Mr Coutts the then minister from Croick Church. Geordie

73

Heatherlea was one of the witnesses. Their first home was at Wester Gruinards where dad was born, then owned by my Grandfather John Matheson who was also born at Wester Gruinards on 13th January, 1859. He in turn inherited it from my Great Grandfather Neil Matheson, both crofters. Other Matheson's like Peter, lived in it as well. I do not remember my grandparents on my mother's side. Granda McDonell, in his later years came to live at Wester Gruinards with my parents. The photograph shows him fishing the head of Moral from the Braelangwell bank and I can only assume he was up on holiday at the time from Roy Bridge where he was a gamekeeper.

Granda McDonell Fishing Head of Moral, Braelanwell.

All of the croft houses on Gruinard Estate are owned by the occupants and have been handed down from one generation to the next. The land the house stands on was owned by the estate as did the out buildings such as the byre and stable. In some instances that may now have changed. On other estates such as Amat the proprietor owns both the buildings and the land. Because there was not a steading at Wester Gruinards my father, helped by a man named Mortimer, at his own expense built one against the east gable of the house. It is still in pretty good shape but some subsidence has caused a crack at one corner.

Wester Gruinards has practically lain empty from the time we moved to Sgodachail with the exception of one or two occasions when it was used as a bothy for woodcutters or fencers. My oldest brother Ian and his wife Marjory were about to move into it when they got married but someone smashed all the windows to prevent them from doing so as they could not afford the repairs. However the house and steading still belongs to the Matheson's and hopefully one day it will be renovated. In fact when I was coming off the hill one day with Jean Matterson and the factor, Mr Milligan pointed out to me that it was about time I repaired the roof at least.

CHAPTER 14

THE JOYS OF NATURE

Living at Sgodachail and later at Gruinard was like serving an apprenticeship with nature and all the joys that went with it. We grew up with the birds and animals around us and learned just about everything we needed to know about them. From Croick School we would go out on nature trails identifying all the plants and insects we could find, drawing sketches of them, pressing flowers and leaves in heavy books until they dried out and building up a large school collection of them. Sadly today when I walk over the moors or up the river banks and I'm asked what certain plants are called their names escape me.

When spring arrived we would be off into the birch woods for hours on end searching for and counting all the different types of songbird nests, at the same time taking care not to disturb or frighten the parent birds to the point of them abandoning their eggs or young. Sometimes we would climb to the top of the tallest of trees just to identify the family from the size, colour or markings of the eggs. The makeup, shape or location of the nest would tell us the same. Up the river banks or burnsides another group of birds and their nests could be found and on the hills and moors it was different again. We could not avoid listening to the lament of the Golden Plover all around us having been told that they had swapped places with the grey partridge and were saddened by it ever after. A good Tale!

The grey partridge disappeared from the croft at Gruinard as it did from so many more sometime in the nineteen fifties. There are odd pairs of redlegs about but they are very much in-comers. Corncrakes were still common in my youth when traditional crofting was carried out. A few years ago I thought I heard one out at Garvery Croft above Bonar but because it is now heavily grazed by sheep and no crops grown there I sort of dismissed the idea until I mentioned it to Ian Bruce who was working with me at the time and he thought it was a corncrake he had heard. One small bird common to the River Carron and other rivers is the dipper which has always intrigued me and still does because of the way it can dive into the fast flowing headwaters of rocky pools and swimming upstream searching the riverbed for food.

Along the brae face of Amat na Tua there were literally hundreds of Lapwing pairs, mostly referred to by us as Peewits because of their song. Their habitat was made up of wet and boggy areas with plenty of knolls and dry banks for nesting on. In the spring when the fields on the crofts were harrowed for the sowing of corn or other crops they would nest and lay their eggs, Olive Brown shells with multi coloured markings, in a shallow scrape. In order for ourselves or the horses not to trample over them you could move the nest several yards each time and still they would settle down on their eggs and go on to hatch out their chicks. In some parts of the country their eggs were collected and sold commercially. When we lived at Lower Hilton at Culrain there were lots of them in the bogs below the house and it was there that Dr. Desmond Nethersole- Thomson often lay quietly sketching and making notes about the lapwings. Sadly like Amat they have all gone and the most you will see there now are crows, gulls and hen harriers. When we first came to live at Bonar, up on Tulloch Hill beside a small lochan six pairs of Lapwings came to nest there in the spring. Both gulls and hooded crows would sit by the nests to get the eggs as soon as they were laid and any chick that was lucky enough to hatch out. After a few years in spite of dealing with the crows all of the Peewits disappeared leaving only the gulls but then their numbers dwindled and the reason for that was buzzards taking their young. At first I thought it was young rabbits they flew over my house with but a closer watch revealed it was gull fledglings, taking them to their young in a nest over on the Golf Course.

In the same area I had two wild duck flight ponds and for a while a Red Kite could be seen flying about. As far as I was concerned they were not a problem but one day I had a visit from a police officer, two RSPB members and a guy from the local agricultural office in Lairg, armed with a search warrant to search my premises at Dalriada. They told me that the Kite had been poisoned six weeks previous and because I was the only gamekeeper in the area I was number one suspect for killing it. I pointed out to them where all the buzzard nests were in the area, also a sparrow hawk's and where a peregrines nest could be found and that if I was using poison the buzzards would be the first to disappear. However, I told them to be my guest and do whatever they wanted to do as I had nothing to hide. As far as I know birds that have eaten poisoned bait do not always die on the spot and can fly considerable distances before "kicking the bucket."

It was quite common to hear the woodpecker in the Clump or Whale Cottage woods before they were cut down but when I went to work at Gruinard I was often wakened very early morning by one rattling away at something metallic just outside the back door. I tried umpteen times to catch a sight of him but on opening the door he flew off. One morning I kept watch from a nearby shed to find that he was on the top of a hydro electric pole and giving "welly" to the metal canopy. I was down at Mid Fearn Farm one day after that when I saw the woodpecker flying from the canopy top of one pole to another and again it was like the sound of a kango hammer. Until then I always believe the drilling noise was the bird making holes into the decaying trees to get the insects . How wrong I was.

I always thought that the seagull nested on the ground or on cliff faces but at Gruinard two of them, about three miles apart at either end of the estate at the river bank, nested in trees. I said this to two of the water bailiffs because one of them was a keen photographer but they would not believe me. I told them to go and look for themselves but they did not go for several days because they thought I was playing some sort of joke on them. At the tail of Pool Moral there was a very large oak tree with some ferns growing in a fork about ten or more feet up where a Mallard duck nested two consecutive years in it. Oyster catchers, which pair up for life, came every year to nest in the gravel just out from the front door of Gruinard Lodge which a friend of mine insisted in calling them pearl fishers.

CHAPTER 15

MY FATHER'S WAY OF LIFE

Before taking the job at Braelangwell my father worked mainly as a fencing contractor or with his pony and gig would run a sort of taxi service for passengers, mainly the gentry from the lodges, using the Railway Station at Ardgay. A busy time for him was just before the glorious 12th and throughout the grouse shooting season when he would also go to the hill with his pony and panniers to carry the lunches and shot birds. He hired himself and the pony to take the stag carcases off the hills at Alladale, Duchally, Langwell, and other surrounding estates. There were not many deer forests or grouse moors in the area that he had not worked on, either as pony-man or fencer and sometimes looking after the spare dogs when grouse were shot over English Pointers or Setters.

He was good with his hands, a very practical man, and I can remember him as if it was yesterday working in the barn at Sgodachail fanks making what we would describe today as a bench seat from fence posts and rails. When used as piece of house furniture it was called a "rest" in those days. It was not something roughly hammered together but properly dressed wood jointed and glued. He had only the basic of hand tools such as a saw, a plane, hammer and chisel. When it came home and into use in the house people travelling up or down the Strath would come in to see it. This made him proud of his achievement and "Dry Rot" was not there to keep him right. He also made a gun rack which took pride and place on the wall above the mantle shelf for his 12 bore hammered shotgun, four ten folding gun with the centre of the stock cut out and often described as a poacher's gun. Probably his favourite was a .303 Ross sporting rifle that provided us with the venison we often ate. The action of it was so smooth and one could be very accurate with the flip up open sights. Unfortunately the rifling in the barrel deteriorated so much so that it was disposed of to a gunsmith in Inverness. I believe only soft nosed bullets should have been used in it but often as not ex army (Home Guard) ammunition was fired through it for target practice, myself contributing to it.

Although he was a crofter my Dad was happier working with other people and continued in latter years as a self employed fencer until ill health took its toll. From an early age Noel did all the croft work and quite rightly fell heir to it when Dad died. My nephew Derek has the croft now and works it in conjunction with a successful joinery business. He built the new house on the croft for himself, his wife Kate and family. My sister in law Margaret still occupies the old croft house which generally still retains its original outward appearance.

When Derek built "Craigmhor" he incorporated stone in the front to enhance the appearance and take away the bareness you see on so many of the houses, including my own, done completely in the traditional harl or roughcast. At the time of handling the stone I don't expect Derek was aware of some family history connected with it. The dressed sandstone came mainly from the remains of old house ruins on Gruinard Estate and one in particular, which I have always known as Bella's. This ruin, which is situated a few hundred yards across the moor from the rear of the old Croick School once belonged to and last lived in by Isabel (Bella) Matheson, widow of Johnnie Matheson, a brother of my father. Incidentally, a short distance east of what is left of this ruin, stands an armour plated target which the home guard used for rifle shooting practice. Bella and Johnie had four of a family, two daughters and two sons. One of the sons' also named Johnnie married an Irish lady and latterly ran a Boarding House just outside Lochinver. His brother Alastair went into the Merchant Navy and was last heard of many years ago in Cardiff. Catherine lived in the Invergordon area and the other "Dodo" Murdina Smith lived in Shetland.

Derek and Kate's house

Three other houses in the same area, lastly lived in by women, are remembered by me by their names simply because of hearing them spoken about so many times by my parents. One house still stands about 100 yards from our old house at Wester Gruinards. It is still in a reasonably good state of repair with a red corrugated iron roof, although probably not the original one, and last lived in by a Grace MacCallum so naturally it has always been known as Grace's. The other one with very little left of it is half way between the old school and Heatherlea and was last lived in by a woman named Effie, short for Euphemia. There still stands some ruins of another house up on top of the hill above Wester Gruinards on an old croft site called Balnachie. Records that I know of go back as far 1838 when Donald and Effie Ross lived there. My father cultivated this croft and grew oats on it. When the corn was in stooks and waiting to be dry enough for stacking I often heard him speaking about sitting under the stooks waiting for the grouse to land on them. The hand would be ready to snatch them by the feet or sometimes he would set snares made from single strand rabbit snare wire and catch them in this way. Before that house tumbled down I remember over a number years seeing a

79

very large bible sitting in an alcove in the east gable end, probably left there by the last occupants. I never did know what became of it but in any case by now with the roof off, the elements would have destroyed it. George Ross from Heatherlea who is keen on ornithology has recently fenced off this croft from livestock in an effort to get back the black game there. At the top of the fields at the east end of Heatherlea Croft is the ruins of Bain's Cottage. Not so much the cottage, but Bain or to give him his full title, Peter Bain, faired prominently in the history of the Battle of Gruinard because of the severe injuries he sustained and his subsequent imprisonment at Tain.

CHAPTER 16

RABBIT MONEY

Even before leaving Braelangwell rabbits became a source of pocket money to me and my brothers. After school, weekends or school holidays we were out there in all weathers ferreting, snaring or trapping them. Following a fresh fall of snow, rabbits always bedded out in the heather for the first few nights before returning to the burrows. We would arm ourselves with a purse net and a good heavy stick and track them to wherever they lay up. In deep heather we would put the net over the hole of entry, go round about and flush them out into it. In small bunchy type places you could judge exactly where they were sitting under the snow and just whack them over the head. Sometimes in the fields you could see the rabbits sitting in the longish grass in their beds and we would circle them round and round each time getting closer and closer until you could throw yourself on top of them. We learned how to do this from watching stoats and weasels doing it. The rabbits just sat there transfixed with terror. In the winter time the white hares would come down off the hill to the turnip pits and in the morning like the rabbits we would track them in the snow where they went back up the hill. The problem with them was the distance they would travel before bedding up. Often you would go round in circles for what seemed like miles to come right back to near where you started. I liked stewed white hare but not brown hare which is much stronger in taste.

As a back-up we always took the collie dogs with us on our missions. They saved a lot of time when ferreting because we could tell from their behaviour if a rabbit was at home or not. They would hunt them out of large patches of bracken and whins and if they could not catch the rabbit before it reached the nearest burrow we would ferret it later after it had time to settle. More often than not we had two dogs and it was amazing how they worked as a pair. One would enter the patch of bracken to flush out the rabbits whilst the other would run around the outside waiting to catch a rabbit as it bolted or to keep it within the patch of bracken. Seldom were the two dogs in the bracken at any one time. I think we ruined every collie dog my father ever owned by taking it to the rabbits. Fan, one of the new dogs my father got was very thin when it arrived. It must have been early summer because Willie Renwick said to him not to worry about it as the dog would put on weight when it got the skins of the new tatties. What kind of new tatties was he in the way of eating?

During the week we sold our rabbits to Ian Ross or McIntosh the butchers from Bonar Bridge, who came round the strath with their vans'. If we had a lot we would couple them up and hang them over the handle bars or the bar of our bikes and cycle to Bonar with them. Often we would be stopped en route, especially at Church Street at Lower Gledfield, by women wanting to buy one or two. Names that come to mind are Bella Watt and Annie Duncan. Annie used one of the rooms in her house for a little shop she had, selling sweets, biscuits and other treats that the children going to and from school would buy. They would ask us to pick good rabbits and get us to skin them as well. For that they would give us an extra shilling on top of what we charged. When dealing with butchers, even as young boys, we would haggle with them and play one off against the other until we got that extra penny or even a halfpenny per pound. From this money we started buying all our own clothes and footwear which must have been a relief to my mother, not so much the sewing for her but not having to find the money to buy them.

We took the skins home to sell along with others and mole skins to the travelling people. I mean real travelling people like the Williamsons and Stewarts from Edderton, Ardgay and Lairg, who came round the doors trading their wares. They were excellent tin smiths and made all sorts of pails, jugs and other utensils. Clothes pegs, heather pot scrubbers and willow baskets were other things they sold. On haloween night you could always get sale for such pot scrubbers even if you were dressed up as a minister. We got sixpence for a rabbit skin and four-pence for a mole one. Sometimes we would send them south with the post. To prepare them, we would stretch them out and tack them on to the back of a shed door and rub paraffin on to the insides. Salt was something else we used to cure them. On the odd occasion Mam would make a pair of slippers or mitts from the rabbit skins and for luck she always carried the front paw of a rabbit in her handbag.

When the Williamsons' Peter, John and Kate got too old for the road they took work locally and many a blether I had with Peter. He came up the strath to help with the hay or harvest and I am sure he enjoyed telling me, with a sense of pride I may add, about his travelling days up the west. Caithness he said was not a territory they entered into. I once had occasion to transport a prisoner by the name of McPhee down to detention centre in Perth and took the opportunity to ask him about his life style as a tinker living under canvas. He grew up after the days of the horse and cart and before the caravans and went from place to place with other members of the family or group in vans or small trucks hawking for scrap metal to sell and did a good deal of thieving on the way. When I asked him about eating hedgehogs he said it was true and that one made a very tasty meal. He described how they were wrapped in a good thickness of clay and put into the fire until ready for eating. When the baked clay was broken off it took all the skin and spiney bristles with it. The meat was then picked off the bones and eaten with tatties and turnips and as he said, "Stolen from some field." He confused me at first when he told me he slept in a stand up bed in the winter-time. I had visions of the bed up on end but all he meant was that it had four legs. On entering the centre which had a reputation for having a very strict discipline it reminded me of my very first days in the Royal Air Force. After the prisoner was shouted at to stand to attention and told to button up his jacket I was conscious of checking the buttons on my own jacket. He was then sent off to march down the corridor with arms swinging shoulder high to be met by another guard who bellowed out more orders, a short sharp shock to his system but an introduction as to how things were to be.

All of this was before the days of myxamatosis and crofters and farmers were only too glad to let us on to their land to kill the rabbits. Our main hunting ground was the crofts on Amat na Tua and The Craigs which Miss MacKay had a tenantcy of and who who ran the Post Office from her house. She also operated the telephone switch-board within the premises but now a new exchange has been built near Coneas Bridge, retaining the name The Craigs as its title. She was very good to us and understanding if we caught one of her sheep in a snare. She did not like the gentry and would rather cycle down and find one of us to deliver a telegram to the lodges. There were very few private phones then and often a telegram was the only means of urgent communication. It was good money for us too. The Post Office paid one shillings for each one we delivered but Miss MacKay always gave us more and often we got something from the person the telegram was for.

My father and Willie MacDonald clipped and dipped her sheep. She did her own lambing and looked after the cows and fences unaided. One day at the height of the summer she was repairing a fence by the roadside and lost her staple punch in the heather, and in her wisdom decided to burn the heather in an effort to find it. The fire took off, burned over the hills for three days and ended up at the back of Whale Cottage house where the last of it was put out. All the men in the area were out night and day trying to extinguish it. She was a proud woman and not even they were allowed to call her anything other than Miss MacKay. Each spring she would employ the MacKenzies' from Dounie to put in a field of oats and to plant a few rows of tatties. Donnie, his father Alec and an uncle, with two horse and carts would go up to the Craigs with all the necessary equipment, plough the field and put in the seed in one day. In the autumn they would return for a day and harvest it for her.

Donnie's mother died when he was very young and the father and uncle brought him up. When they passed away he continued to work the crofts he inherited but was happier doing work for other people. Most of the work was on neighbouring crofts where he would get whatever meal was on the go at the time. He was a great story teller and had a fantastic memory for past events, including the times and dates of them. He could sit for hours talking and most of his stories started with, "And I remember another time." If Donnie was in the middle of eating a meal when telling a story it was amazing how he could stop the fork half way to his mouth and hold it there until the end of what he had to say and even keep it there for longer if he began to tell another story. As often as not he would be travelling about on his old tractor after dark. Not having lights on it, he would switch on a small hand held torch he carried in his pocket either to the front or back when he saw approaching vehicles. At work you would seldom see him without three or four inch nails to replace the missing buttons on his jacket or raincoat and the lapels held together by a nappy safety pin, but for funerals or other such occasions he could dress as smart as the next person with his dark blue suit and bowler hat. I often heard it said he was very, very clever at school and could have gone on to university or become a banker or something if circumstances at home had permitted it.

When George Ross was with the forestry he bought a television set but could not get a good reception. The difficulty was getting the areal high enough, so to overcome this problem he cut down the tallest and most suitable tree he could find in Balblair Wood. His fellow forestry workers, including Al Munro, questioned him on how on earth he would get it home. George assured them that he knew the very man that would do it. Yes Donnie "Dounie" was that very man. He had an old Massey Ferguson tractor and trailer at the time and was delighted to be given the task. After it was lashed on to the trailer with a massive illegal overhang, thirty feet or more, this tree was taken through Bonar and Ardgay and up Strathcarron to George's home. His main difficulty was at corners or sharp bends when the tail of the tree would swing out across the road almost hitting things at the kerb or road side. At times he owned an ex council pick-up truck and would do carting jobs for other people with it. He was very friendly with the McLeans' Kincardine Hill who were very good to him but at the same time they would often play mischief on him like the time they squeased a cockerill sideways through the top of a window. Donnie who was in bed and on hearing this weard noises downstairs had to light the tilley lamp to go down and investigate. The next six weeks or so he spent telling everyone he met about it and trying to work out how it managed to get through the small gap. He was about to set off from Kincardine for Banffshire with a load of boarding on the vehicle but because of the overhang Jimmy said he would tie a red rag on the end of it to make it more obvious. What Donnie did not know was that Jimmy took a pair of his daughter's bloomers off the line and tacked them on to the longest board. Going down the road even beyond Inverness other drivers were tooting the horn and waving to him. This puzzled Donnie because he thought all of them could not have known him.

CHAPTER 17

WORKING FOR A LIVING

On leaving school I worked with my father at the fencing and my goodness he was fussy. He set himself very high standards and any old hole would not do for a strainer post. It had to be the correct shape, not too wide and the depth of the spade we used. Everyone I dug he would drop the spade into it to make sure it was right and if the handle was not level with the top I would be told to carry on until it was. Our first job together was for Colin Campbell who had Creich Farm at the time. We first erected a deer and rabbit proof fence at the top of the fields next to the hill ground. We repaired and made stock proof just about all the other fences. The last job we did for him there was to put up cattle pens and because the finished job had to be six feet high all round I used a stool for standing on to maul in the posts. Although I was still very young I picked up the knack of swinging the mell as we always called it with some force. My father had a habit of saying, "That will do," when he thought the post was far enough in to the ground. At the same time he would put his hand on the top of the post to check for firmness. Well I could not stop the mell coming down on his hand and in doing so I burst the tips of three of his fingers. All he said was "bloody hell," wrapped his fingers in his handkerchief and we both cycled up to Doctor Lindsay at Bonar where she dressed them properly.

After finishing at Creich we took on the job of repairing the dry stone walling along the roadside at Amat Lodge. It was an endless task because after every gale the roots of the huge trees under the wall would loosen the stones and bits of it kept falling down. Another thing I learned from him was how to put steel posts into rock where the ground was not suitable for wooden ones. I would sit for hours hitting away at the rock with a chisel called a jumper, turning it round a bit each time. I suppose it was called a jumper because each time you gave it a wallop it would jump up and sometimes out of the hole. Again when the depth of the hole was right we would pour lead into it and then set the post in it. If water got into the hole in the process we would fill it with oil to get rid of the water. If not when the molten lead was poured in, the water and steam would come spurting out and so easy to get severe burns from it. I was off to the Royal Air Force by the time my father was working as a ghillie at Braelangwell Estate when along with Neil MacKay, he built the shelter at Moral. After the bank was dug out sufficiently large enough he then took stones from the river and built the banks up and roofed it with turf covered corrugated iron. For fishers and ghillies, Ronnie in particular, it has been a welcome shelter ever since.

About a year later he was to get his own back on me, not deliberately of course, when we were fencing at Glencalvie Estate. He was doing the melling that day and we were working on a side slope with me standing below him when the head of the mell came off the handle and was hurtling straight for my face. Luckily I got my head out of the way in time but this fourteen pound lump of metal hit my left shoulder, breaking my collar bone and sent me rolling down the hill. Whatever fencing we did there it was always oak posts from a saw mill at Beauly we used and I hated them. The tops would sometimes break off or they would split and driving staples into them took longer.

The estate was owned by a Mr and Mrs MacLean an elderly couple and from the old school of gentry. My brother Ian worked for them as kennel boy, under keeper and ghillie but had to leave on call up for National Service in the army. We were self employed but because our work entailed a variety of different jobs we were paid on a daily rate. My father and I enjoyed working there simply because of the other company, but there was a lot of infighting went on amongst the permanent staff. I was never sure who was speaking to whom. This was common on estates and still is to this day with workers vying with one another to get further in with the boss, creating a lot of jealousy. We tried as best we could to keep out of it but it was not easy. Every so often one or another would say, "What are you talking to him for".

David MacLeod was head keeper at Glencalvie but left to go to Amat Estate about the same time as we started there. The next keeper to arrive came from the Isle of Mull. He was death on otters and killed many of them up the River Diebidale. He had traps set everywhere for them and got a ten shilling bounty from the owners for each one he killed. It was common practice in those years, in the belief that it would protect the salmon stocks. Now it is banned as is otter hunting with dogs. I am lead to believe that the largest otter killed was by hounds and it measured five feet and six inches long which I assume was from the point of its nose to the tip of its tail and weighed fifty pounds. Yes they killed a few salmon each year but that was a small part of their diet which ranged from eels, frogs, riverside mammals like rabbits, even lambs. Predacious birds such as herons, cormorants and mergansers probably do more damage to young stock.

Every spring above the Moral Falls we often found the odd salmon killed by an otter. As often as not a few bites would be eaten from behind the head. The remainder was perfectly good for human consumption provided you got it before the gulls had messed over it. Down at the Washerwoman Pool one morning I came across an otter feeding on a salmon by the water edge but as soon as it saw me he slipped back into the water. He then must have had second thoughts about the breakfast he left behind and came out almost immediately, snatching the fish and off with it. Usually it was one salmon at a time that was taken but on one occasion I found three dead at the Keepers Pool. I think a family of otters must have been involved. They were put to good use, one for the guests in the lodge, one for Jim and Fiona and the other for Marjory and I. I knew of several otter holts up and down the banks of the river Carron. Very often they were in rabbit burrows or holes under the rocks and occasionally an otter would be seen carrying a salmon in to them. One of the days I was fishing I came across this mess of salmon scales on the bank and by the water edge and at first I thought it was the aftermath of salmon poachers but then discovered a holt up in the rocks. The otters had been taking salmon up the bank to their young for some time.

From Garden Cottage we often watched them at any time of the day swimming about in the Boat Pool or down at the tail in the shallow water turning over the stones with their front feet to get the eels and crustaceans. I often saw them right beside me when I was fishing. In fact I found them to be quite curious animals. It is often quoted by fishermen that you will not catch a salmon if there is an otter in the pool. That is not true. On three definite occasions I caught a salmon in an otter's presence. One early morning at Moral I was conscious of something in the water about ten feet from me. It was only after staring at the spot for a while did I see the nose and whiskers come to the surface and this went on until I hooked a salmon and with the disturbance in the pool it cleared off. After watching them from my kitchen window I went off upstream to fish the Kennel Run. At the tail of that pool there are banks of rabbit burrows and from them came the sound of a rabbit squealing in distress. Then out from one of the holes came an otter with a rabbit in its mouth and together they tumbled down the bank into the water. It was about thirty yards downstream before they surfaced again and I'm pretty certain the rabbit was to feed her young in the holt below the lodge.

At the same warren I watched a rabbit swimming round and round in a back eddy of calm water. I thought it had fallen into the water and that it could not get out but then it sprung out on to the bank and with it forepaws wiped away at its face and ears before going back into the water. This took place several times and I can only assume it was to get rid of fleas which makes me now believe the story of the fox swimming into the loch with a bunch of moss in its mouth to rid itself of fleas.

Something else I witnessed but still do not know the reason for it. I was sitting in my van waiting to be joined by a colleague before going to a nearby fox den. A lot of rabbits were hopping about as they fed but this particular one was munching away at a piece of sheep's wool measuring four inches wide and about eight inches long. It was at the time of year when many sheep lose part of their fleeces before coming in for shearing and this piece looked as if it had newly come off a sheep's back. About an equal amount of the wool was sticking out of the rabbit's mouth at either side but as it munched away it slowly disappeared. There were no signs of the rabbit's cheeks bulging out to indicate that it was still in the mouth so I assume it was swallowing it. Not wanting to disturb the foxes at the den by shooting the rabbit I will never know the reason behind it all.

I had my terriers Jake and Twiggy at the river bank when I went fishing and bearing in mind their attitude towards cats and foxes they took little or no notice of otters. I saw one otter swimming up and down alongside the terriers on the bank of Moral. Moral was a favourite pool for them and you could hear them at dusk calling to each other. One otter was seen there to catch a salmon, swim across the pool with it and deliver it to a second otter, which then went off downstream with it. I can only assume it was for her young in a holt somewhere, perhaps the one at the lodge again.

Not only did the otters work in pairs on the river but in the hill lochs as well. I spent at least half an hour watching two of them doing what I would describe as quartering the water. Side by side they would dive and appear some fifty yards apart. They would simultaneously dive again to appear side by side further on. This system of looking for fish I assume went on for at least the duration of the time I watched them. Otters, like children, love to play in the snow. I have watched them use the snow to make a slide down steep banks and on one occasion I watched an otter sliding down a grass bank into a burn. This was repeated a few times so they must get a lot of enjoyments from it. When I was in my early teens otters had a holt high up on the Braelangwell bank of the Lower Brothers' Pool and you could see their slide mark in the snow below it. It was very distinct because of the red sand coming out of the holt on their wet bellies. It was the same at the kettle pond at Ruin an Taoir where they went back and fore to the Kyle at Otter Point. I watched another climb up a water fall and dive back down again from a rock about eight feet high with barely a ripple on the water as it entered it. Down on the North Esk River I witnessed another display of their aquatic ability when one that had been obviously disturbed downstream came racing up the water edge towards me. When only a few feet from me it plunged into the river and continued to leap up and across the surface of the pool with minimum of splashing. On reaching some rocks it leapt from one to another before getting out on the opposite bank some distance from me and going on its frightened way.

I went to the hill one evening in the hope of shooting a fox that I had been trying to get for about a week. It was using the same sheep track to come on to this particular piece of hill to hunt for rabbits in the rushes. I was spying the ground to see if I could spot it when I noticed that a sheep was lying on its back with it legs kicking in the air. I walked to where it was, laid my rifle on the ground and tried to get the sheep to stand but it was unable to balance itself. I carried the sheep to some deep but dry tractor tracks where I would leave it to get on its feet in its own time. I stood looking at it for a little while and said to myself now you cannot fall over, when the fox passed by a short distance from me. I let it get out of sight, ran back for the rifle and crawled up through some rushes to the top of a knoll. The fox was nowhere to be seen but as I squeaked away to draw its attention an otter appeared eyeball to eyeball less than six feet in front of me. In one movement I jumped to my feet, pointing the rifle at it as if I had a bayonet on the end. The otter to my amazement raised it front paws to an almost sitting position, curious I suspect, to what I was. Cool as a cucumber it turned around and sauntered off.

I do not know how many wild animals do this nor do I know the reason for it but both otters and foxes if they are ill will come right in to where humans are present. It can be farm steadings, estate buildings or even into villages as one did in Bonar. One day it was seen on the streets and next day it was found dead. I witnessed the same once with an otter at Glencalvie and twice with mange infected foxes at Gruinard. Nobody took the trouble to find out what was wrong with the otters and they had no obvious signs of injury.

The only real trouble they gave me was at my current duck flight pond where I found like other animals they will kill just for the sake of it. In one such incident overnight I had eighteen ducks killed. The head chewed of some, others partly eaten in the shallow water and some with little or no marks at all. I thought I had a secure fence round the pond but did not realise how agile the otter can be in climbing. They have a short legged gait and are rather sluggish movers with a thick rooted tapering tail trailing behind. Hence the "otter tail" when referring to well shaped Labradors. I would have blamed the pine martin but marks in the mud and the damage to a cage trap I had set to re-locate the culprit proved beyond doubt which animal was responsible. Now I have an electric fence round it.

Eel is a delicacy, particularly the elver, and very much sought after for big money abroad, particularly Holland, to the extent that river systems in this country are getting depleted of them. I am not suggesting that is the only reason for their decline but it hasn't helped. To eat eel was never a wish of mine even just to try it after watching them scavenge the river bed and feed on a diseased dead salmon or for whatever they could find. On the sea front at Blackpool there were lots of live eel stalls and you could choose the one you wanted and it would be cooked for you there and then. In the East End of London they had similar stalls selling ready cooked eel and molluscs. In the pie and mash cafes they would serve that up with peas and bree from the boiled eels poured over it. I always remember what a shipping pilot from the London Docks said to me, "I would only eat a steak from just behind the head of a conger." He never did explain why.

To us as kids they were a menace when fishing the worm. They would swallow the hook and it was a terrible job to get it out. They also damaged the nylon gut with their needle sharp teeth and I don't think wire traces were invented by then. Although we had no wish to do so we often had to kill them to get it from their gullets. Sometimes we would deliberately go fishing for eels but used teased out wool from our jerseys. We would lie on our bellies and dangle it tied to a short length of line or string and watch the eel get it in its mouth. As soon as you pulled on it the eel would grip all the harder and you could lift it out of the water.

Now you have seen and heard all kinds of animals and machines being raced but I'm pretty sure you have never heard of eels being raced. On the days fishing for them with the teased wool we normally did it in the deep water near the head of Moral. When we got a few out at the same time we would carry them up the steep bank to the top of the field where we would release them all together. The tendency for them was to riggle down hill to make for water and like any other race the first one to reach it was the winner.

When young enough not to know any better we would ask why there were often eels in the pool of a stream where we took the horses for a drink. Stupidly, we believed that hair falling out of the horses mane into the water turned into eels. It was just as ridiculous to believe there were so many midges on the railway track up to Culrain that they stopped the train. Every July or there about I witnessed the many eels returning from the breeding grounds of the Sargassa Sea making their way up the waterfalls at the head of Moral.

It was a sight to behold. Literally hundreds of them at any one time, some only two or three inches long, in rows one after the other could be seen over several days slowly climbing the slimey rocks to make their way to the higher reaches of the river. I think it was only by their closeness together and the sheer numbers of them that they were able to do it.

I thought that a keeper from Mull who came to Glencalvie had very cruel streak in him when it came to hedgehogs. I know they eat bird eggs but his way of dealing with them was to put a ring of twigs into the ground around them and just leave them to die. This could never be justified when there were so many more humane ways of dealing with them. He did not stay very long and a man named MacLennan came from the west coast somewhere. Like the other keepers he stayed up at Diebidale and had to look after a herd of about forty highland cattle and a flock of sheep.

Down at Glencalvie was Ian Thom the vegetable gardener. He also drove the old ex army lorry and looked after two milking cows. His wife was housekeeper. Joe Docherty was general handyman and helped Mrs MacLean in the flower garden. Living with him in the bothy, accommodation for single men, or in Aberdeenshire a chaumer, was another young Irishman who did the fires and helped generally. He did not like working there and out of the blue after getting his wages he did an overnight runner. A Jamaican lady was cook. Two other men, Willie Bain and Jimmy Cameron, came up from Bonar Bridge each day to ghillie for the deer stalking season. In the summer they were both gaffers at the Bonar salmon sweep netting stations on the Kyle.

I worked one whole season on the River Shot under Jimmy Cameron and at other times when I came home on leave. A normal shift was for eight hours from the time the tide started to run out until it came back in again and after that we would sometimes do a further four hours when the tide was in at the bay between Bonar and Ardgay. One week after I returned from leave to wherever I was stationed I was told that some of the crew members had been reported by the bailiffs for leaving the net to hang stationary until the salmon were seen to enter it. Although the temptation was there to do so it was illegal. I cannot remember how much they were fined but I could easily have been one of them.

In those days it was practice for the crews of the different salmon cobbles to take part in a boat race as part of the annual gala. Jimmy Cameron and Johnnie McKenzie the overall gaffer normally won this race so Donald Stewart and I were hell bend on beating them. The race was timed to coincide with the turn of the tide so that you had the benefit of fast water going down towards the bridge. Because of other boats getting in our way Donald and I did not get off to a good start. However, by sheer determination to win we passed all the other boats except one with Willie Bain and partner in it and the leading boat with Jimmy and Johnnie, who by this time had reached the mouth of the River Carron. In the course of overtaking Willie Bain we got too close to the starboard side of his boat and broke both oars as we passed sending their boat up on the rocks at the water edge and breaking the other two oars on the port side. I can still picture Willie standing up but hanging on to the side of the half upturned boat and screaming at us. It was almost a neck and neck finish but the two heroes beat us to the bridge.

Part of Ian Thom's contract of employment was that he could use the lorry on Saturdays to go to Tain for their shopping and to visit their parents. He always came back home through Ardgay at about midnight. The dances were finished by this time and we would be waiting for a lift home. The bicycles were put on the lorry in order of where we lived in the glen with those getting off first having their bikes put on last. By the time everyone got on, there was not much space left but I cannot recall any mishaps. We were all very grateful to Ian for taking so much trouble and patience with us.

The first port of call for Dad and I was to meet in the bothy for a cup of tea with Joe and the ghillies. Then we would go over to the kitchen garden where Dad had a blether with Ian while I had a rummage round the fruit and berry bushes to see what was ripe to eat. Ian caught me out one morning by giving me horse-radish to eat. He already had it all washed clean and told me to munch it up as quickly as possible. Like a fool I did. I was so desperate because of the burning feeling in my mouth that I had to take handfuls of not very clean water from the greenhouse butts to swill it out.

With the young Irishman's hasty departure my father was summoned to the lodge to be asked if they could have me to do the fires etc. The arrangement agreed to was that I would sleep in the lodge and make my own food in the bothy. Everything got off to a good start and the MacLeans' were happy with my work. It was mid-summer and at the height of the growing season in the garden. The salmon fishing was at its best. One morning Mr MacLean came out ready to go fishing and told me I had to go with him as ghillie. I had never ghillied for anyone before but I had watched others doing it. I carried his rod and took a long handled net with me. I did not like the look of the gaff and thought it would be too easy to make mistakes with it. The very first pool he fished, he hooked a salmon and not knowing any better I was at the water edge like a flash with the net at the ready to get my one and only swearing from him. He told me in no uncertain terms to get back out of the way and he would tell me when the fish was ready to net. I went on to land many fish for him but he was a man of few words and I soon got to know when and when not to speak to him. His favourite fly was the blue charm.

Mrs MacLean, who was an ardent garden enthusiast, was easy to talk to but liked to be addressed as Madam. Although they owned a Rolls Royce motor car that sat in the garage and never turned a wheel, Mrs MacLean would make weekly trips by private hire car to Howden's Nurseries in Inverness to purchase plants, fertilisers and anything else required for the garden. The taxi firm she used was Ali Matheson's from Bonar Bridge. He owned a large black Austin Sheerline seven seater saloon, which he drove himself, to take them wherever they wanted to go. Little did she know that he carried a .22 rifle concealed in the boot of his car to nab a bit of venison on the way home. I saw this for myself on more than one occasion when he would combine the school run with a delivery for Glencalvie and I would go up there with him and help to drag a beast to the boot of his car which he had already prepared. He was not adverse to a bit of poaching on the river and the reason I say this is that I found a net stretched across the river near our house. I took it home and about a week later Ali asked me for his net back. When asked to donate a raffle for some local cause, he told me that he climbed over the fence into the butcher's back-yard and pinched a couple of hens for it.

If I was not working in the lodge I would have to help Joe or Mrs MacLean in the garden. When weeding the flower beds it was not unusual to come across a bottle of Gin and a glass which was Madam's favourite tipple. We left it where it was but often she forgot that such a bottle ever existed and mysteriously it would find its way to the bothy. She would come out after breakfast or lunch and collar me to join her, at the same time arming me with a hammer and a basket full of pegs. We would meander about anywhere within a hundred yards of the lodge placing pegs where she wanted holes dug to plant Rhododendrons, Azaleas and other shrubs or the odd tree.

What I never could work out about Madam, was the fact she knew at once if I changed the location of a peg, even only a foot or so to make the digging easier. When all the holes were dug, probably about twenty or so at any one time, Ian Thom, my father and I would go up to Diebidale for peat which we dug out from the exposed banks at the roadside. Ian had no qualms about taking a salmon for the table, and by that I mean their own table, out of the river Diebidale by whatever means necessary. There was a falls pool that he stopped the lorry at to show my father and I where to get one. There was a pot half way up the waterfall and you could see from the road if a salmon was resting in it. He nipped down with a gaff he had behind the seat, took a salmon out, and gave it to Dad to take home. I can picture it to this day unwrapped and tied on to the carrier of his bicycle as we cycled home.

Joe and I would make lots of compost from the peat. He knew the exact mixtures Madam wanted to use for the different plants, either to raise seedlings or for potting on. As soon as the shrubs arrived from Howden's we would get on with the planting under her supervision. I rather liked working with Madam, she taught me much about the plant names, their likes and dislikes, fertilisers that each one got, and any other basic requirements they needed. Many of the shrubs we planted were in a deep hollow across the road from the bothy which now is an ornamental fish pond. The bothy has been completely refurbished for some of the staff to live in. She said to me one day that she wanted to create a path through that area, and whilst standing at the top of the bank, she asked me to walk across it where I thought it should go. Bearing in mind that I was going to have to do the digging and did not have the first clue about landscaping I took the shortest route which was virtually in a straight line. I was soon called back and after suitable advice was sent off to do better by putting in a few twists and turns into it, dropping pegs along the way. She made a few minor adjustments to it and was then happy for me to get on with it.

She gave me the job one day of clearing out a large shed over in the birch wood near the river. It was stuffed to the gunnels with boxes and crates of empty wine and spirit bottles. I had to burn the boxes and take the bottles to a tip on the estate. In the process I came across a full bottle of Sherry. It was not my first taste of alcohol as I used to go down to the Caledonian Hotel in Bonar where Ian was a member of their darts team. I was under age but still had a couple of beer shandies. Dad, Ian and I drunk the sherry and I got quite tipsy on it, but surprisingly no after effects. I must have got rid of hundreds of bottles but only one full one.

In October the cattle had to be rounded up for the sales in Dingwall. Jimmy Cameron and I were paired up to turn them off the hill known as the Face of Glencalvie and drive them up towards Diebidale where they would join up with others before being penned. They were as wild as hell and to escape from us, one of them jumped off the bank into the swollen river making for the other side with only the horns showing at times and then took off up the hills.

Being a bit naive that day I told Ian Thom that I found five red deer carcases up on the hill above the wood. They had been shot, gralloched, with head and feet taken off, not the normal preparation for taking stags home to the larder. I assumed it was the work of poachers. What never occurred to me was the fact that Ian and MacLennan had previously fallen out. Ian took this opportunity to go straight and tell Mr MacLean and needless to say all hell broke loose. Dad and I were finishing off a stock fence round the keepers house at Diebidale and on the Monday morning when we got up there MacLennan was waiting for me and what a ruddy tonguing I got from him. The minister did not have a look in. I would not like to print the oaths. Many a time we would be in their house for a cup of tea and to eat our sandwiches but he left me in no uncertain terms that I would never darken his doorstep again. A lesson learned. They had two lovely boys Gavin and Ewen, both under school age who intrigued me, each of them speaking fluent Gaelic and when we spoke to them they instantly switched to English and were equally fluent in that as well.

Jimmy Cameron had a Norton motor cycle and on one of my trips to Diebidale with Ian and Dad Jimmy asked me to take his bike down to Glencalvie for him. I had never ridden a motor bike before but I agreed to help him out. Ian and Dad set off a short time in front of me and after I got the machine started I gingerly followed on. I was getting on fine until I rounded a bend and there I was confronted with the lorry taking up the full width of the road, a stupid place to stop I thought. Not enough distance with my experience to pull up in I took to a cattle track and went skittering along it until it came back to the roadside again. The next hazard I came to was the gate across the road at Glencalvie. I slowed down and braked but forgot about the clutch, bump and I was into the gate. The tyre on the front wheel was a bit soft so it went round on the rim and sheared off the valve, Although it cost Jimmy a new tube he just had good laugh at me.

My work at Glencalvie came to an abrupt end while I was living in the Lodge. Even as a young man I was a very early riser in the mornings and still am to this day, once I waken I have to get up. This suited me for doing the fires, I could have the ashes off and have the fires reset for lighting before Mr and Mrs MacLean came down for breakfast. On at least a couple of occasion Mr MacLean came down about 6 am to see what the noise was, only to find me going about my work. Doing it this way I could be over to the bothy early and cook myself a breakfast before 8 am when the others arrived.

One particular morning the cook rushed into the bothy, "Shouting the smoke-room is on fire." The men did not believe her and began joking with her that, "That was what a smoke room was for." I ran up the short drive and on looking through the window I could see that the place was ablaze. I ran back to get help and there was no messing about with them this time. I was first back at the lodge and there was Mr MacLean still in his pyjamas thumping the bottom of a fire extinguisher on the floor to activate it. What he did not realize was that the foam was already spewing out of it and hitting the ceiling and walls of the staircase above. My father grabbed it from him and soon had the fire out but not before two easy chairs, carpeting and other items were destroyed.

The kindling I used was tinder dried in the boiler room and the paper caught alight from the still very hot grate setting the chimney on fire and when the hot burning lumps of soot came down it knocked over the fire guard which then acted as a ramp for it to flow out on to the rug and carpet. Everything was taken outside and when Mrs Thom arrived she took charge of a big clean- up operation. The only thing Mr Maclean said to me was, "A fine piece of work this morning Matheson". Mrs MacLean did not come downstairs until her usual time but never mentioned fire to me.

A few weeks later I scorched the polished floor beside a stove in the main hall. I took the hot ashes off into a galvanised steel bucket, stupidly setting it on the floor beside me. Mrs Thom, again came to my rescue. We sanded off the black marks and blistering varnish and then Mrs Thom pressed as much Mansion floor polish as she could into the circular groove that was burned by the rim round the bottom of the bucket. A good polish over a few times, a rug placed on top and nothing more was said.

Soon after that I was asked to light the solid fuel Aga in the back kitchen. No problem as I thought. In with some paper, dried kindling and, "Bob's your Uncle". While I was waiting for the Aga to get going, the cook as she often did, offered me a cup of tea in the main kitchen which I accepted. Then what looked like smoke came wafting through from the back kitchen. Immediately, everyone thought another fire but that was not the case. I used a very wet cardboard box to carry in the kindlers and stupidly again, I left it sitting on top of the Aga but over at the oven side. Unbeknown to me, the flames crossed over to that side before going up the flue into the chimney, and as the wet box dried out lots of steam came off it. No doubt it would have caught fire eventually Again Dad was summoned to the lodge and was told that I was too much of a risk and I could not have agreed more with their decision. The MacLean's thought I would just go back to work with my Dad, and the gardens etc. I declined the offer and came home that morning.

Glencalvie, like many more of the estates in the glen have changed ownership, most of them several times. When I was in my early teens, Gledfield, Dounie and Gruinards changed hands for around twenty thousand pounds. Today that figure is in the millions. Alladale Estate was bought a few years ago by Paul Lister who has set about to restore it to its former natural glory, cutting down on the red deer numbers and planting to restore habitat. He has introduced wild boar and European Elk and has plans to establish wolves and other wild animals in the future. The thought of wolves arriving has caused great consternation not only to hill walkers and ramblers but to the local people as well. He has created much needed employment and long may it continue. Apart from that there has not been much change or excitement in the glen other than arrival of electricity, estates moving from private stalking and fishing to commercial lettings with guests on occasions arriving by helicopter.

CHAPTER 18

FENCING AT FORREST FARM

Dad left soon afterwards and took on the erection of a stock fence for Major Campbell and his son Colin, stretching from the west end of Braelangwell Estate along the Strathkyle march to the Corriemulzie march, the entire length of Forrest Farm, several miles long. He took on the job on the understanding that he would get the rabbit trapping in case of bad weather in the winter, and also that all the material would be put out on the ground for him. Prior to that Dan Campbell from Errogie in Inverness-shire did the rabbits. He was a full time trapper and fox hunter and a very good hand he was. When I first remember him he drove an old ex army motor bike and flat topped sidecar, a regular sight on the road with the sidecar stacked high with crates of rabbits on the way to Ardgay Railway Station or Bonar as it was named at that time to be sent south. Latterly he got himself an ex army American Wyllis jeep and trailer.

Dan was fond of the dram and when he was in the pubs he was always pestered by individuals wanting a pair of rabbits. "Yes" he would say, "Just help yourself" knowing perfectly well that his two wire-haired fox terriers, Saighdear and Fraochie, gaelic for soldier and heather(y) respectively in the jeep would not let them anywhere near the rabbits. Dan was a long term friend of my Mam and Dad, and it was nothing for him to arrive at the house on his way home to Croick from the pub at one or two in the morning with a good shot in. Because our door was never locked in those days he would just walk in and sit on the end of the bed and share a half bottle with my Dad. Mam would get up and make tea for him to try and sober him a bit before going on his way. There was no proper road up Strath Cuilanach to Loubconich at that time, only a rough track along the riverside and it was feared he might end up in the water. If Dan was not at the rabbits he would be helping Dad with whatever he was doing. I believe one of the jobs they did together was to erect a bridge across the river Blackwater a short distance below the Croick falls. I remember Dad explaining to him how they would pull the steel beams across with fence winders because hand winches were not available to him at that time.

At home at Errogie he lived on his own in a little two roomed house called the beehive. In those parts he was known as Donnie Campbell and looked after himself but spent a lot of his time in the bar of the Whitebridge Hotel. At one point, because of Dan's behaviour, the owner banned him from the bar. Not to be out-done by him, one evening Dan crawled unnoticed by the publican into the bar and sat below the level of the counter. His friends bought him drinks and at closing time he stood up and told the owner it was the best night he had for a long time.

The beehive   *Dan as anchorman*

Dad and Dan Campbell

To prepare for the rabbit trapping Dad bought twelve dozen gin traps which were left soaking in the burn to get rid of the smell of the new iron. We made pins out of old whisky barrels for pegging them down. Night after night we made snares until we had a thousand, five hundred for each of us. Pegs for them, we cut out of an ash tree from up at The Craigs and start pins we cut them from hazel, birch or willow but all in all we had a lot of work to do before we even got started. What I don't see any more is the tarry looking treated twine we used for the cords. It lasted for years and was much stronger than the cotton looking stuff you got on readymade snares. Another use for the waterproof twine was the big hooks for taking salmon out from the falls pool. At the end of a season it could be put away until the next year and it would be just as good as new.

Monday was set up day when we would get most if not all of the snares down. Tuesday morning we would lift the rabbits from them and after gutting them would hang them on a fence to cool off. The snares would be re-set and if there were any left from the previous day we would get them down as well. Wednesday forenoon would be the same procedure but when afternoon came we would get down to setting the gin traps. Usually we put them first in the holes along the river bank. Scary rabbits we did not catch in them would make off up the hill and we would get a second chance of catching them in the snares. Friday we would move the traps up on to the hill above the snares and leave them there until Tuesday night. All the snares would be lifted on Saturday or early Monday morning ready for setting again on fresh ground. On it would go like that until bad weather set in and you had to stop trapping because of snow or frost.

Croick and Loubconich was a terrible place for wild cats and they did a lot of damage to the rabbits we caught which made them unsellable. One morning alone I caught three of them. We had another problem with rabbits being taken out of the snares we had set near to the new road that was being made up the strath. Geordie Bruce later confessed to being one of them responsible. When I came home on leave my mother said I would have to do something about the foxes taking her hens. I knew she was in the way of shutting them in at night so when I asked her about this she said, "Some of them roost in the trees." That must be a wild cat I thought so I set gin traps for it. One, I set in a tunnel made from stones with the remains of a dead hen for bait. The second morning my mother woke me about 5am to say there was an awful noise coming from the trap.

Sure enough I had caught a huge female wild cat which I shot. Next morning up on the hill above the house I caught another two; both young ones and Mam had no more bother with the hens disappearing. Mr Kemmis paid five shillings for each tail. When myxamatosis did for the rabbit population that was the start of a huge decline in wildcat numbers and they have never recovered from it since. The cat, wild or domestic, is an opportunist and will pounce on any small animal or bird. They will eat the eggs as well and because of their way of living they are not the most popular animal with gamekeepers or people keeping poultry. The domestic cat is very much responsible for the huge decline in song birds.

Ferreting came into its own then. I preferred the small white jills' and on a good bolting day it was easy enough to make a day's

One night I was cycling home from Croick rather pleased with my catch when I noticed about twelve rabbits sitting outside a bank of burrows up on the hillside. A thaw had set in a couple of days previous so conditions could not have been better. "Counting my chickens before they hatched" I set off again for Croick the next morning and on arrival at the burrows I netted every hole expecting an explosion of rabbits as soon as the ferret went in. When I went to get my Jill she was not there. She had escaped from my bag as I cycled up the road with the postie, Geordie Heatherlea and neither of us had noticed her escape. I never did find her. Almost a year prior to that she stuck in burrows down by the riverside behind our house. For fourteen days I kept checking the holes to see if I could find her but she would not come out for me. Then after a fall of snow I saw her tracks going down to the carcase of a merganser I had shot so I knew she was still alive. I set a rat cage trap and caught her up again but did not use her for the remainder of that season even although she showed no signs of wildness. Perhaps she was destined to go back into the wild. My Mam was lucky the ferret did not make the short distance to the henhouse or the shed where the ducks were housed overnight because from past experiences with escaping ferrets they can do a lot of damage.

That same season I bought an open sighted .22 BSA ten or fifteen shot rifle. I was authorised by the police to purchase three thousands bullets, my allocation for three years. That rifle was hardly out of my hands and what rabbits I killed with it. In my first year I had fired all of the bullets and was having to borrow them from other people like Geordie Ross the keeper. I practised it so much that I could hit rabbits running away from me and on occasions if I threw a tin up in the air I could hit that too. It may have been a fluke of a shot but I killed stone dead a roe deer crossing down-hill at full speed about two hundred yards in front of me. I hit it in the neck and it somersaulted over like a dead rabbit and then each time I came home on leave my shooting got worse and worse until I could barely hit a tin sitting on a fence post. I sold it after that.

Colin Campbell was a very lively go ahead daredevil sort of guy, unlike the more serious nature of his father. At Creich it was quite common to see him hurtling across the fields on a motor bike when he needed to speak to my dad or the tractor- men. He had only one route for his motor bike and that was the shortest one even if it took him across a newly ploughed field. Major Campbell of Balblair Estate who Dad did a lot of work for over the years and who he held in high esteem was sheep farming in a big way at Forrest Farm and other estates up the River Oykel way. Colin, to put the material out to the fence line, hired an ex army tracked vehicle known as a Weasel from Sir John Brooke of Mid Fearn Estate. Colin wanted me to drive it but Dad would not allow it. He thought I was too young. This machine, powered by a V8 petrol engine with brake steering, was used to tow a sledge and as long as you were on flat ground, even soft and boggy, it was fantastic. It had the power and traction to go loaded straight up the steepest of hill faces but absolutely useless on side slopes, when it was oftener off the tracks than on them.

One day when we put our last load out Colin wanted to show my father another small bit of fencing he wanted doing. This was down by the riverside near the shepherd's house at Loubconich.

Behind that house the hillside is very steep in deed and my father refused to go down in the Weasel. He tried me to get off as well but I was prepared to jump off if things did not go to plan as my father anticipated. We had not gone very far down the start of the steepness when the Weasel took off and Colin could not stop it. I made a quick exit to the side and Colin was standing up to do likewise, when luckily the sledge stuck momentarily against a rock and almost instantly freed itself resulting in the sledge shooting forward and the chains getting caught up in the tracks. Colin was almost catapulted out over the front but managed to hang on as everything skidded to a halt and after freeing the chains we took a different route. There were a lot of deer on the hill when we first started this work but Colin, mischief as he was, took a delight in showing how his collie dog could round them up like sheep, and then he would charge into the herd with the Weasel. After a while the deer got wise to this and were off at the slightest noise or sight of it until we saw very little of them.

CHAPTER 19

SHANKS PONY AND ROSY

Up until now to get anywhere for work or pleasure it was bicycle or, "Shanks pony". Only Noel ever had a new bike simply because he had to cycle the six miles or so to Invercharron Farm where he worked and had to have something reliable. Ernest and I had only old bikes made up from pieces we scrounged from wherever we could. Jock Beaton, the old smith in Ardgay opposite the corner shop saw plenty of us. We were forever there buying tyres, tubes, axles, ball bearings or getting him to straighten wheels or do repairs we could not do ourselves. Brakes and lights were a low priority until we started cycling to the dances in Bonar or Ardgay. For brakes we put a foot forward and pushed the mudguard, if there was one, down on to the front tyre. This braking system was a complete failure coming home from a fishing trip to Sgodachail burn. It was my bike and Frankie Sinclair was sitting on the handle bars whilst Ernest sat on the bar. Frankie was holding the rods across his knees and on reaching the school bridge we could not stop and the rods got well and truly broken. A short distance from our house the front forks buckled under the weight and all of us went over the handle bars, back on the scrounge for more bits. We rarely had complete pedals, only the spikey looking axle sticking out from the crank. We did not have proper levers for taking tyres off the wheels and improvised with our mother's spoons. Although most of them showed signs of wear and tear we never got into much trouble for it. Yes for not bringing them back into the house and often had to be sent out to the shed for them before a meal. Because Dad used his bicycle regularly for work we were dared not to use it but before we got our bikes we would sneak it out when he was not there. It was far too big for any of us so we had to put one leg through below the bar and pedal it like that but what a mess that leg got into from the oil or grease off the chain.

Jock Beaton could be a grumpy old man but he was good to us, probably because we always paid him on the spot from our rabbit money. We took Rosy our horse to the smiddy for him to shoe. He never had any bother with her but sometimes, when things were not going well with other horses, Jock really took his temper out on them with whatever tool he had in his hand or what was nearest to him until they behaved, a horse whisperer was not one of his many skills. Sometimes, Dad would get us to take the cart down with us to take home one hundred weight bags of flaked maize for the collies or oats for the hens from Peter MacLaren at the Poplars Farm. Another port of call was the meal mill at Gledfield to collect oat meal or bruised oats for the pigs. Noel bought a sow and bred a few litters of piglets to sell when they were a few months old. Dad trusted us to do this work on our own provided we did not gallop Rosy and cause her to throw off her new shoes.

Rosy was an excellent horse, quiet, easily yoked and handled for any job you were doing with her. Once harnessed for the cart all you had to do was to raise the trams up in the air and from wherever she stood she would back under them, knowing exactly what was wanted. I put the dung from the midden out with her one season and she would go up and down the drills on her own whilst I stood on the back of the cart graiping off the dung into heaps doing three rows at a time. Rosy would move on without being told and stop long enough at the right distance for the job to be done. In later years she did not like the younger members of our family. When you went up the hill where she normally grazed to catch her, the ears would go back and she would rear up on her back legs in a threatening manner then gallop off down the hill to wait for you at the gate. There, all you had to do was to put your hand on the top of her head which she would lower, and you could walk her to the stables with the greatest of ease. Dad only had to call to her and she would come to the gate even from the top of the hill.

I sledged home the peats with her one summer and before leaving for the hill Noel said to me to let her take the lead in getting in and out of the peat bank because she would know the route better than I did. This was to avoid me getting her bogged down in soft ground. He was absolutely right. She would weave about with the nose not too far off the ground and I heard my father say as well that when he was taking deer off the hill in mist he would throw the rein over her neck and just follow on. At feeding time in the stable she started playing us up. When you took a sheaf of corn up to her manger she would swing her backend round and not let you out. She was quite deliberate about this because if you crossed under her neck to the other side of the stall she would swing round that way, and the only exit was to climb over the partition into the next stall.

A man from The Department came round once a year with a stallion and Dad tried several times to get a foal off Rosy but it never worked. Some of the woodmen stabled their Clydesdale horses that they used for dragging the trees out to the roadside with us. It was hard work for the horses and every so often one would die from a racked stomach muscles or colic. It was not unknown for a rope to be tied round the neck of a horse that would not pull its weight or if it got stuck and attach it to the one in front. With the horses came a plague of rats. They invaded the feed boxes to get at the bruised oats to the extent that the horses would back off. We tried killing them in gin traps, with pitch forks, dogs and ferrets, even turning the drum of the threshing mill, but in the end Dad reluctantly had to make up a dish of milky porridge laced with strychnine. That soon got rid of them, rather risky because of secondary poisoning but we escaped any of that.

One of the woodmen who had his Clydesdale stabled with us was a George MacKenzie from Bonar Bridge who had a wooden hut for living in during the week when he was working at Gruinard and Dad would do the horse for him at the weekends. He was a very nice man and very kind and caring to his horse and often came into our house in the evenings for a caleidh but that did not stop us throwing stones at his hut door until he came out and chased us. There was no malice in it just a sort of game for us. When I came back north from London I was having a haircut from Maureen in our local hairdressers when George came in. Maureen made to introduce him to me but instead I asked George if it was not too late to apologise for our mischief so many years ago. George replied, "I think that is better forgotten about." Maureen said, "So you know one another then." I said, "You could say that."

CHAPTER 20

FAILURE AT FARM WORK

Our first tractor, a petrol paraffin grey Fergie, was bought from the owners of Gruinard Estate where Noel, by this time worked. Rosy became redundant and was sold probably to pay for the Fergie. When home on holiday I often did work with the tractor. Simple jobs like grubbing and harrowing but one day Dad and I tried our hand at ploughing with it. Neither of us had the faintest of clues how to go about it and what a ruddy mess we made. The furrows just would not turn over properly no matter how much we adjusted things. Noel was left to put it right but was rather kind to us when he said it was the plough not us. We did not believe him.

Me, Noel, Ernest and Anne all aboard the Fergie

I tried my hand at scything corn and got on quite well with that but the edge would not stay on the blade for long and I had to keep sharpening it. This resulted in the sharp edge taking on a scalloped sort of shape, a series of curves along its length. The department came in after that and cut it with a tractor and binder the driver of which was a man named Morrison I think. Whoever he was he came previously to plough for Dad before we got the Fergie. He had with him a Fordson tractor and trailing plough and he made a bigger mess than Dad and I did and had to come back with disc harrows to put things right. Whilst the cutting went on my brother Ernest and I would arm ourselves with good long strong sticks to kill the rabbits as they bolted from what was left of the standing corn. With the tractor going round and round them they came out a bit dazed so they were not that fast to catch up with. Later in years I would use the shotgun. On one occasion a big rat ran across the stubble towards Ernest. After missing it with the stick he tried to tramp on it but the rat bit him on the calf of his leg and hung on until he took his foot off its tail. At school he had to explain to everyone why his leg was bandaged, likewise when a goose sitting on eggs pecked him just below the eye. Soon after that he had to explain multiple scratches and bruising when he was thrown off a tups back when it bolted along the road. One job I hated doing was gathering and burning knott weed. There seemed to be no end to the amount of it. Gathering stones was another bore.

Traditional crofting is no longer practised nowadays and I don't know of much oats or barley grown now on the crofts round about Ardgay or Bonar but you will find the odd binder or early combine rusting away in the scrap heaps. Down Easter Ross and further afield into Moray and Aberdeenshire the combine harvesters are getting bigger and bigger by the year. To make the most of the few good weather days farmers get, it is not uncommon to see the machines working in pairs well into the night with a blaze of lights and clouds of dust around them. A few months ago I crossed over the Cromarty Bridge on to the Black Isle where I saw the farmer at thigh depth checking the grain in a field of barley. I assumed it was for moisture content but the combine was sitting at the ready nearby having cut its way in from the gate. On my return a few hours later a very good start had been made to demolish that crop with some of it already baled. Within two days, three at the most, you would not have known it had been a field of growing barley with everything securely harvested, the field was ploughed and sown out again for the following season with oilseed rape.

Back in the early sixties when I was in Aberdeen I went for extra money out to Darra Hill Farm at Udny to do some stooking or stocking as they say down south. Dressed in my Barbour shooting gear I was quite happy working away on my own although weather conditions were far from good. I had done plenty of it in previous years on the Buckie farms including forking to the carts and threshing mill but was never elevated to the job on the binder until one morning Mr Barron was short of a man. In about ten seconds flat he sat me up on his one and was shown what all the various levers were for and to look out for this or that. For a start, on take off I was almost out of the rusty old iron seat so now I had more than the levers to think about. Number one priority for me was definitely staying put in the seat and after a few hundred yards Mr Barron realised he had a "thicky" to contend with over and above driving the tractor. When he stopped I thought he was going to tell me to go back to the stooks but instead told me to concentrate on the height of the crop and accordingly to raise or lower the flails, if that is what they were called. Honestly, he might as well have placed the scarecrow from a neighbouring field on the binder.

Another horse that I had the experience of working with, albeit for a short time, was one that Glencalvie Estate bought for taking home the deer carcases, but the ghillies never worked it after rumours went about that she was not good in harness. However, my Dad and I had to repair an old track and ford crossing into a field at Diebidale. Because we needed stones for this we decided to have a go at yoking their mystery horse, even if it was a bit dodgy. I caught her up and between us we put her harness on, so far so good. Next came the cart and she went into that without any bother and off I set for Diebidale some five or six miles up the glen. I was dared not to sit in the cart but to lead her by the head. Once out of sight I grabbed the reins and climbed into the cart, to be joined by Dad at a quarry, where there was a ready supply of suitable stones.

To begin with, taking no chances we took it turn to hold the horse by the bridle whilst the other loaded the cart. After a day or so we got a bit too confident in our mode of transport and both of us set about filling the cart. This went fine for a few loads but then all of a sudden the horse bolted down the road, "Glencalvie here she goes" we thought, but she turned down the track towards the ford at full gallop and over went the cart, dragging it for a short distance and then just stood there as if that was the norm. The cart was in pieces, some of the harness bust beyond repair, and her with not a care in the world. The only way to get her out of this tangled mess was with a good sharp knife Dad carried, and after taking all her harness off we left her in the park. She was not used by us again and I never did know what became of her. The remains of the cart are gone as well.

Before the fallout over the deer carcases MacLennan took my father out to shoot a stag and I was to join them as an observer and help to drag any beast they shot to a more accessible place for the ghillies. It was a misty morning but not too thick to put us off going to the hill. From the house at Diebidale we could hear stags roaring so we set off via a pony path that took us round the shoulder of the Middle Ridge into the start of Coire a Mhalagain, an area normally kept as a deer sanctuary until nearer the end of the season. We reached the fringe of a scattering of the old Caledonian Pines and Birch trees that the corrie was famous for. Long before my time and also my father's, timber from there was floated down the rivers to be milled for the construction of buildings, churches and castles in particular, where you can see so much beautiful architecture and ornate carvings all in pine. When I was building Ruie an Taoir I salvaged much of the pitch pine from the old Free Church at Amat and after dressing it down with a planer used it for window cills and other facings.

A stag was roaring a short distance ahead of us but because of the mist we could not at first see him. The roaring was quite scary for me as this was my first encounter of it so close to hand. We crawled in as far as Dad and MacLennan thought it safe to do so. As we lay there waiting I got even more scared and thought we were too close for our own good having listened to stories told at the fireside of people being attacked by stags during the rut. Other stags were roaring not too far away and in the same direction.

At long last the mist cleared enough for us to see the beast that was making the loudest noise and master of his harem. It was roughly about one hundred yards from us and further than I had imagined. It was not long before he presented himself broadside and when Dad took the shot it crumpled to its knees not to flicker any sign of life again. All sense of fear by now had left me and I was eager to witness the next stage of proceedings, the bleeding and gralloch. We dragged the carcase down to the burn-side for Willie Bain and Jimmy Cameron to pick up with another garron. During the drag I had a few headlong falls into the deep heather and as a result I lost my first pocket watch. It had a chromed body with a stainless steel cover over the face but because it did not have a ring or fixture you could not tie it to your jacket and obviously the hankerchief pocket was the wrong place to have it. I got it from Dad, and on our way back to the house we searched for it but without any luck. It was not the monetary value of the watch that bothered me, only its sentimental connections.

PART TWO

WITH THE ROYAL AIR FORCE

CHAPTER 21

HAIR BRAINED IDEAS

I stayed at Gruinard until I was 18 years old before going off to the Royal Air Force. I was eligible for National Service then anyway. My parents wanted to transfer the croft into my name to save me from call up but I had different ideas. In any case Noel was more entitled to it rather than any other member of the family. My mother and father never influenced me in what I should do with my life. Probably most folk thought I would just continue to work with Dad at the fencing but I had other ambitions or hair brained schemes in mind. I wrote off to a whaling company for a job but was told I was too young for that. I then saw an advertisement for people to go to India to hunt Bengal tigers. Far from the rabbit and wildcat scene but I got the same rebuff. Then it was to emmigrate to Canada and join the Hudson Bay Fur Trading Company. I had no luck with that either but little more than a year later advertisements kept appearing for young Scots to go out there and join them. The Australian Army were looking for recruits but that was no more than a glancing thought.

Not to be done I applied to join the Royal Air Force and was asked to attend the recruitment office in Inverness. My mother was a bit anxious about this and thought someone should go with me, not for the company, but in case I got lost. The furthest I had been before that was on a school bus trip to the open air swimming pool at Invergordon and another to the beach at Dornoch. What I remember of the swimming pool was that the water was freezing cold, it was surrounded by corrugated iron and the water changed each time the tide came in.

After some basic exams and a medical I was accepted, and voluntarily signed on for a four year engagement to train as a driver mechanic. I was sent to Bridgenorth in Shropshire for twelve weeks "square bashing". I seem to remember that town has more pubs per head of population that anywhere else. As soon as we were into uniform our civilian clothes were put back in the suitcase and sent home. I was now into a very different kind of life, bawled and shouted at from daylight to dark by an Irish Corporal, and heaven help anyone who stepped out of line. I would be kind to him if I called him anything other than a bully. My adventure I thought had come to an abrupt halt virtually as soon as it began and I had to come to terms with reality in the forces. Within the first day or so we were marched to the station barbers for a short back and sides, a little less than being scalped. On a regular basis we had to line up for a medical check which entailed everyone at the same time having to drop their trousers and pants. The corporal and medical orderly would then walk along the front of us lifting up our shirt tails with a long cane and then came the order to turn around and bend over for a rear end inspection. It was all quite embarrassing but after we moved on to other stations it was down to the individual to look after personal hygiene.

For unknown reasons he picked on me and two other airmen to be sent regularly to peel potatoes in the cook house. All three of us knew we had done nothing wrong to deserve it. I think he just did not like the look of our faces. On the last week of our training he sent us to see the sergeant who told us that we had been recommended by this sod of a man to do further training for one week. The sergeant was sympathetic but said there was nothing he could do about it. Part of our training was to go into a gas chamber to realise the affects of that and by the time I left Bridgenorth it went through my mind that an overdose of the stuff would have tamed the corporal a bit.

Most of the recruits had no choice in being there. "Call up" or National Service for its proper title, had not ended by that time and they were a disgruntled lot, having made up their minds to do nothing whatsoever, unless the corporal was standing over them. Sometimes in the billet or toilets a heated argument would get up over this and a certain one or two from Glasgow would flash a knuckle duster or razor, just to show that they had them but never threatened anyone with them. On kit inspection days I wondered how they managed to conceal them because the lockers were emptied and everything displayed on the beds.

I was glad to get a week's leave after that before going to RAF Weeton near Blackpool to be taught how to drive. The driving course was for thirteen weeks of intensive instruction, including highwaycode and basic vehicle maintenance. The first half was on a Hillman Minx saloon car. If you passed that you went on to lorries. Each instructor took out two learners and we took it in turn with the driving. The lorry was a four wheel drive Bedford QL, whatever that meant, with a high canvas canopy on the back.

I sat most of my test right in the heart of Blackpool in the narrow streets around the Tower and the Winter Gardens thronging with holiday makers. I'm sure the examiner took us there only to do a bit of talent spotting. I passed but my colleague failed after several attempts on a hill start. After passing the test our final week was out solo with given routes to follow in the Preston and Chorley areas with a set time to do it in. his was to give us confidence before going on to our permanent postings. On one solo run a female driver came back to camp with the canopy of the lorry sitting on top of the tailboard, having lost her way and tried to go under a low bridge. It reminded me of a very large open touring car.

After the course we all went home on embarkation leave and on my return had to go to Lytham St Annes to be told of our postings. Everyone going abroad had to be inoculated against various illnesses. It was a very hot day and the medical team decided they would do it outside. We stood in a long line and took it in turn to walk up to one of the orderlies where they had everything laid out on tables. I think it was two or maybe three jabs we got depending on which country we were going to but what amazed me was the number of guys that fainted in the line up just at the thought of it. Along with some other lads I went out for a farewell drink to Uncle Toms Cabin in Blackpool and on getting back to camp we were a bit noisey and several guys in their beds were complaining and moaning about sore arms. They got no sympathy and told they were a lot of "Wimps".

The journeys then between Inverness and London were made on the old steam engine trains like the Flying Scotsman. It was usually over night and we slept at least the first half of the way pulling down the blinds and stretching out on the bench seats and sometimes, depending on the number of us in the compartment, up in the netted luggage racks. For some reason or another we would wake up as we crossed the border into Scotland to a different tone of the engine. Perhaps the engine had to work harder but without opening the blinds you could tell where we were. An extra engine had to be put on to take us up over the Drumochter Pass and the Slochd. In the daytime after leaving Euston Railway Station on the journey north and passing through Hertfordshire, Bedfordshire and right up through the Midlands you could rest assure it would be misty and not very appealing. Sometimes there were tunnels to pass through and the sooty black smoke could always find its way into the carriages which left a smell on your clothing. However, one very clear day I was joined in the compartment by an Australian who was heading for Edinburgh and he was somewhat overcome by the different shades of green the countryside had to offer. I would imagine most of us would have taken it for granted but he kept bobbing up and down to the window to take yet another 'photo, using up spool after spool on that alone.

Hanging about on railway stations for the right connection was not my "cup of tea". After visiting my sister Joy and family in Cornwood near Plymouth where my Brother in Law Albert was a Chief Petty Officer in the Navy I spent a night at Bristol and the station there was cold, draughty and downright miserable but that was what I had to put up with to get back to Bridgenorth in time for Monday morning parade. I should add that Joy arranged with a young neighbour to drive me about on his motor bike to see the lovely places along the Devon Coast. If I remember correctly it was an alternative to going with her and the children to a school sale of work. I got as far as Carlisle another night but had to wait a further two hours to get a train north but it was going only as far as Glasgow. To pass the time I went out on to the street for a walk and got talking to a driver who was filling his car of petrol. When I asked him how far north he was going he said, "Up beyond Inverness." When I asked him where? He said, "Culrain." I got a bit excited at the thought of a lift all the way home to Ardgay but that was short lived when the the driver pointed out the "Limited Trade Plates" on the car which forbid him to carry unauthorised passengers. He said, "If the police stop me not only will I get fined but probably lose my job as well."

When the train got into Glasgow I asked a porter where he thought I could get cheap bed and breakfast for the night. He directed me a short way to the back of a tenement building and on climbing the stairs to the third floor a very old lady dressed in black answered the door. There was an eerie feeling to everything but the lady was very nice and welcomed me into her home, showing me to a room and giving me a cup of tea and something to eat with it. It was quite dark in the flat and she went about with a paraffin lamp that I was so familiar with before the tilley. She asked what time my train was leaving and assured me that I would be up in time to catch it. About 5am there was a knock on the bedroom door and when I went through the porridge was on the table to be followed by bacon egg and toast, ten shillings worth of anybody's money.

Coming home after a short time away I soon realised the beauty of the glen I had earlier left behind. I remembered saying to my father how boring it was and nothing to see but hills when you looked out of the front window. His reply was, "Go to the back door and you'll get a different view." I said, "What? More hills." Although I never appreciated scenery then I very much do so now. I was speaking to Catriona one day about a possible holiday in New Zealand where I have a number of cousins and their families, descendants from one of two gamekeeper uncles who emmigrated to that country as trappers to help deal with a glut of rabbits. In brochures the scenery is beautiful but Catriona's view was, "Why go there when it is every bit as good in Scotland."

Our current home looks over Marjory's much admired garden, the first fairway of the golf course and Loch Migdale beyond. When the house was being valued prior to a sale for previous occupants the agent put a price of £4,000 on the view. How he worked that out is your guess but it does have a beautiful view. I never tire of staring at the sunrises with ever changing colours from deep red to orange and sometimes with black clouds adding to the picture. With so much Forestry Commission woodland planted during the last sixty years much of the beautiful landscape has been lost for good. I know it gave much needed work when most needed throughout Scotland, but that is not the case today with modern machinery having taken over. I have mixed feelings about large areas of heather hillsides in crofting areas being reseeded for extra grazing with the bulk of it turning into rushes. The latest blight to be seen now is the windfarms springing up everywhere even at sea but we all have to live and eat.

CHAPTER 22

OFF ON THE TROOP SHIP

I went from Lythem St Annes for my posting to Germany along with an airman, Bob Dalziel, from near Dumfries. There were others with us but they were going on to different camps. We travelled down to London and then caught a train to Harwich, where the troop ships went back and fore to the Hook of Holland. During the afternoon that day we went to the cinema at the Elephant and Castle and when we came out from it I had my first experience of London "smog", a mixture of soot from the coal fires and fog. Now that in cities only smokeless fuel can be burned the problem is pollution from vehicle exhaust. I don't know what is worst but my own experience from traffic fumes when directing traffic at busy junctions your lips dried up to the point of being sore and just how much of it were you inhaling. The smog was so dense that you could barely see a yard in front of you and we asked a policeman standing in the cinema foyer to help us. He told us to join hands and he took us across the streets to the entrance of the underground system to get a train to Liverpool Street. From there we took the main line to Harwich and went on an overnight troop ship to the Hook of Holland and then ushered on to a wooden seated train for Oldenburg with one transit stop on route. When we reached our final destination a driver collected us and took us to the station transport depot. After about two to three weeks there, and unbeknown to us, we had been reported missing. We should have been taken to the transport section of 5352 Airfield Construction Wing.

This wing was formed in two parts, transport and plant. Oldenburg was headquarters for both sections and there were detachments at every airfield in the British Zone. At this time all runways were being extended to accommodate the jet aircraft, squadrons of sabres, meteor and venom fighters. I was a bit overawed when I first saw the size of the plant transporters which were lined up in neat rows in front of the hanger. They were made up from a mixture of A.E.C., Krupp, Kaelble and Faun. The A.E.C's were very much older, smaller, real bone shakers with crash gearboxes. I had never seen such large vehicles and trailers before and asked the corporal who drove them. He replied, "You in about three months time."

The first month with about ten other drivers I spent carting top soil into a disused German seaplane base, now called RAF Rostrop, which was being converted to a military hospital. A bit of competition with money involved at the end of each day crept into this as to who would be first back to Oldenburg. Bets were also taken on who could get the most loads in, and this depended greatly on who would give way to the other on the narrow perimeter track we used. A farmer grew cabbages adjacent to this track and each time we had to go off it we noticed that the cabbages got thrown out of their drills. Sometimes the lorries got stuck and had to be pulled out but this only put temptation in our minds and we took bets on who could stay off the track furthermost and the amount of cabbages that got thrown out. I'm sure the farmer could have seen us in hell unless of course he got good compensation.

Another piece of irresponsible driving we got up to was at the end of the day when the lorries had to be washed down before going back on the public roads to Oldenburg. You had to drive them down a slipway to the edge of the lake where they were hosed down by the station fire-engine. After the first lorry went down, the ramp became very slippy and if you were not careful you ended up in the lake and had to be pulled out. It was the driver's responsibility to get out of the cab and fix the tow chain and many a driver went home the road at night with a wet backside. I think we likened ourselves to the American film "Hell Drivers". To get out of the cab whilst the lorry was being loaded by a huge tracked digger wasted time when money was at stake. I was sitting there one day revving at the engine for a speedy take off when the digger driver misjudge the height of the cab and a tooth on the bucket ripped a hole across its entire length. I was not injured but got a good fright just the same. After reporting the damage a written instruction came out to say we would not sit in the cabs when the vehicles were being loaded.

The next tipper job I was put on was with about thirty other drivers, both RAF and German, carting hardcore to a runway that was being extended but behind schedule. I think the entire fleet we had of six wheeled Mercedes and Fauns were put on the job to give a boost to catch up. I enjoyed driving the Faun tippers either empty of loaded but the Mercedes had fierce braking and if empty you were liable to skid all over the place. We were very much better behaved and more organised. Many Germans were employed on all the RAF camps and I can honestly say they were very friendly and easy to work with, although the different language was a problem to begin with. Their movement was somewhat restricted and they were certainly not allowed to go outwith their own country. If I was not out on the road and looking for something to do I would get the overalls on and help the German bloke in the tyre section. It may only have been scraping or wire brushing wheel rims but at the same time he taught me most of the German language I got to know. I regret now not having learned more of it.

Every so often the Germans had a long weekend off and practically none of them would work during it. A D8 bulldozer was urgently required at RAF Wunstorf and at first they could not get a driver and mate to deliver it. When one German driver eventually volunteered the Corporal asked me if I would accompany him, at the same time he said, "If you play your cards right it could be the start of you on the transporters."

I was all for it and before leaving early the next morning I went to the cookhouse and got enough sandwiches, fruit etc for both of us. As soon as we got through the town of Oldenburg, Bernard pulled in and got me behind the wheel, changing over at each town we came to after that. At lunch time he took me into a pub to have a beer with our sandwiches, and as soon as the bulldozer was unloaded and an unserviceable one tied on, we set off for Oldenburg. I got stuck in and helped Bernard all I could and was pleased when he let me drive most of the way home including through the smaller towns and villages. Back at the camp I had sore ribs from steering that old AEC but I never complained. They soon became obsolete and it was a treat to get into the modern German makes with heated cabs, power steering, fantastic lighting, powerful winches and so much more. Bernard must have given me a good report because that was me on the transporters full time from then on. I considered my self privileged to have even been considered suitable to drive such large vehicles so soon after passing my driving test. A lot of responsibility went with it.

The Old AEC Bone Shaker   *Krupp and the Galleon Grader That Hit the Bridge*

The Faun with rear wheel steering and three D 4's on Board – gross legal weight 58 tons

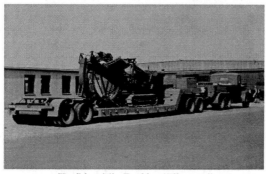

Kaelble – The Daddy of Them All

117

Ernest joined the Royal Air Force as well but was misguided into joining the Regiment side of it. Because of the strict discipline routine and all the "bull" that went with it, he did not like it and after going absent without leave ended up buying himself out. The day the RAF Police came to arrest him they were accompanied by Ken the Bobby from Ardgay but Ernest was along at Willie MacDonalds clipping turnips so they went there for him. Ernest was adamant that he should take his bicycle home with him and the Bobby agreed with this. However, when they reached Coneas Bridge Ernest went down the Braelangwell side of the river and crossed back again at the school footbridge leaving the police with their vehicle on the other side. Ernest could easily have done a runner on them at that point but went home as planned. The escort was not happy with him and wanted to take him away there and then but he insisted on washing and changing into clean clothing which they reluctantly agreed to. After Mam made tea for them all they went off quite happy.

Ernest was stationed for a while at RAF Wunstorf and I would stop overnight there just to see him. On our way to the canteen for supper I took him to see what I was driving. The first thing he said was, "What would Mammy say if she saw that coming down the brae." I would never have got off the A9 at Ardgay far less get up to Gruinard. Probably at that time back in Britain only vehicles belonging to the likes of Pickfords and other heavy haulage companies would have matched them. Even in the early to mid fifties some of our trailers had rear steering on them. One particular type you could switch the towing bar to either end of the trailer and change the lighting and number plate to suit, all of it taking only twenty minutes or less to do it. Now you will see plenty of them on our roads and even much bigger ones usually artics. Apart from the "Queen Mary" aircraft transporters which the RAF had, I cannot recall ever seeing other articulated vehicles in Germany but trailers were common place. All of our plant vehicles were tractor units with about eight to ten tons of concrete ballast on them which in itself was a load for normal lorries. Occasionally if I did not have space on the trailer I would put one or two caterpillar tracks on top of that but not often.

Heading back to Oldenburg one afternoon I came across a six wheeled Leyland lorry laden with oxygen bottles bogged down to the axles at the side of the road. Two airmen from the R.A.F. Regiment were frantically flagging us down but I would have stopped anyway. Their biggest concern was the fact that they were not on the authorised route given to them and the regiment was a stickler for discipline. A German civilian driver was not as happy as the airmen were when I got stopped at the scene of an accident on the autobahn near Hanover. I was asked by him to pull his lorry and trailer back up a steep bank on to the road again. By the marks I think he must have fallen asleep at the wheel. It was highly irregular for me or any member of the forces to do it but being a bit of a hound for the pound I said I would for one hundred deutsche marks. When the driver agreed I should have asked for the money first. However, when the back wheels of the trailer was just about to come on to the road I asked him for it but he reneged saying he did not have any money. I was so annoyed with him I let the winch brake off and his lorry went further off the road than before. If he had said in the first place he had no money I would still have taken the vehicle out for him. A combined piece of equipment to work with the winch was a skid that could be lowered for it to dig into the ground or tarmac to prevent the tractor unit being dragged backwards. It was so effective that on that occasion the front wheels were offering to lift off the ground. The police were not very happy with me either.

The worst ever driving experience in fog I had was on the approach to a rear entrance to Wunstorf Camp which I was always in the way of using. I had to turn left on to a side road that ran alongside a railway line at the same level. I literally was guessing where I was and started to make the manoeuvre but soon realised from the bumps that I was on the line. I reversed back and my colleague got out and walked from there with a red lantern to guide me along. At the guardroom on entering the camp the duty officer said to follow him in his Volkswagen car. He took off and that was the last I saw of him. I carried on very slowly until I felt we were going down a hill and knew that this was not correct. We were then approached by a German guard who said we were heading for an underground firing range. After the fog lifted a bit we got out of there and headed for my usual parking place.

Over the last few years it has become quite common to see young lady drivers behind the wheel of all sorts of lorries and 'buses. Back in the fifties when I was in Germany it was very much the normal thing to see them hauling coal and other goods with their large curtain-sider lorries and trailers from the industrial areas around Essen, Dusseldorf and the Ruhr up the autobahn to Berlin and elsewhere. Most of them were about forty to fifty years of age, severe, swarthy, hard faced women so unlike Liza Kelly from "Ice Road Truckers."

CHAPTER 23

MY FLIGHT COMMANDER

I did have a break when I came back to RAF Weeton for a mechanics course and should have gone into workshops afterwards but as luck had it, I was ear marked by the unit Commander, Flight Lieutenant O'Sullivan, who I got on very well with, to transport an obsolete aircraft hanger which was already dismantled up north at RAF Schleswig and take it south to a camp near Bonn. They considered using railway carriages but when I said I thought I could do it in three weeks they opted for that, being more cost effective as well. The main frame work was of heavy steal with exterior wooden cladding and metal sheeting. Every nut, bolt and fitting had to go with it.

I used the largest plant trailer we had, an impressive outfit with thirty two wheels. Ray Padbury from Leaminton Spa was to be my second man. We had been on many trips together before that and were used to one another's way of working. We also went out socially together. The Germans at either end were to load and unload the vehicle whilst we caught up on our sleep. We carried our own bedding and extra clothing to save the trouble of getting the duty store man out during the night and all the rigmarole that that entailed. We each carried a chit signed by the Flight Lieutenant to say we were entitled to a meal at any camp out with normal meal times. This in its self saved a lot of hassle getting a meal during the night at camps where we were not so well known.

The first load the Germans put on I was not happy with it. I told them we could carry double the amount and to stack it the full length of the trailer and as high that we could still get under the bridges on route, which took us down through Hamburg, across to Hanover and then down the autobahn to our final destination. They did as they were asked and Ray and I thought we were some "Kiddies" with this lot behind us. Because the Germans worked from 8am to 5pm we found ourselves driving mostly during the night so we also carried our civilian clothes and stopped off in places like Hamburg and Cologne for a break and a meal.

After we dropped off the last load I enquired if there was any plant to go back to Oldenburg. We got loaded up with lots of end of season grass cutting equipment and other machinery which I was not in the way of hauling. When we pulled up outside our offices at Oldenburg, Flight Lieutenant O'sullivan, who occupied an office upstairs, shoved up his window and shouted down at me, "What are you doing back here with that load of junk?" He was surprised, but pleased to hear that the job had gone so well, so quickly and under the three weeks I had estimated.

That was not the only time Mr O'sullivan shoved up his window and shouted at me. Two six wheeled tipper lorries had to go to a breakers yard some two hundred miles from our camp and that we had to tow them there. I had better ideas and suggested putting them on the same plant trailer but the Warrant Officer, because of their size did not think it was feasible but left it to me. Although I was not authorised to operate cranes I did for that job. I positioned the two lorries back to back with old tyres between them and the front wheels up on the platform part over the road wheels and securely chained them down. Another impressive load, but soon afterwards I was again summoned to Mr O'sullivan's office. The conversation went something like this "You are not authorised to operate a crane." Reply, "No sir." "I had better put that right then", said Mr O'sullivan, taking a new driving permit, a 1250 as every piece of paper was numbered, out of his desk and deleted only tracked vehicles from it. I was from then on authorised to drive or operate every other type of vehicle.

It became a bit of an obsession with me to get even bigger and heavier loads behind me. That same German crane was one, and the station railway engine was another, both going back to factories for repair. When not in use the gib of the German Crane came down on to a platform alongside the split cab. It was air operated and the safety stops on it went faulty with the risk of it not positioning safely and crushing the cab. At one of the stations I visited, a fairly senior officer was having a look around my vehicle and trailer. Afterwards he said, "Just think of the money you could make if you had this for yourself back in Britain." Two other divers came over from England who I would love to meet up with again, were Johnnie Sprosten from Shrewsbury and a guy called Brian Palin. Johnnie had a very lucky escape when a tractor came out of a field onto the public road and hit his lorry, which overturned and burst into flames. Johnnie kicked out the windscreen to get out but ended up in hospital with severe burns. Brian on his first outing as a driver failed to see that Ray had stopped on the road in front of him. He slammed on the brakes and swerved to avoid a collision but ended up with the front wheels down in a deep, deep ditch, having clipped the rear of Ray's lorry in the process. Instead of accompanying Ray in his lorry I should have been supervising Brian who was actually on a test drive and when this happened he thought his driving career was over barely before it begun but I got his truck out of the ditch and covered up for him over the slight damage.

Johnie Sprosten after his Lucky Escape from Fire   *The 5352 Wing Cranes*

Brian Palin and myself   *Another recovery*

I did not escape accidents myself. It was in the winter time and deep snow was on the ground. I was coming down into Osnabruck with a high load, and knowing there were a number of low bridges ahead, I asked Brian or Ray whoever was with to see what clearance I had on the first one. I thought from memory that it was higher than the others but it was not. The machine, a brand new galleon grader, got jammed underneath, and because we did not have the keys to the grader we had to let down all the tyres on the trailer to get freed. There was pumping facilities attached to the tractor unit so we were able to blow them up again and proceed with a police escort through several railway yards to get to the other side of town. Appearing before the Plant Section Squadron Leader and my own boss regarding the damage, I spun a yarn of misjudging the depth of hard pack snow and ice on the road and the fact the grader was two inches higher than the older ones. They swallowed the excuse and I walked away with a mild ticking off. Under the bridge the road was as clear as if it was the summer.

Another bit of explaining I had to do, not only to my bosses but to the German police as well, who stopped me and accused me of hitting the wall of a house as I drove through a small village north of Hamburg. Because they could not speak the basic of broken English I had difficulty understanding what they were accusing me of doing but I knew very well that I had not hit a house. I then got through to them that because of parked vehicles I had to go up on the pavement but I was not aware of it at the time that the sewage drains collapsed as a result of the heavy load. There was no way of getting out of it when the police found granite cobble sets jammed between the tyres.

During my two and a half years I was there I got to know Germany better than my own country. I was just a glorified lorry driver, away for weeks on end and from all discipline, parades and kit inspections. In fact when I got demobbed at the end of my service, I handed in a deficiency chit for webbing which I deviously escaped getting. The store man could not believe his eyes when he saw it and thought it must have been a record for an airman to go through service for four years without webbing.

CHAPTER 24

OTHER INTERESTING WORK

My work whilst at Oldenburg took me to Denmark for a crashed jet, often to the docks in Holland and Belguim with old vehicles coming back to Britain or collecting new plant required for the construction work. I did several journeys down the beautiful Rhine Valley to Koblenz and often stopped to watch the paddle steamers towing barges or the specially built boats for pleasure trips. The reason for me going there was to haul special timber required for radar masts right up through the British Zone as far north as the Island of Sylt, where we had a camp of that name. From memory I think the wood was called lignum and rated to be the heaviest in the world. Incidentally, a firm of German Civil Engineers called Hochteif, were extending the runways at Oldenburg when I was there, and the same firm were the main contractors who recently completed the hydro electric scheme at Glen Doe near Fort Augustus where my Son in Law Tim worked as a surveyor.

Not far from Oldenburg a Sabre jet crashed into peat bogs and disappeared underground. The pilot ejected at the last minute but did not survive the crash. I was very much involved in the efforts to recover the jet which went on for about a month. The access to the site was down what I could only describe as a farm track and my first job was to shunt a plant trailer down it to use the platform of it as a bridge over a water crossing. I then took a RB 24 crane type excavator to the track end from which it went to the site under its own steam and dug without success for the duration. The hole kept filling up with water and every other day more and more pumps had to be taken there. After a month the search for the engine was abandoned on the assumption that after going underground it had levelled out and travelled an unknown distance.

Another recovery I was involved in was down a similar farm track with ditches on either side when and army lorry on exercise got bogged down. A young army officer in charge apparently kept telling his men to dig round about the wheels and that it would come out but each time it sunk further and further into the peat until you could see the head and shoulders above the canvas canopy of anyone standing opposite you. The same officer was adamant that the bulldozer I took out should be close coupled to the lorry for a short pull. This was against the wishes of the operator resulting in the bulldozer ending up on its side in the ditch. I took a second bulldozer out but this time the operator of it refused to go off the harder part of the track. He then winched out the one in the ditch and from there with one bulldozer anchored to the other the lorry was winched out.

The only other direct involvement I had with the Army was, having to recover one of our own vehicles that had gone on fire either at Celle or Luneburg. The driver had a load of hessian sacks aboard and due to the friction they caught alight and because of the intense heat the chassis melted to the extent that it dropped to the ground other than where it crossed over the axles. For fear of damaging the grass verges or the white painted kerbing on the roads within the camp I was made to walk to where the wreck was to make sure it was feasible to drive there and turn around. It must have been the highlight of their day as so many servicemen of all ranks came out to watch the proceedings. I surprised them all by switching the towbar after loading up and drove off without having to turn the trailer.

Coming home one night to Oldenburg towing a smashed car behind a Scammel breakdown vehicle, or "wrecker" as they were more often referred to, a civilian car coming in the opposite direction bounced off the front wheel of the Scammel and went down over a bank. When the Polizei arrived they arrested the driver for drunk driving for which he got a prison sentence and apparently that was quite common.

On one of our journeys north from Koblenz I decided to take a scenic route through the mountains but when it got too close to the Russian Zone border it became a bit too scary for comfort. Although we carried two hundred gallons of spare diesel in jerry cans we were running precariously low because of the type of terrain and wintry conditions. Taking everything into account including the monthly returns on fuel consumption for each vehicle we just had to abandon the scenic snow covered mountains for the autobahns again. I may be wrong but I feel the winters over there were more severe than what I have encountered at home. Some mornings vehicles sitting outside overnight had to be literally dragged into the hangers to get the oils thawed out with blow heaters before the engines would start or the gear boxes or back axles began turning. Out on the runways there were special machines that blasted out jets of flame below them to melt the ice to keep the aircraft flying.

One of our German drivers, Otto Gross, was towing one of those machines back to Oldenburg one night during a heavy snowfall when his tractor unit broke down. By the time I got to him the batteries in his vehicle had gone flat and he had no lights. I suggested towing his outfit to the nearest camp and leaving it there but in spite of the cold he was adamant that we should take it home. We attached a ridged steel towing bar and off we set and because Otto was limited to what he could see he had to depend on the tail lights of my vehicle and every so often his vehicle would be bumping off the wall of packed snow at the side of the road. Not only was he grateful for being rescued but for Otto's benefit I stopped at a Salvation Army Hostel and the staff, although about 2am, very kindly supplied us with an excellent hot meal. During the three winters I was there I only once had to put chains on and that was because of the depth of snow sitting on ice. Even then we had to punch away at it until we got through the worst.

I set off up the autobahn one morning heading for Hamburg but forgot to lower the radiator muff, resulting in the engine overheating and a big loss of water. In the distance at the bottom of some fields I could see a stream but to get water from it I had to empty one of the cans of diesel into the lorry. I never liked to pour in the last little drop because of the dregs and checked to see how much was left in the can only to find that I had emptied a full jerry can of pure antifreeze into the tank. I was more careful the next time and got the water from the stream. I was hopeful that the antifreeze had settled in the bottom of the tank and when I removed the bung a little diesel came out first but then almost filled the can again with good clean antifreeze. Everything was fine until we were coming up a hill out of Hamburg on our way home when the engine started banging, the likes I had never heard before. I switched off immediately thinking I had knackered the engine with the antifreeze. After rolling backwards down the hill I managed to get into a parking place and just sat there not really knowing what to do. Oil levels were OK and not a trace of spillage or outward damage.

Foremost in my mind was the cost of repair and the time off the road for another Krupp engine when the pistons seized in it. To hell with it I then thought and turned the engine over to see if it would start. It did immediately and to my surprise it ticked over as normal. Gingerly I increased the revs until I was confident that all was well and got out onto the autobahn again. Next morning I took the vehicle to the workshop to have one of the fitters check the engine over and as an afterthought I asked him to drain off any more antifreeze that may have been left in the tank. Immediately he said that that would have been our problem when a small drop had gone through the system and entered the injector pump thus causing the banging noise. He assured me everything would be fine and not to worry about it and that was the way it turned out.

We had a German clerk in the office who kept the servicing records for all the vehicles including the fuel consumption. On one of my journeys down south into the American Zone I stayed overnight at an American camp. Firstly, I found it unusual to be served huge steaks at supper time and bananas and ice cream at breakfast time, a bit up market to what we were used to. Then it came to filling up with fuel. I cannot recall how much we got from them but it would easily have been in the region of two hundred gallons. I asked for documentation for this but no way would they give me anything. A present form Uncle Sam the serviceman kept saying. I did not even have to sign for it. Go back and tell the clerk that.

To get to the Island of Sylt you had to drive the lorries on to a train which took you over on a causeway. On one crossing a tarpaulin covering the load came undone and was blowing in the wind like a parachute, held only by a rope at two corners. Whoever was with me and I had to climb out of the cab, crawl over the back of the tractor unit to get on the trailer in an attempt to secure the cover but all we could do was to hold onto it to prevent it blowing off into the sea. A big attraction on that Island for us was the nudist colony. To get to our fuel depot we had to drive past it. I cannot think of any other in existence during the early fifties. Were they ahead of the times? On another trip to Sylt with a bulldozer we came to a temporary bailey bridge over a canal. It was of a wooden structure and built on top of the existing bridge. There were no weight limit signs to be seen so we took a chance but once we were on it we realised it was not as stable as it looked. It swayed slightly from side to side but we had to keep going and what a relief it was to get back down on the tarmac.

CHAPTER 25

ROYAL NAVY RESERVE

During the four years I had in the Royal Air Force I never even saw the inside of any of their planes but on a three months attachment with the Royal Navy Reserve at Schleswig Holstein I could have gone up every other day in their two seater Sea Fury training planes. They were the fastest of the piston engine planes and their wings folded up for taking less space for storage on the aircraft carriers. It was a novelty at first but as time wore on I just went up to please the pilots because they liked the company and for someone different to talk to. Most of the time it was pretty normal flying but on one occasion on take off this other plane flew into a flock of birds. The pilot called up the pilot of the plane I was in and asked him to make a survey for damage. He got so near to the other plane and at different angles I was not very comfortable with it. My job there was to refuel the aircraft so I had plenty contact with all of them. They had a five or seven seater Dominee plane that went up every so often just for sight- seeing trips. I joined them a couple of times and on one occasion the pilot was stuffing chewing gum into a hole to stop an oil leak. When I questioned him about the safety of this he assured me that the oil was not under pressure and that all would be OK.

I enjoyed it so much in Germany that I was tempted to sign on there for another six months but opted to come back to Britain instead. We were entitled to take ten days local leave each year but I never bothered with that. I saw plenty of the country without it. As far as sightseeing goes I think the driver's job was second best to the pilot's. I took all of my UK leave and came home to Gruinard for that. One such leave was just after Xmas and I bought a couple of pounds of Black Twist tobacco or Bogie Roll to some smokers to take home to my Dad. Then I thought I might as well buy him a pipe as well. A few days after I gave it to him my mother said, "You're a fine person buying your father that tobacco. It was bad enough Joy sending him some but you had to give him a pipe as well. Did you not know he had stopped smoking about two years ago?" After I went back to Germany my mother told me that temptation got the better of him to try the pipe and he started to smoke again. However, years later he stopped again and this time for good.

I was posted to Hillhead of Tyrie near Fraserburgh which was an old radar station that was now defunct. I was collected from Aberdeen Railway Station and at first taken to RAF Buchan near Peterhead. After two or three weeks there, and reported missing once again, they realised I should have been taken to Hillhead. When I did arrive there I found there were only one sergeant a corporal and fourteen men there. Most of them were radar mechanics that had just completed dismantling all their equipment, dog handlers and two cooks, and one by one they kept getting posted down to England. On our way there we stopped at the Post

Office in Fraserburgh to ask directions to the camp but the lady not knowing where it was said, "Al gang an spear." The driver who was from south of the border and I just looked at one another rather questioningly. When she returned a few minutes later she told us how to get there. That was my introduction to the Buchan dialect but after meeting many of the friendly "Broch" folk and being invited to their homes I picked up the brogue very quickly, not only to understand it but to speak it as well. Having married a Foveran lass it has stood me in good stead ever since although she only uses it now when with her own kith and kin.

For those who are not familiar with "Spiken" the Doric, the dialect and local lingo in the North East of Scotland, particularly Aberdeenshire, and out Fraserburgh way it is as broad as it gets so I'm going to quote a few sayings:-

Your tea break is a fly an when ye gang hame it's lousing time so keep her chappin.
You don't start anything ... ye get yockit.
When ye start spiken the incomers dinna unnerstan fit yer sayin.
Don't think yer glaiket if ye dinna ken the difference between a roll, a safty, a rowie or a buttery.
If yer cald, ging to bed and coorie doon.
When yer feeling doon a bozie will pick ye up.
If ye gang up Deeside ye may wint tae visit Bunkry, Abine, Bulter and Brimmar.
Ye may ken fit a lad or a lassie is but in these pairts it's loons and quines.
Burns nicht is when ye eat haggis, neeps and tatties for twa weeks.
If yer nae weel get a baggie o peels.
Now pit yer sheen or sluppers on and read the rest o it.

There was very little for me to do apart from the collection of rations from the cookhouse at RAF Buchan, one laundry run per week and a dog meat run to Aberdeen. Pretty boring stuff compared to what I was used to. Because there was no public transport to or from the camp we were allowed to use the two ton Austin truck for one or two social outings, mainly dances, per week. Instead of buying a car I went into Aberdeen and bought a brand new Ariel Red Hunter motor cycle from Shirlaws. On my way back to the camp with it and after about ten miles the engine started to heat up although I was not going very fast. The shiny new exhaust pipe where it came away from the engine was well discoloured. After it cooled down I set off again to find that there was a fourth gear. That shows how much I knew about motor bikes.

I ran that bike about Fraserburgh regularly with no L plates and sometimes with a pillion passenger. The Bobbies saw me about town a lot and must have assumed that I had a full licence. During my driving test two of them turned round sharply and stared in my direction. It was pouring rain at the time and I did not put on a jacket thinking the examiner would take pity on me and cut it a bit short, but no he kept me out in it until I was soaked to the skin. He kept stopping me several times and asked what the procedure was for making right hand turns. I answered this correctly but each time he told me to put into practise. However, I passed the test but after a few minor incidents I sold it and bought a car. One such incident was early morning when I arrived home from the salmon fishing at Bonar. Heavy dew was on the ground and Mam was feeding the hens at the time and as I banked over to enter the peat shed the bike slid out from below me giving my mother a terrible fright and for the hens to fly everywhere even up on to the roof of the barn. I took the bike up onto the road for a test drive to see if it was damaged and I convinced myself that the handle bars were twisted. Noel, who was working at Gruinard Lodge at the time, came along every morning so he took it for a ride. He came back with his hands up in the air and demonstrated that there was nothing wrong with the bike. I fell asleep one night on my way back to Fraserburgh and fortunately the jolt I got from going up on the grass verge woke me up. I was near to Loch Oire so I stopped and washed my face in the cold water and was more alert afterwards. The one that finally made up my mind that motor cycling was not for me was when near Ballater on the North Deeside Road on a very wet day I could not stop the bike from drifting across the road until it got a grip on the sandy stuff at the opposite side. Luckily for me there were no vehicles coming from the other direction.

My mother was totally against motor cycles and was far from happy when I bought my one. I could understand her reasons for being that way after my brother Arthur was killed on one. He was still very young in his early twenties at the time and working as an under shepherd at Mid Fearn. In his spare time he snared rabbits and came up that morning on the motor bike to sell them at the butchers in Bonar and on his way home at Kincardine Church Yard he was involved in a head on collision with another vehicle and fatally injured. In later years Ernest, my younger brother give her cause for much worry having had several bad motor cycle accidents, the last one leaving him permanently injured.

Just before the Sergeant got posted he asked me to use the truck to go to RAF Boddam where a dance was being held in a nearby hotel. While at the dance, I was aware that an off duty RAF policeman was there but never thought much about it. He was often on duty at the guardroom when I booked in and out, so we knew each other reasonably well.

The sergeant was courting a barmaid from another establishment and it was prearranged that I would pick him up there for the return journey back to our own camp. I never give it a thought but I had one pint of beer at the dance and I did not change back into uniform before driving to the guardroom to book out, where I was expecting to be waved through at the barrier. The same policeman was on duty and he came out and arrested me for what I thought were very minor misdemeanours. What I did not know at that time was that my sergeant and the RAF police sergeant had some previous altercation and that I was the piggy in the middle. I seem to recall it was about the same barmaid.

During the night I was not asked about anything and went from close arrest to open arrest, and back again several times, with freedom to go about wherever. I chose to stay in the guardroom until I was then free to go back to Hillhead, but not before putting my uniform back on. Both the sergeant and I, before the disciplinary hearing, were invited to make written statements about the chain of events. We had no problem with this and just told the truth, but in mine I embodied all of what took place in the guardroom after my arrest, bearing out all the indecisions that were made.

Crunch time came a few weeks later when I was frog marched into the Station Adjutants office at RAF Buchan. He was second in command and told the police escort to leave the room. He spoke about the night in question and then went on to say I was promoted to Corporal. I am more than certain the promotion was down to Flight Lieutenant O'sullivan, and I was a bit vexed that it did not come through while I was still working under him. The adjutant went on to say that from then on I was to be in charge of RAF Hillhead which by now was down to five men. The sergeant had already got his posting date and was there for only a few more days. Now to be marched in on a discipline charge and come out promoted must be another record for the forces. Before leaving the adjutants office he said to me, "Now you are both of the same rank I don't want you going out there and trying to get even with him." Not long after that the same policeman asked for a lift on the motor bike into Peterhead which I thought was a bit of a cheek. Because of all the bends in the road I gave him something to think about and he never asked me again.

I was courting a girl from Cairnbulg by this time and her parents were not happy with me taking her on the back of the bike. The night of a dance her father would come up to Fraserburgh to take her home but we would leave early to avoid him. I then decided to go back to Shirlaws and they gave me a good price for the bike which I spent on buying a car. I don't know why I did not do that in the first place.

The day before I was due to go to RAF Buchan for the rations I would load up with firewood from a collapsed radar mast for the catering officer. In return I could get anything I wanted from the cookhouse much to the annoyance of the Flight Sergeant in Charge who kept reminding me that he had hundreds of men to feed instead of my five. One day I was loading the truck with concrete slabs for another Flight Sergeant. It was very warm and I had removed my collar and tie and went into the guardroom to have cup of tea with our own policeman. He was similarly dressed and unexpectedly who turned up at the gates but the Adjutant from RAF Buchan being driven in his official car. We had a brief argument as to who would go out and meet him. The policeman did and I went back to the truck and carried on working. Being in charge of the camp I know I should have gone to speak to him as well but I thought I was better out of the way in the circumstances.

When the Adjutant got back to his station he sent a message for me to report to him the next morning. With the uniform nicely pressed I set off but stopped in Fraserburgh for a haircut I badly needed. To put it mildly I had quite a mop and without going for just a short back and sides I had the top cut well back as well. The adjutants opening words were, "What has gone wrong with Hillhead since you took charge of it?" "Nothing Sir." I replied. He then went on to relate his findings about his visit the day before. How the two airmen in the guardroom argued with one another, neither wanting to come out and speak to him. He then described one of them as having a head of hair like the Highland Cattle you see up north. He then said, "Who was he anyway?" I replied, "That would have been the orderly from the cookhouse at RAF Buchan who was at Hillhead only temporarily and would be going back there very soon." After commenting about a nice stew simmering away on the stove and vegetables all ready for the supper he talked about the living accommodation and for me to go to the stores and get whatever I wanted like carpets and armchairs to make the place more comfortable. Just before leaving he sprung another pertinent question on me, "So where were you when I called?" I don't know if he already knew it was me who was in the guardroom and was not letting on but I said, "Oh, I was away over at the other side of the camp loading the truck." The same day he authorised me to use my own car, a 1947 Austin Eight, instead of the truck for our social outings and was paid accordingly. That was the last time I saw that officer until the day I got demobbed.

That was not the first car I owned. When I was on the mechanics course at RAF Weeton I bought an American Hudson at a car auction. It was large and roomy and I reckoned I could make money out of it by charging guys from the camp going in and out to Blackpool. It was two shillings and sixpence in or out and I had as many as fourteen in it one night. After a dance one night and driving alone out of Blackpool some young lads were thumbing a lift so I stopped thinking they were from Weeton. It turned out they were from RAF Kirkham nearby and just after I dropped them off I got stopped in that village by the local policeman. He did not believe me that I owned this big car and took me into the police station for further questioning. I had all my documents with me and after studying them for sometime he told me I was free to leave but I could see that he sensed something was not quite right. I told him that I had dropped off some fellow airmen but not that I charged them for the taxi ride back to camp.

My first car

I was at Weeton for three months during the summer season. It was a favourite place for holiday makers, young and old. For people of my age the Tower Ballroom and the Winter Garden were the main attractions. Billy Dunbar from Ardgay was doing a six months welding course there and shared the same billet as me. Often I would be leaving for Blackpool with my first load when Billy was just getting back to the billet having had his supper at the canteen. We often laughed about this and how I would have washed a shirt and dried it with the iron. Everything else went to the station laundry for cleaning. The mates I went out with, including Billy, thought the Harris Tweed jacket with leather patches on the elbows and flannels that I wore clashed with their style of dress and talked me into buying a suit and a more adequate supply of shirts to match. Apart from Billy they were all "townies" and thought I was a bit of a "country yokel". A Johnie Porter from Edinburgh was one of them and by coincidence some four years later I was waiting for a 'bus in Edinburgh to take me out to the Police Training School at Whitburn, West Lothian when I met in with him again. He had joined Edinburgh City Police and was on the same course. As you can imagine there was a lot of catching up to be done. I had long grown out of my first tailor made suit from Tain so with them in tow I bought one off the peg in a gent's outfitters in Blackpool.

When the auctioneer's hammer went down and I was asked to drive the car out of the ring, a man walked over to me and offered to take it out for a fiver. I was naive about the remark and said I would drive it out myself. He followed me outside and told me he was a taxi owner and had been bidding on the car with a view to adding it to his fleet of Hudsons. He said, "I know what you will be doing with it." I agreed to sell him the car when I was due to go back to Germany and he gave me the hundred and five pounds, the same as I paid for it. In 1955 that was a lot of money to the likes of me. Some would say I was a good boy to save that amount on forces pay, 28 shillings for those on call up and 49 shillings for regulars, but others may view it differently. I did not smoke and I drunk very little, but did go out to restaurants for good meals with Ray and others. Many of the airmen, especially those on National Service, smoked and drunk heavily to the point they were always broke. Every week if I was around they wanted to borrow money from me. Yes I loaned them various amounts but only to the ones I could trust and even then I made sure I was there on a pay day to collect the rewards. Call me a loan shark if you may. From non smokers I would buy their weekly allocation of cigarette coupons, buy the fags, usually Senior Service in packs of two hundred and sell them to the German drivers. They could not get enough of them and I could not get enough of the coupons. Cadbury chocolate was something else they were keen to buy, all for a profit of course.

The numbers at Hillhead dwindled until there were only myself, one other airman, and a civilian caretaker. He was a little cripple man called Davie Birnie from New Pitsligo. He was at the camp for many years and was very popular with everyone. He thought nothing of rustling up a good fry of bacon and eggs for us on the billet stove if we were out the night before and late in getting out of our beds. I was doing the cooking and returned the compliment with having him for lunch each day. Sometime after I left the air force I stopped off in New Pitsligo to see him but sadly he had passed away. I had no training as far as the cooking was concerned. I had often stood and watched my mother doing it and by trial and error I can honestly say the other airmen, about five of them when I first started it, were quite happy with the food and I can't ever recall getting a complaint. The first time I tried to make rice pudding I had no idea just how much it swelled out. As it crept up to the top of this large pan I used, I had to ladle half of it out, add more and more milk until it settled at the amount I wanted. I often made it after that because the men liked it and often asked for it. I shudder to think what the mess in the oven would have been like if I had done it mother's way. To this day Marjory keeps telling me to follow the recipe book which I seldom bother about and at Hillhead I don't think there was one.

PART THREE

A POLICEMAN'S LOT

CHAPTER 26

INTO A DIFFERENT UNIFORM

Just before my demob I applied to join the Aberdeen City Police and also the Scottish North Eastern Counties Constabulary or SNECC as it was more commonly known. I passed the exams for both forces and when I went down to RAF Buchan for by demob briefing, it was the same adjutant, Flight Lieutenant Tommy Ross, I saw. He tried to get me to sign on for another term but when I told him I had been accepted for the police he tried to persuade me to go down to Edinburgh City where his brother Hugh was a Chief Superintendent and was commandant at Whitburn Training School . I later learned that the Ross's came from Ardgay and that their father was a local postie and gent's barber who had cut my hair on many occasions. Their Grandfather, Alexander Ross, during the infamous evictions of the mid nineteenth century was born within the confines of Croick Churchyard where so many of the Glencalvie and other people took shelter. I considered myself very lucky to have had so many options and not least to have served under both those distinguished gentlemen.

On my way home to start my month's demob leave, I called in at SNECC Headquarters in Banff and was asked to come back the following day for a medical and an interview with the Chief Constable, George I. Strath. I went back to the camp and spent an unofficial night there. I was told that it was to close down completely the following day and the only airman left was to be transferred to RAF Buchan. Davie was to continue as caretaker. Two other airmen who came from the Glasgow area got demobbed the same day as me but stupidly they never handed in their bedding and got arrested on the way out at the guardroom with the blankets in their suitcases. It was not the norm for airmen to be caught stealing but at Hillhead items like shampoo, toothpaste and other toiletries were going missing. The only policemen left at the camp and I narrowed the suspect down to an acting corporal from the Ferrier area of Aberdeen. He went home every weekend so we decided to search his case as he left camp but Charlie refused to open it and went back to his billet rather than go home. The pilfering stopped so we knew we had the right man. After he got posted we learned that he was in the way of stealing tea, sugar and other foods from the cookhouse and before my arrival he would fill bags of coal and get the previous driver to drop them off at his house when he collected the dog meat.

After a successful interview and medical the Chief Constable talked me out of having the months demob leave I was entitled to and to join his force the next Monday. When I got home my mother was disappointed in one sense because she thought I would be home for a while, but then happy for me when I told her I had joined the force. That weekend when I went to a dance at Rosehall I lost my wallet and although I returned to see the caretaker the next morning we could not find it.

A couple of weeks later Anne forwarded a letter with my driving licence in it. The accompanying letter suggested that if I could identify the remaining contents of the wallet it would be sent on to me. This was not difficult to do and I told the finder to keep two pounds plus postage for his troubles. A little time later the wallet arrived complete with all its contents including the cash except for what I told him to keep plus another two pounds which he said he would send on when he got his pension. I was grateful for getting everything else back so I wrote him and told him to forget about that money. One of the less interesting things in the wallet was a railway warrant for me to travel down to Kent to collect my demob suit. I never did go and after hearing so much about them I don't think I missed a bargain.

My first week was spent at Banff where I was fitted out with uniform and other kit. For the records I was photographed and my fingerprints taken. Two books, one almost three inches thick on Criminal Law, and another smaller one on Road Traffic Law, were thrust into my hands with instructions to read both of them. My introduction to real police work was to happen that week as well when a very badly decomposed body was retrieved from the sea, the worst type of remains you could ever wish to deal with. Another recruit and I had to go to the mortuary and search the clothing for signs of identification.

The raw recruit

Eight o'clock the following Monday I was off up the road in my little Austin to Buckie to begin my two year probationary period, the first four weeks of such, would be under the supervision of a senior constable. On my approach to the station I met Fred Argo and he came back and introduced me to the other officers

136

on duty. I was initially to work alongside him, Norman Moir, Bill Burnett and Andy Birse. Recently I called on Fred and his good lady Maureen, at their Buckie home for a quick chat in the passing. Fred reminded me of his first meeting with me as I arrived in the car. He never said anything to me at the time but he thought to him self this young bobby must have money. That idea was based on the fact that out of all the officers at Buckie at that time only the Inspector, the Sergeant and one senior constable had cars. Little did he know but I did change my cars fairly frequently after that which again he reminded me of.

Andy Birse, so to speak, took me under his wing and helped me a great deal. We were out on patrol one night when he got me my first arrest. We caught up with a very drunk man staggering down the street, bumping off doors and windows as he went his way. I was ready to have him for being drunk and incapable but Andy said to wait. He was then just about to enter a pub when Andy said, "Grab him." Between us we manhandled him up the streets to the station where he was locked up until sober. Andy sat down and scrawled out a report for me to read. I cannot remember the exact wording of the charge but it was along the lines of entering licensed premises whilst under the influence of alcohol, contrary to a section of the Temperance Scotland Act of 1913.

The next task for me was to sit down and type the report and I shudder to think how many attempts I had at it before getting it passable. Like everything else the more you practice the better you get at it. Any spare time I had, I would get on the typewriter, chap away with two fingers as I am doing at this very moment, until I reached an acceptable standard. I came across an article in a police magazine about "Jack the Ripper". I decided to type a copy of it, not only for the experience but for the interest in the story.

I had a short spell under Sergeant Cassie who was renowned for having a bad temper because of his ulcers that bothered him. I fell fowl of his wrath one day for not going to look for a missing pedal cycle where he thought it would be. After leaving the office I met in with Bill Burnett and he talked me into joining him to serve a summons on someone and that we could look for the bike later. Because we had to report back to the station on the hour or half hour depending which beat we were on, the search for the bike was left for our next patrol.

It was not to be as simple as that for me. The sergeant was waiting in one of his moods for me to come in. In the occurrence book it was shown that Duncan Kerr another officer had found the cycle right where I was told it would be. When I tried to talk myself out of my disobedience, at the same time not dropping Bill in it, the sergeant knew I was waffling or in other words telling lies. After giving me a good dressing down, he asked how much I had earned since joining the force and what I had to show for it. After a few stutters and stammers from me he told me to get out on the street and not to come back until I had something to show for it. He also tore a strip of me for slashing the peak of my cap to make it look like a guardsman's. I did not do this myself. Norman, who was an ex guardsman was responsible but I did not blame him either. On that note the sergeant told me that when I got rid of my baby face and looked more like him I would not worry what my cap looked like. After all that was said, I went out at the door feeling a bit hurt, probably because I was not really to blame for any of it and later to hear that the sergeant on my departure just laughed and said, "That will give him plenty to think about."

Cassie left and Andy Birse took over as acting sergeant and I got on ever so well with him. He was a great help to me, as was most of the officers, but he went that extra mile. He had well over thirty years service before he was promoted and retired and most of that was spent in Buckie. He saw the younger generations grow up, knew who was related to whom, and generally speaking everything a good bobby needed to know about the environment and the people he worked within, something that cannot be said in modern times. Andy would often tip me off about offences he knew were being committed and after my bollocking I was ready for anything no matter how trivial it was.

The very first serious crime I was involved in was when I was out alone on my first night shift. A young lad cycled up to me to say that a girl had been badly assaulted. Just before that, a young man carrying his raincoat ran past me, and the description of the assailant that the lad gave me, matched him. I instructed the lad to go to the station to get help and to tell them that I was off after the person I thought responsible. Somebody else was looking after the victim.

I could still see this guy in the distance and set off after him, taking a short cut through a new housing scheme, at the same time he would not see me coming. He was not carrying the raincoat he had earlier, having stuffed it into a hedge. When I finally caught up with him I found out he was a native of Newcastle and was a serving rating from the Naval base at Lossiemouth and had his passport to prove it. Bearing in mind that I had less than two months service, never been to training school, and still had nine months to go for that, I tried to prolong the interview as long as possible until help arrived. Even although I was raw to the job, I involved a courting couple at a house nearby to witness his presence before letting him go. I knew he would be easy enough to trace.

No sooner than he had gone off up the road when Sergeant Cassie and another officer arrived. He was arrested and charged with serious assault with intent to ravish and sentenced to six months in prison. The disappointing aspect of it for me was the fact that I got no credit for the part I played in it and not even a mention in the report. Andy Birse, I know would not have allowed that to have happened if he had been involved, in fact he told me so. The victim, apart from being very traumatised, had some devastating injuries to her scalp where she had been struck umpteen times with her own stiletto shoe.

The next night shift, with Cassie gone, Andy asked me to look for a man wanted on warrant. He thought he was sleeping rough in one of the many derelict houses in the old part of Buckpool. With a feeble police issue torch I set off after midnight for this eerie experience. Practically the whole street was empty of people and as I entered each room I was far from ready for the unexpected. I did not find him but Andy himself arrested the man next morning somewhere near the harbour. I was quite relieved to know this.

In the first few months I discovered that all men lying on the street were not drunks. This was brought home to me one night when along with another officer we found such a person. He was beside a stack of fish boxes beside the harbour. When he became conscious and stood up he told us that the last thing he could remember was a fall out with his girl friend and standing up against the boxes to think things over. We came to the conclusion that a box had fallen from the top of the pile and hit him on the head. He had quite a bump on it to confirm our theory. A second time was a man out for the count at a telephone kiosk. Apparently he decided to urinate in it and got an electric shock from some cables. Both victims declined the offer of going to hospital for a check up.

Andy sent me to deal with many different complaints and incidents. One day, according to him he had the very job for me, and told me that a dog belonging to a man living next to the Star Bar in Buckpool had bitten a lady. He briefed me as always on what evidence was required and to take the lady to the man's house to identify the dog, and just as important to see the injury. What he did not tell me the lady was a local prostitute. Now she was a long way short of being the most glamorous of women I had come across and when she indicated that the bite was to her crutch I decided to give that part of the investigation a miss. She was probably more than willing to oblige and maybe in more ways than one. I knocked on the dog owner's door and when the man came out to answer it, the dog flew past him and bit the woman a second time in the crutch. I was teased back at the station about having missed the opportunity to have two looks at it. I wonder what they meant.

The Fishermen's Hall was a favourite place for dances on Friday and Saturday nights. It was always a busy night for the police because it was the venue for all the young for miles around, including the army personnel from Pinefield camp at Elgin, the navy from Lossiemouth and the RAF from Kinloss. Regular punch ups took place where they tried to settle their differences only to find themselves sharing cells for the night. Saturday night was very much a local affair with little or no bother. My self and some of the other single bobby's would attend them when off duty. One night though two of the local councillors made a name for themselves when they came to blows and ended up brawling with each other on the floor.

I have never heard of it being done since but after the local elections every three years there was what was called the "Kirking of the Council". They marched with a police escort from the Town Hall to one of the churches for this service. I was not long at Buckie when I was one of the officers accompanying them but I cannot remember what really went on in the church.

Kirking of the Council at Buckie, 1957. Fred Argo on my right

CHAPTER 27

ALIAS HARVEY WILSON

The night before I was due to leave for my initial training at Whitburn I was at one of the dances when I met a girl for the first time and offered to walk her home. During the course of conversation she asked what my name was and I jokingly replied "Harvey Wilson". There was absolutely no ulterior motive for me to say that. That name was only mentioned the once and just before we parted she said she would write to me.

I was at Whitburn two or three weeks when a notice in large print appeared on the blackboard requesting the officer expecting a letter from this girl at Buckie to report to the Chief Superintendant's office. Curiosity got the better of me so I plucked up the courage to go and see him. He was mystified by all of this because there was not an officer of that name on any of the courses. "You're the culprit," was his opening words. He never made an issue of it but did tell me to use my real name in future. Not like Sergeant Cassie he believed me. When the girl said she would write I dismissed it immediately thinking she did not have the college address anyway but unbeknown to me her sister was married to a bobby in Elgin and she got the address from her.

As the Inspector at Buckie always said, "And get on your bike you'll get there quicker." Not always strictly true in my case. I cannot remember where I was going but I was pedalling quite hard up this road and pulled out to overtake two teen aged school girls who were cycling in front of me when one of them suddenly cut across my path to enter a side street. The front wheel of my bike hit the rear wheel of her one, and both of us, bikes included, ended up in a heap on the road.

Quicker than me she was back on her bike and away. A couple of men delivering coal nearby started shouting remarks like, "If that was me you would be testing my brakes." Although embarrassed I just laughed it off and called back, "Feel free to do so." Before the other girl left she told me where her friend lived. As a result of the collision my mudguard got buckled up and jammed in the forks. I straightened it out as best I could and set off to speak to the girl's mother and to enquire if the girl was injured or not. She turned out to be fine but a bit frightened for having knocked a bobby of his bike.

On my way to the girl's house I had to cycle past some council workers who had previously dug a track across the street, with about three inches still to fill in. When my front wheel went in to this, the sudden jolt caused the same mudguard to catch against the tyre and the wheel jammed again. Over the handle bars I went and with me spread-eagled on the road with the workers fussing about me to see if I was alright. More sympathetic than the coalmen I can add. Needless to say I pushed the bike back to the station before getting a new mudguard.

At my expense the public had another good laugh, and most of them were school children waiting to catch their buses home. It happened in Cullen when I was relieving the constable there for his holidays. I was walking briskly up through the square when I became conscious of a toffee paper stuck to the sole of my boot. Without breaking my step I bent down to pick it off but instead of being smart I went headlong on to the pavement to cheers from the kids. I brushed myself down, gave them all a good wave and went on my way. It was a good story for them to go home and tell their parents and I'm sure they all did that.

Our Inspector, behind his back, was always referred to as Jocky Simpson and umpteen occasions he was caught ear wigging behind doors. When the sergeant typed out and signed a report of any significance Jocky would re do it and put his signature on it instead. I was in digs in a local temperance hotel when he came to stay for one night only, when he retired. There was no farewell party or anything for him, in fact I saw him as a lonely old soul. I was hurrying to get off to a dance that night and he was pleading with me to stay and talk to him. I got on well enough with him but I had better things on my mind and before I left he told me how he thought I would do well in the force but to watch the fly men. Rich coming from him I thought. Perhaps the young man with mental problems who, one morning, was brought into the station from a nearby monastery, summed him up pretty well. As he lay on a mattress in the tea room waiting for a doctor and mental health officer to arrive he talked about having invented a dry gearbox. He was full of praise for us but as soon as the Inspector came in he changed his attitude and got somewhat aggressive in his mood towards him. He told the Inspector many things that I'm sure some of the officers themselves would liked to have told him.

Most of the bobbies at Buckie were friendly with the Territorial Army Sergeant from the drill hall. Bill Burnett, my self and one other went out with him to an old railway line between Buckpool and Portgordon to shoot cormorants and mergansers perched on the rocks at the sea front. The sergeant took with him a variety of military weapons which we took in turn to fire. Today, or even then most if not all of the birds we fired at would be protected but at that time the public were more tolerant as to what went on. I don't know what the army authorities would have thought about it if they found out. I'm sure they would not have regarded us as potential recruits.

At thirty years service everyone one was expected to retire but in those days many of them went well beyond that with one reaching thirty eight years before calling it a day. Duncan Kerr was one of them who were well past the sell by date. He was partial to a dram and when out on patrol with him he always had an excuse to call on a publican. He must have thought I was naive. I would go back and meet him at a set time so that we would return to the station together and no questions would be asked.

One day I asked him to come with me to keep me right in dealing with my first suicide. I knew it was going to be a very messy one and I thought a bit of support would not go amiss. Try as I did he just would not come with me and his final words were, "You have dealt with a drunk haven't you?" Of course, "I said." "But what has that got to do with it?" His reply, "Well a suicide is just as easy. Off you go laddie." When still at Buckie I dealt with two more and many others after that. A farmer did not get on with his neighbour and for spite shot his horse. The same day he turned the shot gun on himself and made a right mess of it in more ways than one. He blew his jaw off but lived.

A lady tried it by drinking Lysol but recovered from it. Because of the state she was in, I said to myself that she would not try that again but she did and was successful the second time. Another old man in his sixties who I had charged with using lewd and libidinous practices towards two young girls in the afternoon, shot himself at night. It did not register with me at the time when he said, "The balloon is up for me now." The following day the sergeant instructed another young constable who I was in digs with to strip the body ready for a post mortem. He refused to go to the mortuary until Norman Moir said he would help him. Norman told him to undo the trouser belt and to pull the trousers off at the same time as he was pulling the jersey off. When the jersey came free, one of the arms came down and hit the young officer on the back of his neck. Out at the door he went and would not go back in to finish the job. Our landlady told me that he came home and threw his gloves down at the door and barely ate for days. I lost touch with him and never did know if he completed his two years probation.

The reporting officer always had to attend the Mortuary in Aberdeen where the pathologist would carry out his examination to establish the cause of death. The attendant there who prepared the corpse for him was what I would call a rough diamond. He was nicknamed "The Ghoul" and took a delight in trying to make you sick, even to the point of eating sandwiches whilst he went about his work in the place. Notes had to be taken down for the pathologist and if he came across something unusual he would go to great lengths to show and explain it to you. He was also a lecturer at Aberdeen University and when I moved to Aberdeen I chose him as my GP.

It was Hogmanay day when I had to call him to the digs where I was in bed being violently sick every so often. I had a bottle of whisky sitting on my bedside table which luckily had not been opened. I decided it would be better out of sight so I put it down on the floor between the bed and the wall. When the doctor came into the room the first thing he did was to push the bed away from the wall and kick over the bottle. He accepted my assurance that it had nothing to do with my illness and diagnosed gastro enteritis. I had to call him a second time when he diagnosed jaundice and signed me off work for eight weeks. It is still laughed about to this day because I jokingly blame my mother in law for causing it. She gave me tattie soup the day before but not the kind I was used to having. In Aberdeenshire it is made from tatties and mince and although I know it was not the reason for the jaundice I still on occasions remind her of it. Most people have their potatoes boiled enough so that they are soft enough to stick a fork into them. In Aberdeenshire some people, Marjory included, likes them fairly firm in the centre and for this they speak of a bone in the tatties. When Tim first started coming up with Fiona on holiday Marjory said one day that there was a bone in the tatties. Understandingly, Tim as he was eating his meal kept looking for the bone until all was explained.

In my second year at Buckie I just about lived out of a suitcase going from one single man station to another as holiday relief. Each officer had two holidays a year, a fortnight at a time. I would start at Portgordon and do all the villages down the coast as far as Portsoy and then have my own fortnight off. When I came back I would do the same thing again and then have my second holiday. It was good experience for me and no fellow officer by your side to turn to for advice. You just had to get on with it, making decisions as you went.

At every one man station each day of the week you had to cycle to a fixed point some five or six miles away to a shop, farm, post office or other establishment and get your notebook signed to confirm that you had been there at the appointed time. If you were unable to be there you had to have a very good reason and include that in your weekly report. I enjoyed the cycle runs and it was a good way of meeting and getting to know the local people including officers from neighbouring stations. We got a new Chief Constable from Edinburgh and he put a stop to all of this including the weekly reports. When I was walking along the main street in Portsoy I came across this odd looking character. He was very scruffy with a soft hat tied down over the ears with binder twine. His opening words were "Where's Massie?" I said, "On holiday." "I'm going to shoot him." Was the next thing he said. He refused to tell me who he was and because I thought he was just some crank that the regular bobby would know I did not pursue it. When Alan Massie came back off leave I told him about it. Alan was curious about this and told me he knew the man well and that he did not have a firearm but in any case we would pay him a visit. When we got to his house the man was no bother and handed over a humane killer, a weapon used by slaughtermen. I reported him for the appropriate offences and he was dealt with at Banff Sheriff Court.

One of the officers I relieved was Albert Davie from Findochty who tried his hand at writing a book but could not get a publisher to print it and for different reasons that will probably happen in my case. They told him it was too far fetched and did not think it would sell. The story was along the lines of a mail train being hijacked and driven into a tunnel where a large consignment of money was stolen. It was not long after that when the "Great Train Robbery" took place, making the book look rather insignificant in comparison. Albert was very musical and tried his hand at song writing as well, but that was not very successful either. He composed one to a very catchy tune I thought, about a girl he saw on a poster and how she smiled at him each time he passed.

An engineer friend of mine worked up Speyside at the distilleries and from time to time he would give me a bottle of the neat stuff. To me it was like firewater and I hated it, but Duncan would lick his lips and mustache even at the thought of it. If we were on night duty together we often had a game of snooker before going home and I would give Duncan a glass or two of it. I convinced myself that it was a better way of beating him. The only drink worse than the raw distillery whisky I ever tasted was when Fiona came home from France after a school exchange and the couple she stayed with give her a gill bottle of home-made brandy, "Explosive stuff". Another source of distillery whisky was from Bell's at Inchgower and many a party I was at when a white enamel bucket three quarters full was carried in, to be replenished if necessary later in the night. Yet I cannot recall anyone being the worse of it. It was mature whisky so maybe that had something to do with it or they were all just hardened to the stuff.

CHAPTER 28

THE SPINNER - A GREAT INVENTION

Bill Burnet and I became very good fishing friends. We each had a permit to fish the River Spey at Spey Bay. It was an excellent place for sea trout and finnock. We found the best time to be there was just as the tide turned to run out, or when it was coming in. It was Bill who first introduced me to the spinning rod. Prior to that I did not have a proper rod and for worming which was the only method of fishing I did, was with a long thin tapering branch cut from a Rowan tree. I was invited by a guy called Phipy Ross for a day's salmon fishing on the Spey just below Fochabers. He told me it was a one off invite and I may not get the chance again so be at the water for daylight and don't expect to go home before dark. Bill loaned me his spinning tackle and armed with plenty of food for the day I was at the water edge by six am.

Phipy and I fished the whole day until the light began to fade. I was coming down this pool behind him when I hooked a salmon out in the strong water. I had on a brown and gold three inch Devon and quite a bit of spiral lead weights on. Bill's rod was light enough for the job but I landed the fish which weighed seventeen pounds. Phipy asked where exactly did I hook it and then set off to try his luck over the same spot. I went back in behind him and on reaching the same spot I hooked a second salmon and landed it. It was a pound less than my first one but why it did not go for Phipy's Devon I do not know. Was I fishing deeper than him? I was going to cut one of them up to share out but Phipy would not let me. He made me go to Cruickshank the butcher in the Square and sell them where I got £2 per pound for them.

Phipy and his mother had a shop in the main street of Fochabers from which they sold fishing tackle and did rod repairs which was just as well because Phipy in the darkness and excitement stood on the tip of Bill's rod and broke about six inches off it. Soon after that I saw an advert for second-hand fishing tackle for sale. The seller was offered a job on one of the estates up Spey Side but had to have a Spaniel dog and to raise the money to buy it he decided to sell his spinning rod, reels minnows and whatever else he had. It was actually a split cane trout rod with an Ambidex reel but the price was right so I bought all of it with the money I got for the two salmon.

That outfit was to be the first spinner used on the River Carron which was supposed to be a fly only river but then Braelangwell started to let their fishing commercially and the first of the guests brought spinners with them. They then had to fall into line with the rest of the beats on the Carron. I was fishing without permission anyway so what did it matter. Every pool on the Gruinard stretch was hoaching with salmon and so easy to catch on the brown and gold Devon. One had to resist the temptation to take more than one at a time. Giving them away or selling them would only have brought notice to our selves. On the odd occasion I would take two home and my mother would be frantic with worry in case someone came in and saw them. She had to make space in a small outside larder for them when I was at home. Ronnie Ross's father, Geordie, was keeper at Gruinard by then and he sometimes asked if I had caught anything but did not know I was spinning for them. He would take out his fly wallet and give me one of his favourite flies to try.

In his boyhood Geordie and his brother went to Croick School. They were living at Alladale where their father was stalker. He would bring them down in the spring cart on a Monday morning and come back for them on Friday evenings. In between they would lodge with my parents at Wester Gruinards. Years later when Geordie was himself keepering at Langwell up on the Oykel my Dad went there to ghillie for the grouse and stalking seasons. I used to hear him talk about the Debenham family who owned it.

A Misty Day at Langwell with Geordie Ross

Another Day at Langwell

147

To get into where the keeper's house and the lodge were situated, it necessitated travelling over a very rough and long track and I'm not sure if it is that much better today. My nephew has been doing work there and because of the weather has temporarily had to call a halt to it. If the river was low they would walk across on stilts at the ford. On a Sunday Geordie would sometimes take Mrs Ross and family on the motor bike and sidecar round to see my parents at Wester Gruinards or Sgodachail with the baby carried in a gamebag on his back.

Word of this rod soon went round the crofters and I think just about everyone of them on the banks of the Carron got one. George, Elsie, Brian and Sheila all fished successfully with them. The Munro's at Corvost and those further down the strath got into them as well. I eventually left this rod with Noel and I would not like to guess how many salmon he caught with it. It got broken several times and in the end was no longer than three feet with the point of it drooping like the nose of concorde. I offered to make a new six foot piece for it but Noel declined the offer saying he could walk up or down the river bank anywhere with it in his hand or down the leg of his trouser without suspicion. The reel and short butt he could stick in his pocket.

I bought a fibre glass rod after that. It also was a trout model but very strong. Ernest and I went up the river one evening when it was in flood. I first caught a thirteen pounder in the field pool which I halved with Geordie Heatherlea who happened to be checking his sheep at the time. We then went up as far as the Lower Craigs and I hooked a salmon over in the quieter water on the Braelangwell side. I foolishly played it over there and when I took it back to our own bank it did not have the strength to hold itself in the strong water and got swept down towards the start of the gorge. Each time I got it up to the tail of the pool Ernest was not able to hold on to it with his hands. He even put a handkerchief over them to get a better grip but each time it slipped away. To get the fish back up I had to wind the nylon round my hand as it came inch by inch. The strain was just too much to operate the reel. The rod was bent double and Ernest kept shouting above the noise of the rushing water going down over the rocks that I would break the rod if I did not let it go. I got it near enough to get down on my knees and take hold of it by the tail and throw it up the bank. It was some fun I can tell you, even at the risk of breaking the rod and the pain of the nylon cutting into my skin.

Ernest got his own rod and was spinning for salmon at the Keepers pool when George Anderson the keeper came along. They got into heated row about this and George reported the matter to Mrs Kemmis. It was Noel who was summoned to the lodge to get the telling off, not the real villain, but all that Mrs Kemmis could say was, "Spinning, Spinning of all things." Later when I went to work there she told me not to be hard on the crofters as they were the best bailiffs we had. Little did she know.

As I said before, you could not safely give salmon away but one person outside the family I give bits to on a casual basis was Billy Dunbar, the son of the local river Superintendant in charge of the bailiffs. When he first asked me for a bit I said,

"What about your father?" His reply, "He likes a bit of salmon the same as the next person". Billy's dad never mentioned salmon any time I was in their house. The one and only time I sold salmon from the Carron, I took some I caught on the spinner down to Aberdeen. I was in the way of selling Don and North Esk salmon to the Scottish White Fish and Salmon Company. The boss was pleased to see me with them because that weekend he had an order for the Royal Households. I still wonder on whose plates they were served up on.

Billy Dunbar and I along with about fifteen to twenty others used to meet every Sunday evening on Carron Bridge. Sometimes we would go into the nearby field and play rounders or something but for most we just sat about and talked, probably about the dance the previous night. Occasionally one or two of the Ardgay youths would go off to pinch apples or plums from the gardens they knew and bring them back for us to share. When I came home on leave I used to borrow my Dad's car and on a Friday night I picked Billy up in Evanton where he worked and we would go off to dances anywhere in the Black Isle or Inverness. One night we went to a dance at Fortrose and I had most of the petrol siphoned out of the car and on our way home at Wester Fearn it ran dry. Billy walked home and told his Dad. There were no full cans of petrol about so he told Billy to drain the petrol from two of the fishery board motor bikes and to use the third one to take the petrol back to me.

Incidentally Carron Bridge was built by Thomas Telford and during the First World War when the American Soldiers were carting timber down from Strathcarron to their sawmill at Ardgay the bridge was inspected every Sunday for signs of damage caused by the lorries. At that time the vehicle and load would have weighed about 4 tons. Today, huge articulated timber lorries with a gross weight of almost 40 tons use the same bridge regularly and nothing has been done to it to strengthen it.

From what I recall of Billy and Joan in their early courting days it was a little bit off and on with their relationship. We met in Inverness one afternoon when I was on my way back to Aberdeen and I was to give Billy a lift to Elgin to see his sister. When we discussed going for a meal beforehand Billy quickly named this very good restaurant he knew and in we went. The penny dropped when the waitress came to the table and it was obvious that she was the attraction not the cuisine. This was the start of them getting together again.

On our journey to Elgin in my 1947 Hillman Minx I had by this time, the clutch burned out at the village of Alves and the only place I could take it to was the local blacksmith's. It was my own fault because when I put the engine back in it I did not put on the return spring for the clutch pedal. Instead I would stick my foot under it to keep it up but it was so easy to forget. He agreed to repair it and that I would pick it up a few days later. In the car I had a huge bunch of sweet peas that Noel, who was an expert in growing them as cut flowers, gave to me to take back to Marjory and her mother. There were many more perishables like fruit and honey in the old Hillman which Noel also gave me but were not suitably wrapped for carrying on the 'bus. I told the blacksmith to help him self to whatever he wanted, hoping he would be a bit easier with the bill. During the repair he accidently set the engine bulkhead alight and scorched a lot of the paintwork on the bonnet.

The car only cost me forty pounds as a part exchange when I sold a Vauxhall Wyvern with a suspect engine to a car dealer and it was not one of the prettiest motors on the road. I remember Johnnie Hutcheon looking round it one day and telling me that putty was only a shilling a pound. For most it got me there and back until one day I was heading for Gruinard just west of Elgin when the big ends started to rumble. After checking the oil level I carried on knowing that the car was reaching its time for the graveyard anyway, and keeping my fingers crossed I could maybe make Forres with it. It made Forres and then Nairn but didn't quite make Inverness. I was at Tornagrain when there was an enormous clattering and banging from the engine. I could even hear bits falling on to the road.

I coasted into a nearby side entrance and was standing looking at the engine when a lorry driver from the Scottish Agricultural Industries stopped to see if he could help. When he asked if I had a problem I said, "You could say that." The end of the connecting rod had come out through the side of the engine casing. The piston was no longer attached. The lorry driver said, "Well if ever. I've heard of that happening but have never seen it before. What will you do now?" I asked him to give me a push up the side road to some cottages.

He told me it was company policy not to give lifts to anyone far less tow their vehicles as well. However the kindly good soul took pity on me and towed me all the way to Milburn Road in Inverness. He was happy with an extra days pay and wished me good luck. A local car breaker was more interested in selling me another engine than buying my car for scrap. As luck had it a person I recognised as a police instructor I knew from college days intervened and told the guy not to be so miserable and pay me something for it. As they say "Something is better than nothing" so I took his four pounds but the story did not end there. When I returned to Aberdeen I never told Marjory or anyone else what happened to the car and for them the mystery remains to this day.

Billy and his wife Joan got married and after living in Peterborough for some years are back in Ardgay and every so often I meet in with him for a blether. Joan used to help Marjory in the lodge at weekends for the big clean up and what a good worker she was.

To show how easy it was to catch salmon with the spinner on the Carron in those years, I was about to leave one lunch time to go back to my digs in Stonehaven where I was at that time and Anne was nagging me to take a salmon back to my landlady. I had been eating it all week and I knew that I would be eating it for another week if I took one back with me. With the suitcase in the car ready to go I changed my mind, ran down to the Pigeon Rock pool and in my hurry had five salmon on and lost them. The next one I dragged it in but unlike the others it stayed on and I landed it. Up to the car, I rolled it up in a wet sack and went into the house to say I was off. Anne having the last word said, "So you're not going for a salmon then." She would not believe that I had been and got one. She said, "You have not been out of the house for more than five minutes." I showed her the fish to please her. Incidentally, there was a cookery book or one on good housekeeping in Gruinard Lodge where proprietors were advised not to feed salmon to staff more than twice a week. This may have come about after the staff at Balblair House, Invershin, sometime during the 19th Century, went on strike for being given salmon for too many of their meals.

CHAPTER 29

TRAFFIC PATROL

Still in my probation I was selected to join the traffic department at Banff for six months for what was called the turkey patrols. Leading up to Xmas the theft of poultry, particularly turkeys was prevalent, hence the reason for extra staff. At first I was paired up with Geordie Robertson or "Speedy" as he was better known, but later I was replaced by Alistair Gordon a fantastic pianist. Before joining the police Speedy drove a lorry for Calor Gas out of Grangemouth. Because of a severe snow storm we were confined to the office for a month unless we had to go out and Geordie had an endless supply of stories to keep us in suspense about his exploits on the road in particular across on the Islands. Geordie was also a time served motor mechanic and was renowned for his ability to tune twin carburettor engines. He and I were sent down to Luton to collect two Morris Isis patrol cars. Chief Inspector Patterson "Winky" gave us strict instructions that the cars were to be properly run in on our way north and that none of the recommended speed limits were to be broken. He expected us to have at least two over night stops on the way back.

Traffic Patrol and Lodge Walk Days

Coming out of the factory gates Geordie was to take the lead as he was more senior and familiar with the route than I was. When we came to the first set of traffic lights Geordie got through but I had to stop Geordie never waited for me and that was the last I saw of him until I got back to Banff. I stayed the first night in Lincolnshire and the second near Arbroath. Speedy never stopped until reaching home and by the number of hours he took it was obvious that he had thrashed the car up the road. The Chief Inspector was far from happy. Geordie kept telling him that new vehicles should be run in at the speeds they would normally be driven at and not what was recommended by the makers. In fact Geordie had the last say when after six months the engine in the one I drove north packed in and had to be replaced under guarantee. I had a clear conscience that I was in no way to blame.

Until then I did not appreciate piano music but Alistair could hold your attention for hours playing any tune you could throw at him. Classical music was a definite no and still is to this day. I was brought up to the sound of the accordion and the fiddle but none of our family was musical. My Mam could sing in tune with a very soft voice, whilst Dad could sing but had a very deep tone. However both Marjory and I can recognise when string instruments are out of tune or wrong notes are played and it is difficult to dance to if the timing is out. After a party one night I said to Willie MacDonald, "Well whose fiddle was out of tune last night?" He agreed but assured us that it was not his and I had no reason to doubt him. Another instrument I enjoy hearing if played in a dance band is the saxophone. When at the police training school at Whitburn Alastair always played the piano at the weekends in the Double Five public house until it was time to go to the local dances. A colleague, Wattie Greenlees and I used to play darts beforehand for pints of beer with the local miners. The very first evening we had no less than fourteen pints on the counter which they had to buy for us and they were not too happy with that. When it was time to go upstairs for the music we left all the beer with them and after that, win or lose, they were only too keen to play us.

Latterly at Banff I went on the car with Norman Michie for the remainder of my time there. Most of us shared the same digs until one day we planned a mass walk out. The landlady's family owned the butchers shop next door and talk about being mean I had not come across anything like it. The tea was made for the first officers going out to start the early morning shift at 6am and that teapot sat on the Raeburn stove simmering away until 9am by which time it was as black as tar and tasted like it as well. For breakfast it was not unusual to get a single fried egg on your plate and nothing else. When we complained she would just say, "I don't know what to give you that will please you. A tinny of beans will do Bob."

Crunch time came when money started going missing from the shop and we were all suspects although at first we did not know that. Apparently the C.I.D. kept watch on us and the shop but then the message boy was caught red handed and everything came out after that. Our "walk out" came as big surprise to the people in Banff and was seen as a disgrace to Jess Wood the landlady and her family. We all found much better lodgings and Norman even stopped tossing his sandwiches over the hedges to the birds and eating mine instead.

We were boozing buddies, including Alistair, and went to the dances together. One night we went with others to a near all night party in the local Bay View Hotel. At that time it was owned by a member of the Edwards family who owned the Bridge Hotel in Bonar and also Swordale Farm. Everything would have been fine but Bill Gerrard, a bus driver was unfit to take out the first 'bus in the morning. Stupidly, he told his Inspector the reason why, and he in turn reported the matter to the police Chief Superintendant, who then ordered an inquiry.

He delegated the local Inspector to make the enquiry but as it so happened he was at the party along with his wife. Although he was none the worse of drink like the rest of us he thought his name should be kept out of it. I told him to think again as we are all in it together. Alistair was the only one with some sense and decided to sign the visitors register as having stayed the night as a resident. When it was known that the Inspector was involved, the enquiry was dropped. Chief Constable Hunter an ex Glasgow City officer, who was only too fond of the drink himself, may have intervened but we will never know if that was the case. When we went on duty after a night out the typist, Milly Potter could tell straight away if we had been drinking. That was the signal for Norman and I to raid the bag of pandrops the Chief Constable always kept in his car. I think he was worse than us, at least we never drunk and drove when we went out, always taking the 'bus. I don't think I could count the number of times Norman or I took the Chief's car to the body repair workshop for scrapes, dents or bashes to be sorted. Eventually he was caught after an accident in Aberdeen, lost his licence, and ended up resigning his post. Pandrops were not much good to him that night.

Soon after that an unmarried officer was required for six months at Stonehaven for the busy holiday season, so that was me on the road again. Once again I was to meet more officers for the first time. One in particular was Fred Argo's brother Gordon. He had about eight more year's service than me and our shifts seemed to coincide quite a lot. One night he asked me if I fancied a bit of fresh sea trout or if we were lucky, a bit of salmon. Arming him self with a sack we walked along the foreshore to the mouth of the river Cowie. Each night about the same time the distillery discharged the wash from the mash directly into the Cowie. This affected the fish in as much that they came right into the shallow water and lay there as if dead. We picked some up with our hands and took them back to the station. Amongst them was a small grilse which I had, and the rest was shared out with whoever else was on duty, including Sergeant Jack Ewen. He was an ex wartime pilot with the RAF and lived in the flat through the back. I was a bit suspicious about giving him any but it was obvious that this was not a first. When the tide came in it swept all the fish out to sea where they made a full recovery or at least that is what we thought happened. I don't think SEPA was in existence then but later they put a ban on all such discharges.

My lodgings at Stonehaven were above the Fire Station. They were very good, comfortable, plenty of food with one minor complaint of getting fried fish twice or more per week. Don't get me wrong. It was of the best of quality but the landlady liked to stand out on the street talking to friends and neighbours, lose track of time and on seeing me on my way home she would dash into the fish shop for something quick and easy to cook for my supper. I was courting Marjory at the time and one night when I got back to the digs I found that unintentionally I had been locked out. With the help of whoever was on duty at the station we tried pushing the front door key out on to a sheet of paper and pull it out below the door but that did not work. We then got a ladder from the station and from the back of the fire station I climbed up the gable, crawled along the ridge and then over the slates to my bedroom window which was partly open. I could have been a cat burglar as no one seen or heard a thing.

On one of my trips up to meet Marjory in Aberdeen I filled up the car with petrol at the Check Bar Filling Station to find that I had no money to pay for it. I had left my wallet back at the digs. The attendant was far from happy about this and went on and on about not being able to balance the books at the end of her shift. After a lot of cajoling she let me go but not before I agreed to leave my wrist watch to ensure I returned and paid for it. A similar embarrassment for me was when I stopped at the Cocket Hat pub for a drink to put in time before I was due to meet Marjory. I ordered a Gin and Bitter Lemon which I was in the way of drinking and no sooner was it on the counter when I knocked over a glass of beer. I immediately turned to the person whose beer it was and after apologising offered to buy him another drink. I asked his friend what he was having and then asked the barman to give them each a drink. Thus done I made to pay for all three drinks but again my wallet was back in the digs. I had not touched my drink and offered the barman to take it back but he declined and we all had a good laugh about it. I paid for it the next time I was in. I did the same again at the barbers near to my digs in Aberdeen.

When I first arrived at Stonehaven one of the senior constables warned me about the Inspector who had a reputation of being a bit of a bully with young newcomers. He said, "Don't take it off him and you will be alright." The sergeant was frightened of him and you never got his backing. The Inspector and I had several rows, usually over where I parked my car in the garage and he wanted it out of there altogether. In the adjoining workshop one of the other officers was doing some joinery work for him self and the floor was a mess of wood shavings. I had the engine of my car neatly stripped down on the bench with newspapers below to put new piston rings in it to stop it burning oil. What I now know I should have put big end bearings in at the same time. The Inspector accompanied by the Sergeant took me out to the garage and created merry hell about the mess on the floor. I was not having any of it and gave him as good back and then said to him, "If you want it cleaned up I am more than willing to do it." I spent the remainder of the morning at it much to the annoyance of the Sergeant. I must admit having spun the job out much longer than what was necessary but the Inspector and I got on a lot better after that day. Every time I see the advertisement on television for the Churchill Insurance Company I see the face of the bulldog a splitting image to that of the Inspector.

At the end of my six months at Stonehaven I returned to the traffic department but this time at Lodge Walk in Aberdeen and latterly at Bucksburn and stayed there for about six or seven years. My first turkey patrol from Lodge Walk was with a CID Officer, Bill Falconer. He handed me a list of country shops and other premises and asked if I knew where they all were. I recognised some of them but was fairly confident that we could find the rest. As we went we ticked off each of the premises that we checked for security but at one point we came out on to a main road but did not know which way to turn as there were no direction signs. In our wisdom we decided to stop the first vehicle that came along but not to say we were lost. When the first car arrived the driver produced his documents and at some stage I had asked him where he was going to which he replied, "Aberdeen." I was convinced Aberdeen was in the opposite direction and stupidly said to him that he was taking a funny route to get to Aberdeen. "Tell me a better way?" he replied. Get yourself out of that I thought. I ignored what he said and bade him goodnight. As he drove off, Bill pointing to the disappearing car said, "That way." By the end of the night I think we found most if not all on the list.

Following a light fall of snow one evening another officer, Bob Davidson and I were driving along Countesswells Road, Cults when we got interested in a man's footprints going in the opposite direction. Earlier a burglar had been disturbed in Cults and we thought there may be a connection. We then decided to turn around and follow the marks which took us first in about a few caravans parked at the edge of a field. Whoever the man was he did not actually go close up to any of them. Instead he came back on to the road and then went down a farm road and made across one of the fields in the direction of Cults. Bob went off on foot to track him whilst I went ahead with the patrol car thinking he would come back out on the road somewhere. After a while when Bob never came back I decided to follow both of their tracks which took me to the corner of a high walled area which at one time had been a water reservoir and close to the caravans. I saw where they had climbed over the wall so I did the same to find both of them in a disused corrugated iron shed.

I could not believe my eyes to see that this other person was dressed in women's clothing. In the shed he had a metal trunk stuffed full with similar attire. We arrested him and with all the gear we took him to Cults Police Station where we made him change into his own clothing. I could not help from laughing as each item was removed, more so when he removed the brassiere he had on. Underneath he had two half tennis balls with a condom pulled over each of them I suppose to give the breasts a more realistic look. His day job was a docker from Aberdeen Harbour and at night got pleasure of a kind, only to him, by walking about the streets in this way complete with high heels and handbag.

When questioning him about having so much women's clothing he told us he had stolen the items from washing lines and wash houses in that area. Many of the thefts had been previously reported so we were able to write them off as "clear ups". He was given a modest fine at the Sherrif Court but lost his job at the harbour ending up as a rabbit trapper for a Clearance Society in the Bucksburn area.

Jimmy Ellis from the one man station at Echt was another officer I took out with me on the turkey patrols, in fact most officers from single stations took their turn. I don't think I came across a more meticulous officer than him. His reports were in such detail that they were amusing to read but the Procurator Fiscal told an Inspector who was apologising for their long windedness that he never had to return any of them for more information. Anything superfluous could easily be deleted at the stroke of a pen.

One such report started off when he got a telephone call during the night to attend to an incident, how he got out of bed, changed from his pyjamas into uniform and got his bicycle out of the shed, then after checking the brakes and lights how he cycled as fast he could to the scene. Another related to a complaint about motor cyclists speeding through the village and the length he went to curb it. When he stopped one of them he asked if he had been speeding and Jimmy described in great detail how the offender removed his fly bespattered goggles and arrogantly replied, "No.".

Motorists then were frequently reported for failing to stop at "Halt" signs and a lady pleaded not guilty to one of Jimmy's cases. When her case came up in court the defence solicitor asked Jimmy if he was watching the lady from a distance behind how he could tell she had not in fact stopped. Jimmy replied, "I could see from the circular motion of her hips that she had not stopped pedalling."

We were checking traffic near to the Cross Roads at Lumphanan one night when Jimmy told me he had not been in that area for nearly thirty years and asked if he could go and have a look at something. He never said what but when we got to a garden gate leading to an old cottage He said, "It's still there." and pointed to a "Beware of the Dog" sign on the gate. I don't know if there was any significance to it or not. He said everything with such seriousness that when he asked, "Would it be the same dog" I did not know what to make of him. Incidentally I passed by that same gate about two years ago and the sign is still on it whether it was the same gate or not. When Jimmy retired he got a job as a precognition officer with a firm of Aberdeen solicitors and I could bet he never left a stone unturned.

In an old Log Book at Banff Police Station which originally was the Headquarters for that County Constabulary there was an entry from the policeman stationed at Balindalloch. It read something like this, "Drunk again. Wire instructions." A week or so later another entry showed that the same officer was fined a few shillings for being drunk on duty. Anyone setting their chimney on fire was reported for that offence and was usually fined a couple of pounds. The sergeant at Turriff I understand reported himself for the same offence.

At that time there was a villain from Aberdeen, Arthur Bell Burnett and his accomplices were breaking into country shops on a regular basis, doors jemmied, 1cwt. sacks of sugar or animal feed emptied out on the floor, and the saleable stuff taken away in them. He had a newsagents and tobacconist shop in the city which was the ideal place to sell his ill-gotten gains. To be honest he gave both the City Police and the County the run around for a long time. He would be clocked leaving Aberdeen and sometimes coming back but nothing was ever found on them or in their distinctive car, a silver Austin Atlantic ERS 777. Unbeknown to us they had a caravan in the woods near Kinellar in which the stolen goods were left until taken into Aberdeen during daytime in another vehicle. Eventually we got a tip off that they were going to do the shop at Whiterashes and this time about a dozen or more of us were waiting for them. We spread out behind other buildings, in the fields and anywhere else to hide to make sure they did not get away.

At the south end of Kincardineshire and the County of Angus another guy, Alexander McBain Ettles from the Kirriemuir area was giving the police the run around as well. In addition to the usual saleable things, he went for safes he could carry out of shops and garages and then bust them open in a quiet location. When he got arrested I had the privilege of conveying him to Perth Prison and on the way he was obviously annoyed at having to do time for something not that profitable to him. He went on to say, "When I get out I'm going to rob a bank or something and make it worth- while."

Some months after his release a man in motor cycle gear including a crash helmet went into a bank in Forfar and held up the cashiers, making off with a considerable sum of money. On leaving the premises his accomplice, suitably attired, was waiting with a motor cycle at the ready. For good measure and to avoid being chased they poured a can of petrol across the street and set fire to it. They were to my knowledge never caught but for me it did not need two guesses who one of them may have been.

Just about every district in Aberdeenshire held their agricultural shows or Highland Gatherings like Aboyne, Braemar and Lonach and many other events. The traffic officers were responsible for parking and traffic control so we attended all of them. After the Ellon Show one night when the marquee dance was in progress a complaint was made by a female teenager that a man had indecently exposed himself to her through a join in the canvas. A married couple she was with witnessed the incident and he took a swipe at the offender with his shoe but did not make contact. The initial search for him was unsuccessful but half an hour later he did the same again and I was able to arrest him. His only excuse was that he had been neglected as a child. What that had to do with it I do not know.

The Royal family always attended the Braemar Highland Games and I was on point's duty at the main junction to make sure they got a clear run out when it finished. The last chauffeur driven car to come along was that of Lady Haddo's from Tarves who had already left in one of the Royalty cars. Who was sitting in the back of her car like lady muck herself, was Rosa Dickie, a family friend and who was personal assistant to Lady Haddo. She asked the driver to stop so that she could speak to me which he did. After a short conversation they went on their way to Balmoral. Some very senior officers standing nearby, thinking she was one of the Royalty, were anxious to know who the lady in the car was and why she wanted to speak to me. I never made them any the wiser and passed it off as friends in higher places.

It was about that time that we got our first Jaguar as a patrol car, for the simple reason when escorting the Royalty, and it was no secret, His Royal Highness the Duke of Edinburgh took a delight when he was driving to leave us trailing behind. Off all the Royal cars I escorted the late Queen Mother was by far the best. When her car broke down near the Spittal of Glenshee she walked back to the police car and asked that in the event of it not starting could she get a lift in the police vehicle to Birkhall. So sweet of her I thought. On arrival at Birkhall she always instructed us to go into the kitchen for a cup of tea.

The queen mother's ghillie at Birkhall, Jim Pearl, was a long time friend of my parents and my mother kept asking me to go and see him. Jim was sending messages via my mother inviting me to fish at Birkhall the first two weeks in April each year. I know I was disrespectful in not accepting the offer and just by chance I met in with him at the Balmoral dog trials when he left me in no doubt as to what he thought of me. I'm sure it was a privilege to fish on that beat. Prior to going to Birkhall Jim was a gamekeeper at Amat Estate for Lord Conygham and also at Gruinard Estate for Mr Lewis. When out looking after the dogs on the Gruinard Hill during the grouse season he was accidentally shot in the face by one of the party and as a result lost an eye. The surgeons were unable to save it and in its place fitted a glass one. The following season at the grouse he was shot in the leg. Willie MacDonald who was ponyman one day escaped getting shot in the face as well. The horse however was not so lucky and was well and truly peppered on the head. Mr Lewis and others from the party came back and were petting the horse and asking it if it was alright. Nothing was said to Willie if he was alright. The gamekeeper at that time was Harry Munro and to get his own back on Mr Lewis Willie, in spite of strict instructions not to, allowed a setter bitch to get mated on the hill. Nothing was said until after the pups were born when Harry asked him if he wanted to buy a pup.

Jim's brother Jack, or to give him his full name Alister John Pearl, was a wartime Royal Air Force Sergeant Air Gunner and got shot down over Holland and killed on 12th August, 1942 on one of his many bombing missions. That particular one was when he stood in to do an extra one to help out a colleague who wanted a day off. That's fate for you. The family grew up at Gruinard where their father Robert Pearl Senior was head gardener. He was a native of Hertfordshire but came to Gruinards after a spell at Auchterhouse Estate, near Forfar, but I seem to recall that he or his son, also Robert worked at the Royal Botanical Gardens, Edinburgh or London and was responsible for planting out the lovely show of rhododendrons along the bank below the lodge on either side of the stone steps leading down to the river, the gardens and park I have previously described. His son Robert was under gardener with him and with his family lived in the flat over the coach house where their daughter Daphnee was born.

Robert Senior, with his wife Virginia lived in Garden Cottage and he was known to tell ghosty stories or weird happenings about the estate, particularly the pair of white horses he often saw drawing a coach down the drive. Another one was that the door knob of Garden Cottage would turn minutes before anyone would arrive. He would tell people the lodge was haunted as well. Of all the people I know, including Marjory and I, who lived there never saw or heard anything unusual about the place. When a party of tradesmen were working in the lodge they tormented an apprentice about the place being haunted until he came to me about it. I assured him that it was not and to wait until they got on to him again and then to say, "That's enough. I'm off home." and to walk out. He called their bluff as I suggested and that was the end of their mischief.

Tom Chasser the deputy got the Chief Constable's job and I was to become his driver until I got posted to Fettercairn. By this time Headquarters had moved from Banff to Bucksburn and Mr Chasser had bought a house in Anderson Drive. About once a month he had to attend a Chief Constables Association meeting in one force area or another. All the time we were away he insisted on paying for everything unless we were at a bar and then he would let me buy a round or two of drinks. On our way to Dunoon we decided to stay overnight at Arrochar in the hotel of that name. He first went in to check if they had vacancies. He came out to say that they had only one room with two single beds and gave me the choice to look elsewhere or to share the room which was fine by me.

So in we went with our overnight bags, in which I had a pair of pyjamas given to me as a birthday present by my mother in law, Edith Shepherd. After supper and a drink or two we retired to our room, and if I did not mind, he was going to do some reading in preparation for his meeting the following day. I was not bothered what he did but we both undressed to get into bed. When I put on the pyjamas the legs barely reached below the knee. In this day and age it could be quite normal but not then. I could not get into bed quick enough in case he saw them. He never said anything so I assumed he had not. Minutes later the bulb fused and that put an end to his reading. The next hello he called out, "I know where we are." And repeated it once more then saying, we're below the cobbler. I had no idea what he was talking about so he got me out of bed to come to the window where he pointed out the skyline of this mountain that resembled the face of a man lying on his back, hence the name cobbler. It was fairly dark in the room by this time so he would not have noticed my predicament. Next morning I was up and dressed before he woke. Thinking back on it, and knowing him a lot better, I'm sure he would have seen the funny side of it.

One month when we arrived at Hamilton far too early for his meeting he asked if I was familiar with Lanarkshire. When I told him I was not, he took me on a grand tour of the county, pointing out places of interest and his old haunts as a Chief Superintendant there. When we came up to Strathpeffer he insisted I would use the Jaguar to go up and see my parents at Gruinard. I did this and when I arrived my father was out at the end of the house. I knew he would not recognise the car so when I pulled up I jokingly asked him where Glencalvie was. I made sure my face was out of view, and assuming I was some toff or other with such a posh car, he politely started to give me directions until I stepped out of the car, but that quickly changed.

A twist to this story was at a Traffic meeting in Aberdeen which my Inspector, Charlie Cruickshank, attended.

He told me how a Sergeant MacDonald from Dingwall asked if he was aware that I had been up at Gruinard with a police car. The sergeant then went on to say, "I just thought you should know bla bla bla." The Inspector already knew about the visit and cut him short, telling the sergeant that it was the Chief Constable's decision in the first place.

I knew Sergeant MacDonald, a brother of Willie, very well but thought, "You two faced sod" or something perhaps not quite so polite.

From Maclennan, I learned to hold my tongue and to use discretion before repeating things, a quality that Tom Chasser appreciated. He had no fears about telling me what went on at the meetings, and often asked my opinion before and afterwards. Coming home from a meeting in Elgin one night, he along with the Deputy Chief Constable and another person I cannot remember who were discussing what I thought should have been a very confidential matter. An indirect remark was made about my presence in the car but the Chief assured them of my discretion and I thought a lot of him for that. McLennan certainly must have done some good.

I was chosen to chauffeur a Chief Constable from a central Scotland force who came up to attend a police meeting in Aberdeen and to look after him during his stay. In the evening after the meeting I had to take him to Turriff where he was a guest speaker at a Burns Supper.I got him back to his hotel at 4am, and had to book the police car in at the same time. A lot of officers, including Charlie Cruickshank and Tom Chasser, were asking questions as to where I had been to that time in the morning but that was for me to know and for them to find out. One thing I did learn that night was how outside influence could affect an officer's promotion or not. I have been to several Burns Suppers and none of the speakers could hold a candle to the likes of Tom Chasser and other high ranking officers. Not only were they great orators but they knew the subject well. I would go as far as to say they must have made an in depth study of the poet. By this time Norman and the rest of Headquarters staff had transferred to Bucksburn and Norman and I were back on the cars together. I enjoyed working with Norman. We had so much in common and always on the same wave length. He was to become best man at my wedding and just recently he came up to Inverness to join us in our Golden Wedding celebrations. It was there he became aware that I was no longer able to drink alcohol as a result of an allergy. His response was, "I wish you had been allergic to it when I first met you."

CHAPTER 30

BACK AT GLENCALVIE

I was to return to fish at Glencalvie in later hears when it was owned by Mr and Mrs Hickley and Noel worked for them as gardener handyman but had to help out as ghillie on the river and the hill. Tommy Gordon came there from Wyvis Estate as stalker and later, John his son as shepherd. John has been employed there all his life having taken over as head stalker on the death of his father, witnessed many changes and has seen numerous owners and workers come and go. I am sure he personally will have lost all account of the thousands of guests who came to stalk or fish there, many returning year on year. One thing I'm pretty sure is that no other person connected with Glencalvie past or present will know the place better than him. Well perhaps that may not be quite true if you read the next three paragraphs.

Extract from the Inverness Journal, 24th February, 1815 - There is a notice of a veteran named Alexander Campbell or "Iverach", residing in Glencalvie, Ross-shire, who was said to have reached the age of 116 years. Six Ross-shire gentlemen in London contributed a guinea each to enable him to dress in tartan and refresh himself with a drop of liquor. The editor was requested by the minister of Kincardine to announce Iverach's receipt of the bounty and to express his thanks. The veteran is well, and prays for as many days to each of his benefactors as he has seen, and an equal `portion of health. He longs for the weather getting a little milder that he may take a walk to see friends at Gledfield and the manse and to tell them of the tide of riches that has set upon him. He danced two reels at the last Kincardine cattle Fair, and a few days ago entered as a scholar in the Gaelic School at Glencalvie. It is supposed that he is the oldest Campbell alive.

Extract from the Inverness Journal, 3rd May, 1816 - Died lately at Glencalvie, Parish of Kincardine, Ross-shire, Alexander Campbell, alias "Iverach", at the advanced age of 117 years. He was born in 1698, carried arms in 1716 under William, Lord Ross and, till his death showed the characteristic hardihood of a Highlander to an uncommon degree. In the severest weather he went with neck and breast bare and, to the last, walked perfectly erect: his dress the short coat, kilt and plaid, and his staff generally across his breast. Till the uncommon storm of last winter fell, he could walk down to Gledfield and the manse in a day, the distance being about 11 miles.

He entered as a scholar last year in one of the Gaelic Society schools in the parish, actually learning the alphabet, and began spelling, when his further progress was arrested by the failure of his eyesight. He waited last harvest on the Rt. Hon. Lord Ashburton of Rosehall when his Lordship, with his usual benevolence, gave him a shilling for every year of his life, and further sum to buy a little of his favourite resquebagh, in all upwards of 6 guineas. His Lordship's donation outlived Iverach's days and helped to put the hoary veteran decently under the turf.

At first I thought the name Iverach was Gaelic but a friend of mine has informed me that it is not and that it probably comes from the name "Ivor", possibility his father's first name. I guessed resquebagh was not Gaelic but could not find it in the dictionary. Again my friend was of the opinion that the journalist of the time got this spelling wrong and that it possibly relates to uisge deatha but in any case the money was for his favourite whisky, the water of life. John could equally match the bit about the severest of weather and walking upright with bare neck and breast. Well the breast may be bare of clothing but not of hair.

The Hickley's, for whatever reason took a liking to me and as soon as they knew I was about they would ask if I had my fishing rod with me. For most I did not, and would be instructed to take the guest rod and go and get them a salmon. A smoker as Mr Hickley called it. One morning I was sent off as usual and I caught a beautiful freshly run sea liced salmon on a stoat's tail from where the water ran out of the falls pool. So many salmon from that pool were caught by fowl hooking, whether you liked it or not. When I told Noel where I caught it he said, "Tell Mr Hickley any pool but the falls pool, he won't believe you that it wasn't foul hooked". I decided to be truthful and told him exactly where it took the fly but the expression on his face said it all, more so when he turned around and walked away. Noel was absolutely right. From that day onwards I told him only what he wanted to hear. By this time I had bought my first fly road.

Being mean I suppose I was never one to spend money on the latest gadgets or equipment whatever they were for. It is the same with clothing. I tend to wear the same things until they are almost dropping off. When one lot is in the wash another lot will be on. There are items of clothing in my wardrobe that have been bought for me which I have not yet worn or even tried on. Last Xmas Marjory bought me a jumper and soon afterwards she asked if I had tried it on which I had not. Five months later I decided to wear it but could not find it. When I asked Marjory where it had got to she replied, "Back to the shop." I'll have to do better next time. I got my first shot gun from my Uncle Don a retired game keeper when he was finished with it. It was a very old under lever hammer gun, well pitted and showing the worse of wear where a crack in the stock was braced on either sides with steel plates, but as Don said, "Point it in the right direction and it will kill everything you want to kill." How right he was but because of the pitting, not nitro proofed and the loss of one of the hammers I disposed of it. I am not sure if the reason for it was the Damascus barrels but it gave off an unusual report. Fellow shooters would come and ask me what kind of cartridges I was using but as often as not they were no different to their own.

I had three spinning rods in my lifetime, one I gave to Noel to be replaced by a solid glass fibre trout rod, and the salmon one that I have at present which I bought in Aberdeen in the early sixties. The salmon fly rod was also solid glass fibre and measured about thirteen feet. I bought it in Inverness on my way north to fish at Amat where on the River Carron it was "fly only". When Scott came up to Gruinard to fish I gave that one to him and told him to take it home with him as he had permission to fish on a beat on the River Dee. I bought myself a fifteen foot Bruce and Walker carbon fibre road which I use for most of the time. Just before I left Gruinard one of the guests was desperate to sell a Hardy salmon rod because he could not cast with it. None of his fellow guests were interested in it so I made a ridiculous offer for it which he accepted. My intentions were to sell it for a profit but never got round to doing it. I do fish with it from time to time but I cannot say that I have caught any more salmon with it or that my casting is any better or not.

At the end of a fishing season the rod would be stuck up in the rafters of the garage and literally forgotten about. January or February depending on the circumstances out it would come again and when not in use it would be propped up at our back door. The line, the nylon and fly would still be on it from the last day it was used at the end of September. I never changed anything not even the knots. A blood knot was all I needed to know and the nylon was usually about twenty pounds breaking strain with one of lesser weight in the summer for grilse or sea trout. I had two lines, a fast sinker and a very old double tapered floater and if I was to check it today I don't think I would find much taper left on either end.

No one will change my views that luck is what it is all about, being at the right place at the right time. Fish can be caught on the crappiest of equipment and in the most unconventional ways. Supposedly perfect casts at the correct angle downstream are not for me and to say that in the thirty or so years of salmon fishing I have caught over a thousand salmon goes to prove it. I have consistently casted straight across the pool or stream unless circumstances does not permit it and probably caught more salmon with a huge belly in the line or nylon with the fly or lure coming straight back across the water. I have caught salmon casting upstream and saw others doing it as well when fishing the "Yellow Dolly". I have dropped a silver toby directly down on to salmon lying deep at the bottom of a very narrow gap between rocks. There was no other way of doing it but yet two salmon were caught within half an hour of each other in this way. Bert Riddel the keeper at The Burn would not believe me when I told him where and how I caught the first one. He thought it was nigh impossible to fish the gap. I then had to demonstrate to him and Irvine Barclay how I went about it and it was then that I caught the second one. I was fishing a brown and gold wooden minnow on the River Don at Persley one day when I saw a salmon head and tail in the pool above me. I assumed it had newly gone over the dyke behind me and from where I stood I cast up into the pool a little ahead of the fish. A salmon took the lure immediately and came down over the dyke beside me, nothing traditional about catching that one either. Half way down the Washerwoman Pool on the Gruinard side there is a very deep part where the salmon often settled in low water. Guests fishing there one day got frustrated at seeing the fish because they would not look at anything they were offered in a conventional way until a 2 inch Willie Gun was dropped directly down on to them. As the fly sunk at least two salmon took the fly so there was nothing magic about that either.

From the MacLean days when the staff were allowed to fish the Diebidale River with either worm or fly I taught myself the art of worming for salmon, something to this day frowned upon by ardent fly fishers but I can safely say not everyone can do it with success. This was very much a spate river and from July onwards large numbers of both salmon and sea trout went up it. I was there on a Saturday fishing the worm in the bridge pool when I hooked what I could clearly see was a fairly large salmon. I played it until it was ready to land, but having no net or gaff with me I had to do it by hand. Because of the rocky nature of this pool I could not beach it leaving me with the only option of hand lining it up the rocks. It was barely out of the water when the nylon struck the sharp rocks and off it went with hook and about three feet of nylon attached to it. To my amazement, about three weeks later and a mile or so upstream, I caught the same fish with my lost tackle still hanging from its gob and the hook securely entrenched well down its gullet. It turned out to be a thirteen pounder.

When the water was low and clear the art of worming came into its own. Invariably you had to crawl in on your belly to near the head waters of the pool to avoid being seen, or vibrations from walking was enough to scare them off as well. On three separate occasions I tried without success to catch a lone salmon from a shallow pool using my normal tactics. This fish became quite a challenge for me and on my fourth attempt I went on my belly no nearer than twenty yards upstream from the head of the pool and floated the worm down from that distance. This ploy paid off. Mr Hickley preferred you to fly fish on the Diebidale but would not stop you from worming if that was your choice.

I was up there again on holiday when Mr Hickley sent me off this time to the Diebidale for another smoker. I disturbed three salmon in a very small but deep pool not far up from the lodge. The water was running crystal clear that day so I knew I had to be extra careful when I returned to try my luck a second time. After my usual belly crawl, in went the baited hook. My preferred choice of worms were the reddish purple type from the garden, around the midden or from under slates or old sacking, not too big and several of them on at the same time, with one inch of tail left wiggling. What right minded salmon or trout could resist such a lure? I could see the worms float over the salmon and that they were not interested. Twice I retracted the hook and each time I put on a lead weight until the bunch of worms almost went straight into the mouth of one of the salmon. Right away one of them went for it and this is when it becomes a bit nerve racking. You know the hook is in the fish's mouth, do I strike, or do I leave it or what?

From experience, patience is the answer. Leave the fish, be it salmon or trout, to make the first move when it will head upstream in to the white water of the pool. By now you are almost certain that everything is well down its gullet with little chance of getting away. Strike too early and you risk the chance of pulling worms and hook from its mouth. I landed that salmon, after it, and the other two thrashed about in the pool for some time. I immediately re-baited the hook, stood in full view of the remaining two fish, and to my surprise no sooner was the hook chucked back into the white water when the second salmon was on. The third one came out equally as quick. I have never fished the prawn but I'm told that salmon in a pool can behave in the same way or you can frighten them altogether with it.

I took Noel's advice on this occasion and presented only two of the fish to a delighted Mr Hickley, both caught on the fly and from different pools. He told Noel to prepare the larger of the two to go for smoking and said to me to take the other one home to my father and no, the largest of the three was not the one hidden in the boot of my car. I then had to go into the lodge to have the records written up and the offer of a whisky. The next day he asked me to take the children to fish on a hill trout loch. When they appeared I found them to be older than me by a good number of years, but we had to abandon the loch because of mist. On getting back to the road we had difficulty finding the Landrover because we did not know whether it was further up the road or down the way.

CHAPTER 31

THINGS DON'T ALWAYS GO TO PLAN

When I went out for a beast on Carn Bhren I had the experience of getting lost in thick fog. I disturbed a Sika stag which headed off in the direction of a corrie where I thought it would settle. Instead of making a wiser decision to go home I carried on and knew I had to walk round the top of Carn Sallachy to be on the right side of the wind. What I did not realise was that I gone round the top and half way again and I found myself heading down in the wrong direction. I sat down to see if the mist would clear. It did a little bit and I could see some greens and water down below me which I recognised as being on Gledfield ground. I took my bearings from that and set off again. The mist got thicker and I had to sit down a second time. I got my bearings again about a half hour later when the crofts above Bonar became visible and I was able to continue, making home a good deal later than I should have. I saw the same stag sheltering behind a rock but I chose not to shoot it because of the weather conditions. Not far from home I jumped over a ditch and damaged the cartilage in my knee which sometime later required an operation to put it right.

About 11am one morning snow was falling and there was a good covering already on the ground with much more up on the hills. I said to Marjory that I thought the deer would be down somewhere about the loch and that I was going up to shoot a hind or two. Marjory asked if it was a wise idea but I assured her all would be fine and carried on in the argocat saying to her I would be back home by lunch time. When I got to the loch the deer were higher up near to the eagles nest but I still carried on because in the snow they would be easy to drag down to where I could get the argocat. I shot four and dragged two of them down as planned and then climbed back up for the other two. I was late but things were going to plan until I got back to near the loch. A blizzard got up and I could not see where I was going but it was obvious I was going round and round in circles because I kept finding my own tracks again.

Eventually I saw in front of me the ice and snow covered loch and knowing that there was a small burn that ran out of it, I made my way round the edge to follow the burn until I picked up the hill track down to the public road. That should have been simple enough but I had to cross the burn a few time on my way resulting in the wheels on one side of the argocat sliding off the bank and getting bogged down. At first I had no success in getting out and had visions of walking home. I then decided to unload and luckily with me pushing from the front and keeping the throttle open I managed to get reversed out. I then lost my direction again by following the burn too far and found myself between a fence and a steep bank down to the water. It was dark by this time and it was too chancy to sit in the argocat so I walked along side it at the same time hanging on to the top wire of the fence until I got past this precarious bit and lo and behold I came on a gate that I did not know existed. Through I went and headed for the track at some speed not realising it was nearer than I imagined. The next minute I was off the bank and nosed dived on to the road, later to find that I bust the welding on the front cross member of the chassis. When I got home at 7pm Marjory was just about to call Ronnie and others to mount a search party.

Because of constant changes in wind direction much of the Gruinard hill is not easily stalked. Many a time I set off up one end of the estate to find that the wind was in the wrong direction. I would change plans but by the time you got to the other end it would have changed again and change again as you got to the higher ground where the deer were. I preferred to start the day dogging into the wind for the grouse but that could go "hay wire" on you as well. For gamekeepers stalking dear on high ground it is not uncommon for them to find ravens following them to get at the grallochs. This was apparent to me at Duchally Estate when dogging for grouse on the lower reaches of Ben More. Donald Clark the stalker explained that they did not distinguish one party from another but it was a gralloch they were after.

CHAPTER 32

HOLIDAYS AT GRUINARD

Lord Bolton took over Glencalvie from Mr Hickley, and although Noel continued to work for him, I did not have the same enjoyment of fishing there. Glencalvie changed hands yet again when Mr Peter Fowler bought it. Noel left soon after that and worked for Lord Bolton again who leased part of the salmon fishing on Amat Estate and rented the Old Manse next to Willie MacDonald's house for accommodation. I was in London by this time and Noel would telephone me in the spring, usually the first week of May, to say the salmon were up at Amat. John Gordon always said their arrival coincided with the buds coming out on the birch trees. At Gruinard for most they arrived in any number the same time as the Oyster Catchers. The number of Oyster Catchers up Gruinard way has been declining fast and I put it down to the Peregrine Falcon. We were constantly finding dead birds with the head off.

I would catch the night train from London and be on the water by lunch time the next day. One time I arrived at a pool just beside Coneas Bridge, where the water after passing over a series of waterfalls went through a narrow neck where Noel said the fish lay and to be very careful not to be seen. I think the pool was called The Steps. I crept forward on to the steep bank with the point of the rod over the water. No sooner than I dropped the fly down towards the water when a salmon was on. It happened so quickly that to this day I am not sure whether or not the fly had actually touched the water before it was taken. I did that for many years and had great fun with Noel when he could spare the time to be on the water with me. He was so occupied building up a successful painting, papering, joinery and building business, the croft and much more. In fact he could turn his hand to just about anything. When I asked him one day how it was going, he said, "Open that box down there" and when I did it was full of labelled house keys from many of his customers who had holiday homes in the surrounding districts. He said "That speaks for itself." On leaving school his son Derek worked with him and is equally knacky with his hands, subsequently putting himself through college to qualify as an architect. John my other nephew went to college and learned the trade of welding which has taken him to many parts of the globe. When ringing home from the college he would ask, "Anything doing on the pools?" and he did not mean the football coupons. In those years it was quite common in Strathcarron to get a crossed line so you could never be sure as to who was listening in.

When we were in London we were friendly with Andrew and Sarah Cunningham and their two boys and one summer we decided to come north together on a camping holiday. The first night we stayed at Buxton in Derbyshire and then came on to the Lake District but the site was over crowded and noisey so we only stayed there for the weekend. Our next stop was Gruinard and we set up our tents on the field along from the house. We cheated to some degree by accepting Margaret's kind offer of having supper each night in the house. The bathroom was always available to us as well but during the night I am not sure if it was David or Brian that often needed a "Wee Wee" and had to resort to an empty bean tin. Probably today one will blame the other. I will also remind them that as boys they were so confident because of previous camping experience their tent would be up before ours and that Marjory and I would need their help. Things did not go to plan with them and we were well into cooking supper by the time they finally got their one up.

Marjory and I had our very first holiday together in a two man tent that was not very waterproof. We set off from Aberdeen to go to the West Coast but the weather was so bad that we changed plans and headed south. Just before dark we reached Stirling Bridge and set things up there. To keep the bedding dry we wrapped a polythene sheet round everything. In the night we were awakened by what sounded like a mouse crossing over the bed but it was only a spider. It was amazing how the sound was magnified by the polythene.

Next stop was a camp site just out of Blackpool. We picked a nice spot where fresh green grass was growing. About two mornings later when we woke up we were surrounded by water after heavy rain during the night. In that site it was the highest bit of the ground and the campers who had recently left it probably chose it for that reason. Marjory did not like Blackpool so we up-tailed and headed north to Ayrshire to try it there. I think it was Troon where we intended stopping but there was a sand-storm blowing and we ended up in bed and breakfast. We set off in the morning for Gruinard and the further north we went the rain got heavier and heavier. The sight of the water cascading down the mountainsides at Loch Lomond was spectacular. In Glen Coe you felt it possible to stretch up and touch the Black clouds in the darkness.

When I was unloading the roof-rack Noel told me to leave the fishing rods where they were. The river was dead low and no fish had been caught for more than a week. Undaunted by this I was up very early the next morning and did a recce of the pools and located one salmon in the white water of the Brothers Pool and a second one in a narrow neck down towards the tail of Lower Brothers. A jar of worms was dug later that day and everything else was got ready to try my luck early the following morning. I went for the one in the white water first and cutlets from it for everyone went down a treat for breakfast that morning. At 5am you don't expect many people about but the following morning when playing the salmon in the Lower Brothers a guest from Braelangwell Lodge came down and started fishing the head of Moral less than a hundred yards from me. I stood behind a large willow tree keeping one eye on the fish and the other on the guest. At no time did he look in my direction so when the fish was played out I nipped down the bank and grabbed it. Because of my luck the verdict from Noel was to take the .22 rifle and try and shoot a sika deer that was often seen in the wood above the lodge. I never did see it.

When I finished in London I made arrangements to buy a .222 rifle from Tom Breckan, a registered firearms dealer from the Borders. He came up regularly to Ronnie's at Braelangwell and I met him at one of the parties where he played the Cumberland pipes. What a fantastic rifle it turned out to be and many a beast I shot with it until the barrel wore out and its accuracy faded. I had two does lined up to shoot with it at the same time but whilst waiting for a third to come into line a .22 shot went off from the road above me and all three ran off. I know people will only be too ready to condemn me for even considering it. I guessed it was George Anderson the keeper and when I saw him next day I ribbed him about spoiling my shot. He replied, "Why did you not tell me before hand. I would have left them for you to shoot." In my early years it was more important to me to fill the bag or to put food on the table. As such I had no qualms about lining fur or feather up to get more than one with a single shot. I did it with shots from a hide at pigeons or when I arrived at the Minnes Dam and ducks were already in it. A little patience to wait for the right moment and it was amazing just how many you could get with one shot. I am pretty mediocre with a shot gun so perhaps the sitting targets did nothing for my swing through.

Spinning in Moral was always a risk of being caught by the owners or guests from Braelangwell Lodge. From the top of the field above the Moral Falls you could see them leave the lodge on their way to the river and sometimes one of us would keep watch from that spot and fire off a shotgun as a signal to run for it. Because of the rushing water coming over the falls it was about the only thing you could hear. If we were down near the tail of the pool we would slip away in the direction of Gruinard Lodge and then double back out of sight. Derek, who grew his hair long and was wearing a raincoat, did just that one Sunday morning which everyone considered to be the best time to get one for the pot. However, he was spotted but mistakenly identified as Miss Jean from Gruinard Lodge. George Anderson was keeper there at the time and he got an irate phone call from Braelangwell complaining about her fishing on a Sunday. They were so adamant about it because of the long hair and the direction of departure that was taken. However, the complaint never went further than George.

I knew there were no guests in Braelangwell Lodge this particular week so about seven in the morning I went down to the head of Moral with my spinner. I hooked a salmon and after I played it for a short time it began to dive deeper and deeper as I thought. John the "Pecka" in my presence once measured it with a brick tied to the end of a tape to a depth of seventeen feet but with the amount of nylon the fish pulled off the reel I knew something else was wrong. It transpired that the nylon had snagged round a rock in the deep water and the fish was away down about fifty yards in the main pool. Each time I put pressure on him he only wanted to go further downstream.

I was frightened of breaking the nylon at the rock and leaving this fish with a mess of nylon trailing to it so I drove round to Braelangwell to get Ronnie's assistance. Ronnie had been at a wedding the night before and was still in his bed. I went back to Moral and the fish was still on. I tried again without success to get

Ronnie to help and just as I was driving away from his house I saw Doctor Graham senior arriving. He scrounged salmon fishing from wherever he could get it but still had the audacity to report anyone who he thought had no right to be fishing.

Hell for leather I returned to Moral to get there before him. I cut the nylon from my reel knowing that the fish was still on at the other end and then tied on another spool of nylon to it and fixed that spool to a fence. I had to go off and help Derek that day with a shed he was roofing but on our way home late afternoon we went via Braelangwell. Ronnie was speaking to the doctor who was in his car and in the process of leaving. We pulled up a little distance past them because I did not want to get into conversation in the doctor's presence. Ronnie then came to speak to us and his opening words were, "I know what you "Buggers" want. It's round here." From one of the rod boxes he produced the brown and gold Devon with reams of nylon attached to it. I said to Ronnie, "But where is the fish?" I then told him the story and both of us were convinced that the salmon was on its way to Tain.

I thought it would be fun for all of us to go off up the glen on the Fergie tractor for a picnic. When I suggested this to Noel he thought it bit daft and suggested borrowing the Landrover from Alladale but I did not see so much fun in that. With bales of hay on the trailer for seating and plenty of food and drinks we set off like a band of tinkers. On the trailer were Marjory and the two girls, Andrew and Sarah and their two boys and Noel and Margaret's two boys John and Derek. I cannot remember how far we went but everyone was on a high with plenty of shouting and singing along the way. The next day we went up to the beach at Scourie and almost froze to death. A bitter cold wind was blowing and it was no fun waiting for the heater in the car to warm up and trying to change out of wet costumes. When I drove on to the ferry at Kylesku I asked the attendant to tell Andrew and Sarah that he could not take them on board and that they would have to wait for the first ferry in the morning. Sarah kept saying, "But you will have to. We are with them."

It was hay time and Andrew and I were helping Noel to take in the bales. Because of thistles amongst it I used a fork to put the bales up onto the trailer and because Andrew was struggling to put them up by hand I said to him to give them a heave with his knee at the same time. Because of the thistles his legs were red raw and blamed me for it. Many years before that when hay was in the same field Ernest, myself and two other boys were playing there when we came across a foggy bee's nest. One of the boys came from the old manse at Amat and we often played mischief on him. He did not see us find the bees so we put a basin over it and then drummed the ground round about it until we could hear a lot of activity under the basin. I cannot remember the boy's name, Edward I think, but when he arrived we asked him to go and get the basin. He got some fright when all the bees got up around him and flung the basin away as he ran off. We knew that the foggy bee was pretty harmless and not prone to stinging but he did not know that.

172

Andrew and Sarah were excellent company and many a good laugh we have had together. One glass of wine was enough for her to get into a fit of giggles Andrew was a very good and keen golfer winning lots of Police Trophies. He collected and restored old clubs but was not a D.I. Y. enthusiast. For most Sarah took over that role in the house and could turn her hand to most jobs. The plastering in their bathroom was only one of them and it was lot better than my one and only attempt. I remember when they arrived in London having driven down from Edinburgh in a little A40 car which had seen better days and took twice the normal time. Soon afterwards he was telling colleagues in the canteen that he was having trouble with the rear brakes coming on but no matter how much the adjusters' were slackened off it made no difference. After listening to what he had to say for a while I asked him to check the rear springs and told him the cause could be a broken main leaf. His reply to that was, "I've heard it all now, are you taking the pis" A second hand spring from the breakers cured the problem.

Sarah rung me in a big panic one morning to say that Andrew had smashed his car and could I come out and have a look at it. She went on to tell me that he had been at a retirement party the night before and went through a garden wall at Rainham on his way home to Upminster. He had a BMC 1100 by this time and when I went out to see the damage the entire front was stoved in but the engine was still intact. Sarah will tell you that I was more interested in hearing about the night before than the car but I had already made up my mind in the passing that the easiest thing to do was to get another shell and transfer the good bits to it. A few days later I bought a similar car minus its engine from a breakers yard at Plaistow for twenty five pounds. Andrew and I towed it to his home and in a day or so Sarah got all the details registered at Swansea and they were on the road again.

Sarah got home sick for Edinburgh so when Andrew got re accepted for that force they moved back there buying a house at Penicuick. One of Andrew's colleagues who was having an affair with another woman and fancied a weekend away with her, volunteered to drive his furniture up to Edinburgh if he could get someone to load the lorry. I had done plenty of flittings for myself and for other officers in London so he asked me to do the needful. I agreed, but told the two of them I would require plenty of old blankets or something similar to wrap around the furniture to prevent it getting damaged. Andrew knew of a firm of upholsterers who sold bales of foam cuttings and I told him it would be ideal. When he brought it home it was put into a small tatty old garden shed with two doors for the roof and a bit of felt to keep things dry. Sarah, or Hazel as I for some reason always called her, required some of it for packing and when she cut the straps the bundle exploded and lifted the roof of the shed.

When the lorry was picked up the morning of the flitting it was smaller than what Andrew and I expected but if careful with the loading I was fairly confident everything would get into it. Neither Andrew nor Sarah could make up their minds whether to take their old gas cooker with them or not. They changed their minds about every hour but finally decided they would take it. It was the last item to be put on the van but on arrival at their new home the next morning it was the first item off and went straight to the tip. Andrew not wanting to leave anything behind at Upminster gave me eighteen concrete slabs he had for a path. After the lorry was loaded I put them in the boot of my Triumph 2000 and took them home to Gidea Park for the same purpose. I can picture the wheels yet, splayed outwards at the bottom, as the suspension went right down to its lowest point.

Andrew was a bit of a comedian in his own way and on a visit to Gruinard he went into my bedroom and dressed up in one of my plus four tweed suits, complete with stockings, brogues and a fore and aft. He took one of my guns and went parading about outside. When I returned to the house there he was in all his glory and the fishing guest who was with me thought he was someone who had arrived for the start of the grouse shooting the following day. Sadly, Andrew over the last ten years or more had to cope with "M S" but in spite of this both Sarah and him made the most of their retirement, visiting friends, eating out and taking holidays every so often to spend time with Brian and family in Edinburgh and likewise with David and family in France and latterly Swizerland. Just a few days ago his health took a turn for the worse and he passed peacefully away leaving many, many happy memories for all of us.

CHAPTER 33

HOLIDAYS WITH OTHER GOOD FRIENDS

Other good holidays we had, were with Helen and Irvine Barclay, Linda their daughter and son Ian. When they came to stay in London with us we spent some time on the south coast. Another holiday we met in a self catering farmhouse near Bala in North Wales and toured most of that area on day trips, one of which was a boat crossing to the Isle of Man. After that trip I could safely say that it put Marjory off sailing for life. The previous day the crossing was cancelled because of the stormy sea and the damage that was done to the boat and pier. It did not improve much by the time we sailed. We enjoyed all the scenery including going up Snowdon but we were put off by some of the local people when you went into a pub or restaurant. For instance they would stop speaking English and revert to their Welsh language. I thought they were bad mannered and those who I came in contact with in the Met. did not impress me either.

We chose Nethybridge another year and again went self catering. It was good and we had a lot of fun. Pony trekking did not go down quite so well with the girls that year but the canoes on Loch Insch they enjoyed. I could not master it and spent more time crawling through the muddy water to get back to the bank. On a walk back from Glen More to Nethybridge I left the party to do a spot of fishing on the River Nethy, again without permission but this time with the worms on a hand held line. I said to the others to go on ahead and that I would catch up with them later. Expecting them to be home before me I was surprised to find they were not. I took the car and went back looking for them to be told that they had taken a wrong turning and was heading out on to the hills where a gamekeeper found them. Stretching the point he told them they were heading into Deeside but took them back to the track they should have been on. Irvine, being a member of the police Mountain Rescue Team, as you can imagine, took some stick over this. Ian was the oldest of the children and was always left in charge if we were out. One night we went to a local ceilidh dance and on our return we found that the girls to get their own back on Ian took all the alarm clocks they could find and hid them in different places in his room including the inner's of a piano so that he kept getting wakened up at different times.

With Margaret and Frank Mussard, caretakers of Balblair Estate we flew over to Vancouver where a coach was waiting for us. We had an excellent driver and courier who looked after us well and went out of their way to make the holiday a very enjoyable one. We stopped off for few days in various towns and cities en route through The Rockies to Calgarry from where we flew home. From Victoria we went sightseeing trip from a sea plane and when in Jasper we flew over part of The Rockies in a helicopter. Marjory did not enjoy that so much because of the transparent floor but she was not alone. The gentleman sitting next to her she thought never opened his eyes for the duration. I sat next to the pilot and thought it was fabulous. Marjory and I went on another coach trip to Kilarney one year where we had another enjoyable time, plenty of blarney but no sign of the leprachauns. It coincided with a Country and Western week and the hotel we stayed in laid on dancing every night.

The four of us went to Spain to play golf a few times and another occasion Bill and Marrion Luke joined the four of us on a golfing holiday to Portugal. They were good holidays taking more or less the same pattern each year. The golf was pre booked and we would be out on the various courses soon after 8am to avoid the mid-day heat. Lunch at the Club house, a relaxed afternoon and out for dinner every evening to different restaurants. Golf to me, although for a while I was a member of our local club at Bonar, was never taken serious and I fell foul of the etiquette so often to be told off my Marjory who plays competitively all of the time.

When we went to the Costa Del Sol Marjory and I decided to play an extra round on one of the other courses at Mijas and chose Alhaurin El Grande an eighteen hole, Par 72 course designed by Seve Ballesteros. It was carved out of the natural surroundings of the steep hillside with almost every green or fairway with a slope on it resulting in the ball running off and bouncing from one rock to another. An exciting course to play but even more so for Marjory who had a "hole in one" on a Par 3 which entailed hitting the ball across a sort of gorge to land it on the higher part of the green and let it roll down into the hole. I had no problem reaching the green but took eight strokes to conquer the slope.

Alan, Catriona and the girls took up the offer of a free apartment in one of Portugal's seaside towns and holiday resort. We were invited to join them which we did and again it was a most enjoyable holiday. The apartment had its own swimming pool and the girls just wanted to stay at it all day. The complex had other swimming pools which they tried out and the beach was nearby. We played golf there as well but I'm afraid I have not yet managed to impress Alan. The worst ever round we have had together was at Golspie which was a total disaster on my part. Again we went out to different restaurants for dinner at night and one of the days coincided with my birthday and Alan through his office in London arranged for a chauffeur driven car to take Marjory and I to wherever we wanted to go for the day.

My sixtieth birthday did not go by without something special laid on for it either. We were living at Gruinard at the time and I had the fishing for the week. All of the family were at home on holiday and Marjory and Margaret Mussard planned a surprise party at the Meikle Ferry Inn. They lead me to believe that there was a ceilidh and dance there on the night and asked if I would like to go to it and see Alan and Lippy Ross's girls we knew doing highland dancing. One of my friends who I invited to fish for a day at the beginning of that week blurted out, "Thanks for the invite to the party." He then realised the mistake he made in letting the secret out of the bag and said, "Just forget I said that." I promised that I

176

would but he felt awful about it. I then started to quietly take note of what was going on but never said anything other than we should all go for a meal beforehand. Marjory's reply to that was,"No no there is plenty in the fridge for a meal." But that was not the case. Another good friend, John Mortimer from Cumbernauld was up fishing with me and I asked him if he got an invitation to the party. When he first made out he knew nothing about a party I did not believe him because I was sure Marjory would have invited him. I then said to him, "If you have not been invited to my surprise birthday party John you are now." John just laughed and I still did not know if Marjory had said anything to him but the following day he told me he got his invitation but was sworn to secrecy and could not speak about it. It was my turn to laugh then.

On the night of it when we were all getting dressed Catriona and I were in the living room when Fiona came in and joined us. She was wearing stockings or tights with really bright colours and Catriona without thinking said, "What will granny say about them?" Fiona snapped back, "She's not likely to see them." I made a discreet move to the kitchen and waited for the mini bus to arrive. On the way down the road I saw that this person's car was not in the drive or that another car was missing so I was building up a picture of who was going to be there. Marjory said later she was worried that I would go off round to Culrain and find all her people in the holiday houses. It would also have saved a lot of bother if I had just told her I had found out about it. John Gordon provided excellent music; memorabilia decorated the walls, a fantastic buffet and a jolly good night had by all.

CHAPTER 34

HAPPY TIMES AT FETTERCAIRN

After about six years in the traffic department I came to the top of the list for being allocated a police house. The one to come vacant was in the village of Fetercairn in Kincardineshire and I was to be the village bobby which also took in a fairly large landward area made up mostly of farming and sporting estates, a lovely part of the country. Fasque was still in the hands of the Gladstone family and Fettercairn Estate was owned by a cousin of the Queen, Lady Dianna Bowess-Lyon, and her husband, Peter Somerville. The Police Station was attached to the house and situated on the edge of the village next to the playing field and bowling green. It had a large walled garden and as soon as I saw the place I knew the time was right for me to have the black Labrador bitch I always wanted to own, but previous accommodation was never suitable. One of the first people to introduce himself was Frank Low or better known to others as, "Punk Low." It turned out he was a special constable for the area and was head-keeper to the Somervilles so we had lots and lots in common. I bought my puppy from him for £4.00 which was the going rate in the mid sixties whereas it would cost at least £400.00 today. Frank had a large kennel of Labradors of all ages, some for his own use, some he was training to sell to sporting people and the best of them he kept for trialling and breeding from. He was one of the top Field Trialers and Judges at the time. One of his proud moments was to be presented by Her Majesty the Queen with a trophy he won at Balmoral. A photograph of the presentation to him by the Queen was proudly displayed on the mantelpiece in the living room of their welcoming home.

I named the puppy Jewel, and under Frank's influence I set about to train the dog, but another gentleman who I met in the course of my work and was to play an important role was Colonel Harland from The Burn House, originally the big house for the estate of that name, before it was broken up. Professors came there with their students for reading parties and he loaned me a book titled "Dog Training by Dick Sharpe" which proved invaluable to me. I followed the guidance in that book meticulously, and kept referring to sections of it time and time again.

The Colonel rang me one morning in a panic to say the house had been broken into. When I got there I found that it was an upstairs window that had been smashed but with only the minimal amount of broken glass on the landing inside. On the ground below lay a part emptied whisky bottle, all of it giving the impression of a party that had gone wrong. In my opinion it was not the crime of the century but Colonel Harland did not see it that way and was adamant that we should get to the bottom of it. Two other officers came to assist with the enquiry which meant interviewing over a hundred occupants. All of them including the staff were first taken into the main hall and told that if the culprits owned up it would be dealt with as an internal matter if not it would mean a police prosecution.

About five o'clock that evening and after everyone had been spoken to we were none the wiser. When the other officers had gone home I took the whisky bottle which had a serial number on it and went to the local hotels to see if they could help. It was identified as a bottle coming from a particular case of whisky but no one could say who it had been sold to. On my way home I decided to call on Henry Littlejohn the head keeper at the Gannochy Estate to tell him of what had been going on and to see if he could throw any light on the matter. All he could tell me was that the grouse beaters had their last day on the hill and most of them would have left by then. We were having a cup of tea and still talking about it when there was a knock on the door. In came three young student lads who were rather surprised to see me. After each of them thanked Henry and his wife for their stay in the bothy and were about to leave I said, "Before you go I want to know about the broken window at the Burn House?" Straight away one of them replied, "First of all he had nothing to do with it", pointing to one of his friends and then went on to tell me how they had a party the previous night, knew about the Burn House and went there looking for female company, but got disturbed and had to make a run for it out through the broken window.

In one of the gate cottages lived an old family friend, Mrs Grieve and her daughter Betty. My mother, in her younger years, was in service with Mrs Grieve and I used to call on them regularly. Betty was agent for a local Member of Parliament and for most spoke with a very posh accent but often forgot herself, reverting to her mother tongue, adding plenty of expletives on the way with mother sitting there shaking her head at her. One day when I walked in on them Mrs Grieve was eating roast pigeon for lunch. I was teasing her that she had been poaching partridges. She thought I was serious and went on to tell me how Betty shot pigeons and rabbits in the garden. Betty then produced a gun case to show me what she had in it. I was a bit gob smacked when out came a matching pair of Purdy twelve bore shot guns in mint condition.

I had never seen a Purdy gun before, far less a matching pair in the original leather case. It transpired that Betty's father Wull was head-keeper for the previous owner of the Burn Estate, who left the guns to him in his will. Because of the value of the guns, even then, I persuaded them to deposit them with their bank manager for safe keeping. The guns were eventually gifted to a nephew of the previous owner. Betty had another old Spanish gun for "blootering" as she called it, the little b****s in the garden. Frank Low was an under-keeper to Mr Grieve at The Burn and to get a rabbit or anything else off the estate for a dinner Mrs Grieve had to rely on Frank for it. On a pay day the two men would go to the pub in Edzell for a "booze up" and next day they would be counting the money they had between them to see if they had enough for another drink. Frank used to tell me how they would raid Mrs Grieve's hen house and pull the necks of a couple of hens to sell to the butcher for the price of a couple of pints.

179

Betty and her mother came up to Gruinard for a holiday and it was the first time she had been in a public bar. We took them down to the Bridge Hotel and she got a little bit tipsy and of course enjoyed herself. On the same visit Betty took her mother up the East Coast for a run and stopped off in Helmsdale where they watched some fishers below the bridge. Betty got talking to one of the locals standing on the bridge and enquired about buying a salmon. The guy said, "Leave it with me. Go and have a cup of coffee in the cafe and I will see you in half an hour." Sure enough he returned with a salmon concealed in a bag which was hurriedly placed in the boot of Betty's car. Two pounds it cost her, little more than the coffee and a biscuit each of them had in the cafe. Some of them may have been fishing legally but in all probability they were ripping the water to foul hook the salmon.

Most of my spare time, and I had plenty of that, was put into dog training sessions. Some of the villagers who did not know I had Jewel thought I was practicing my traffic signals, as if. I used to walk over the fields and throw dummies into the hedgerows for her to find. Jewel soon worked out the easy way to find them without waiting for my directions was to follow my scent to them. To overcome this, I would enlist the help of boys going to or from school and ask them to cycle over the field for me, and place the dummies. I never quite worked out which they enjoyed the most, the dog work or just helping the local bobby.

Unless I was off duty for a complete day I always wore my uniform. After breakfast I would walk up to the village post office for our mail and do a bit of shopping for Marjory. I took this opportunity to get to know the local people and for them to know me. The practice in single stations was to work then until 1pm and be off duty until 3pm and then go back on duty and work into the evening or as late as you wished to. I was running a Mini van at the time which was handy for the dog and my fishing rods, guns and a waterproof jacket were seldom out of it. The registration letters were BUS and in Union Street, Aberdeen a bus inspector pointed out to me that it did not entitle me to park at bus stop even if only temporarily. Leaving the station to deal with routine matters I would tell Marjory where I was going but no sooner through the gates I often changed my mind and sometimes be away all day leaving her unofficially to hold the fort.

Jewel reached a very high standard in her training and was very popular on the shoots. As soon as keepers got their shoot dates they would be knocking on my door to get them into my diary if the days were not already booked. Within a few days of Frank calling to introduce himself he drove me down to Sauchieburn Wood and told me I could go shooting in it any time I wanted. This was to become a great facility for training Jewel, not to mention a pigeon or other bit of game for the pot. A nice roe buck fell to my temptation one day and after it was hanging in my garage, skinned and ready for butchering, I thought I better let Frank know and get his approval in retrospect. His response was, "I'm partial to a dinner of roe venison just as I think you are." That was as good as a nod and a wink and the carcase was shared between us. Over the years he had eaten plenty of venison and after I gave him a haunch from a red deer hind I shot with the .22 coming home from Glencalvie one night he told me it was the best venison he had ever tasted and was interested to know where it came from. Amat wood did provide good eating beasts, red, sika and roe.

It was in Sauchieburn Wood with some regret that I shot my first and only Capercaillie. Frank had a keepers' day there on one of my excursions from London and I was a standing gun. There were some shots fired down the line and I could hear other guns calling caper. I picked it off in a gap above me in the tall pine trees as it flew past. It was the last drive of the day and all the game was laid out for the count to see who had won the sweep. Frank told everyone to take a brace of birds but that I was to have the Capercaillie. There was no shortage of well meaning advice as to how it should be cooked, including the usual one of first burying it in the ground for two weeks. This apparently was to get rid of the taste of pine needles which the bird fed on. For my opinion, after trying to eat it, a young keeper when advice was being dished out, summed it up pretty well when he said, "Yes, and just leave it there."

A Met police officer stationed at Barking in Essex came from Caithness and one winter holiday up there he took back with him a Capercaille from Berridale which he placed on one of the busy junctions for all to see. It was expected that a member of the public would report it or bring it to the station and sure enough they did. The unsuspecting officer on duty at the desk contacted a particular Superintendent who was a bit of an ornithologist and he came to identify the bird. Straight away he said it was a Capercaille and that no such bird was indigenous to England. He then volunteered the theory that it must have been hit by a high lorry and came all the way down from Scotland on its roof, falling off as the vehicle negotiated the junction. Subsequently he took the joke in good part.

Another good friend I made at Fettercairn was Alec Downie, head keeper at Fasque Estate the home of the Gladstone family for many generations. Alec used to borrow Jewel for the grouse season and while she was with him she lived a life of luxury sleeping at night in an easy chair by the fireside. I called one evening to see how Alec was getting on with her. It amused us, when I got no welcome from her whatsoever. I could have been anybody who walked in. She raised her head slightly and then went back to sleep and when I was leaving she did exactly the same. Alec took me deer stalking, out for duck and goose flights and had me there for the white hare shoots.

One evening we went to shoot pigeons as they flighted in for their night time roosts. We were up on a hill face with our backs to a pine wood and could see the pigeons coming at least half a mile away. As they weaved about, ducked and dived I picked one, would then change my mind and choose another, thinking it would give me a better chance of hitting it. I could hear the pellets rattling off their feathers but the disastrous result was three or four pigeons for seventy odd shots. Alec had not done much better. In contrast with this I went with Alec and Sandy Sipmson (Ecky Doo) to Inglesmadie Forest and standing in a narrow ride I had eight pigeons for twelve shots. You heard them coming, got a glimpse of them overhead, threw the gun up and fired with the pellets raking up the braches as they disappeared. The bump on the ground told you a connection had been made.

Alec Downie took in stray dogs handed into the police. He was required to keep them for a minimum of seven days before disposing of them if they were not claimed, but if they were nice dogs he would often keep them longer or try and find them a home rather than put them down. He got in touch with me to say that a collie he was looking after matched the description of one reported missing from near Arbroath. This was about thirty miles from Fettercairn and I did not think it would be the same one but I got the local police to inform the owners to give them the opportunity to come and see it. They did come and it was their dog. They told us that they had recently moved home from the top of Glen Clova and that the dog must have been making its way back there with the last stage of its journey across the Fasque Hills and then through Glendye. I don't know what the exact number of miles would have been but certainly considerable for a dog working under its own instinct

As a result of a chimney fire at the keeper's house on the Burn Estate I met Bert Riddel and his wife Agnes. We were to become very good friends for many years until Bert suddenly died from a heart attack. We were in London by this time and gradually we lost touch with Agnes and the boys. Agnes would look after our children if we were away anywhere. Bert was an Aberdeenshire man from the Insch area where he previously ran a syndicate shoot along with his father known as "Roarin Rab", both very knowledgeable men in the keepering world.

Bert's boss was an ex army officer but never used his title preferring to be known simply as Mr Kennoway. I got very friendly with him and got to know him ever so well. He owned a single bank salmon beat on the river North Esk where he invited me to fish at any time. In fact, to encourage it, I was told to keep every second salmon for myself. There were two reasons for this. One was that they wanted to boost the catch numbers because no records were kept previously, secondly, to keep me off a neighbouring beat where I had a similar arrangement and Mr Kennoway did not get on with the owner of it.

One morning I turned up at Bert's house to go fishing but Mr Kennoway and his family were there. After getting my usual welcome from him I went to speak to Bert who was getting fishing rods ready for everyone. They were one rod short so I offered Mr Kennoway my one. He asked what I would use then. Without thinking I said "I can come here any day." Quickly he retorted "So can I," and then said "No, you and I will go together." We were allocated a couple of pools by Bert and I hooked a salmon in the one known as the "Snake" because of its narrowness and long winding shape. I offered Mr Kennoway to take the rod and play the fish but he declined. Because of his earlier observation I did not press him but soon saw that it was a Kelt I had on. It was well mended and very silvery. In the water it had all the appearance of a fresh one.

Mr Kennoway was adamant that it was a freshly run salmon but I was one hundred per cent sure it was not and even more so once it was on the bank. I said it would have to go back. Mr Kennoway, bless his soul, said "If you say so" and picked it up with both hands, raised it above his head and flung it back in the water, and then stormed off. The fish quickly recovered from its ordeal and swam off. I later caught up with Bert to be told that Mr Kennoway was not a happy 'chappie' and was just as adamant with him that it was a fresh fish and perfectly edible. Bert jokingly said to me, "You should have let him eat it, maggots and all." Apart from the Carron, the North Esk was one of the finest rivers I was privileged and had the pleasure to fish, great pools like the Gannochy, Snake, Lyn Martin, March and the Chappleton on the Arnhall beat.

The pheasant shooting at The Burn was leased to a syndicate in which Mr Kennoway retained a gun for himself but he was not that interested in shooting. I would be standing nearby with Jewel picking up the dead birds and sometimes even before the end of the first drive Mr Kennoway would thrust his gun into my hands, empty his pockets of cartridges and go off home, leaving me with a day's free shooting. I knew most of the syndicate members anyway but they were a bit surprised with Mr Kennoway for doing this, but when it became a habit it was accepted as the normal thing.

Bert and I spent a lot of time together either fishing, shooting rabbits for the dogs or general estate work. I was often teased about being his under- keeper and Marjory still claims that she was the un- paid police officer at Fettercairn. I was the last to arrive there one day to join others for the end of season keepers shoot. Making sure everyone heard him, Sandy Simpson, a retired landscape gardener from Helensburgh and who Bert knew from his Aberdeenshire days, shouted out "That just leaves the bobby's licences to be checked." Putting my hand up to my breast pocket I said "That is fine by me. But you will all have to do likewise." Bert shouted out "Don't bother, let's get going." Half way through the morning when a police car was seen approaching in the distance most of the party was over the fence like scalded cats into a field. I think that spoke for its self. Another laugh that day was when we were walking through a birch wood one of the guns shouted "Over" alerting us to something was on the wing. Someone else shouted, "It's a buzzard." Bert shouted, "Shoot it." Next call, "The bobby's here." Bert crowned it all with a final call, "Shoot the bloody bobby as well."

CHAPTER 35

FISHING A FROZEN RIVER

On the river South Esk the bottom beat was another fantastic place to fish. The late Fred Walker, a neighbour of mine from the village leased the first week or so of the season there and always invited me to fish for him, even after I moved to Peterhead and London. I was still at Fettercairn when Fred and I set off in his car for the opening day to find six inches of frozen snow on the bank and the pools iced over. This was not new to Fred and he assured me it would be alright. We immediately set about throwing large stones or boulders onto the ice to break it up and prepare it for fishing later in the forenoon. To give the pools a rest we fished the streamy bits between them. No sooner than we got started when my brown and gold spinning lure snagged on something. I waded out to free it and on my way back Fred hooked a salmon just above me. Paying more attention to him and the fish, I slipped on a flat stone and went head first into about three feet of the icy cold water. Fortunately for me I had a very good water proof Barbour jacket on and of course wearing thigh waders. The water went down from the top around my neck. Standing barefoot in the snow I stripped off all my clothes, not a pretty sight on such a wintry day, including the pyjamas I left on knowing that it was going to be very cold. The wettest clothing was the "Jim jams," and my underwear which I hung in the branches of a tree. I put the remainder of my clothes back, on starting with driest. I had no dry socks so they just had to be rung out and put back on after pouring the water out of the waders. In weather like this one cannot have enough clothing on in the first place.

By the time Fred landed his salmon I was raring to get back into the water again. Too much valuable fishing time had already been lost that morning. Fred came over to me with his fish but I could tell he was not very pleased with me. Having given me a lift in the car to the river he thought he was going to have to take me home to get changed, and that would have been a disaster as far as he was concerned. He laid off about it and me getting my death of cold. An alternative suggestion of his was to go to the keeper's house for a change of clothing but I was not having any of it, having made up my mind to continue fishing. I felt good and even better when Fred plied me with steaming hot coffee laced with whisky. By this time the pools were rested long enough. I went up to the top of the beat and Fred went down below with us meeting later for lunch. I never got further than the top pool and was still there when Fred came looking for me worrying that something had come over me.

Far from it, by this time I had three lovely fresh salmon on the bank and thirty two finnock, young sea trout, alongside them and much to Fred's relief. He weighed each fish caught as soon as it was knocked on the head, labelled it ready for going by train from Montrose to Billingsgate Fish Market. I'm sure he was like a walking calculator counting out the value of the fish and matching it to the rental to establish a profit or loss. One fish would be cut up for the week and he was very fussy who was about at the time, you had to earn a piece.

He could not work out how I was able to catch so many finnock. He had been striking at them as well but was unable to hook any of them. I then told him the secret that the finnock were not going for the lure but instead the swivel which was about three feet up the nylon. I then showed him how I tied on a very small treble hook on to the swivel and the number of the fish on the bank spoke for itself. I went on to catch another two salmon in the afternoon but we had to cut the day short because of the rings on the rod kept icing up. The day ended with a hot bath, a hearty supper and out on patrol for the evening.

Fred, who was a great bee keeper, lived almost across the road from the Police Station and I could see him most days in the summer working on one hive or another. He never wore a vale, gloves or anything to protect himself from stings and I don't believe he got that many. For his age he had a good head of hair and you could see him picking the bees out of it and tossing them aside. He told me he made most of his money during the war years hiring out plant and machinery to the Ministry of Defence at the many airfields in that district alone. Apparently half of the so called equipment was on paper only. He then became a dealer in second hand tractors and other farm machinery. He and other dealers formed a purchasing group. For instance, on arrival at a farm sale or auction, they would decide which item each person wanted to buy. Only one person would bid for it so that they were not competing with one another even although more than one of them was interested in the same item. At the end of the sale they held a mini auction between themselves to see who was going to get what and any profits made on the original price was shared between them and you did not have to be at the sale that day to get a cut of the profits. He was a good neighbour, kind and helpful but him and his wife apparently had not spoken to one another for over twenty years. Any conversation was done through the dog. If any note had to be left for the other it was addressed to the dog. If they were all in the house together and one had to say something to the other it was said to the dog for the other to hear. I found it difficult to believe but so many people there assured me it was a fact.

My experience of keeping bees was short lived. I was cutting out queen cells one evening and I thought I was properly dressed for the job but the whole hive went wild and attacked me. I got stung round both of my wrist, my neck and everywhere the bees could get at me. I bunged everything back together and got away from the hive, at the same time brushing off all the bees on me. I went to the kennel to put the dogs in for the night but felt faint and had to hold on to the wall and put my forehead on the cold stone.

When I got into the house I was itching all over, my heart was beating extremely fast and I had difficulty in swallowing and my tongue felt funny. I just collapsed on the settee. Marjory rung Doctor Dally from Edzell to ask if there was anything I could take for it. He came to the house immediately and as he walked through the door he was getting a syringe from his bag. I tried to speak to him but he told me to lay still and be quiet. He never took the precaution of swabbing my arm, just stuck the needle into it and beckoned Marjory through to the kitchen. After a while he came back in to see how I was and gave me eighteen tablets and told me I had eighteen days to get rid of the bees. The swelling of my tongue and my heart beat got more normal but I had to stay in bed next day. The following one I tried to walk to the village shop but had to sit down half way and then return home. My eyesight was affected that day as well in as much as about forty yards in front of me everything looked like a heat haze. What I now know is that I am lucky to be alive and can only thank Doctor Dally for his promptness in attending so quickly. I understand up to twenty people die from the same thing each year.

Another gentleman from Fettercairn who I fished with was George Pirie a tenant on one of the local farms but lived in the village. In the mail one morning an anonymous letter arrived stating that this farmer was employing a tractor driver who was disqualified from driving. Because of my relationship with his employer certain innuendoes were made by the writer. The writer also said if I wanted to catch him whilst driving he would be carting potatoes the following morning. As soon as work began in the morning my colleague Irvine Barclay and I stopped the driver and reported him. Because the employer was responsible for allowing him to drive and to drive without insurance I had no option but to charge George as well. I do not believe in making fish of one and flesh of another. Both he and his wife created quite a scene in the house calling us the Gestapo and all sorts of other names. The nicest thing he said, "I thought you were my friend." My reply to that was, "Yes George and if we are no longer friends we never were in the first place." For the best part of a year I tried to make conversation with him but I was blanked at every turn. I knew that mutual friends were putting pressure on him to turn the clock back to the way we used to be and he eventually warmed to my presence at the Polling Station on Election Day. Soon after that he approached me for a special varnish I used for the brown and gold fishing minnows which he could not get from any paint supplier My source was a company in Aberdeen who made wooden fish boxes and he knew I had half a gallon of the stuff.

For a few days of receiving the letter I racked by brains in an effort to come up with the author of it. Then it dawned on me that the page had come from a writing pad used to write a previous letter and I could faintly see the imprint of an address on the one I had stared at for so long. I lightly shaded over it with a pencil and there was no doubt where it came from and who had written it. He also was a local tractor driver and by coincidence I met him coming out of the Post Office one morning and I casually said to him, "Thank you for the letter." He smartly replied, "I don't know what you're talking about." I then said, "It's alright. Don't worry about it but thank you all the same." Talk about "taking the bull by the horns" when I next met him, he challenged me as to how I knew it was him who had sent the letter. I never made him any the wiser but assured him his secret was safe with me, bless his soul he went to the grave not knowing.

Another farmer who kept getting reported to me for driving whilst under the influence of alcohol was not so easy to catch. He and his wife tried to hand in bags of potatoes, oven ready chickens and more. Each occasion they were sent packing or I took the stuff back and dumped it on their own doorstep. When they resorted to handing sweets over the gate to our children I thought enough was enough and a concerted effort by my self and others was made until he got disqualified. His wife then hid the car keys from him and locked his clothes away but not to be out done he would walk to the village hotel in his pyjamas. The hotel keeper and his wife were no help to him either. They would take him through to the kitchen and ply him with whisky neat or put it in his coffee. It was not uncommon in London to be offered money for not arresting drivers who were over the limit with drink. In Aberdeen my self and a colleague were offered a hundred pounds each from a haulage contractor if we did not proceed with an overloading charge.

Not far from the village there was a government underground telephone system linking Britain with America and it was manned by civilian security people. I had nothing to do within the site but I often called and spoke to the staff just in case I was ever needed. One day we got talking about shooting and the officer on duty said, "Why not come here for a shot? There are plenty of hares and pheasants." I said to him that I would have to get permission from the Officer in Charge and he lived in Dundee. When it was all set up for me and I thought everything was in order I went along with Jewel and the gun. I had a nice bag for the few hours I was there but in the evening I got a 'phone call from an adjacent farmer asking me who I got permission from. After explaining the position and offering him the game he assured me that all was well. His farm was part of a larger picture and when he bought it from the Ministry after the war he got all of the shooting rights and the security firm did not have leave to give anyone permission to shoot on it.

A lot of my police work at Fettercairn involved me going to the American Naval Base sited at the old Royal Air Force airfield. Those guys thought nothing of driving down on a weekend pass to London to see a show. I never once had to take any of them to the Sherriff court. Their commanding Officer would deal with them himself internally, less fuss and officialdom than our ways and the men did not like that one bit. It was a big loss financially for them to be sent back to the States and worse still if it was to some punishment posting. Outside the gates was a pile of car wrecks supposedly to warn other naval men the dangers of driving on our roads but it did not appear to make any difference. Although they changed the vehicles regularly they were never short of having freshly damaged ones to display. They were mostly left hand drive so that may have had something to do with it.

One morning I was summoned to the Base Bowling Alley where the safe had been bust open and the contents stolen. A door from outside the premises had been jemmied. Preserving the scene for clues never entered their heads. As I walked in one officer was sitting on the corner of the safe and another was sitting on a desk top with his feet up on the safe. The CID came out to take fingerprints but that was a waste of time. An examination of the door damage indicated that it had been done from the inside so this ruled out a forced entry. Suspicion then fell on the caretaker and closer examination of the damage to the safe suggested that it had been done with the door open. The top of the safe immediately above the lock had been struck three or four blows with a sledgehammer which was still on the premises. The Americans, not doing anything by half, got two brand new safes out from the stores. With the first one in the locked position, no matter how many times they hit it with the hammer in the same way it could not be opened. With the door open on the other safe after three blows the damage was consistent to the original one. We had our culprit including the contents.

CHAPTER 36

GOOD ADVICE

During my three and a half years at Fettercairn I can honestly say I never once reported a juvenile to the courts, that was not to say that they did not get into bother but I was always able to deal with it via the parents. They were on my side and appreciated my approach. Before going there my Inspector in the traffic department, Charlie Cruickshank, reminded me of the reputation that traffic officers had, and that I was no different. "I'll give you a bit of advice Hugh," he said. "Leave your note book in your pocket for three months. You will not have a witness sitting beside you all the time. You will need to win over the confidence of the people first. Better still, make it six months." I never forgot what he said and I got on very well with the residents. Overall they were very good people and did not give me much bother. I could honestly say there was not a rotten egg amongst them. On leaving school several of the youths came to me for references and I was only too pleased to help.

I do not watch modern day police programmes on television but have to admit watching "Heart Beat" much of which I can relate to myself and Fettercairn. The local Bank Manager complained to the Inspector about the youths in an evening congregating in the bus shelter. The Inspector said to me afterwards, "I just told him that Fettercairn had the only 'bus shelter in the County that did not have broken glass in it."

One very grateful family was the parents of a secondary year pupil who stole five pounds from a house on his evening paper round. At first it was not reported to me because the victim a retired baker was afraid he might have to go to court. This was one of the questions I put to him if the culprit was caught. He assured me he would if it was necessary but I could see he was quite worried about it. However, I thought the paperboy was a likely suspect even although he had not been in trouble before. When he came to the police station to deliver our paper I closed the door behind him and accused him of it. Straight away he admitted the theft and told me where the remainder of the money was hidden in an old teapot. He took me there and then we went to his home where it was like dropping a bombshell on the parents. Unbeknown to me the following week they were due to leave for emigration to New Zealand. If the boy had to go to court you can imagine the complications that would have caused. The money was repaid in full and it was a huge relief to all concerned. When I took the money back to the baker you could almost see the horror on his face at the thought of going to court. On the same sideboard where his money was taken from sat a large round biscuit tin and in it there were hundreds and hundreds of pound in cash of all kinds of notes.

I persuaded him to take it to the bank and arranged for one of his friends to accompany him.

Three girls stole over a hundred pounds from one of their mothers' houses. She was saving up to buy a television set and had it hidden in a wardrobe. The girls went down to Montrose and spent it on clothing and shoes that did not really fit them and all kinds of rubbish. After school they would dress up in it but on hearing that I was making enquiries about the theft they ditched everything in a nearby burn. I retrieved most of it but it was not much good for anything. The granny and mother of one of the girls got quite stroppy with me and accused me of all sorts. I invited their girl to come on her own to the Police Station to have a chat with me about it. After school the following day she came to the police station and told me it was them, at the same time asking me to go back home with her to break the news to her mother and her granny which in one sense I took a delight in doing. They never went to court either.

One night, about 2am, a school teacher living on her own 'phoned me to say that someone had just been in her bedroom and shone a torch in her face. At first I thought of a burglary but a purse on the kitchen table where entry had been made via an open window was untouched. Along with other officers a search was made of the area but no one was found. Next morning I went to see the lady again and when I asked her about some men friends who were known to pay her a visit she assured me that was not their style. I had another idea that it could be an eighteen year old youth from a nearby farm which could explain the sudden disappearance of the culprit. Again she would not hear of it being him and went on to say how well she knew him having taught him years earlier in school and how nice a boy he was. Whilst this conversation was taking place in the school playground the young man came along the road on his bicycle. I jumped over the wall and as he cycled up to me I took hold of the handle bars and with him still sitting on the seat I simply asked him what he was doing in the teacher's bedroom during the night. His reply was, "Will I go to prison?" No, just a twenty five pound fine was the outcome.

Another nice little clear up I had while at Fettercairn was a trail of damage by shooting at road signs and other property mainly filling stations and AA boxes stretching from Aberdeen to Fettercairn. It was fairly obvious that it had started at Fettercairn or ended there where a telephone kiosk was blasted with a shotgun by someone driving off in a bright red Riley car. Luckily only one such car was known in the area and my enquiries took me to interview a student working on a Hill Research Farm. He admitted being involved but did not have a firearm himself. He told me of two others involved and a colleague and I drove up to the head of Glen Esk to interview one of them. A group of students were there for the grouse beating and that evening they were all playing football in a field. When we stopped one of them singled him self out to come and speak to us. Unwittingly he kept tossing a .22 bullet from one hand to the other. I told him I would have it for starters and then asked him where the rifle was. He took us up to his van and produced a sawn off rifle and very roughly adapted to replicate a pistol. He also told us that the shotgun used was owned by the third person who was known to us and lived in Laurencekirk. All three went to court charged with about twenty or more offences and had to pay if I remember correctly eight hundred pounds to make good the damage. They were given time to pay but the Laurencekirk youth got arrested as a "Peeping Tom" at a hospital and ended up committing suicide.

Twice a year at compulsory dipping time it was the duty of police to visit the farms to make sure that it was being done properly and that each animal was completely submerged for a set time. If you arrived at the farms un-noticed the sheep would be going through "jig time" until they became aware of your presence. It was impossible to visit every dipping but it was good to cycle out and get to know the people, sometimes having a cup of tea with them if it happened to be at meal times. Every stock holder had to submit a return of the number of sheep dipped and of those that had still to be dipped with reasons why they were unable to do so. At the end of each period an overall return had to go in from each police station to the Department of Agriculture. Other form filling with the farmers was the movement of pigs. This was less complicated but you often got awakened early morning by the farmer, usually the same ones, leaving it to the last minute on their way to the auction mart or slaughterhouse, to get a movement licence.

Sometimes I would be over on duty at Laurencekirk Auction Mart issuing the pig licences and got to know a number of the retired farmers from that area. Any day other than mart day you would find a group of them putting the world to right on a particular street corner. I heard from someone who had been at one of the regular furniture sales that when the auctioneer could not get a bid for a chanty or chamber pot he knocked it out to one of the retired farmers who was far from pleased about it. The first time I saw him after this was with his friends on the usual street corner and in the passing I said to him how pleased I was to see him well again. He replied, "What do you mean? There's been nothing wrong with me." I said "Sorry", I heard you were unable to come down stairs at night and had to buy a chanty at the mart." It was taken in the good spirit of things but to the amusement of his fellow cronies he threatened me with his walking stick.

Marjory and I arrived at Fettercairn a couple of months or so before Xmas and the New Year. On Hogmanay night they held a dance in the village hall and I was on duty until midnight. I was up at the hall to see the end of the dance and the sizeable crowd dispersed quickly, probably to go home and take in the New Year. A few of them asked if my door was open to "first footers" and I assured them it was and that it would always be to anyone. Some of them were already in the house by the time I got home. I immediately got out of uniform and we soon got into the swing of things with a party. Revellers came and went as that was the tradition, some merrier than others. About two or three in the morning a farmer, David Brown came in. He was quite sober as he was driving. I asked him where was his friend Gordon Reid? "Out in the car the worse of drink he replied." I went out to the car and there he was slumped asleep in the seat. I woke him up and said

I was arresting him for being drunk in charge of the car. It dawned on him after a bit where he was and that David was in the house. I took him into the house but soon afterwards he fell asleep on the mat in front of the fire. David and a couple of the others wanted to leave the party to take him home. I encouraged them to carry Gordon through to the spare bedroom and put him to bed where he could sleep it off. When the last of them left Marjory and I got to our own beds.

I was up and having breakfast when Gordon sheepishly appeared with not a great deal to say. Then the 'phone rung and this was another farmer, Norman MacWilliam asking if Gordon was still with us. When I said, "He was", Norman said he would arrange a lift for him to get home. Then, yet another farmer, David Middleton, rung to ask if Gordon was getting bail. I twigged right away that he had been asked to come to the police station and bail Gordon out. I said, "Yes but to come straight away as I was going to a white hare shoot at Glensaugh." He arrived a few minutes later and I thought I would carry the joke on a bit further. David again asked if he was getting bail and I assured him he was. I then invited him into the house for a New Year's dram which he accepted I could see that he was not happy with Gordon although they never spoke to one another. David again asked about the bail and how much it was to be. £50.00 I told him but when he took a cheque book from his pocket I thought it had gone far enough and told him the truth. Gordon knew nothing about what was going on. David quickly jumped to his feet and beckoned Gordon to follow him and he was not too enamoured with me either. Norman rung me later in the day to see if it was true what I done on David because they did not believe I would have carried it on as far as I did.

I met Norman a few times and Marjory knew his wife quite well. A number of the ladies arranged to meet at the police station before going on to a W.R.I. outing at Brechin and Mildred MacWilliam left her car in the drive while she travelled with some of the others. She made a comment as they left that she hadn't locked the car but because of where it was it would be safe enough. To get my own back on Norman I decided to put their car in my garage and shut the doors. When the ladies returned no car, panic, panic, no, Norman had not been to collect it. Then they found it in the garage. Alan Wilson, the dairy farmer from Gosesslie was another mischief. You never knew what next would come crashing in when you opened the back door in the morning. He could always find something to prop against it to give you a fright. Hiding things was another bit of fun for him.

Alan was good to me when Jewel had a litter of pups. Every day he gave me extra milk and took a keen interest in their well being. Jimmy Oswald from Glen Tanner Estate came over to look at them and ended up buying one. He had already seen Jewel working at the trials in Deeside. In the course of conversation he asked me to come over for a cast on the River Dee on the opening day of the salmon season. Jimmy was head ghillie and Irvine Barclay's uncle worked with him. We went over together but on arrival the prospects did not look good. A thaw had set in, the river was quite high with huge pieces of ice about four to six inches thick were going down it. Undaunted, Jimmy took me to a pool to get started. Watching the ice to clear a bit he would say, "Wait, wait, wait, now go for it." That was the signal for me to make a cast, and then hurriedly I would be told to reel in. As the day went on the ice cleared a bit and I caught three beautiful springers. We all had fish that day but I was amazed how far up the river they were so early in the year with temperatures as low as they were. Where we were it must have been something like forty miles from the sea and Jimmy said that fish had been caught previous years higher up the river. Jimmy went on to become head keeper and in the course of that work he made a study of the native wildcat. He also laid claim to being a distant relation to Lee Harvey Oswald, the sniper who killed John F Kennedy.

Alan, his wife and Marjory and I went up to Stonehaven one night for the police ball. When they dropped us off at the police station I bent down to put the slip bolt for one half of the gate into its position, a piece of piping in the ground. At the same time Marjory slammed the other half of the gate shut but my head was in the way. I often had a headache after a night out but this time drink had nothing to do with it. I think Alan told everyone on his milk round what Marjory did. He reported the theft of a drive shaft from a piece of farm machinery and when I called on him to see a similar one we both suspected the same person for having taken it. He was another farmer but had a suspect character. On leaving Alec Downie's house one afternoon he was seen to pick up a box of cartridges from the stair and put them in his pocket not knowing that a lady at the top of the stair had seen him. I took it upon myself to have a look around his sheds one night to see if I could find it. So at 2am when all was quiet, in about I went, but had to run for it pretty quickly. About twelve geese flew out of their shed making a terrible noise and chased me out of the yard. Alan and I had a good laugh about it but he then told me to forget about the shaft.

CHAPTER 37

HITTING THE HEADLINES

Jewel hit the national press as a result of her part in tracking a prisoner who stole a car in Perth and abandoned it at the North Water Bridge before decamping into the woods nearby. A full scale police search was mounted, including a dog handler from Aberdeen City Police. We were not allowed into the wood because of the police dog and while we were waiting for the word to go one of the officers asked why I had brought my Labrador along. I said there was every chance she would sniff him out. They scoffed at this idea but changed their minds when they saw me throw my car keys in to a field of hay. I sent Jewel for them and in no time at all she was back to me with the keys. What I did not tell them was that I had taught her to seek out people from hiding places by using the words, "Who is it"? I had previously put her to the test on my nephew Geoffrey when he was hiding behind coles of hay. My brother in law, Eric, got quite a fright one evening in the dark as he finished work. I was standing in a doorway a little distance away from where he garaged his tractor and I just asked Jewel who is it? She ran forward and starting barking at him. When I called her off he said he knew it was Jewel but next day he said to his mother, "That was not a fine thing Hugh did to me last night." Both Geoffrey and Eric disbelieved me that she would behave like this but knowing she would not harm them I decided to prove my point.

Word came out that the prisoner had broken cover and was seen running across fields. My neighbouring officer, Irvine Barclay from Auchenblae Police Station and I went to where he was last seen while all the other officers including the dog handler went away ahead to cut him off. Irvine and I walked along the edge of a barley field hoping to find tracks of him going into the crop but there was no sign of that. Both of us, at the same time, got a strong smell of cigarette smoke. I said my normal to Jewel, "Who is it?" quite confident that she would find him. I practised this with other friends and families and when she found them she would stand barking at them but would not touch them. She was very intelligent and knew exactly what you wanted her to do. The hairs on her back got up and I knew then she was aware of another person's presence. She crossed into another field and then went up a ditch with steep Broom covered banks to it. We went for about two hundred yards chasing after her and all of a sudden she jumped up the bank and went under a large patch of the Broom. Almost in the same movement she came out with her tail between her legs and growling over her shoulder. At the other end of the Broom patch out rolled the guy and after a short chase I caught hold of him. He came quite quietly and after getting transport he was taken to the police station.

When Jewel was still a pup Marjory told me a white linen table cloth was missing. At first she thought I had taken it in off the washing line but when I assured her I had not, suspicion then fell on the dog. The garden, kennel and every other possible place was searched but there was no trace of it. It was far too big for her to have eaten it so the mystery went on for weeks. Then one day I noticed in a puddle where I had lifted early potatoes a rather off white piece of something sticking out of the soil. No it can't be I thought, but yes it was the table cloth, buried all that time in the red clay soil that the Howe of the Mearns is noted for. It could have stayed there for all the use it was. In spite of all the washing and bleaching it was never white again and ended up as dusters.

Jewel got her Kennel Club prefix name Sauchieburn from the small district around the hotel of that name in the Fettercairn beat. The building itself was the old farmhouse. It was run by the two farming brothers and their elderly mother Mrs Watson. I paid my first visit to it after about a couple of months of arrival at Fettercairn and what a surprise I got. It was a Saturday night and about half an hour after closing time. The place was packed. The back door was the main entrance and it took you directly into the public bar as it was called but there was not an actual bar as such in it. Most people sat round a very large pine table or on other odd chairs or just stood about wherever there was space. All drinks were brought through from the kitchen. The sitting room was what at one time had been a large bedroom upstairs and the furnishings were as scant and not un-similar to the bar downstairs

On entry I greeted everyone including the brothers' and walked through to the kitchen and sat down to talk to their mother. Old as she was she was still the licensee and a very interesting person to chat to. The brothers' panicked a little bit not knowing what I was going to say about all the people still drinking in the place. After they all left we continued to chat to get to know one another. It was not an establishment I needed to visit very often and by the time I left Mrs Watson's health deteriorated to the extent her conversation made no sense whatsoever but still knew I was the bobby and they insisted I would go through and talk to her. I have not been in it since but I understand it has all been modernised and extended.

Near to the Sauchieburn Hotel was the village of Luthermuir and each year in the playing field they held a marquee dance to raise funds. Along with another officer I was on duty at one of them when fighting broke out between two guys. Both of them were arrested and taken out to the police van. The first one went into the back of the van voluntarily but the other got quite stroppy and made a run for it. I chased him down the street for some distance until he jumped over a series of garden fences with me still on his heels and confident that I would get hold of him again sooner rather than later. My luck ran out when I took a nose dive into a strawberry plot and the buttons on my uniform jacket got caught up in some herring fishing net that was covering them. It took some time to extricate myself without ripping the buttons off and when I did I thought there was not much point in continuing with the chase. On returning to the van the other officer and I decided to let our prisoner in the van go and to kick his arse up the road. He had no complaint with this course of action.

A few months later I was in Strathcathro Hospital for a cartilage operation and in the course of conversation with a nurse who knew I was in the Police at Fettercairn decided to relate this story about her boyfriend who escaped from the police by running through some gardens. He could never understand why the policeman had not followed him over a low wall into a builder's yard with no easy means of escape. She was a bit gobsmacked when I told her I was the officer concerned but had to laugh about the strawberry net. I teased her about arresting the boyfriend when I was well enough and back on duty but saw the funny side of it instead.

Like many of the one man stations that closed in the force area Fettercairn and Auchenblae fell to the axe as well. Residents on my beat still regarded me as their local bobby even although I was working out of Laurencekirk police station. They did not want to travel there with their problems and speak to officers they did not know. They were loyal to me and I could not turn them away and this upset the Sergeant at Laurencekirk, resulting in me being transferred to Peterhead.

It was just before our move to Peterhead that Mrs Garvie reported her husband Max missing and all enquiries relating to it were being made by the Sergeant from Laurencekirk. Intensive searches had been going on for sometime in the Fettercairn/Auchenblae areas for a body. We went off from Peterhead on holiday after that and on our way stopped overnight at Fettercairn to visit the annual Agricultural Show. I met in with Fred Walker and soon the conversation got round to the Garvie mystery. It stuck in my mind what he said about it, and to me it made a lot of sense as well. Fred's opinion was that the police were searching in all the wrong places. Tavendale, who Mrs Garvie was having an affair with, came from St Cyrus and was born and brought up there. He was unfamiliar with the surroundings of West Cairnbeg whereas he would have intimate knowledge of every hiding hole in the vicinity of the hotel where he lived. How true it turned out to be.

I went fishing and shooting with Max and thought I knew him quite well but obviously I did not. I knew he liked a good time and was a man for the women but what I was not aware of was that a group of them rented a cottage at Tough near Alford where they went for wife swapping parties and other kinky goings on. Mrs Garvie and Tavendale were subsequently convicted of charges in connection with Max's murder having shot him with a .22 rifle whilst he was asleep in bed and hid the remains in a culvert near to the hotel at St Cyrus. By coincidence not that many years ago I bought a Landrover Discovery which had the registration number J 2 WCF (West Cairnbeg Farm) and previously owned by Max's son.

Our neighbours at Peterhead were Colin and Loraine Donald. We lived in a police houses in Golf Road overlooking the mouth of the River Ugie and the Golf course beyond. It was November and sleet was falling that day. Loraine had a big coal fire on for us and the kettle was on the boil. She also put old newspapers down on the floor so that the removal men would not make too much mess. They were excellent neighbours and were to become long lasting friends. Many an evening we would play whist or scrabble in one or other of our houses. A tap on the adjoining living room wall was all that was needed to signal that they were ready for a game. We would do likewise. Loraine and I were regarded as card cheats and that was why we won so often. Marjory would dispute the "Always winning bit." Throughout our life we have been fortunate to have had excellent neighbours and it is no exception here at Dalriada. Hamish, Meg and family are great so what more could you wish for.

One of the first jobs I had to do on arrival at Peterhead was to make a kennel and run for Jewel and her daughter Gem. Gem was a good enough retriever but never reached the standard that Jewel attained. I ran Jewel in several trials and won a couple of prizes. I was at a trial with Jewel at Balmoral Estate and Her Majesty the Queen came out to watch the dogs running. Bill Meldrum, her own handler was there to run dogs from Sandringham for her. I saw Her Majesty in a different light that day. It was pouring rain and she was dressed in waterproofs, complete with wellies and so informal. She mingled with everyone and when progress was slow she sat down in the heather and talked to whoever happened to be nearest to her, so different for her, being away from all the pomp at official engagements. At the end of the day she presented the prizes. Unfortunately I was not amongst the winners but Frank was.

To amuse the children I would set out a line of shoes, one belonging to each of them. I would hold the corresponding shoes and let Jewel have a sniff of each one in turn and then ask her to retrieve the matching one from the row. She got it correct every time. I was fishing the Lyn Martin one very wet night and I thought I got a glimpse of somebody up the bank in the field. I looked at Jewel and the hairs on her back were standing on end. I said to her, "Who is it?" and off she went. When I climbed up the bank I saw that the person was a local farm worker and that he was standing with his back to the fence with his arms up and calling to me that he would wait. Jewel stood there barking at him. The man had a fishing rod with him and it was obvious that he was down for a sly cast on the river thinking that nobody would be about because of the stormy night. I asked him if he knew who I was. He replied, "The Laird." I then mischievously said to him, "If I catch you here again I will get the police to you" and off he went. I told Bert when I next saw him and he was not that amused. He knew the farm worker personally and knew he was only out for a fish for the pot, something I had done so often myself. He described me as a rotten so and so. I did not feel too bad about it because Bert himself called me to the river when he caught two guys fishing without permission. They had hitched a lift up on a lorry from Glasgow and when subsequently charge with the offence it transpired that they had previous convictions for the same thing elsewhere.

Frank Low told Marjory years before that I would never in a lifetime have another dog like Jewel and how true it turned out to be. Another comment made by Frank about Jewel was at a shoot at The Burn. They were sitting in the barn when his under-keeper asked him if he had heard about the bra retrieve the bobby's dog had the previous day. Apparently, without lifting his head from eating his sandwiches he replied, "I've told you all before, buy the right material and you can't go wrong." The remark related to a retrieve that Jewel had at eleven months old when she crossed the Lyn Martin, went up a bramble covered bank, over a stock fence and took back a cock pheasant from a field of turnips. Mr Kennoway did not want me to put the dog in the river in the first place but later congratulated me on the fine piece of dog work and then to my embarrassment poured me out a glass of Glenfiddich whisky. What made matters worse was that no one else got a dram. Roarin Rab posed for an advertisement for Glenfiddich whisky and the distillery gave him a case each year for life. Rab in turn sold on the whisky to Mr Kennoway.

CHAPTER 38

PETERHEAD DAYS

My work for the dogs at Peterhead was pretty limited. On a Saturday I went rough shooting with Alastair Gordon and some other friends but game was sparse in those parts. I also had the odd outing to the Loch of Strathbeg for a shot at the geese and ducks but now that loch is a nature reserve. Tom Ferguson who I met at the dog trials was keeper to Captain Curzen at Saplinbrae near Minlaw. I went beating for Tom there and also at Esslemont Castle when Tom went to work for Captain Wolridge-Gordon. At Esslemont the Captain always wore the kilt in true Scott fashion. Perhaps it may have been better for him if he hadn't. After one pheasant drive when crossing a fence with barbed wire on the top he embarrassingly got his you know what caught up in it. He had plenty of female volunteers to help but he was having none of that.

When Eric Kite and I came up from London Tom always asked us to his keepers shoot at Esslemont. The party was divided into two teams. I was with Tom whilst Eric went with the Captain. It was supposed to be "cocks only" but the very first bird of the day was a hen pheasant that I shot. Tom placed me in a very narrow gap among fir trees and when I said to him I would have no chance of seeing what was coming he said, "Just listen for them and let fire." My neighbour was a young keeper with a Labrador that took the bird back to him. He could not get rid of it quick enough in case he got blamed for shooting it.

At lunch time everyone was taken into the large dining room in the castle and wined and dined to the highest standard and with all the staff looking after us. Some discussion arose as to why our team did not shoot any birds in the drive immediately before lunch. Without thinking I said they were all hens. Well if I did, time was right for the other team to make the most of the hen I shot and I was told in not so polite language that I did not know the difference between a cock and a hen and it would be better if I just shut up. Most of the regular guys, keepers and beaters, said the lunch to them was the highlight of the day and I was inclined to agree with them. It was the Captain who first introduced me to the "Rusty Nail".

Pranks seemed to follow me. At Saplinbrae, Captain Curzon at lunch time always came in to give the beaters a drink. This day he poured out a very generous glass of Vat 69 whisky to everyone. At least that is what it said on the bottle. Some had it neat, others had water with it and I opted for lemonade. A cry got up from the old hands taking it neat to ask, "What the hell is this?" Cold tea was what he poured into the glasses. Tom's wife, who was in on the act, then brought in another bottle, placed it on the table and told everyone to help themselves. We all had a good laugh about it and at later shoots the Captain was always challenged when he came in with the bottle whether it was the real McKay or not.

Across the mouth of the River Ugie there were rabbits amongst the sand dunes and whins, and when exercising my dogs I would take them across to the top of the steep bank by the old fishing bothy and send them over the river for a run around. I had an audience of retired fishermen from the local fleet, who sat on a bench nearby putting the world to right. When swimming, the dogs were always side by side and not one nose further forward than the other. I would whistle to them to turn back and each of them did it outwards from the other and when I sent them on again they would take up their original positions. Sometimes I would send them out in the sea from one sandbank to another to scare off the seagulls without letting them chase the birds. When it was time for them to go back to their kennel all I had to say was, "Bed" and they would cross the road, go up a side street and enter the kennel a back way. I took a short cut through the front garden which amused the fishermen no end.

In Peterhead I was tempted by a neighbour into trying out another form of fishing. He was the owner/ skipper of a forty foot sea going vessel known locally as a day tripper. Him and his crew of two would leave Peterhead Harbour at 3am and go roughly to about 12 miles off shore, fishing for haddock, cod, whiting, and other species. The skipper put me off from joining them on several occasions because of a bad weather forecast. Eventually I made up my mind that I was going come what may. I enquired about taking sandwiches or any other type of food with me but I was assured there would be plenty on board. We had not gone very far out of the harbour when the skipper told me that all the bacon, egg and sausages and other food had been stolen the night before but not to worry, there was plenty tea and biscuits to keep us going. I was never a good seafaring person so perhaps not having hot food during the trip was a blessing in disguise. I was fine until I went below deck into the small galley and the diesel fumes then got to me.

I experienced the same affect when I went out with colleagues on a sea fishing trip off Hastings in the English Channel. For line fishing it was not a very eventful day with little or no fish caught. A friend and I decided not to go home empty handed so between us we bought a box of haddock when we came ashore. A little laugh I had with Marjory about this trip was when she asked if there were toilets aboard. I said, "No there was not." So she questioned what the only female member of the party did about it. I told her two of the guys just held her up and she did it over the side of the boat just like the rest of us.

More successful fishing trips I went on were out of Kinlochbervie with a party of local tradesmen where we all had a good catch for the day. The skipper new the waters well and took us over some very good shoals. I treated two of our nephews, Andrew and Duncan Shepherd from Lincolnshire to line fishing for mackerel from a small boat out off Portmahomack. Again the skipper was excellent and we all got a good catch. The treat of the day was when the skipper took the first few fish caught down to the galley and filleted and fried them in oatmeal. By far the best mackerel we ever tasted.

Andrew and Duncan came up from Bourne to Gruinard most summers for a holiday and spent most of it either fishing or out shooting rabbits. One evening when they were shooting from the van they got stopped by the police and it took a lot of explaining to do after giving the officer their names and addresses. All was well after I confirmed that they were staying on holiday with Marjory and I and had my permission but if that was today they would most likely have found themselves handcuffed and taken to the station. I had an old pickup truck that I used on the estate for taking home firewood. Neither of them was old enough to be driving but I let them play about with it. Duncan came into the house one day to say that they had a problem and could I go out and help them. "It will not be a problem to you" he kept saying. He took me along to the Dutch barn where the pickup was jammed against one of the brick built pillars. I could see from the damage to the door that they had been trying to free it but was unsuccessful. I showed them by putting the vehicle in reverse and a different lock on the steering wheel it would come away quite easily. That done I asked what they had been doing and they told me they had been trying to drive in and out between the pillars. I then noticed that the opposite wing was dented to be told that they had hit the corner of another barn. I left the pair of them to repair the vehicle the best way they could and I was surprised how good a job they made of it, including the mixing of old paint to get a half decent match. I knew the vehicle was going to be scrapped but it was a good little exercise for them.

Because of my job I got very interested in the theft of food stuffs from the fishing boat at Peterhead and made up my mind to find out as much as possible who the culprit was, I was aware of several other thefts and on chatting to the skipper it was obvious that it was an ongoing thing. Before it became common knowledge among the fishermen some of the seine netters had set off to sea for a week or more and had to go in to places like Wick to replenish their larder, causing delays and extra expense in getting to the fishing grounds. The skipper told me that the suspect was a guy sleeping rough on a small boat in another part of the harbour. We had a very good trip, plenty of haddock and some cod but by 2pm the sea did turn very choppy. The waves came crashing over the bow, then split to go either side of the small wheel house. I stood behind it grasping on to a hand rail on either side of the door trying to judge whether to be further over to one side or the other. On occasions the boat would keel over to one side or the other and the water would slosh across the deck and all this time the two crew members would carry on without a care in the world gutting the catch and putting them in appropriate boxes ready for the market.

The chatter and jargon over the ship's radio that day intrigued me. It was practically none stop from the time we left the harbour until we got back in. They all got to know about the missing food so you can imagine the wise cracks, "Perhaps the bobby will do something about it this time since he has had to go without his breakfast." The skipper wanted to show me some rock formation on the way home along the coastline known as the "Boulers of Buchan". I was taken in between a huge rock and the cliffs, a bit too close for comfort as far as I was concerned but they obviously felt safe in doing it. On the radio, I could hear another skipper saying, "Are you trying to frighten the bobby." Another said, "Make sure he does not jump overboard and swim for the shore," and so on. Good craik as far as I was concerned.

Before entering the harbour on our way home the skipper took the boat alongside the break water wall built by the prisoners from Peterhead Prison who had to do hard labour as part of their punishment. Huge slabs of granite rock in regular rectangular shapes which they quarried at Stirling Hill was taken by rail to the site. Each piece would have weighed anything up to ten tons but the power of the waves pounding against the wall lifted several out at different heights along its length and were lost into the depths of the sea. The wall across the bay was to provide a refuge for boats to come in and shelter from storms in the North Sea. During one of such storms I was on duty when the maroons were fired to call out the lifeboat crew. When this happened a large crowd gathered near the harbour and we watched a Danish fleet of fishing boats trying to come in. They were literally bobbing about like corks, one minute on the top of the waves and then disappear into the troughs with even the top of their masts going out of sight. It seemed ages before you got sight of them again and each time everyone including the coastguard thought that they had disappeared for good. The lifeboat was launched expecting the worst but all of the fleet made it into the safety of the bay. I think it was said that the lifeboat had to go two miles further out to sea before the crew felt it safe to turn around. On an "open day" at the Lifeboat Station visitors if they wished could be taken for a short trip in the bay. Albert Davey went on one of them but without thinking took a position up front at the bow of the boat. When the boat went down the slipway and hit the water pretty hard the wave not only drenching Albert but sent him flying as well. Colleagues said, "It could only happen to Albert." My first night duty there Albert would show me round the property that had to be checked each night including the academy. Because there were a lot of drains dug up around the place he said, "Just follow me but be careful." The next hello Albert was stretched out face down in the bottom of one of the trenches.

All the boats came back to the fish market about the same time and the catches sold soon afterwards. Fish from the day trippers, because of their freshness, were in great demand by the smaller merchants. One in particular, known as "Killer" had his premises about fifty yards up a narrow lane from the harbour and not much bigger that a good sized hen-house, but he knew how to smoke haddock. No artificial dies, only the smoke from oak wood shavings. If you went in to buy fish from him they came straight off the hook and you asked for two shillings or half a crown's worth rather than by weight. You always got good value for money. To the shops he sold them in special card-board boxes, and if you wanted one of them, as I sometimes did for friends like Frank it cost ten shillings or fifty pence in today's money.

It was not often that we needed to buy fish. We got so much of it straight from the boats as they were landing. You only needed to show your face there and one or more of the skippers would be wanting to give you a fry as they called it. A fry to them was a third of a creel of un-filleted haddock which took two of you to carry it up the street. It was very kind of them but you can get too much of a good thing. One late night a fishing boat from Burghead was tying up at the pier and I stood up to watch them. I got chatting to the owner/skipper who wanted to know where they could go for a meal. He called down to a deck hand to bring a fry up to the bobby. I did not catch what the reply was but the skipper said, "That's what I mean. Bring it up." When I told him that we got plenty fish of the local boats he said, "I bet not like the one I'm going to give you." Up came this enormous halibut which I struggled on my own to carry up to the Police Station. I think, probably about twenty people in all had several steaks from it.

One fry of fish I had no wish to even think about was when Sergeant Florence and I went to a house in Peterhead in search of a man wanted on theft charges. This house was occupied by a couple of men who were down and out and often found lying about the streets suffering from the effects drinking mentholated spirits and other concoctions. The door was open so we just marched in and searched the place. The two alcoholics were stretched out in another world and we had to waken one of them to enquire about the guy we were looking for. In a drunken stupor he said, "Just a minute." He then walked over to a butler sink with about a dozen un- filleted haddock in it and urinated over them. We were both convinced that when they sobered up the fish would have been eaten for supper.

Day or night the harbour and its activities always fascinated me. There was one place if you were very quiet and shone your torch on the water you would see a seal slip off its sleeping berth, an old fishing box and some flotsam. It remained in the harbour as long as I can remember feeding on spillage from fish landings. A satisfying night for me was when I saw a lone man coming across the bridge from the "Queeny" a name given to a particular part of the harbour. He was carrying the usual white pillow slip which fishermen used for taking their laundry to and from the boats. I knew that a boat had not tied up so I challenged him as to who he was and what he had in the slip. It transpired the pillow slip was full of items and food he had stolen from a boat. When the boat he was sleeping rough on was searched I found lots of stolen items. This piece of news soon went round the fishermen quickly and the good natured banter started again. "See what a bobby can do when he has to go without breakfast etc". I lapped it up, not only was it good for the crime clear up figures, but also for good public relations. With Buckie or Peterhead fishermen you were either in or out with them and often I got good information from them. It was a bit of an ego boost to me when the Inspector remarked about the success I had in clearing up outstanding crimes. I put a lot of it down to luck but in any case there was a lot of self satisfaction to it.

A young probationer and I were on duty one night when a guy known as "Snakey" Geddes came in and reported that he had been assaulted. I was dubious of this because he was known to be a bit of a karate man. I told him before accepting his allegation I would go and see the other party. He did not want me to do that which made me even more suspicious. However, on our arrival at the other man's house, Snakey was waiting for us having taken a taxi to get to the house first and tried to prevent me from getting to the door. When I told him I was arresting him for obstructing a police officer he said, "You and whose army?" It ended up with the two of us having a bundle on the pavement with me trying to put handcuffs on him. I got one on before he pulled off my whistle and chain and whacked me round the face with it causing me to lose my grip on him. We both got to our feet and he took up a karate position with the handcuffs dangling from one wrist and was making various threats at me. I called to the probationer who was terrified of what was going on and standing back about twenty or more yards for his baton. He threw it along the pavement and armed with this I moved in to get to grips a second time with "Snakey" but he ran off down to the sea wall where he jumped down on to the beach and swam out to some rocks. I often wondered if that young officer ever made a career of it. He certainly had no "bottle" for what went on that night.

From there he continued to shout abuse until he disappeared from view because of the incoming tide. At first we thought he had drowned and a crowd gathered on the seafront and a search was set up along the beach, but then an arm kept flicking up by the waves so we knew he was still there but did not know if he was dead or alive. My self and another man who knew him went out almost waist deep towards him on a ledge of rocks. We kept throwing a rope as a lifeline to him but he would not take hold of it. We ourselves were in danger from the incoming tide and gave him one more chance to grasp it. He did but first we had to promise not to touch him. He was taken by ambulance to the local hospital but because of his violence in Casualty they discharged him only to assault me a second time. After spending a night in the clanger the Sheriff sent him to Craiginches Prison as a guest of the government for six months.

It never ceased to amaze me how people could turn against you even when you were doing them a favour. I remember them telling us at training school if two Paddies are knocking six bells of shit out of one another to leave them until they were finished because both of them will set about you instead. I was on duty outside West Ham Football ground when a man in his early twenties during a fight was pushed backwards through a plate glass shop window. A large triangular shaped piece of glass fell from above him and embedded in the front of his thigh. To stem the severe bleeding I first had to remove the shard and apply pressure to the wound until the ambulance arrived. The crew took over but before they took him away for some reason or other the victim decided that I deserved a smack in the face. Whether or not he thought I was responsible for him going through the window I don't know but I awarded him with a visit to the Magistrates Court for his troubles.

The TA Sergeant from Peterhead decided to join the police and him and I were out on patrol quite a lot. One morning he kept asking me to get him a case to report when I noticed Marjory driving up the street towards us. I asked him to get out on the street and stop that car as there would be something wrong with it. I stood back on the pavement and watched Marjory's face change from concern to a smile and back again. It then dawned on the young officer that all was not quite right and when he turned round to look at me he saw that I was having a good laugh. Afterwards he said he should have carried on until he found something wrong.

Another day the same officer and I were chasing up drivers who were wrongly parked in the town centre, something we got lots of complaints about. When they got their warning I would say to them that the two pound fine was better off in their pockets than in the courts. In my absence this officer decided to adopt the same style but one motorist before driving off told him he would be the better judge of that and introduced himself as the procurator fiscal. Had it been me he said it to I would certainly have booked him.

I often played practical jokes on Marjory and following an accident she was involved in where another driver ran into the back of her car I got the reporting officer to write out a fictitious witness summons for her to attend court. I was night duty at the time and the officer came to the house and delivered it by hand. I was not there at the time and did not have the opportunity in the morning before she went off to work to tell her it was a joke. She told everyone she knew about it and asked for a day off work. I was not the most popular guy when she found out it was a hoax. At the time of the accident I went to the scene to make sure her and the girls were alright. Marjory at first did not realise that the car had actually hit hers. She thought she had just stalled the engine but Catriona said, "Mummy that car has hit us." Then a man on the street corner said to her, "Ye better hurry lassie he's done a runner." He was referring to the other driver who decamped leaving a Morris Minor with a damaged front and water streaming from the radiator. I got speaking to a villain who I had previous dealings with and he told me who the guy was. He had seen him a short time earlier trying to get into a parked Jaguar. I told them at the office and another policeman picked him up after a stolen Mini crashed through a wall on the outskirts of Peterhead.

In one of our garden magpies use to frequent a particular laurel bush and I was convinced that they would nest in it. I said this to Marjory and she just accepted what I said. A week or so later I was out on patrol and saw a notice for geese eggs for sale. We used to have geese at home so I stopped and bought a couple. When I showed them to Marjory I said to her that I was sure the magpies were going to nest and this was their eggs. For a few seconds it never dawned on her that I was stating the ridiculous. When I kept hens myself I was given what was thought to be china nesting eggs. I duly put some of them in the hen's nesting boxes but when they went missing I thought the rats had gone off with them. They were not china eggs at all but very old iced chocolate eggs and where did they go? They were brown sticky messes stuck to the hens' rear ends. Mischievously I put one in the bowl of eggs in the house for it to be boiled up in a similar mess.

CHAPTER 39

ITCHY FEET AGAIN AND A STEP INTO THE UNKNOWN

Leading up to the early part of 1969 with two of family things got pretty tight financially. Police pay seemed to be worth less then than in previous years and Marjory had to take part-time cleaning work and looking after a dentist and schoolteacher's children to make ends meet. Without those extra funds coming in it would have been very hard going. For instance if we were in Aberdeen for any reason we had to look in our pocket to see if we could afford a meal out.

I got unsettled and applied for two sub-postmaster jobs, one in Muir of Ord and the other in Conon Bridge. I rang Miss MacGregor, the Muir of Ord post mistress on the Sunday evening to make an appointment for the following morning. She abruptly told me that she did not talk business on a Sunday and put the phone down on me. My cousin Alastair was up from London on holiday with us at the time and after an early morning breakfast of fried cutlets of freshly caught salmon we set off to call on Miss MacGregor who by this time I realised must belong to the Free Church of Scotland. Not that I have any qualms about a person's religion, race, colour or creed. Our visit to some extent was an amusing one. As soon as we entered the Post Office and introduced ourselves to the young counter assistant she immediately demanded a pay rise if I was to be the successful applicant. She went on a bit about not having a rise for years. Talk about taking the bull by the horns.

When we met Miss MacGregor she told us that whoever got the post would have to purchase the house as part of the deal. On showing us around we noticed a bible on just about every work surface there was. I knew I could not afford the money expected so we looked about for alternative premises. We found a vacant shop with a flat above it. There was plenty of space for a separate sorting office and parking for official vans. When I spoke to the owner of this property we came to a provisional agreement about renting it. We even made a quick call on the selling solicitors to have a note of interest recorded before going on to Gruinard to see my parents.

I went for an interview with the Post Master in Inverness but a couple of weeks later he wrote to me to say I had been unsuccessful. One of the references I had to send with my application was from Inspector MacAulay who had retired from the force and was working as a security officer at a distillery. When I called to see him I got a great welcome and he was only delighted to oblige. The sub post master from Conon Bridge got the job. His vacancy and property was then advertised and I went through the same rigmarole again. When shaking hands with me the Post Master in Inverness before leaving told me I had been unsuccessful again but third time lucky. He also said to me that I should go south where salaries were much higher and, "Yes" I said, "And get a gun stuck in your face." I went home rather disappointed and that same night while on night duty I wrote the Commissioner of the Metropolitan Police in London (the Met.) about transferring to his force. I got a nice letter back, rather formal, setting out answers to all my queries and inviting me for an interview if I was still interested. I never told Marjory what I had done until later. She agreed to go and I continued with my application and went for an appointment. I was accepted and a transfer date was agreed.

I sold Gem to a local fisherman who went shooting on a cousin's farm at Udny. He also bought my car. Jewel went to the owner of a grouse moor near Newtonmore and who also had an estate in Gloucestershire where Jewel would be in her element at the pheasants. Everyone was taken by surprise when they heard of our plans to go south, not least Irvine and Helen Barclay from Auchenblae. A year or so previous Irvine rung me at Fettercairn and suggested we both should transfer to the Met. I said, "No way, you must be off your so and so rocker." And that was that. Irvine on hearing of our plans rung me up and said, "Who is off his so and so rocker now?"

I was allocated a police flat opposite the 'bus station on Greengate Street, Plaistow. I could not afford the expense of going down to see it and just accepted it. We were on the bread line anyway even after selling our dogs, car and surplus furniture. I was in the Royal Air Force with a guy from Aberdeen who set up his own furniture removal business, so I contacted him about moving us. We agreed a cheaper than normal price provided I drove the van down to London so that his driver would be well rested and within the legal driving hours for coming back on his own. The journey went without a hitch but on arrival at the flat we could not get a key for it. We broke a glass panel in the door and got in that way. To put it mildly the place was filthy dirty. Marjory and the girls were to join me two days later by train. I spent that time scrubbing and cleaning until my fingers were red raw. When Marjory came in and had a look about she said she was going to do one of two things, either catch the next train home or go to bed. I suggested she went to bed which she did. There we were in a strange place with no friendly neighbours and only twelve pounds in our pockets between us. Another down-side to the flat but we learned to live with it was the noise from the very busy London Transport 'bus depot. When winter came it was even worse with the drivers revving up the engines at five and six in the morning to get their windscreens defrosted.

When the first Hogmanay arrived we decided to visit one couple that we sort of got to know and I took a bottle of whisky in with me. We had a few drinks including a couple from my bottle but when we got up to leave I did not get the chance to take my bottle with me. The guy said, "Thanks for the bottle," so I just left it on the table. Today whisky and other drinks flow like water with a Hogmanay any night. When we were in Sgodachail I remember my Dad and others talking about how scarce it was and how difficult it was to get a bottle for the New Year. There were no "Off Licences" then and you could only buy it from the pub. Dad came home one night and Mam asked him if he managed to get one. He said, "Yes" and produced a bottle of White Horse from his raincoat pocket. Most people I have spoken to including my doctor have never heard of anyone being allergic to alcohol but almost ten years ago I had to give up my favourite tipple because of tummy upsets and the spoiling of many a good meal. Sherry in trifle and wine in a sauce are only two of the things I have to look out for. Some medical dressings will cause blistering of the skin. I do not miss having a dram but going back to my father buying a bottle the pubs closed at 9pm which changed later to 10pm. Now you can get a drink somewhere at anytime day or night. In London coming off duty at 6am some pubs were open then where you could go for a drink but I never did.

On Monday morning I was off to Hendon Police College to start a thirteen week training course. It made no difference that I had twelve and a half years previous police experience. The same applied to driving police vehicles. I had to sit my first test in a Morris Minor panda car then on the van or the blackmaria as it was called, and finally did an advanced driving course. My first visit back to the flat was two weeks later when I took my first pay home to Marjory and was she not glad to see it. I enjoyed the training and got on very well with the younger entrants. Yes they poked fun at "Poor old Jock" as they often referred to me as, but I could hold my own with them even on compulsory sports day. Fitness was something I did not lack.

At the same time as I transferred to the Met. about twelve officers came down from Ross-shire. This was a huge loss to such a small force with only about a hundred and twenty in it prompting the Chief Constable to write to the Commissioner asking him to put a stop to it. A reply came back that regulations permitted it and as long as they were suitable he had no intentions of doing so. My brother in law Eric came down to stay with us for a few days and I arranged for him to meet all the north guys for a drink at a pub in Fleet Street. I cannot remember the name but it was very much Scottish orientated and used in the day time by many of the journalists. After getting sloshed we all got on the underground to go to a dance in the Police single men's accommodation at Kennington. A Section House it was called and when I think back on it and Eric would have agreed we should all have been sectioned that night. On the way the whisky bottle was being passed around and the other passengers in the carriage entertained with a good selection of Scottish songs which they all enjoyed. At the dance they were on a high and did the Strip the Willow and Eightsome Reel to music for the twist and other pop stuff. The night ended with us missing our train out to Plaistow and having to walk home in torrential rain. Marjory thought we had been jumping about in the fountains at Trafalgar Square.

At the end of the course we got our postings and I was sent to Bow Road right in the heart of the east end but quite close to Plaistow. Tibbs country, where their gun battles were fought with the Richardson gang from South London to take control of the protection rackets. They were very much into boxing and had their gym about a hundred yards from the police station. Traces of their shootings were still evident at the doorways to some of the pubs. The only dealings I had with any of them was after I went to Plaistow. I arrested one of the younger brothers for theft. It took me some time to settle into the way the Met. worked but guys like

Alan Brooks, Charlie Given and later on Malcolm Campbell were very good to me and went to great lengths to help me. Little blighters about seven, eight or nine years old would give false names and addresses without blinking an eyelid. Something I never came across in Scotland and one had to be in constant touch by radio to have the voters roll checked to see if parents or older members of the family lived at the addresses.

It was compulsory to work three out of eight rest days in a month, a London allowance towards the higher cost of living and other voluntary overtime such as at football matches, demonstrations and marches boosted my pay in a big way. I arrived there just after the Grovener Square riots but was very much in the thick of it at the National Front demonstrations at Southall where Blair Peach, a demonstrator lost his life. Looking at the aftermath that day before going home it was surprising that no more lives were lost. On one side of the road there was a building site for new houses and on the other a public park. Officers lined along the front of the new houses had tins of paint poured over them and just about everyone within distance was pelted with bricks and other building materials. Across the road small trees were up-rooted, fences torn down and used as ammunition or weapon against the police but in the process many of their own kind fell victim to their behaviour. I can only describe it as a scene from a battle field.

Although our earnings increased our standard of living did not so we were able to save a lot of money, something that was impossible to do in Scotland. From the outset we had made up our minds to buy our own house which we were permitted to do and which was one of the attractions of going to the Met. Catriona had been to school in Fettercairn before we moved south and had got off to a very good start with her education. It was Plaistow Primary she first went to which had a very high ratio of black children of various ethnic origins who could not speak English, far less read or write it. Poor Catriona, even at her tender years, found herself day after day having to write out lots of word or sentences, for the other children to learn from. We saw this, not un-similar, to a pupil getting a hundred lines to write as punishment.

Marjory, for days, tramped the streets looking for a better school but in that part of the East End there was very little to choose between them. My cousin Alastair suggested we should consider a Church of England school. The nearest one was in Barking, Essex. Marjory got good reports about this one and she set about to get Catriona and Fiona into it. Fiona was due to begin school after the summer holidays so we made this the target date. We had a hard fight on our hands, the headmaster, the vicar and the education officer were all approached in different ways but none of them would make up their minds, each saying it was down to the other. Only days before the new term started we still did not know if they were to get a place or not. Just by chance on visiting the school in the hope of meeting the headmaster we found that he was still on holiday and apart from the caretaker there would be nobody else there either until the Monday morning. When our predicament was explained to the caretaker, he of all people threw a glimmer of hope when he said to bring them along to the school on the Monday morning. Both girls were admitted, did very well and came home with good reports. Marjory got very much involved, not only with the school but also with the church, typing their magazine on a monthly basis and much more and because of that we got to know the vicar and the curates very well. Depending on which shift I was on they would for most find me crashed out on the couch and sound asleep which became a bit of a joke with them.

CHAPTER 40

BUYING OUR FIRST HOUSE.

Not only were you permitted to buy your own house but encouraged to do so and got a very good rental allowance towards it. The Met. was moving away from a free house policy. The amount you got was based on the value of the property for what it could be rented out at. With the girls both settled into school, Barking was our obvious choice. We had saved enough money for a deposit on a house and also for the solicitor's fees. Gazumping was rife at the time because of the demand in a rising market and we were let down several time by sellers accepting higher offers.

Eventually we bought a lovely big terraced house just out of the centre of Barking within walking distance from the school, shops and railway station, both underground and mainline. To begin with we thought we had gone over our budget but soon afterwards the rent allowance went up considerably to offset the rise in house prices. It was definitely the start of the first property boom and I'm sure, had we not bought at the time we did, we would have struggled to get on to the property ladder at all. However, with both Catriona and Fiona at School, Marjory was able to take on secretarial work throughout the remainder of our stay in London. Over and above saving for the house deposit etc we were able to have three holidays to Scotland in our first year. Had we stayed in the same old rut in Scotland we could not have done any of it so one can see why we had no regrets at having gone down there.

It was in this house I tried my hand at D.I.Y. (Do it Your Self) for the first time. Whoever fitted the kitchen worktop did not notch it where it passed a conduit pipe coming down the wall and the gap got wider the further it went. When I suggested cutting a channel in the wall for the pipe and fitting the worktop properly Marjory was not too keen on this because I had never done anything like it before. After she went to bed I made a start and that was the beginning of much more. She even bought me a Readers Digest book explaining how most things should be done. I taught myself how to rewire the house and get rid of the lead covered cables. I fitted a modern type consumer unit and the night I decided to connect it up to the mains Marjory deliberately took the girls to the cinema. How about that for confidence?

When I was fitting the the socket boxes for the ring mains Fiona had the school hamster home with her to look after during the school holidays. It went missing for a day or two until I heard noises coming from behind one of the boxes which I had plastered into the wall and yes there it was, a bit hungry but none the worse of its ordeal. We were having a gas fire fitted in a down-stair sitting room which necessitated cutting a channel through the concrete hearth. The hamster went missing again and it never turned up. We learned of its fate from our next door neighbour a few weeks later when he told us that he must have killed it thinking it was a mouse. With a good deal of soot on its coat it was understandable.

They were good neighbours and the kitten I took home from a Bow Road telephone kiosk thought so as well. Two young girls brought the kitten to the station after the parents refused to let them keep it. We took in stray dogs only and after a long chat with them I did not have the heart to send them away. We called it "Hidey" because it kept hiding behind the settee. When we came up to Aberdeen on holiday our neighbours were asked to feed it and to keep an eye on it. They had a key to our house so we did not expect them to take the cat into theirs. However that is what they did and the cat made its home with them. Each morning it would come to our patio doors wanting in and it went straight to the cellar for a look around before going home again. I never saw a cat do it before but when my neighbour threw a rolled up piece of paper along the lawn the cat would go and get it and wait for it to be thrown again. I often watched it hunting the songbirds. The cat would sit below our apple tree and wait for the birds to drop down on to the ground for food. To begin with it would unsuccessfully leap at them but after a while, obviously having studied there get away, it would spring into the air between the bird and the tree and more often than not kill one.

Another job I was doing there that normally would have got me into trouble was it not for our understanding neighbours. I set about to replace all the windows at the front of the house and to complete the job all I had to do was to finish painting the new ones. Lunch time came and leaving the ladder propped against the wall I went in doors for a sandwich or something. I heard this loud noise of breaking glass but did not think much about it because builders across the road were converting a house into two flats and they were forever making a noise throwing things into a skip. Then the door bell rung and there was my neighbour. He said, "I thought it was the cat knocking something over in the front room but it's your ladder." And yes it was, blown over and the end of it through one of his bay windows. Off I went to the allotment and recovered a matching window, came back and changed it for his broken one. A lick of paint and all was well again. On my way home from work when the tradesmen started to remove everything from the house across the road they left a three piece suite in the front garden. Jokingly, but with a straight face I asked them if they had found the money the old lady was supposed to have had but which was never found. It was not long before the suite was ripped to shreds and other items were being retrieved from the skip. When I next spoke to them I said, "Did you find the money then?" "No" was the answer I got. "Well keep looking it will be there somewhere." I said.

The kitchen was very small and I looked several times at the possibility of doing away with an outside toilet to make it bigger. One morning when Marjory was at work I took a hammer and knocked a hole in the brickwork of the adjoining wall. The first brick landed in the frying pan so I thought; now that I have started I might as well carry on and knock it all down. Marjory came home for lunch, something she was not in the way of doing, and was furious with me. I never considered the fact that Granny Hutcheon and Aunt Madgie were arriving the following day. She stormed off leaving me to clean up the mess which I would have done anyway.

I was then promoted to Sergeant and was working long hours very often doubling my wages and more. Still our way of living did not change. The first carpet we bought for the flat at Plaistow was a "roll end." Knowing we were determined to stay there for the shortest possible time the carpet was never cut down to fit the room. This was amusing to Alastair and our Scottish visitors who talked about it in later years. "Prudent" as Gordon Brown would say. Food, clothing and other day to day purchases which Marjory bought at the street markets were cheaper than in Scotland. Travel and entertainment within London was definitely dearer but we were not much into that anyway, only occasionally going up to the West End for a show and usually that was when we had visitors. A few years later because of the trouble on the underground we were allowed to travel free if we were in uniform or produced our warrant cards when a ticket was requested. When younger family members came for a holiday it was more often or not out on boozy nights visiting clubs in the west end or some of the popular pubs with entertainment like "The Grapes"on the Isle of Dogs.

What they were not used to in Aberdeen in those days were men in drag. Some of them really did look the part and could pass themselves off as good looking women. I am not going to mention names but one of the guys this night took a fancy to one and thought his luck was in until I took him aside and advised him of his folly. Another pub one night a lady member thought she would get up on stage to do a bit of dancing only to find herself alongside a stripper. In spite of many taunts to get her clothes off as well she did not. On a pub crawl in the Fulham and Putney area we had another good night. Whilst walking home over Putney Bridge a London 'bus driver going past got an unexpected surprise when a bra was thrown through his window. Not Marjory's I may add. There were other good nights down at Southend for them when the singers took to the stage. Karaoke I think you would call it today.

Our first trip back to Hill of Minnes in Aberdeenshire came up during the August bank holiday weekend while I was still at the training school at Hendon. At that time Marjory's brother Bob was in the Parachute Regiment at Aldershot and he happened to be going home on leave at the same time. Marjory and our two girls travelled up in his car but there was no room for me but since I was quite used to hitch hiking a lift during my Royal Air Force days I thought I would have a go at that. I was a little bit apprehensive about it because it would be overnight. However, the first vehicle I thumbed had three young men in it and as it happened they also were from the police training school. So that was me off to a good start, more so when they were going up the A1 as far as the Middlesborough turning.

The A1 was still the main route to and from Scotland and used by all the long distance lorry drivers. On our way up through England we stopped first for something to eat and then to refuel and each time an Aberdeen lorry heading north went by. We commented, because of its destination and the progress it was making, that it would be a good one to get a lift on. We knew that the driver had not stopped anywhere so we were pretty sure he would do so at the next transport cafe. The first one we came to was close to the Middlesborough turning so I asked to be dropped off at it and sure enough the lorry pulled in behind us.

I approached the driver and asked him if he was going all the way to Aberdeen and he said, "Hopefully yes." I asked him if I could get a lift to Aberdeen as well and he agreed to that. I treated him to his supper and in the course of conversation he asked if I was a policeman. When I told him I was he said, "I thought you were, you have the look of one." It reminded me of the other lorry driver, Roddy McLeod from Bonar. I was only in the police for a matter of weeks and he said more or less the same words. I guessed that this Aberdeen driver would be over his hours if he went on to Aberdeen but I was not going to say anything. When we were about to set off he said, "Now, if I get stopped by the police on the way you tell them that I gave you a lift from a little bit back the road and that is all you know." I got the message and we had a good journey together. We stopped a few time, to check the vehicle, for the driver to have a short sleep and for an early morning trucker's breakfast near Airdrie. The driver said he would take the vehicle only as far as Perth as he did not want it to be seen in Aberdeen by his boss. His overnight stop should have been back down in England so he was well and truly over his permitted driving hours when I first met him. At the transport cafe in Perth, and over a cup of tea he introduced me to a driver from Fraserburgh, who said I could get a lift with him the remainder of the way. He arranged for a lift to Aberdeen for himself on another lorry. I got dropped off at Foveran only a few minutes from Hill of Minnes. A quick phone call and I had a car to pick me up to find that Marjory and the others had arrived only an hour or so earlier.

We did without a car in London for about two years, always hiring one when we needed to do a trip north. The local garage could fix me up with a vehicle of some sort depending how much notice they got. It varied from a van for half a day, a brand new car for a fortnight to a clapped out mini for a holiday arranged at the last minute, lots of knocks, bangs, squeaks and rattles, but it did the job.

CHAPTER 41

PROMOTION TO SERGEANT

Ten per cent of promotions in the Metropolitan Police were by way of a selection board. First you had to apply to be considered, the application being similar to a C. V. today. The Chief Inspector and the Chief Superintendent both recommended me for it and the next step was to go up to New Scotland Yard to be grilled by three Commanders. This was only my second visit to New Scotland Yard. The first was on joining the Met when a group of us had to be "sworn in" but the wording of that has long been forgotten. Only two things stick in my mind about the promotion interview. The first was about the crime fibre in the Scottish force I had transferred from. I did not know what they meant and had to ask them to explain it a bit more. The other was about accelerated promotion or fliers as they were referred to. Sitting in front of three elderly uniformed gentlemen who had come up through the ranks put me at ease with this one and I was confident that my views would be a winner. A few days later the Chief Superintendent came into the canteen to congratulate me on being one of the successful ones. Following the promotion I was transferred to "K" Division and posted to Plaistow, E13.

At Bow Road I did quite a bit of duty as Acting Sergeant, usually as desk sergeant, responsible for the prisoners brought in, all callers for whatever their needs, supervision of the communications room and the general running of the station and often the officer who took the brunt of things when all was not going to plan. It was a very busy station with lots of officers coming and going from different departments such as the C.I.D., Juvenile Bureau and Mounted Branch. Going to Plaistow as a sergeant was not that huge a change for me. By this time I had a good grasp of how the Met. ticked and had a few eye openers on the way. I was surprised to find that discipline was slack and that a good many of the constables were lazy and had to be hounded on a day to day basis. The majority of those who had completed two thirds of their potential service thought little other than the day they would get their pension, a sad outlook.

I was on communications one night manning the switchboard and radio when the flap came down for a call coming in from a police box outside the Earl of Aberdeen Public House. At first I thought it would be one of the officers out on patrol calling in for some reason or other but then I realised it was a member of the public messing about although it was not beyond one of the officers to do that. He kept asking to be put through to a telephone number in Helmsdale. I tried to explain to him in a nice way that I could not do that but when he persisted I had to warn him that I would get a crew from one of the vehicles to come and arrest him. He then recognised my north accent and asked where I was from. When I told him he said he often had a drink in the Lady Ross and went on to say he was the son of a butcher from up Helmsdale way. He had been drinking in the pub across the street and said to his mates he had to 'phone home and they told him to use the police box. I could have dialled the number and put him through but I did not. After a chat about other things he happily put the 'phone down and off he went but what a coincidence.

A personal call came in for an officer who originated from Aberdeen. There were a few of us beside the switchboard and the handset was handed to this particular officer. After listening to the caller for a little time, much to the surprise of the southerners, the Aberdonian said, "Hae a look in the hip pooches o ma aul breeks an yeel maybe find them there." It turned out it was his father in law who was down on holiday and needing the keys to the garden shed. I know I have a funny accent on the phone or radio which I would find difficult to describe and I'm often mistaken for Marjory or other women. Officers in London were not slow to imitate me over the radio when I was sending out messages or replying to ones intended for myself. If it was not me they were making fun of it was someone else. Some of my friends are quite blunt about it and tell me that I talk on the phone like an old woman.

Another night I was Station Sergeant when an off duty Special Patrol Group constable brought in a prisoner for an assault and disturbance on the underground railway. I dealt with it the normal way but noticed the officer kept going back to the cell. On investigation I saw him assault the prisoner which I reported to the Duty Inspector. A month or so later I was at a social evening in a club run by the Thames Dock Police at North Woolwich. I was playing cards with some others when a pint of beer was poured over me. Everyone thought it was an accident but when I saw who did it I knew it was not. It was the same constable that I had the altercation with over the assault. He apologised and offered to buy me a drink but I got the message.

I did nothing about it but news travels fast. Next day the Chief Inspector asked me what had taken place and why it was a deliberate act. After explaining the details to him he told me that he knew the officer who was in charge of the Special Patrol Group and that he would have words with him. A week or so later my Inspector told me that this particular constable had been kicked off the Group and was coming to the Division where I worked. He went on to say that if I wanted it he could be posted to Plaistow and put on my shift so that he would be under my supervision from then on.

I told the Inspector that I would leave that decision entirely to him. Sure enough the guy arrived and it was made clear to me that the senior officers wanted him out of the force. At the beginning of each shift all Constables were inspected for cleanliness, smart in their uniform and to make sure they had all the official kit that they were supposed to carry. This individual was scruffy to say the least, uniform torn and generally dirty. I gave him one hell of a dressing down in front of the others and told him he was not fit to work alongside any of the rest of my men. I told him he would go immediately to the force stores for a new uniform and that he would parade for a full kit inspection the next day. I dared any of the other officers to help him out with anything he had missing. Next day after the inspection I posted him to a short foot patrol between two sets of traffic lights and again dared other officers not to take pity on him. The long and the short of it was, within a month he tendered his resignation and out of the force he went and with good riddance everyone thought.

In conjunction with a drug squad, a raid was planned on a particular property where rowdy parties were regularly held and it was known to be a place where drugs were being supplied. On the bus to this raid someone said a distraction of some kind was to be made and on entering the house each officer had to grab an individual and prevent him from escaping or disposing of any drugs or offensive weapons. As officers jumped from the, bus a dustbin was thrown through a ground floor window which was thought to be the room where the party was going on. Unfortunately it was for next door but at police expense it was repaired next day and no complaint was received. We were never sure for certain but it was thought the occupants were the informers as to what was taking place next door. It was enough though for someone from the party to come outside to see what was going on and allow us a sudden entrance. For my part that night I received my first of many complaints against me. The person I searched alleged that I had stolen cash off him. It was a recognised fact in the Met that if you were a worker you were more likely to get complaints made against you or to be injured whereas those who sat on their arses got neither. Not many weeks later a man was hit over the head with a meat cleaver and a huge raid was made on a seedy night club. When we stormed that place the floor was strewn with knives and other offensive weapons and quite large quantities of drugs discarded by guys who got rid of it pretty smartly. A number of arrests, plenty of complaints made but no sign of the man with the meat cleaver.

As they say a Leopard never changes its spots and on some of the crime squads I was in charge of I would get the officers to search through the records to see who previously had been dealt with for burglary, theft or handling stolen goods. It was easy to find many with several convictions so we would get search warrants and "Spin Their Drums" as the saying went and it was amazing how often we came up trumps. Although every effort was made to get the addresses correct before executing warrants mistakes sometimes did happen. On one occasion I went to a flat and on producing the warrant at the door this dear old Irish lady invited us in at the same time making the point that neither she nor her husband had anything to do with the IRA who was active in London at the time. Of course not we assured them and after declining a cup of tea we sheepishly went on our way.

My Inspector was a Gerry Goodall who originated from Inverness. I think he said it was the Tornagrain area. We joked about me going to Kyle of Lochalsh when I was next up north to claim a motor- cycle of his. Apparently, years previous when it broke down he put it into a local garage with a view to having it repaired but never went back for it. Gerry tried on numerous occasions to find out if I was a

"Mason" or not. The Chief Inspector in Charge of the station was also in the same masonic lodge. Commander Neivens who I first met on the Promotion Board was in charge of "K" Division and he also was a mason. It was rife within the police service where ever you went and I'm sure many officers rose in ranks that way rather than through ability. Over the years I got to know their supposedly secret signs but in desperation, and I had to laugh, when Gerry one day said, "Are you a bloody mason or are you not." I was not one. I could have become one for the social side of it but felt from past experiences that it would have been a hindrance in my work rather than an advantage. Although it was supposed not to interfere with the law of the land it did not stop members of the public trying to get off the hook.

Normally two sergeants and one inspector were in charge of each shift. The sergeants took it in turn to do one week on desk duties and the other on the street supervising the constables. Soon after going to Plaistow I had to deal with a rowdy prisoner one night. He kept throwing himself headfirst at the cell walls and with other officers we had to go in and restrain him. He quietened down after a bit and I returned to the front office to call in the police surgeon to confirm that he was fit to be detained. A little later I went back to see if he was still alright but on opening the hatch on the cell door I could not see him. When I tried to open the door I had to get help again. The prisoner was lying behind it partially unconscious with my clip on police tie round his neck. He was attempting to strangle himself but I got him in the nick of time. I did not and neither did any of the other officers involved notice that my tie was missing but can you imagine had he died convincing senior officers or the coroner how he came by it.

To safeguard myself from criticism I had no hesitation in calling out the police surgeon when there was any doubt about detaining a person. One night a junky or drug addict found in possession of drugs was brought in and normally would have gone to court in the morning. Because of the state of his arms and legs from injecting himself and gangrene to both feet the surgeon was called out again. He certified him as fit to be detained but recommended bailing the prisoner who he thought would be dead by morning. No officer had any desire to have a prisoner or anyone else die in the station because of the paperwork it entailed so out he went on bail. He did not die by morning but did so before his court appearance.

I was not actually involved in this case but a 'phone call came into the station one afternoon to say that a lorry was travelling down Prince Regents Lane with no driver in it. A bit odd to say the least but a patrol car nearby responded and found that there was in fact a driver who could barely see over the steering wheel. It turned out to be a well known boy who had driven away the lorry without consent. I subsequently arrested him in his later teens for taking away a number of vehicles without consent and in the course of questioning him he implicated no less than thirteen other youths who were variously charged along with him. It was chaos in court that morning and the Clerk got a bit hot under the collar, more so when I asked for amendment to be made to some of the charges. It was as a result of mistakes I had made in typing up the charge sheets and using a wrong act of

Parliament. The Magistrates were very good about it and told the Clerk that it was better for it to be done before proceedings went any further. Most of the offenders pleaded guilty and I asked for them to be dealt with that day to ensure that they did not get involved in other crime which would complicate things even further. This was agreed to and I then asked for the others to be remanded to a later date for their cases to be heard in full. Luckily they all changed their pleas on that date to one of guilty.

A few years later I had the same youth in again for questioning regarding stolen vehicles to which he put his hands up to and because he was desperate to get bail he was in a mood for talking about other crime. As a result of that I decided to get a warrant and search his house where I found in the attic a rubber mallet type hammer with his initials cut out of the handle. I also found an imitation hand gun, both weapons having been used in a robbery at a butchers shop. He went to court the next morning to be re-arrested afterwards by officers from another station in connection with the robbery.

CHAPTER 42

THE START OF PLAIN CLOTHES DUTY

It was not long after going to Plaistow when I was selected to do a three month tour on Kilo One One, the call sign for "The Q Car" on K Division The crew for this vehicle, which was unmarked, was made up of a driver, a C.I.D. officer and a sergeant, all in plain clothes with a roving commission throughout the Division and elsewhere if necessary, such as following suspects, executing warrants or simply to make an arrest.

My first tour of duty in this car went very well with plenty of good arrests. The only down side was an assault on me which ended up in a bitter court case where I thought it was me that was on trial and not the accused. At one stage during my evidence I surprised everyone including the Magistrates when I was being pressed to answer a question with a simple yes or no. I picked up the bible in front of me which I had previously taken the oath on, stared the senior magistrate in the eye and said, "I swore on this bible to tell the truth and the truth is I don't know." The defence lawyer was then instructed to move on. We clashed again when my credibility was being attacked. This kind of behaviour by defence solicitors was not unusual when they had no better defence to offer their client and I told this particular one that was the way he was behaving. The magistrates, who chose not to get involved in this ding dong, found the accused guilty. The accused's father apologised to me for the behaviour of their solicitor, and the solicitor himself said in a loud enough voice for everyone to hear, "That's another police area I cannot safely drive through." Council from the Director of Public Prosecutions Office who was supposed to be representing the police that day virtually sat on his backside and said very little but I did not let him off either. All he said was, "I did not need to. You were doing fine on your own."

I was in and out of court several times a week and more than ninety percent of my cases were guilty pleas so when a case went to trial I'm sure on many occasions I got the benefit of the doubt. Magistrates in the lower courts because of their inexperience often relied on the guidance of the clerk whereas in the Crown Courts or the Old Bailey protocol was very different. I preferred the Magistrate Courts. Going to court for me was a better pay packet at the end of the month and I took advantage of the fact that many officers did not like presenting their own cases. My motto was, "You arrest them. I'll prosecute," and for me that was often worth six hours overtime. I know it is different in the Met. today but when I went down to London there were no public prosecutors or procurator fiscals as they are called in Scotland in the Magistrate Courts and the whole thing was a new ball game for me. In not guilty pleas for drink driving and careless driving Sergeants were allocated those to prosecute. I did not mind the drink driving ones but never got to grips with the careless driving prosecutions. The clerk or the magistrates kept interrupting you and in the end I used to say to the witnesses, "Just tell the court what happened," and then sit down and leave everyone else to get on with it. It was frustrating but I never resorted to the behaviour I witnessed at Stonehaven Sheriff Court when the Procurator Fiscal made a spectacle of himself by picking up the glass of water from his desk and pouring it over his own head. When it came to my turn for questioning the defendant or defence witnesses I was in the driving chair and was never slow to make the most of it.

For some reason I had a case come up in one of the Magistrate Court over in the West End, Well Street comes to mind but it may not have been. One of the Magistrates there had a reputation of getting the cases through the court as fast as he could and even more so when it came near to the time his train left for home. For straight forward drunks, street traders and prostitutes they would all be lined up in their respective groups even although arrested separately, and dealt with en masse. The court officer warned me about this and to make sure I was ready. As soon as my case was called I got up in the witness box and before the defendant got barely through the door, the Magistrate said to me, "Ready go." I said what I had to in the briefest form and the guy was fined before he even got into the dock. That's the way to do it I thought.

After the Q car tour I was selected along with another sergeant and an Inspector to run a squad of twelve officers from the uniform branch to combat the theft of cars, mostly old ones, which were disappearing from the streets over the whole of "K" Division and elsewhere in unprecedented numbers and without a trace of them. It was Commander Neivens who came up with the idea that we should target all car breakers and scrap yards who had the facilities to crush or shred a whole car at one time. This type of machinery was relatively new at the time so our first couple of days were spent locating suitable observation points and then put the plan into operation the following morning at 8 am when they opened for business. By 9 am the first of the car thieves were arriving at the police stations. Each of them had a small break-down truck with a crane type jib on the back. They stuck the jib through the back window or windscreen, up with the old car, and off with it to the nearest yard, collecting £25.00 with no questions being asked and the only evidence left behind was the broken glass on the street. After a week or so we scooped up all of the culprits including the yard owners involved.

We then switched our attentions to long stay car parks where a better class of vehicle was being stolen very often to be sold abroad. Many of them were recovered but as often as not they were stripped of everything and even burned out to destroy fingerprint evidence. The plan this time was for two officers with binoculars to keep observation from the top of selected high rise flats. After about two weeks we had a meeting to discuss our failure to get results because the same crimes were being committed right under our noses and we were taking a lot of flak for it from fellow officers. The outcome of the meeting was that we were not concentrating enough on the streets and car parks immediately below us, and trying to observe too big an area. From then on we disciplined ourselves in that

221

way and in the next six weeks we made seventy six arrests but by that time all and sundry were looking up and waving to us.

Following that successful stint, we switched venues again to target crime at the local swimming pool and more than one building site. Because some of the officers were afraid of heights I probably had more than my share of being up there. In fact I rather enjoyed it, but never got the same feeling that some officers did, from watching small birds flying around you, that you could fly as well. One Saturday afternoon alone, I put up a call to officers on the ground that five youths working as a team were stealing hand bags from the outdoor swimming pool seating area. Some were on the inside who threw the bags over the fence to the others. On hearing the police sirens on the cars the youths made off in the direction of a very busy road junction with footpaths and flyovers over a dual carriageway and the side roads. I was able to direct the officers to them then sat back and watched with amusement the chases that followed.

Outside a public house I had a youth arrested for threatening others with a knife. On one building site two men were caught stealing new timber and on another two security guards were observed stealing rolls of loft insulation and making off in their vehicle with it. Every available officer was tied up with one or another of those crimes. Even the desk sergeant at one station had to leave his post and take out the "Black Maria", the name given to the station van. The security men were not arrested on the day but were traced from the registration number of their vehicle. Warrants were obtained and their houses in West London searched. Loads and loads of electric and plumbing fittings were found, over and above several times as much insulation that they were seen taking. Even a complete set of musical instrument from a band were recovered, all stolen by them when they should have been looking after the security of it. Whole kitchens or bathrooms fitted out one day in several houses under construction and stolen by next morning was not uncommon and that was the way things were in one police area alone.

Being on the top of one of those high rise flats and doing what we were paid to do instead of pushing a pen in the office was more to my liking. Joined by a young probationer one day we saw two men carrying heavy sacks along what we called the sewer bank. Directing officers to strategic points to intercept them, we then watched events unfold and in most cases I can see a funny side of things. One was, when an obese sergeant tried to climb over a high corrugated iron fence, failing on several attempts, fell on his backside and rolled down the embankment at the crucial moment. As the two suspects were about to emerge on to the public road where fortunately for them only a single CID officer was waiting, the two dropped their sacks and innocently walked towards him. The officer grabbed one of them and put him in the back of the police car. He then turned round and arrested the second man but the first one went straight out the opposite door and made a run for it. When more help arrived, to begin with I was able to direct them to where the guy was heading but lost sight of him after he climbed over some back garden fences. The first man was charged with the theft of brass bushes from a nearby railway engineering yard.

Some months later I was in court when the same CID officer had the escapee in the dock for another crime. The binoculars we used for the observations were so good that you could read the numerals on officers' epaulettes and because of this I immediately recognised the accused as the guy who did the runner and mentioned this to the officer and told him that I was going to arrest him for the original crime. To save embarrassment, I did not but we did have a good laugh about it.

During the time I was on the crime squads and because there was so much crime taking place, some of it very serious like murder, we were often called in to assist the CID with their initial enquiries. We were seen as a ready available source of manpower that could be called on at short notice but I was never interested in high profile cases that the CID got involved in. I had no wish to go on boring door to door enquiries, filling in and ticking boxes on prepared forms from people who for most did not want to be involved. Another aspect of it was the fact that no officer of junior rank was ever shown on the charge sheet as the arresting officer and as far as I was concerned that mattered most. One such case along with other officers we staked out a pub in the East End where a man wanted for murder was known to frequent. I was first to get my hands on him but a, Detective Chief Inspector who I don't think was even at the pub, went down as arresting officer. It reminded me of my early days at Buckie but having said that I gave evidence at all the major courts in London including The Coroner's and The Old Bailey. I cannot recall the reason for it but I also had to give evidence at a General Medical Council Tribunal.

One sunny afternoon a probationer and I were watching a man acting suspiciously at the edge of a public park. Something told us he was up to no good and sure enough when a lady with two young girls came along he got up from the grass and started masterbating himself in their direction. I said to the young officer, "Look at him now, he's pulling his pudding." At first he did not understand the expression but on seeing the man for himself he excitedly shouted out, "He's having a hand shandy." When I got a car to pick him up it transpired he was a prisoner from Wormwood Scrubs who failed to return after parole. An ex prisoner was charged with harbouring him.

Just after returning from holiday in Scotland I went on to another plain clothes squad to combat a spate of house breakings in the Forestgate area. Many of them were happening during the day time and this particular lunch time a fellow officer and I were walking down the street to look at a second hand pedal cycle for each of the girls. Rather than take their other ones back from holiday I asked my father in law to sell them. Everything looked very peaceful until a man screaming his head off, ran out from a house on to the street. He was followed by a person in female attire branding a bread knife in his direction.

What's going on here we wondered? Both of them stopped when I shouted at them that we were police officers and I approached the one with the knife and asked him to hand it over. No resistance was offered and both people were arrested. On arrival at the station the desk sergeant referred to the one who had the knife by a man's name. It was only then that we realised that it was a man in drag and was a regular at the station. Next morning I took him to the Magistrates Courts and he was on the list to appear in Number One Court. I have to admit from his dress and general appearance I was fooled into thinking he was a woman.

To save any confusion when he went into the court with this lovely outfit on and the flowing blonde hair, I briefed the court officer who in turn briefed the clerk of the court and the magistrates that the accused was in fact a man and that the name on the charge sheet was correct. However, things did not go as planned. The court officer from Number Two Court came out rather hurriedly and asked if anyone was ready to proceed. Without thinking I said, "Me" and in we went with "blondie" climbing up into the dock. From the name on the charge sheet which everyone had a copy, it was obvious that all was not as it should be, and as I explain the position to them a few smiles, winks and elbow nudging went on.

I arrested a very tall man in his late teens who was stupid enough to leave a stolen pedal cycle in his front garden. He tried to say that he was going to return it but in any event he went to court for his troubles. When I was walking him to the station I had a hold of him by the arm and he bent down and shouted, "Boo" in my ear which made me jump and lose grip of him. He thought this was a great joke and emphasized the fact that he could have run away. Yes he could have done but I knew where he lived anyway. A few months later I was on plain clothes duty at Stratford when I saw the same guy up on the top of a fire escape trying to open a fire door. I called to him to come down which he did and I invited him to walk along to West Ham Police Station with me where we could sit down for a chat about car radios that frequently were stolen from a nearby car park. He recognised me from my previous encounter with him but he was of no help regarding the radios. I actually thought he was a burglar that I had arrested but he went on to say that the door he was trying to get in at was to a night club and that his mate was on the inside intending to open the door for him so that he did not have to pay at the main door. To get my own back on him for the boo bit I charged him under a very old Vagrancy Act for being on private premises for an unlawful purpose. He was not fined very much but I'm sure he learned his lesson to be more respectful to police officers in the future.

During the sugar rationing in the seventies I was on duty in Canning Town when I saw this Asian guy walking up the street towards me. He was carrying something heavy in a shopping type bag and when I stopped him to see what he had in it I found that he had seven pounds of sugar. He readily admitted that he had stolen it from his place of work, a jam factory at Barking but according to him that was all he had taken. In mitigation of his wrong doing he kept saying to me, "I'm a poor man. I don't steal. I come from a big family with seven children and if you come to my house you can see for yourself." I caught him by surprise when I took him up on his invitation and went with him to his house where I found more sugar and quite a lot catering size tins of jam. When he went to court the

Magistrates adjourned the case to allow time for me to get an interpreter for him. He made out he did not understand English. At the next hearing the interpreter sat in the dock beside him but when I stood up to outline the case against him he told the interpreter to be quiet as he wanted to hear what the officer had to say.

Within the Met if you suspected anyone of committing a crime you had the power to stop, search and summon that person. In practice they were always arrested and then charged at the station, going to court the next morning. Using this type of policing it was amazing how often you came up trumps and for such a variety of offences. Like the guy with the sugar I stopped another man carrying a crate of gherkins along the street. He was a lorry driver from Liverpool and was on his way to lodgings for an overnight stop and the gherkins were stolen from his lorry and were for the landlady. His firm had been trying to catch him for some time and they sacked him on the spot, sending another driver down to London to take over the remainder of the deliveries and to take the lorry back home. What appeared at first appeared to be petty turned out to be quite serious when the company got to hear about it. For a few months afterwards I earned the nickname, "The Gherkin Kid."

I spent just about all my Met. years in the east end of London going from one crime squad to the next, both in Uniform and plain clothes, during which I got the chance to go into the C.I.D. I did not want to get involved with them permanently for so many of them were corrupt and Sir Robert Mark, the then Commissioner proved it but having said that there were many more good hard working detectives. There was a general feeling however, that they thought themselves above and apart from the rest of the force. When I was on one of the squads an ex-flying squad officer was in charge. He came to work early one morning and told me that he had to go up to New Scotland Yard, assuring me that his work was all up to date, that he had cleared his desk and may not be back. Neither he was. He was forced to resign from the force that day and I never saw him again. So many of them went out on their "ear" like that. Sir Robert was followed by a Glasgow officer nick named "The Hammer" but as an ex colleague and friend said, "Yes the hammer with the rubber head." He was supposedly knighted for his work in London but got it before the seat in his office was barely warm.

CHAPTER 43

BUYING OUR SECOND HOUSE

Catriona was successful in being accepted for the then two top secondary schools in that part of Essex but still within the Metropolitan Police area. One was St Edwards Church of England at Romford and the other was Coopers Coburn at Upminster. Because we were more than satisfied with her church schooling at Barking we chose Romford where we soon found that the headmaster, Mr Thomas, was very much a disciplinarian. Before the intake, there was a parents meeting to hear about the way the school was run, and Mr Thomas made it very clear then that if pupils misbehaved he had no qualms about using the cane, and that if parents did not like what they were hearing they were bluntly told to find another school for their child. Everyone just sat there in silence.

To begin with Catriona travelled by bus to St Edwards but knowing that Fiona hopefully would be following her we started looking for a house in that area. Because house prices had risen considerably by that time, we first looked in the different boroughs near to Romford rather that the houses itself, and set our sights on Gidea Park. Next to Raephal Park were a large number of individually designed houses as a result of an architect's competition. No two of them were the same, beautiful houses with large gardens and some occupied by celebrities. On the other side was Gidea Park private golf course and a Municipal one close bye as well.

Perhaps we were just dreaming but I was still earning big money, and the break we needed came by way of a private advertisement in the local paper for a three bedroom, detached house on the fringe of this development. It only took about five minutes to walk through this park and you were into the centre of Romford, its street markets and every type of shop and store you could wish for.

We drove past this house many times before even enquiring about the price. We were so sure it would be out of our league but Marjory said there would be no harm in ringing them up anyway. We did, and the sellers were very keen for us to come and view it which was on the market for just under twenty thousand. The owners said, "The price is not as important as a genuine buyer." Apparently they were let down badly several times by buyers dropping out at the last moment. We told them we had already had a buyer for our own house and were aiming to move during the school holidays. We looked over the house and spent quite a lot of time with the couple. The husband had been an educational officer with Havering local authority but accepted a similar post right across London with Brent. All his travelling costs and resettlement allowance were being paid for in the meantime but this was due to run out. We ended up agreeing to buy the house for just over nineteen thousand, but then our own troubles started.

Buyers we had started dropping out but luckily Marjory and I had just returned from putting the house back on the market yet again when the phone rang to say a prospective buyer wished to come and see the house. When I asked when, I was told, "Now." Five or ten minutes later a Mr MacKenzie was knocking on the door and he turned out to be one of the most eccentric persons I had ever met, but yet a very interesting man to talk to.

It was not a case of waiting to be asked into the house, with a fag in his mouth he barged past me and to start the conversation I said to him that Marjory was making a cup of coffee and would he like one. "Yes but I will have a look around the house first." He never entered any of the rooms, only sticking his head in at the door and then on to the next one and making the briefest of comments. There was a cellar in the house and he was more interested in that than anywhere else. Although the flit round the rooms was very brief he smoked at least another two cigarettes and over the coffee he filled an ashtray with tabbies. He continually lit one from the other the whole time he was in the house, obviously a chain smoker.

He told us he came from Inverness and studied history at Durham University and at that he was working as a steel estimator with Mowlems the building consortium. He went on to say his furniture was in storage down on the south coast and needed into the house the following week. I said to him that was a tall order but perhaps in two weeks time when the schools broke up for the summer holidays. We already had our finance and legal matters in place as did the couple in Gidea Park. Our chain smoker assured us that he was in the same position so a date was set to coincide with us going up to Hill of Minnes the night the school closed for a pre-arranged two week holiday.

Because we could not get into the Gidea Park house for six weeks all three parties came to a rather controversial agreement, and certainly one that solicitors would not have agreed to, where our furniture would be stored in their garage until the house was vacant. We would go on holiday as planned and Mr MacKenzie would move into the Barking house. For the other four weeks Marjory and the girls would stay on in Aberdeenshire with her Mam and Dad. As agreed, when I came back off holiday and moved in with Mr MacKenzie for a month or more and everything went according to plan.

Mr MacKenzie as I thought turned out to be a bit of an odd bod. Every ashtray in the house was left full, not a plate, cup, saucer or bit of cutlery was washed in the two weeks he was there on his own and I shudder to think what a mess the place got into after I left. He used to come home and tell me what I considered "ghosters". I was never sure whether to believe him or not. For instance, bearing in mind the steel job he had, he told me he got a contract at a holiday camp at Bognor Regis to take over the security there. It was only a couple of nights later when he asked me to carry in piles of complete uniforms did I believe him.

Some nights he would not come home at all, once for three nights and another time for a whole week. It suited me in one sense but I did worry about him because he never thought of giving me a ring on the 'phone. One of the occasions, he said he had been over in Canada in connection with a government contract. The other time he arrived home in crutches having been involved in an I.R.A. bomb explosion at a hotel foyer in the West End of London resulting in him being blown across the street and escaping with only a broken ankle.

About the end of my stay with Mr MacKenzie he asked me if there was a Sergeant Sloan at Plaistow. It so happened that he worked on the same shift as me and when I told Mr MacKenzie this he said, "Tell him Ben Gunn was asking for him." I never did see the connection but as requested I passed on the message much to Sergeant Sloan's surprise. Apparently Mr MacKenzie from his Newcastle days knew the sergeant as a little boy. Curiosity was then to take over as to how I met in with him, the story of him buying our house and me living, albeit temporarily, with him. This colleague said he could not wait to tell his Dad about him. They had been good pals but just lost touch, something I could relate to. Sergeant Sloan assured me he was a very genuine man and a truthful one, so your first impressions are not always right. There is an old saying in the Highlands, "You don't know the person you live with until you have burned the stack of peats." He moved from that house soon afterwards and I never did know where he got to.

Our stay at Gidea Park was to be a very busy one in many different ways. After getting on top of our mortgage payments once more, Fiona now at St Edwards as well and no more bus trips to Barking we were able to centralise our activities closer to home. Marjory got a full time job as a personal assistant with a local firm of printers. A vacancy came up for a Sergeant at Upminster and I applied for that because my blood pressure was on the high side. I was given this posting which turned out to have a large country beat to it making it similar to working in the "sticks" again.

We were apprehensive about our move into the new house with posh neighbours and Jaguar cars, and there was us with a broken down Triumph 2000 and an old banger of a red mini with a lime green door that the previous owner picked up from a breakers yard. However, our neighbours were very friendly and chatty. Ken and Pauline Cutler next door invited everyone in to their house for coffee so that we could be introduced to them. Coffee mornings were quite common with the ladies but Marjory never got involved. The neighbours were mostly professional or business people and although they lived in posh houses, they themselves were not. One thing that really did annoy them was a market trader who lived in the street and a colleague of his who came at 4am every morning to pick him up in his lorry before going to the vegetable and fruit market. Other times they would have two lorries parked there doubling the amount of noise in the early morning.

Very soon into our coffee morning the question of the noisey lorries came up and it was suggested that I might do something about it. My reply, rather jokingly was, "I distil my own whisky. I don't want anyone interfering with that so fight your own battles." Oh alright, alright was the response and the subject of lorries ended on that note. A few months later and after I transferred to that sub-division I did sort the problem out. I was awakened to the usual noise and got out of bed in my pyjamas and went into the street and read the riot act. After reminding one of them about a previous term in prison they agreed to leave the lorries elsewhere and take a car to work.

Overall it was a very friendly place to live, relatively free of crime, house parties held quite frequently, including a big one at Jim and Joan Clarke's house every Hogmanay. One Sunday the neighbours were invited to our house for a pre lunch drink and nibbles supposedly, but Marjory laid on a huge spread suitable for a buffet lunch to feed about twenty to thirty people. When everyone was really merry and had no thought of going home, although some did to switch off their cookers, I produced several boxes of breathalizer kits. One of the biggest surprises from that was Marjory, who had only two glasses of wine and she was away over the top. I think just about everyone else was as well but with a lot more alcohol.

Richard Cutler next door, a young eighteen year old, was probably the worst. His mother, Pauline was adamant that he should not go for a pre arranged skiing lesson but he was just as determined because Valerie his sister was going to drive him there. Through a defect on the slope Richard had a tumble and broke his ankle. Pauline in no uncertain terms went through the "I told you so routine" but Valerie assured everyone that it had nothing to do with the drink. Well that was their story and were sticking to it.

When I came home from work one Sunday afternoon Marjory told me how the two couples across the road went about cutting down a tree at the front and between their respective houses. Jim a professional commercial photographer and his wife Joan occupied one of the houses and Jack Clark, the owner of a motorcycle sales and servicing business and his wife, also Joan, occupied the other. What amused Marjory was the system they adopted. Jim was up the ladder sawing of the branches and cutting down the trunk log by log from the top down and passing the pieces to his wife. She, in turn passed them on to Joan Clark who put them in a barrow for Jack to wheel round to the rear of the house. Although the tree was not a particularly large one this went on for about two hours until the job was complete.

At this time there was an enormous amount of Dutch elm disease about, and within the Borough of Havering where we lived it was no exception. Hundreds of mature trees were dying every day and the odd thing about it for me was the fact they would just topple over in the calmest of days, the roots having completely rotted away. Always ready for a laugh, I concocted a spoof letter supposedly from the Council's Parks and Trees Committee stating that the efficient and effective work they had carried out in cutting down the tree between their houses had not gone unnoticed and that a contract to cut down all the diseased trees within the borough was being offered to them.

Marjory typed the letter on the best quality paper from her office and we posted one to each couple. Neither couple nor anyone else in the street mentioned anything about it to us so I began to wonder if they had taken offence at it. About two months later we were invited over to Jack and Joan's house for the evening when Jack produced the letter. He went on to say how they made up an appropriate reply and sent it to the Borough Engineer who lived down the street a bit. He could not make any sense of the letter not having seen the original one. He went along to Jim Clarke's to see what it was all about and on seeing the fictitious address immediately said it was a hoax. Now there were five or more trying to work out who the author was. They came to the conclusion that it must have been a car dealer further down the street, but no, it was not him either. They were afraid to accuse anyone else but still mystified as ever. I could not help but laugh as the story unfolded and Jack was quick enough to guess that I was involved. They thought it was a great joke and talked about it a lot going through all their suspects but never had me on their list.

You will go far to find another Post Master like Martin Calder who we have in Bonar Bridge Post Office. He is so helpful in every respect taking all the time in the world to explain procedures, forms that come with all the red tape, to the extent of filling them up for you. Above all is his sense of humour and everything you buy from him is a bargain, even the postage stamps. I have an old Post Office Savings Book issued on the 11th April, 1957, with a balance of six shillings and four pence in it. For a bit of fun I compiled a letter along the lines that Marjory and I were about to go on a world cruise and that I was consolidating our finances to pay for it and obviously not wanting to fall short of money on the way. I posted the letter to Martin asking him to make up the interest on the balance from 1957. My address is not shown in the book so to begin he wondered who the crank could be. When he gave me back the book he told me that it had more of an antique value for a collector than what was in it as the rate of interest it qualified for was nil, a half penny for each complete pound per annum.

Hoax letters with no sinister motives were common around that time and within the Met. in particular. I'm sure they originated from people sitting in offices with little else to do although mine was done one Sunday afternoon in the comfort of my own home. Today they are often in the form of emails. Just recently, Stephen Franks, who is mentioned elsewhere give me a copy of one sent to his father as far back as 1910 so it has been going on for a very long time. I will reproduce it herein but beforehand my apologies go out to all cat lovers.

Universal Provider
LONDON.

Mr Frank Esq.

Dear Sirs,

Knowing that you are always interested in, and often for an investment in a good live business proposition, I take the liberty of presenting to you what seems to be a most wonderful business, in which no doubt you will take a lively interest, and perhaps advise me by return of post the amount of stock you wish to subscribe to the formation of the company.

The object of the company is to operate a large cat ranch near London, whereland can be purchased cheaply for the purpose. To start with we would want about 1000,000 cats; each cat will average 12 kittens a year; the skins run from sixpencefor the white ones and two shillings the blacks.

This will give us 12,000,000 skins a year to sell at an average of one shilling and sixpence, making our revenue about £2,500 per year.

A man can skin about 50 cats' per day at five shillings a day wage, and it will take100 men to operate the ranch therefore the net profit will be £2,475 per day.

We feed the cats on rats and start a rat ranch, the rats multiply four times as fast as the cats, and if we start with 1,000,000 rats we shall have four rats per cat per day, and then we shall feed the rats on the carcases of cats from which the skins have been taken , giving each rat one quarter of a cat.

It will thus be seen that the business is self supporting and automatic throughout.The cats will eat the rats, and the rats will eat the cats, and we shall get the skins.

Awaiting your prompt reply and hoping you will appreciate the opportunity to get rich quickly.

Yours faithfully

A.S.Windle

Manager.

P.S. Eventually we shall try to cross the cats with snakes so that they will skin themselves twice a year thus avoiding the men's wages for skinning and also getting two skins from each cat.

Another couple, John and Jean Bolding lived three doors along from us. He was a surveyor with the council and I got on very well with him, playing pranks on one another and him referring to me as the "Gremlin" of Brook Road. During this time I was building a very large extension on the rear of our house. I did all the work myself with the exception of the wiring for the lights which entailed some two and three way systems and also the plastering which I had previously tried on a kitchen wall and turned out to be a complete mess. Eric Kite, a Home Beat Officer from Upminster helped with the concrete work and carted the tiles up for stacking on the roof. Although the extension went right up to the ridge of the original house I did not have proper scaffolding, using only towers and ladders. One evening I finished felting the roof and the plan was to come back down inside by leaving a small piece undone. Then I thought I would just finish it and get someone to put a ladder up for me.

The only neighbour physically capable of doing this was John and by good luck he came out into his back garden. He was always watching my progress so it was not long before I got his attention. Taking advantage of my predicament he came out in to the street shouting about me being stuck up there until he had all the neighbours out with him to see what the commotion was all about. Leaving me for sometime John eventually put the ladder up for me. When we came to selling that house I did it privately and put my own "For Sale" sign up in the front garden. John just had to add the words, "By Hughie." When I told him that we had sold the house but the sign was still up, again he had to add the words, "Sold by Hughie."

John was friendly with another Met. Sergeant. I never did meet him but one day when we were talking about him, John said what he like about both the other sergeant and I, was the fact that we left our work at the office and did not talk about it.. This was true of me throughout my career and many a dig Marjory got in the ribs if for instance in a restaurant or pub when she let the word police slip out. I was far from being ashamed of the fact that I was in the police but did not want the hassle of hearing tales of woe from strangers and their experiences with them. Other officers and wives talked about nothing else to the point their whole lives revolved round it, some with no hobbies or other interests. Statistics prove that the life span of retired officers is generally very short and I am convinced that that this along with lack of exercise is the reason for it.

CHAPTER 44

THE CAR LOT

Always ready to make that extra shilling and not doing so much overtime I got into the buying and selling of second-hand cars. There was an excellent market for "Cheepies" as we called them. Mum would buy a car in the £400 price range for her son or daughter who had newly passed their driving test. She would have the use of it during the week and they would have it at the weekends. The most common or popular buy was the BMC mini or 1100 models. Over the years I had several of them and unlike modern vehicles they were easy to work on and I knew them inside out. I bought my cars from advertisements in the local papers, "trade ins" at garages, or from the car auctions at Enfield or Southampton. One of the 1100 cars I had, Marjory drove Catriona over to Paddington Railway Station with it and soon after starting her journey for home the clutch cable broke but still she managed to drive it all the way across London to our home in Gidea Park, slamming it in and out of gear and at the same time coping unbelievably well with traffic at lights or busy junctions, not to mention the London buses that hogged the roads. Marjory preferred to leave the car business to myself and not get involved but at times I had to get her to tow a car home for me. One evening coming home on the A127 from Chelmsford I was doing the towing and decided to go over the flyover at the junction for Romford. Marjory had a different idea and stuck to the nearside lane thinking I would change my mind but I didn't. She then had to get on to the flyover with only yards to go.

It has been a standing joke amongst the family after I bought a BMC 1100 from Marjory's brother Ian. It was a good car but after a year or so rust appeared along the bottom of the doors and Ian was told that it looked as if a machine gun had been fired at it. It was no big deal because I was into doing that sort of repair. Through friends I was asked to find a car for two New Zealand couples who were coming to Britain for three months and required a car. Knowing that the 1100 was a reliable one I sold them the car and they toured the country, Wales, Scotland and even went as far as Spain with it. One couple thought about taking it back to New Zealand but import duty there made it prohibitive. I bought the car back off them and then sold it to Richard next door who had crashed his one. When it was parked outside his house a drunk woman reversed into it and damaged the wing, front door and pillars. It sat there until the licence ran out and I bought it off him for scrap. However, after having a good look at it I decided to repair it and Marjory could use it again. She did for a while but when the rust started to become obvious again I decided to sell it once more. Eric was down on holiday and he got an eye-opener when he saw how things could be tarted up, nothing illegal just the cosmetics. Some Asian lads took it for a test drive and afterwards went away delighted with it. They were probably not interested in getting an MOT or a licence for it in the future anyway.

I was friendly with a garage owner who often tipped me off about a car that had come in for repair or an M.O.T. and because of the costs involved the owner would change their mind and buy another vehicle instead. The gearbox in the mini or the 1100 was a common but major fault and to fit a new one would cost sometimes more than the car was worth and I could buy them for little more than a breaker would give for them. I dealt with a particular car breaker for second hand spares and instead of fitting a gearbox he would sort me out with a good engine and gearbox combined or lump as he called it for £25, and I would fit that instead. The old lump I would take back for him to scrap. I would then do any other repairs and after a good valet I would get a new M.O.T for it which was always a good selling point. To make certain it was not seen as a business I was running I registered all the vehicles in my own or Marjory's name and transferred the insurance as well.

I was always honest with prospective buyers even the three Asians. I told them everything I knew about the vehicles, pointed out anything not quite right, such as rusty bits and told them if they wanted to they could have the car inspected by anyone else. But the best guarantee of all was to tell them just to bring the car back for a full refund of their money if for any reason they were not fully satisfied. I can only remember two cars coming back. One of them was from a policeman and his wife who should not have bought it in the first place, they came to look at a Triumph 1300 for the wife but the husband wanted to buy a battleship grey Wolseley 1600 automatic. They argued away about it for a while and then the husband won the day. Within the week they were asking for their money back and enquiring about the Triumph again. Although it was not I told them it was sold. Many of my customers were serving police officers so everything had to be above board not that I would have wanted it any other way.

An experience never to be forgotten was a day at Southampton Car Auction. Chris Gollard, an ex-butcher turned car dealer, and I went down by train to look for a mini a friend of mine wanted. On finding one in the rows my first approach as always was to walk round about the car to inspect the body and paintwork. Chris always had to hear the engine running. I was down on my knees inspecting the floor well at the passenger side while Chris sat side saddle in the driver's seat and on turning the engine over it started up and the car took off. Not only had the car been left in gear but the throttle was stuck open as well, a recipe for disaster. Chris, with one hand on the steering wheel and trying to hold on to the open door and balance himself with the other, tore up and down between the rows with perspective buyers running everywhere for their lives. As he changed rows his feet sometimes were trailing in the gravel or up in the air until eventually he ran into a dead end and had no option but to crash into an angled iron fence writing off the mini.

The auctioneers and everyone else came out to see what had happened and Chris was told he would have to pay the market price of the car. He refused to do this and many letters exchanged hands before he got a final demand stating that if he did not disclose the name and address of this, "So called Police Sergeant " he would be taken to court. I compiled what I thought was a very good statement laying the blame fairly and squarely with the auction company and pointed out that because of the dispute, Chris, myself and one other had stopped coming to their sales. Chris then got a letter back stating that the matter was closed and inviting us all back to do business with them again. We never did go back but Chris, for a long time afterwards, was teased about going down to the dodgems.

CHAPTER 45

MY LAST YEARS IN THE MET

Whilst working at Upminster I was assaulted a second time. It was on Hogmanay night and I told the officers we would see the pubs closed at midnight and then come back to the station for a drink which was the normal practice and never abused. I was heading back to the station when I was flagged down. One of about eight youths walking up the road was being accused of kicking in the tail lights of a parked car. I drove back to them but they ran into a garden and when I tried to arrest the person responsible the others set about me as well. Urgent assistance was summoned by a member of the public and cars came from just about everywhere in North East London and up through the Dartford Tunnel. I briefed the crews on the various descriptions and it was not long before they had them all rounded up and in the police station. I can distinctly picture one of the guys going through his pockets at the time as if looking for something. Was it a knife? I will never know but I am convinced it was better for me that he did not find what he was looking for. What went through my mind at the time was a call I answered to deal with a man with a mental history who was creating a disturbance at his home address. After I got him calmed down and waiting for a doctor to arrive we each sat opposite one another by the fireside having a cup of tea. All was well until he threw his cup in the fire and he got very restless again. A pair of scissors was hanging on the wall right next to the armrest of his chair and he kept looking at them. I kept talking to him to try and divert his attention from them but all of a sudden he grabbed the scissors and lunged towards me. On the hearth nearest to my chair was a fireguard which I used to protect my self with, at the same time disarming him. Taking no chances after that I hand cuffed him and sat on him until the doctor and an ambulance arrived. He was then put in a straight jacket to contain him from further violence.

So much for a quite celebration drink! The ring leader went to the first available court and went down for three months only to come back out again to commit an armed robbery for which he got eighteen months inside. The others were all fined for the various parts they played. This attack on me aggravated a previous back injury on duty and I was practically living on distalgesic pain killers. In spite of seeing a Harley Street specialist and attending St Thomas' Hospital for three months I never really recovered from it. Going to that hospital on a couple of occasions had a lighter side to it, although at my expense, when the male physiotherapist was on his day off and two young girls were on duty. They were physically unable to carry out my normal treatment in the way he did but instead got me down on the floor with one of them lying across my chest to hold down one of my shoulders whilst the other tried to roll my hips in the opposite direction creating this twisting action to my lower back. Another day for the first time they would try traction. No, they did not have a steam engine but they might as well have had. While they went for coffee I was left on my back on this bench type of thing that rattle away supposedly to stretch the muscles. They got the settings all wrong and I was in sheer agony with sweat pouring off me by the time they returned. Not a good day but we still managed to see a funny side to it. I was then put on light duties which amounted to me sitting behind a desk all day.

On night duty at Hornchurch or Upminster there was always an officer ready to cook a hot meal for everyone, each specialising in a particular dish be it a curry, chilli con carne or biryani. On occasions a rabbit would somehow be got from down on the Rainham Marshes or meat would be bought and the costs shared. A panda driver came in one night from a patrol and had the carcase of a fully feathered chicken with him. Apparently a fox tried to dash across the road from a farmyard with the chicken in its mouth. In the panic it dropped it and made off without his supper. Barry White or "Chalkie" as he was better known did the business the following night. Fallow deer that fell victim as casualties on the A127 were soon put out of their misery by Eric an authorised police marksman and parts of them found their way into the stew pot as well.

Barry was adept at imitating the accent and the way people from eastern countries spoke and specialised in imitating Idi Amin the brutal dictator and ruler of Uganda who was never out of the headlines. When his next door neighbour advertised a dining room suite for sale in the local paper he rang him up supposedly as a gentleman from Pakistan living on the other side of London who was interested in buying it. After the usual questions a prospective buyer would ask, Barry then suggested that the seller should take the suite to him so that he could inspect it. Barry made the excuse that he had a large family and that the expense of travelling to Upminster was out of the question. After putting a number of obstacles in the way such as getting to and from the station Barry's neighbour got a bit short with him. Barry seized on this and accused his neighbour of being racial and that he did not want to sell him the suite in the first place and said he was going to report him to the Race Relations Board. This went on a bit and eventually the phones were put down. Barry then 'phoned his neighbour again purporting to be from the Board and of course using one of his other accents and told him he was to be reported. The end of this saga came when Barry's wife 'phoned the neighbour and told him the truth of what had been going on. His neighbour did not find it amusing and never spoke to Barry again.

When you were on night duty at stations in the met you always got your fair share of "cranks" 'phoning in. I generalise with that term of name for them because sometimes they were just lonely people living on their own and wanted a chat but even they could be a nuisance. One such lady who definitely fell into the former category was a regular and no matter how quick you could put the 'phone down she would ring again. All officers recognised her voice immediately and Barry would kid her on it was an Indian Restaurant she had rung and in his best Indian accent would talk a load of "cobblers" to her. Sometimes we would get her and another of her kind on the 'phone at the same time. The keys could be left open for them to speak to each other and that was an experience to listen to. Ann as she was called, rung one night to lodge a complaint as she put it about a certain sergeant who consistently crapped down her chimney. She did not mind that but the problem was the broken tiles on the roof of her bungalow. At Upminster station alone there were hundreds of 'phone messages recorded from her and in an effort to put a stop to it I took her to court for wasting police time and asked for her to be bound over to keep the peace. This was the course of action taken but it never made a whit of difference.

At a neighbouring station an Inspector had a distinct dislike for her; in fact the feeling was mutual and not many officers cared for him either. He was having a retirement party which she got to hear about and wickedly an officer said to her, "Of course you are invited." And along she went to end up making a scene and getting thrown out. Another unpopular Inspector on coming to work one day found pig tails in his uniform pockets. They had been retrieved from bins at a local slaughterhouse and not the cleanest of items to find. Because of the ill feeling on that shift the Chief Superintendant wanted to transfer me on to it but I declined knowing that I could not work harmoniously with the Inspector either. During the Chief Superintendant's discussion about the problem another Sergeant said, "I don't find him a problem." This gave me the opening I was looking for and said, "There's your man, transfer him."

I was desk sergeant at Hornchurch Police Station when a panda driver brought in a prisoner for creating a disturbance at a doctor's surgery. Everything was going well in the charge room until I tried to explain to him that he was going to be bailed in the sum of £25.00 to appear at court at a later date. No matter how much I explained the system to him I could not get through to him that he did not have to hand over the money there and then. Suddenly he jumped to his feet and said, "You are treating me like a little boy." I put one hand on the desk and the other on the arm rest of the chair and leaned over to the side to stand up and could not have presented my jaw to him any better even if I tried. Wallop and I got this almighty swinging punch to my jaw. Somehow or other I managed to grab him and we both landed on the floor with me trying to stop him escaping. When the arresting officer came in with a drink of water which the prisoner had requested he found the desk being shoved about, chairs overturned and nothing like the peaceful situation he had left a minute or so earlier. Other officers in an adjacent room heard the noise and thought I was moving the furniture for some reason. Yes I was, but not in the sense they thought. The prisoner became very violent but between us we got him to the cells but in the process my back give in completely, leaving me writhing on the floor.

I was helped by fellow officers to the surgeon's room to await his arrival. After an examination I went by ambulance to Harold Wood Hospital where a fracture of the jaw was diagnosed. I was off work for a very long time and when I did return I was to have no contact with the public. I supervised a small number of uniformed constables who were responsible for investigating complaints termed as minor crimes. In the minds of the victim they were not minor and because of complaints they were then recorded as beat crimes. Serious crime was investigated by the C.I.D. and if they got half a chance they would down-grade it to a beat crime. Likewise, the beat crime officers were encouraged to write a lot of the complaints off as "no crime" as the classification, when the victim could not substantiate the allegation, or for instance if you put doubt in their minds as to whether something was indeed stolen or simply lost or mislaid. Statistics can be massaged one way or another to make things look better or worse and I am sure the same thing goes on until this day.

From the same office I compiled the duty rosters for officers at three police stations, Hornchurch, Upminster and Rainham. In total there were over a hundred and it involved a lot of work getting every position covered. Annual leave was registered through me and that was a bit of a headache with so many wanting to be away during the school holidays. Each station had a minimum strength that you could let the number of officers down to but no allowance was made for calls coming in from the "Yard" requiring aid for demonstrations, football matches etc. This was often at short notice when sometimes you had to cancel days off. No matter how well you jiggled things you could not please them all. If, to cover the requirements you give officers overtime, you then had the bosses on your back for that. During all of this time The Police Federation was fighting my case for criminal injuries compensation. I asked for an interview with the force medical officer which was granted. Basically I told him I could not carry on in the way things were going and agreed to be medically discharged. He put me on three months sick leave until the final date of my service.

Knowing that we were to return to Scotland I rung Frank Low to see if he had any young Labrador bitches that would be ready for my return but all he had were puppies so I got him to send one down by train. It was a lovely black bitch and we called her Tara. There were plenty of places for me to exercise her and to do a bit of training which went well with no hickups. She stayed out of doors having a brick built shed for her bed and the run of the garden. I think she was well used to seeing foxes come into our garden for one afternoon we were sitting out doors on the patio when a fox crossed the fence and then went over into our neighbour's garden only to return a few minutes later. Tara never batted an eyelid. London, like many other cities and it is worse now, is infested with them. When I started for early turn duty at 6am I used to watch them scavenging the dustbins up and down our street. Across the road a vixen had a litter of cubs under a garden shed.

When I was at Hornchurch Police Station an unusual number of reports came in about cats going missing and some owners were convinced they were stolen for vivisection. Knowing that there were lots of foxes in the area I would suggest to the owners that a fox could have taken them but they would not accept that. While this was going on a car breaker rung the station asking for an officer to come to see what he found in his yard. He had a huge clear out of old car bodies and under where they had been stacked next to a railway embankment was a large fox den and strewn about was bones and complete carcases of cats. The local newspaper did an article on it and that was the end of complaints we had about cats going missing.

When still very much a puppy we took her indoors now and again and if the 'phone would ring she would stand and bark at it and one evening when I dialled a number there were two men talking to each other. When they heard Tara barking one of the men said to the other, "I did not know you had a dog." The other man replied," It's not mine it's yours." This argument went on for some time and each of them got more and more annoyed. At one stage I passed the handset for Marjory to listen to them before gently laying it down. When we eventually started to pack our things for the flitting back to Scotland Tara was just about in the boxes herself. She knew that something was going on and would not leave our side. She came up in the lorry with us and spent most of the time asleep in the floor well at Marjory's feet.

PART FOUR

COMING HOME

CHAPTER 46

HEADING NORTH FOR GOOD

Catriona was at Cardiff University taking a degree in European Studies. Fiona had finished an Art and Design foundation course at Kingston Polytechnic and was at Winchester College of Art studying textiles. So with both girls away from home Marjory and I decided to put our house on the market and move back to Fettercairn in Scotland. It was soon after my leave of absence when Noel had his accident and I went north to see him and to help out in any way I could. While I was there Marjory rung to tell me that two guys had been to view the house and that they wanted me back in London immediately to complete the sale.

In England it was possible for you to do your own conveyancing and I had everything in place ready for a sale. The two guys gave us the asking price and wanted into the house in two weeks time which we agreed to. Panic then to arrange our move to Scotland. Years earlier I negotiated the lease of an old smiddy and house at a "Pepper Corn Rent" on the Burn Estate from Mr Kennoway where we might do Bed and Breakfast. I thought also of buying a gun and fishing tackle shop and to prepare myself for this I went on a 12 week business study course. Finally because of Noel's accident and at his request we decided to move to the Ardgay or Bonar Bridge area.

Miss Jean Matterson, granddaughter of Commander and Mrs Kemmis had Gruinard Estate put in trust for her. With it went the fishing, shootings, farms and all the properties except those tenanted or owned by the crofters. Mrs Kemmis, leased back the lodge and the policies. Jean was visiting Noel in hospital in Edinburgh and told him she was looking for another game-keeper to replace the one she had because of problems between him and the farm manager. Noel told her we were moving north and could well be interested in the job. She telephoned me in London and we discussed the possibility when she more or less said the job was mine. Marjory would have to work part time caring for Mrs Kemmis.

Jean then changed her mind about sacking George Anderson, or "Jim Reeves" as he was nicknamed because of his choice of songs he sung, and decided to let him continue working for her until his 65th birthday which was about eighteen months or less away. The farm manager, by mutual agreement, ceased to work for her and took a lease on the farm. I was then promised the keeper's job when the time came up if I was still interested in it at that time.

I spoke to Noel about me buying a house in the area and he put me in touch with a Niall Graham Campbell a local estate agent who informed me that there were only two cottages for sale that may suit our requirements. One was Lower Hilton, Culrain and the other was at Woodside, Ardgay. Both of them were in need of renovation so I did not offer the asking price for either. Niall ruled out the Woodside one and told me to put the offer for the other one through a solicitor in proper legal terms. He gave me the name of one in Dornoch so I rung him up and asked him to do the needful but subject to being accepted or otherwise by noon on Friday of the same week which was only three days away. The next day I got a call from him to say the offer had been accepted and that the house was legally mine.

A farewell party was quickly arranged for all our neighbours and other friends down south. Marjory prepared a huge buffet and good music from tapes got the dancers on their feet, Strip the Willow and Eightsome Reels once they got the hang of them were favourites. One guy even danced the Sailors Hornpipe. Another neighbour came to the kitchen to see if there was any more of the meat he was eating. A haunch of venison had been roasted and sliced up and it went down a treat with all who had it, but although he was very complimentary about it to begin with, he spat out what he had in his mouth when told it was venison. The mind boggles. That same guy who was a retired school teacher was a bit of a social climber and forever name dropping of the people he met. One day he came over to the front garden where I was working to specially tell me that a Chief Superintendant from the police was coming the following day to give a talk at the Rotary Club. "Oh" I said. "You mean T.N.T." He got a bit excited by the expression thinking they were to meet some explosive sort of guy. His jaw dropped a bit when I said, "No it really means "Think Noddy Think". One lunch time he and the Superintendent arrived at Upminster Station to coincide with the 2 o'clock change over and they found the early shift had already gone home having relieved by the late turn. Because I was in charge of the morning shift I was summonsed to his office later in the afternoon with a view to being disciplined. After he rambled on about it for some time and it was getting near 4pm I said to him you realise that if this goes on much longer I will be claiming overtime for being called out. I left his office at that point and never heard another word about it but I still got my two hours.

When I was night shift at Plaistow a CID officer made some derogatory remarks in a report he had to do about myself and another Sergeant. We knew we were one hundred per cent right with the procedure we adopted and I lodged a formal complaint about the officer concerned. We were both summoned to appear idividually before our own Chief Inspector, The Detective Chief Inspector and the Uniform Chief Superintendent. They tried to brow beat me into withdrawing my complaint but I would not back down unless I got a written apology. The Chief Superintendent then said he wanted to speak to me on my own and the other two left the office. I got on very well with him but every so often he kept pulling up one side of his trousers and I accused him of having a tape recorder in his pocket. He shouted at me, "Search me if you wish." At the same time he thrust open his jacket without undoing the buttons and they went flying across the floor. The day was saved when the CID officer who caused the entire rumpus knocked on the door to say he had come to make a personal apolgy to me. On the Monday morning I was told to form another crime squad, half uniform and half CID, no doubt to improve relations again.

Previously on a shooting trip to Scotland with an ex-colleague and very good friend, Eric Kite, I hired a furniture van and took all surplus belongings including building material, tools and other equipment, with us to store at Hill of Minnes. Rather than drive that van around on our shooting forays including up to Gruinard, my brother in law Eric arranged for us to get the loan of an old Escort van from a friend of his, Bill Clark, who had an agricultural contracting business at Udny. The van, apart from the half gallon of diesel that sloshed about the floor-well in the back, was ideal for our purpose and all it cost us was a haunch of venison.

I hired the same furniture van to do our proper removal, moving out of Gidea Park on the date agreed. With the help of Marjory and our neighbours, mostly women the van was finally loaded and we were on our way by lunch time, arriving in Ardgay at seven the next morning. After a good breakfast in the Lady Ross cafe we set off on the last leg of our journey for Culrain to look at the house we bought without even seeing and against the wishes of my nephew, Derek, who advised us of the state the place was in.

We had no idea where the furniture was going to be stored but when I stopped at the seller's house to collect the keys he immediately told us to put it in the house and to take some pieces of furniture belonging to him down to his place. We then went up to Noel and Margaret's and Derek arranged for further help to unload the van. The next morning we set off to take the van back to the hire company in Hornchurch and to collect our car and caravan. We had a few days holiday on the way north at Cambridge and York.

Because the previous owner had done a number of botched jobs in the house I made up my mind to gut the place and start from scratch. Over the winter months' plans for a complete modernisation and extension were drawn up for this in readiness to start work in the spring. In the meantime I knocked up a large wooden shed and when work started we moved into it, eating, sleeping and everything else. I think we had about eight square feet to live in with the remainder, including the loft, was taken up with storage of furniture, unpacked tea chests and building material for the renovation. When the girls were home they slept in the caravan. When Andrew, Sarah and the boys came up for a visit on seeing this little cottage in the distance up on the hillside, like Edith and Charlie Shepherd they likened it to "The Broons" one in the comic strip of the Sunday Post.

We set a target for all work to be completed by the 1st of August because of Marjory's brother and family were coming for a holiday. Geordie Bruce a retired road construction worker lived in the village. Marjory, him and I did all the donkey work, first stripping the walls bare, lifting all the old railway sleeper flooring and getting rid of the rubbish. Jochan a local crofter from Bonar Bridge had an old JCB and also a tractor and trailer. He was up at Lower Hilton for weeks on end carting in material for the garage base, digging out the footings for the extension and making the site generally friendly. Jochan was not the most regular time keeper and one morning I arranged to meet him to take a load of firewood up to Culrain for me. After waiting for more than an hour and Jochan had not turned up, I set off to look for him and to tell him to get lost, thinking I would get someone else to do the work. However, when I met him on the road I said to him, "What time is this? His response was, "Get yourself a new watch," opened the throttle and drove off for the firewood. Over the years since he has done lots of different work for me with the digger and incidentally with him now into his eighties he continues to run the croft and go out on hire with the machine.

Tradesmen who were in full time employment came in after work and at the weekends to do the professional work, George Johnson, mason, John Ross and Calum McKinnon, both joiners, Bobby Bain, farmer and electrician, Alan and David Cowie, plumbers and a guy Inkster for the roofing. An excellent team they turned out to be. We were also very fortunate to have two very good council building inspectors, Peter Harrison and John Sutherland. John was better known in the trade as "Stop the Job." We had no problem with either of them in fact they went beyond the call of duty to be helpful. I often had to phone one of them up for advice and they were only too happy to oblige. Geordie was very fond of the drams and I had to be careful when I paid him otherwise I was without a labourer when I most needed one. He was a hard worker and between us we laid all the concrete, mixing it by hand, for the footings and floors in readiness for the mason to start building the walls. When it came to renovations and other building work my biggest failing was under estimating what things would cost and at the end of the day we were laying out a lot more money than expected. If you do not get a grant for a renovation my advice from experience is to flatten what is there and build a new house because it will not cost you any more at the end of the day.

Originally Lower Hilton was two cottages for workers employed at Hilton Farm just up the hill a bit.

Although it was converted to one residence you could still see from marks on the walls traces of the old layout and how small the rooms had been and as I said that conversion and every other piece of work carried out to the property was of very poor quality. There was no form of electricity in the house so I bought a diesel generator as a temporary measure for lighting only. It was not strong enough to boil a kettle and that had to be hidden to stop people switching it on and tripping the fuses. It was so well hidden that it only turned up about seven years later. We took advantage of a subsidised hydro electric scheme and got mains in for £250.00. It was only then that Marjory was able to use her washing machine and other electrical goods, prior to that it was done by hand with aid of a washboard and an old hand wringer. There were no units or storage cupboards in the kitchen so Marjory had to improvise by stacking cardboard boxes on their sides to put things into. One thing she did enjoy using was the old Rayburn stove once she got it cleaned. The oven was fantastic for baking We moved into that house on 1st August, 1984 and moved out two months later to take up the job at Gruinard.

CHAPTER 47

POACHER TURNED KEEPER OR
THE OTHER WAY ROUND?

George tendered his resignation and we got a firm date for starting work with Jean Matterson. Over many previous years I got to know George very well. He would ask me to fish for the estate and turned a blind eye when I wanted one for the pot. The same went for venison from the hill. If I'm correct, I seem to remember George telling me that he caught twenty three salmon in one day from the Moral Pool. For most he fished with a floating line with a couple of yards of other line with the silicone coating stripped off to act as a sinker. His favourite flies were roughly tied by himself with hair from his golden Labrador on brass tubes. George kept saying that I should apply for his job and that he would give me a good reference. I did not tell him to begin with that it was already more or less mine anyway. He was an ex-bailiff from the river Brora and was not adverse to a bit of poaching himself. He was fined heavily for drink driving and a local hotelier paid the fine with George promising to pay the debt off with salmon for the hotel. From all accounts he was a successful one with cages supposedly set for otters to send south.

The main cage was set in a narrow stream right below the windows of the lodge. Stones were built up on either side directing the salmon into it as they made their way up stream. An otter did in fact go into it and George ended up waste deep in the Lodge Run, the pool below trying to recover it. There was a market for otters in the south but I do not recall him selling any. At first George never spoke to me about any of his poaching exploits. When Noel told me, I was not that keen to believe it but when I was told to go and look at the salmon scales on the bank, it was pretty obvious what was going on. Sure enough there was a trodden track down to the water edge. The stones were still in place and a rope hanging from a tree to secure the cage. Sometime later, along with Ronnie Ross the keeper from the opposite bank, I happened to be walking past that spot. Ronnie pointed to the track down to the water and said, "There was a time if you set a fox snare on it you would catch a poacher." The other tactic he employed was to go out on the fords or waterfalls with a landing net and as the salmon riggled their way upstream he would jab the net down in front of them.

At one stage on the upper beats there was such a shortage of fish that he had to be spoken to about his activities. I don't think he was entirely responsible for that. A lot of netting went on by professional poachers and I'm sure they were doing most of the damage. Poisoning of the rivers had mostly petered out by this time but there was one very bad case at the Glencalvie Falls where over twelve hundred salmon and other fish were recovered from the pools downstream. It was said at the time that this poisoning was done for spite. On the rock face at the falls the word "Think" was painted. It was also said that it would ruin the river for years to come but it had no effect whatsoever.

When I was stationed at Fettercairn I dealt with a case of poaching on the North Esk at the falls known as "The Loups" where we filled the back of the bailiff's landrover with salmon we recovered that were killed by the powdery cymag as it floated from one pool to another, a reckless way of using it. If there was a responsible way it was to put it in a stocking, or a sock tied to the end of a stick and dip it in the water taking only a manageable amount of salmon to carry away. Often a net was strung across the tail of the pool to catch them. By morning there was little evidence that anything had gone on. Perhaps a few scales on the bank.

From a police point of view the "Loups" job went extremely well. Following foot prints in the early morning dew covered grass, not only did I find a pile of salmon close to the public road, but a net, sacks, cymag and other gear. With the help of the bailiffs, other officers, Bert, Frank and other keepers, we kept watch for those responsible coming back in the darkness for their spoil. Sure enough a car driven by a woman dropped off two men and then drove on up Glen Esk where she was arrested.

In those days the police did not have hand held radios. The plan was to let the men fill the sacks with the salmon and as soon as they got them on their backs myself and another officer would spring out of the bushes where we were hiding and arrest them, at the same time alerting the others for assistance. I grabbed my one and handcuffed him to a tree but the other got away. Whilst a big search got underway I questioned the one we had, and managed to get the name and address of his mate.

It transpired that the two of them were from Arbroath, some thirty miles away. The police there arrested the second man as he hobbled into his street and went to a nearby van and in it they found gelignite explosive and other poaching equipment. Both got six months in prison for their troubles more than likely because of the explosives. Frank, with others was up on a knoll overlooking the road that night, and what he was going to do if he got his hands on the poachers was nobody's business. When the shout went up, in his enthusiasm he tripped over a tree stump and hit his head on another, putting him out of the scene for the rest of the night. When the prisoner was taken to Stonehaven he was handcuffed to Bert. After I got home Bert rung to say that I had gone away with the handcuff keys in my pocket and that he had to take the prisoner home to bed with him. The officers found another key to fit them but thought it a good laugh to phone me just the same. The other prisoner arriving at Arbroath only had one shoe on and he told me that in the process of escaping from us he climbed up on to the boughs of a large beech tree and it was then that he lost the other one.

Although I was well aware of George's poaching forays I never mentioned it to him, instead waiting for him to bring the subject up. There were mornings when I went into his house he would have his tweeds drying at the fire and not because they had been washed. You could see the odd scale on them. It was only on the day he was flitting that he spoke in any depth about it. I went up to give him a help and when the cages were put on the van he proudly showed me how to make and work them, also how to net the fish on the fords. He explained how it was important to buy a rectangular shaped landing net so that the flat area on it was less likely to let a salmon get past when it was jabbed down in front of them. George went to another ghillie's job at Lochcarron but I never did know if he got up to mischief there. I did visit him there and also when George and Margaret, his wife, retired to Banffshire.

Marjory and I had our first official interview for the job with Jean and Mrs Kemmis at the lodge. Noel, as well as about every other member of my family, at some stage in their lives, worked on the estate for one employer or another. Noel was teasing Marjory about what she could expect from Mrs Kemmis who was quite old by this time but had all her faculties and because she was confined more or less to the lodge had not lost many of her wicked ways towards the workers. He said, "Don't laugh when you see her false teeth rattle up and down in her mouth as she speaks." It would not have been so noticeable or funny if he had not mentioned it. Mrs Kemmis was not that interested in talking to Marjory and sent Jean off with her to show her round the house.

Noel and my sister Anne and anyone else who knew Commander Kemmis spoke very highly of him, even Geordie Heatherlea, although in unusual circumstances. At Braelandwell Lodge there was a public bar and one evening Geordie was drinking in it. He wasn't drunk by any means, just enough to loosen the tongue, and told the story how he met in with Commander Kemmis at the river bank and told him it was not his son who was fishing the river and that it was a bobby who should know better. It did not leave much of anyone's imagination to work out who that was. The Commander, according to Geordie said to him, "Mr Ross I would like to think that I am enough of a gentleman if I saw someone fishing without permission to turn my head and walk away," and at that he just walked off. My father was one of the ghillies at Braelangwell at the time and when he met in with Ken the bobby who was the barman there, he was told of the conversation that took place.

Apparently he was a gentleman to work for as well but got a hard time of it from Mrs Kemmis. Anne said that at the table at meal times, because of the nagging, he would often shove the plate away from him and walk out of the lodge. Bread pudding was a favourite of the Commander's when he was there on his own and would often have a second helping but was worried that Anne would get into trouble if Mrs Kemmis missed the dried fruit she put into it. It was not just in the lodge but outside as well. Noel and the two of them were planting young beach trees for a hedge. As far as Mrs Kemmis was concerned the Commander could not get it right. They were either too close, too far apart or something else. The Commander told her to do it herself and walked off. Mrs Kemmis, as usual having the last word, said to Noel, "Now you have seen how to do it carry on yourself." Marjory can relate to the planting of the trees by the Commander to her own experience with my Dad when planting potatoes. They were the same either too close or too far apart but I don't recall her storming off although perhaps she would have liked to have done. I had only one conversation with the Commander albeit a bit one sided. I was cutting some firewood near to the riverside path and clearing up all the brush to tidy the wood up. I thought I was doing the right thing until the Commander pointed out to me that I was spoiling the cover for woodcock which he was so fond of shooting.

Noel was cutting a plot of grass in the vegetable garden when Mrs Kemmis came in and accused him of not oiling the wooden rollers on the hand mower he was using. They were squeaking as they always did whether or not they were oiled. Noel said there was no oil anyway and Mrs Kemmis wanted to know why not. Commander Kemmis forgot to get it the previous day from the garage. Mrs Kemmis gave him hell and sent him off for it. He brought it back to Noel in the garden but he could see that the oil made no difference to the squeaking. Mrs Kemmis came back at that point and could not accept the fact that she was wrong and orders from her then was to remove all the turf and dig the plot over for another vegetable patch. Tike her terrier always sat on the front passenger seat of her car and anyone else had to take a back seat.

The staff in the lodge were not treated any better. My sister Anne was the cook, and two cleaners, Mrs Sinclair and Mrs Hay were not allowed to have a break for a cup of coffee or tea and there were many rows over that when she caught them. They then decided to hide the cups and other items under one of the baths up stairs and would lock the door when having it. She later relented to them having coffee but would not allow them anything to eat with it so Anne made toasted sandwiches when she was doing the breakfast and hid them in her coat pocket in a cleaning cupboard until one day the Weimaraner dog sniffed them out and was heading for the dining room with them but luckily they were rescued in time.

At dinner at night, particularly if they had guests, she would play the Madam to the extreme to the point of being nasty. Anne would be instructed to bring the soup in whenever she heard them settle down at the table, but when she did this she would be ordered out of the dining room. No sooner was the soup back in the pan to keep it hot and a start made to wash the bowls, Mrs Kemmis would be shouting for it to be brought in. For some reason when the proprietors from Amat Estate were there for dinner Mrs Kemmis decided to serve the soup herself and do it differently. She set out the bowls on the table first and then filled a filthy dirty rusty old jug normally used for watering cut flowers or giving those in pots a feed of Baby Bio and poured the soup from that into the bowls. Heaven knows what the guests thought but they ate it just the same.

Mrs Hay had an allergy to T.C.P which Mrs Kemmis used a lot of. It caused Mrs Hay to sneeze constantly so she gave in her notice to leave and gave that as her reason for going. She got no sympathy from Mrs Kemmis who instead went about sprinkling T.C.P. wherever she thought Mrs Hay would come in contact with it. Anne by this time had enough and she left as well.

For few years before Croick School closed the pupils and parents were invited to the lodge for a Xmas party. Anne took her boy Ronnie to it. When they were seated round the dining room table Mrs Kemmis was dishing up the treats to everyone but left Anne out and went on to the next person. Games to the music of a piper were played afterwards in the hall. By the time Marjory and I went to work for her she had mellowed greatly and as Noel maintained that we probably had the best of her, if there was such a thing. Kim Sawyer met her one day on the public road at Dounie and she told him off about shooting on a Sunday. He and the other keepers had made plans for a fox drive soon after that and he took the opportunity to ask Mrs Kemmis if she would like to contribute a bottle of whisky for the day. "No." She said. "I don't believe in drink and driving." He never did get the bottle he was hoping to get.

Like most estates, staff were hired and fired just as quick at Gruinard. More than one person told me that Mrs Kemmis longed for the days when twenty or more people would be queing up at the lodge gates waiting to get the one job. No consideration was given for sickness. If you were not fit to work after being off for a week or two, it was a case of down the road. One handyman arrived and on his first morning saluted the Commander, at the same time saying, "Good morning Captain." That was enough for him to be shown where the gate was. As Willie MacDonald often said, "There's a slippery stone at the front door of every big house," and how right he was.

The Commander himself got a rather quick dispatch from the estate but in a rather sad way. Moral was the perfect height for fishing and he invited Mr Hunter from Dounie Estate to join him. Leaving Ronnie Ross to wait for the guest to arrive he went off to fish Moral. When Mr Hunter did not arrive Ronnie went up to Moral to join the Commander who was changing a fly at that time. Ronnie noticed that all was not well and within minutes the Commander collapsed unconscious. After making him comfortable Ronnie ran for help and on the way met Mr Hunter. Between them, using an old door as a stretcher, they carried Mr Kemmis to the lodge and got medical help. He never recovered and died in the lodge from a cerebral haemorrhage.

I am no historian of naval history or for that matter a historian of any kind but Mr Kemmis served as a Sub-Lieutenant on the HMS Onslaught a destroyer during the Battle of Jutland when it came under heavy fire and its Commander and 1st Lieutenant were both killed. Mr Kemmis, assisted by a Midshipman, took the vessel successfully out of action and back to her home port. On coming to Gruinard many artefacts, both personal and pertaining to the HMS Onslaught, were evident throughout the lodge.

By the time we got there she certainly had mellowed a great deal but her and I had our differences to sort out on more than one occasion. Admiral Mason and Captain Lloyd would sometimes go in to see her. She told me one day that if there was not enough space in my freezer they could put their fish into her's which I did before we went to Aberdeen to attend a wedding. She did not like Marjory having time off and we expected trouble when we came back home. True to form she got stuck into me for putting the fish in her freezer without permission. That ended up with me having a good slanging match with her and me threatening not to take her for her shopping. For a change when Marjory went in to work on Monday morning Mrs Kemmis could not have been nicer to her. I suggested to Marjory that a row now and again may not be a bad thing but as it turned out that was the only major one. Not long after that row I was driving her down to the village for her shopping when she started speaking about Neil Graesser. She did not like him and said he was a very thrawn man and then looked up at me with a wry smile and said, "But all men can be thrawn."

All the time she was in Gruinard she had a drink problem but worse in her later years. When I took in the shopping it was on average six bottles of whisky and six bottles of dry sherry per fortnight. When it was still available for sale she regularly bought bottle after bottle of Kaolin for her upset stomach. This mixture had a certain amount of morphine in it and people got addicted to it and for that reason it was taken off the market. She treated Marjory as if she did not drink, yet the sherry glass was hidden in a drawer beside her chair in the sitting-room and the whisky one beside her bed. One evening we thought she had fallen off the chair in the lounge and knocked over an electric fire but fortunately no damage was done. She had actually fallen in the kitchen and dragged herself through to the lounge and in the process put the end of her stick through a lead water pipe as she tried to push herself along. She was a bit shocked so we decided to get her up to bed but before that I asked her if she needed a drink, whisky of course. She drank one good one in the lounge and I put the bottle, glass and a jug of water up to her bedroom which was her norm but next morning she told Marjory to take the bottle down stairs at the same time saying, "I don't know what Hughie was thinking about last night." As if she never did have a drink. The pantry next to the kitchen was so full of empties that you could not open the door. Food wise she ate very little, cornflakes for breakfast and mainly tinned rice or tinned macaroni the rest of the day. She would never put out milk that had gone off even if it got to the stage of being like sour yogart. It went on the flakes just the same. Having said that she was in remarkably good health and the only time she was in hospital that I know of was in her dying days.

Mrs Kemmis's main concern was to know if I would be able to drive her car. One would have thought it was something special but it was only a BMC 1100 automatic. She asked what our plans were for Lower Hilton. My reply to her was quite clear, that it would always be there if for any reason we had to walk out of Gruinard over night. That did not go down well with her. The next step was for me only to go to Inverness for an interview with the factor, a Mr Kenneth Hughes. The interview went well enough but I did not get the pay or perks I was expecting. The excuse was that I did not know what the job entailed and that my wages were paid by both Jean and Mrs Kemmis and that Jean could not afford more. He promised me that I would get a substantial rise after one year. I was not too bothered because I had my police pension and I got a very good tools and equipment allowance for using my own. The estate had none anyway and they certainly did not go to Lochcarron. One may ask why I went to work there in the first place and the answer was simply free sport. Within two weeks of starting the job a local farmer's wife said, "You've made it official at last then."

A price could not be put on the free sport I would have, which Jean and the factor both reminded me of later. To begin with there were four letting rods and a house rod which Jean and I fished. There were plenty of salmon in the rivers in those days and on average we would catch about 150 salmon a season at Gruinard alone. That tailed off a bit before I left but Jean doing her calculations for returns at the end of the season reckoned I caught about a third of them. I made my own rules as to when and where I would fish. I never fished a pool before the guests had and most of my fishing would be done in the evening and some weeks I would not fish at all because I knew the paying guests did not like it.

CHAPTER 48

ANOTHER KIND OF BATTLE

At the end of my first year and when I thought I had acquitted myself very well, I asked for the substantial pay rise as promised. Well what an insult. I got a letter saying my pay had been increased by £1.00 per week. The shit hit the fan over that. I had a huge row with the factor and I told him how two faced he was. Mrs Kemmis was not much better. Jean kept out of it but then she had the factor dealing with it for her. I told Hughes I would make my pay up in other ways and that took him by surprise, he was sure I was going to start selling salmon and deer, but I never made him any the wiser. That would have been the same as going to the safe and taking money from it.

My pay went up by £4.00 per week and I was given an extra ton of coal. I asked for two salmon and one carcase of venison per year and he would not agree to that either, so I just told him quite clearly that I would help myself as and when I needed one and stormed off out of his office. I was not that bothered about the salmon because some of the guests often left Marjory and I with a fish or a side of smoked salmon. I never did know if he told Jean about this row and what I said. Jean never mentioned it and we never went without our bit of salmon or venison. I did say to her that I told one of the crofters that as far as I was concerned they, meaning all of them, need not go without their bit of venison. During the night for most they were down on the crofts anyway. She never said much but I could see she was not pleased. Every season she give each of them a salmon but that stopped when they became less plentiful.

Mrs Kemmis was concerned that we would leave, and on her table where she sat in the lounge was a letter from Hughes assuring her that we could be easily replaced and that there were plenty of other suitable people willing to take the job. By this time I took a distinct dislike to the man and I made up my mind there and then that I would see him out of Gruinard before me. It has often been spoken and sometimes written that when the gamekeeper was asked if there was much vermin on the estate his reply was along the lines, "A few hoodies and the factor." That of course is not the case with all of them.

From then on if I could find fault with anything to do with his office I complained to Jean and Mrs Kemmis about it. The first big opportunity came after Mrs Kemmis agreed with me to have the outside of the lodge painted. Much against my wishes a firm from Inverness was given the job. I kept a close eye on their work and noticed that they were not keeping to the specification, primer where necessary, an undercoat and two coats of good quality gloss.

No primer was used, a combined mixture of gloss and undercoat for the finish and painting continued even if it was pouring rain. This ended up with Hughes and I thumping the desk at one another and the surveyor from his office who chose the contractors coming up to Gruinard to look at the mess. He did not want to believe what I had to say and tried to fob me off with how good the firm was and that they would never do a shoddy job, but the blisters the size of my hand on the new paintwork, spoke for itself. He even tried to tell me that they used blow heaters when it was raining Not before we had a good ding dong did he agree to getting them back to put it right. I hate to see people being ripped off irrespective of who they are.

To show how stupid Hughes was he told me one day that on no account was I to discuss estate matters with Jean. If she needed to know anything I had to refer her to his office. Myles Larby, a very nice man, dealt with all sporting matter in his office so I asked Hughes if Jean wanted to know how many fish were being caught, I had to refer her to him. The answer was yes and the same was to apply if she wanted to know how young trees we planted were doing? Had I to refer her to the forestry man in his office? Jean had the good sense to over- rule all of this nonsense.

James Munro who rented Invercarron farm from Gruinard Estate was having a new barn and steading built at Jean's expense. We were out stalking one day when this came up in conversation and Jean told me that the old farmhouse was going to be burned down as an exercise by the local fire brigade and the rubble used in the foundations. When she told me it was to include the slates on the roof and that of the farm steading I pointed out to her that they were of value and enough for about eight bungalows and that I myself would be interested in some of them for another house I was building up Strathkyle. She had been advised that it was too dangerous to remove them from the roof. I said to her, "Sell them on the roof and it would then be the buyer's responsibility to remove them."

Jean promised to speak to the surveyor from the factor's office about me getting the slates I required. I was having difficulty in getting a decision from Jean but was then told to speak to the surveyor, who in turn said I would have to buy the slates from the firm in Dingwall who bought all of them for a hell of a lot less than what they were worth. It was said at the time he paid the equivalent of one bungalow, far less eight.

One almighty row broke out between Jean and I over this. I telephoned her that night in Edinburgh and told her what I thought of her. She came up at the weekend and spoke to me about the rude 'phone call I made to her and at one stage told me that I was being childish. I was still in such a rage with her that I found it difficult to express myself. I did however, point out to her that every minker, tinker from Wick to Inverness was at the farm helping themselves to what they fancied. A lorry load of dressed sandstone and lintels went up to Amat Estate and the farmer himself, took the old brass bell that hung over the steading from the time it was built and had it mounted in his garden at Ardgay. All of this was without permission of anyone, and here was me the only worker in her employment could not get a puckle slates even although I was willing to pay for them. The convenience of where they were made them more attractive to me. I have to say though that after that row I was offered anything else that Jean was disposing off or others seeking to have. Regarding the farmhouse it was a lovely old building but needing a lot doing to it. Several approaches had been made to the estate with a view to buying it but they were turned down each time. It angered me at the thought of it being demolished so I brought it to the notice of the authorities dealing with listed buildings and they fully agreed with me and slapped and order on it straight away.

Luckily soon after that I bought slates of a barn up at Shinnes and organised a party to strip them off the roof with me. Geordie Bruce and I carted them home with two tractors. Everything went without a hitch until we were crossing over to Rosehall when the pin jumped out of the draw-bar of my tractor and the trailer went sliding down the hill past me. With the loader on the other tractor I was able to couple up again and complete our journey with no serious damage done. By coincidence the owner of the barn at Shinnes was Bobby Ramsay whose mother was the last person to live in Ruie an Taoir and locally it was always referred to as "Ramsay's" cottage.

Call it childish if you like but the outcome of this row was me not speaking to Jean for about two months or more. I told her she could buy her own tools and equipment and that I would not be using mine any more. It was a very unpleasant situation. It suited me to use my Argocat to take deer off the hill even although I was not being paid for it but after a few seasons I could see that Jean was not going to get one of her own so I sold mine. It was decided to buy a Kawasaki four wheel drive quad bike. The first day I took it to the hill I had to take home a stag which I shot. Because there was a steep hill to climb on the way home I tied it on to the front carrier. I had not gone very far when I changed direction for another route home. This necessitated going down a slight hill and half way one of the front wheels went into a hole and the bike somersaulted twice, throwing me over the handlebars. I tried to get out of the way but the bike landed on top of me before rolling down a side slope. When I picked myself up off the ground I found that blood was streaming down the side of my face. I knew I had a wound to my right temple but did not know at that time if it was serious or not. I applied pressure to it with my bonnet until the bleeding stopped.

After finding my rifle and binoculars I was just about to set off for home on foot and then thought I would check the condition of the bike which was lying upside down with the stag half off it. I cut the ropes and rolled the bike over on to its wheels. The only damage I could see was to the name badge attached to the front of the radiator grill. I never thought the engine would start but it did straight away. I drove home and when I walked into the house Marjory got quite a fright when she saw the mess of blood. After I give myself a good wash up it did not look so bad but obviously required stitching. I was amused at the local doctor who kept apologising for hurting me and for breaking a needle in the process. I had to tell him to leave the pain to me and for him to get on with the stitching.

I knew the doctor quite well because of my back problem and on another occasion I had to ask him to remove a fish hook from my eyebrow that I was not able to do myself. Most ghillies are quite familiar with this task which entails pushing the point of the hook and barb back out through the skin again, then snipping that part of it off. The remainder slips out no bother. On my way to the doctor that day I met in with a neighbouring ghillie and he saw for himself what had happened but next day when I went into the fishing tackle shop in Tain the staff there was told that I had lost an eye. This relates very much to a local saying, "A fart in Ardgay is something more by the time it reaches Bonar."

Next morning I rung Ronnie to ask him to come with his Argocat and take the stag home to the larder. My legs, arms and ribs were aching pretty badly and I was not able to help very much. When Ronnie hung the carcase up and split it down the breast bone he asked me how many shots I had fired at it. At first he did not believe me and pointed to several holes in the rib cage. I assured him that I only fired one bullet and the holes were from the stags antlers as the bike rolled over. We agreed that I had a narrow escape when the holes could easily have been in my rib cage. I then rigged up a sledge from quarry belting to drag the stags home until we got a trailer.

Kenneth Hughes relinquished his position with the firm and Myles Larby took over. The surveyor remained the same. Myles never came near me for at least two months but kept asking the keeper in Amat if he thought I was ready for speaking to. The message really got home to them. It was not long after that when Mrs Kemmis died in Golspie Hospital. I went there to see her the previous day and was the last one with any connection with the estate to see her alive. She held on to my hand and pleaded with me to take her home. Had she repented by then? When the family arrived, a service and burial was arranged to take place at Croick Church and cemetery respectively. Everyone was then invited back to the lodge for drinks, tea etc. Jean fell heir to the estate in its entirety and her mother was left the contents of the lodge and whatever else. Marjory and my self, to our surprise, were each left a considerable sum of money but peanuts to what she was worth. Jean's mother, Mrs Matterson, came up to Gruinard Lodge several weekends after that to sort out the contents and to arrange the various methods of its disposal. There were rich pickings to be had for Marjory and I from what was thrown out for burning or other means of disposal.

Jean, soon afterwards had plans drawn up for a complete refurbishment of the lodge in readiness for the fishing guests staying in it from the beginning of the following season and I think about one hundred and fifty thousand pounds was set aside for doing this work. I was to play no part in any of this. The same surveyor was in charge of it. With exception of the plumbing all work was contracted out to the surveyor's cronies, tradesmen from Inverness. The only reason the plumbing stayed local was the fact that Moray Munro, who was in the way of doing the plumbing, complained that he was not even invited to price for it.

Because valuable pieces of antique furniture and other things were left in the lodge I suggested that they were moved out before work begun and put in storage in the garage buildings or perhaps do one half of the lodge at a time. But no, the builder arrived one morning and started in just about every room, taking out holes in the stone and lime walls for new doorways etc. By evening there was not a room in the lodge or piece of furniture that was not covered in lime dust. You could watch clouds of it blowing over Garden Cottage where we lived. When the electrician started, not Bobby I may add, he went from room to room and just climbed over the furniture to get to the ceilings. Furniture was only removed as a last resort.

I never forgot, and I'm not likely to, what the surveyor did on me over the slates. Every night I would go over to the lodge and pick fault with the work being done and next day or so I would ring Jean up and bring it to her notice. She in turn would speak, either to the factor or the surveyor. Without consulting the plumber who installed the heating and hot water systems or myself who was to look after it on a day by day basis, incorporated a sophisticated electronic control box of gadgets to regulate everything. This piece of equipment cost several thousand pounds and neither the plumber nor I or anybody else could understand how it worked and every time something went wrong I had to telephone the installer and get him out to fix it, costing a fortune. While this was going on I learned that the same system had been installed in schools and other similar sized properties and it was just not a success. I convinced Jean to cut her losses and go back to a simple time clock that her, and all concerned could operate. The new equipment worked satisfactorily long after we left until new boilers were installed.

Mid stream of the works going on in the lodge Jean rung me up to say she had sacked the firm of estate agents who were running things for her, and engaged an Aberdeen firm to take over, with a Mr Michael Milligan as her factor. I just laughed. It was what I wanted to hear for a long time and Jean herself knew I would be pleased. I just felt that I could draw a line under the past and start afresh. I can honestly say that Mr Milligan, who I always regarded as a gentleman and I never had a wrong word or disagreement the whole time I had to work with him. I also have to admit that troubles in the earlier years between Jean and I could have been avoided had she been better advised. I had a lot of respect for Jean and over all she was a very good boss. In her day job as I would call it, according to an article in a financial magazine I read she had risen from tea-girl to the top. She was exceptionally competent and highly respected but did need the right person to run the estate for her. The surveyor was allowed to carry on until the work in the lodge was completed but by this time the budget was well over the estimate and was to be even more so by the time the painters were finished.

Again it was an Inverness firm who arrived to redecorate and I learned from one of them that they were being paid an hourly rate and to get the work done as quickly as possible even if they had to work round the clock. They had caravans on site and only went home at weekends. I could see quite plainly that for five of them, they should have been making more progress than what they were, and decided to keep a closer watch on them. I did this over a few evenings when I found they spent an awful lot of time in an upstairs kitchen with blankets over the window. When I walked in on them they were playing cards and had been doing that all the time they were there. After the surveyor got an ear bashing the knock on effect was that the boss of the paint firm came to the lodge and sacked them all bar an apprentice. Two other painters arrived and completed the work within a matter of days. We then learned that the sacked four had previously been given redundancy notices and were spinning out the work as long as they could. That was the end of the Surveyor as well.

It was then over to Jean, Marjory and myself to get the lodge ready for the fishing guests in the spring. What time we had was pretty limited but we made it. Because the painters thought it would be carpeted throughout they never bother to put down dust sheets and I was left to clean up this mess by sanding all the floors, staining and varnishing them sometimes going back late at night to give them a second coat or for a first coat so that I could start early again next morning. A few carpets went back down where they had been previously but others from an old store room were cut up to make do elsewhere. Marjory had an even bigger task washing and polishing all the furniture and helping Jean with beds and bedding and so much more. Every Friday night Jean would arrive with more and more stuff. Soft furnishings and pictures for the walls were also in her domain and generally deciding on how she wanted things.

Jean had her own self contained flat upstairs at one end of the lodge but later had part of the garage buildings converted for accommodation there. Originally it was the coach-house, tack room and coach-man's flat above, limited for bedrooms, but otherwise very compact and comfortable. My nephew Derek drew up the plans and supervised the building of it. It was more private and quieter than the first flat she had in the lodge.

By this time Marjory had got to know a lot of the local people but was confused with their names. So many of them had bynames and often it was the same person that different people were talking about when either one or the other of the names was used. Nicknames are interesting and I often wonder how they came about although most of them originated from School days, at work or in the forces. For amusement I'm going to list a few of the ones I have come across but no offence is intended towards the bearer of any of them:-

Kipper; Jeely Heels; Jinty; Tort; Forty Five; Knocker; Forty Nips; Pot Licker; Sheepy; Pimpo; Spivey; Oracle; Dry Rot; The Shark; Shiner; Bull eye; Bubbles; The Mole; Cheese and Egg; Wissen Pug; Country Road; Dew drop and last but not least Shuggie. No one could tell me where "Tug Wilson" came from.

As I said before, I promised Hughes I would make up my earnings in a different way. I investigated the possibility of buying another old cottage, Ruie an Taoir, which was in a worse state than the first one, which was being sold by sheriff's warrant. Marjory and I went to look at it more than once. It was a complete wreck of a place, cattle and sheep having free access to it, holed and rusty corrugated iron over turf for the roof and walls bulging and falling down. One good gable end, three quarters of an acre site, and no water supply. The selling agent, Peter Graham, happened to be fishing with me one day and I told him that I was going to put an offer in for it. He immediately tried to put me off, but I insisted I was serious, in which case he agreed to put the offer forward.

I did my home work and found out why it was being sold under warrant. The previous owners, an unmarried couple, had borrowed a small sum of money to buy it, but then could not afford to do any work and in the end they split up and the lenders wanted their money out of it. When I, in a roundabout way, found out the amount of money involved I then added on a ten per cent here and there to cover selling costs to solicitors and agents. I gave the sellers a few days to accept it which they did. When Peter told me that my offer had been accepted he was curious to know how I arrived at this odd figure. He had no idea how much was owed on the property and I never did make him any the wiser. It was about two years later before I did anything with the property. Because it was to be our main residence on leaving Gruinard we lavished more money on it than we would normally have done.

Charlie and Isabel Hutcheon were up at Gruinard with us for few days and they decided to go and have a look at our latest purchase. Before leaving I said to Charlie, "You better get the key to the house from Marjory." When he asked her Marjory said, "When you get there I don't think you will require one." When they came back Charlie said to Marjory, "I understand what you meant now."

Burning turf off the roof   *Base for the turf*

Peter Harrison drew up the plans and got me grant aid for it. Almost the same team of tradesmen did the professional work but this time Alan Ross was the main joiner. Geordie was number one labourer again, Charlie Povey a local water bailiff and Robert Sawyer, a schoolboy made up the rest of the team. Robert was strong for his age and had plenty of common sense, having worked so much with his granddad. He was really good for operating the tractor and loader. I always said he would move Cairn Bhren if he was behind the wheel of a tractor or other machine. Yes I used to shout and swear at him almost on a daily basis but he took it all in good fun and would tell his mates to take no notice of me. Incidentally, Robert lives a few hundred yards along the road from me and now has his own successful builders business and we have remained good friends ever since. Only this week he has started the ground work for a new house for himself, Nicola and their little girl Chloe. I was cutting the grass on our lawn down next to the road when an empty beer can came flying over the hedge. I immediately stopped the mower and shouted a few expletives at whoever was responsible then this grinning face appeared from the roadside delighted with him self at having got one over me. Another joiner who worked for me was Willie James. He was something else. I had to keep re-assuring him that I was not that much older than him self and that I did have a mother and father who were wed when they had me.

The Safety Inspector

I had to be away from the estate a lot of the time while this project was ongoing even although the bulk of the work was done at nights and weekends so I paid Geordie to come up and strim the river banks, cut firewood and other odd jobs on the estate. This balanced the books one could say. I never told Jean I was doing it, I just did it, and I was to do it again for two other properties I was involved with in the Culrain area, one for a lady who was moving out of a large house to down-size and the other for a couple from Wilshire who bought a house site. As far as I was concerned it all came within the terms of the statement I made to Hughes.

Ruie an Taoir, gaelic roughly for the slope of the joiner, not very exciting and Lower Hilton was let out as holiday homes but financially that was a dead loss. When Marjory and I decided to leave our jobs at Gruinard we went as planned to

Ruie an Taoir to live. By that time I had bought about seventy five acres of rough grazings next to it which was good for me because as a hobby I got into training pointers, setters and other gun dogs. I also created a duck flight pond and the odd roe deer or sika could be shot on the land as well, good for keeping the freezer topped up. Trout fishing rights went with it along the bank of the Kyle. An unusual part of its topography was what is known as a kettle pond. This dates back to the ice age when a very large area of ice got surrounded by gravel and silt. When the ice eventually melted it left a deep tapered circular hole some one hundred yards across at the top and probably the same in depth. It was half full of water which I stocked with brown trout but the otters which had a Holt on the edge of it saw to the last of them. Divers I believe went down into it but for some reason they said they would not go back into it again. When there was a snow fall you could see where the otters were sliding down the slope to the water. Just below that pond, at the edge of the Kyle there was a piece of land jutting out into the tidal water, known as otter point where they were frequently seen. Before the Forestry Commission cut down a nearby wood there used to be a heronry in one part of it and they were regulars at the kettle pond as well. At the boundary fence there was a large badger set and one day the local farmer asked me if I knew who was taking soil away from under the cow pats in the field nearby. It was no one, only the badgers digging for worms.

Marjory and I got fed up having to look after Lower Hilton. If either of us was not available to do the cleaning on the Saturday change over days it was not easy to get suitable people to do it. Marjory suggested selling Lower Hilton but my view was to sell both the houses and move to Bonar Bridge either to buy or to build. Andrew and Sarah Cunningham who by this time were living in Dalriada where we are now, told us they were going to sell it because of the excessive number of golf balls coming into the garden, so many, that they wore cycle helmets when working in it. I along with other members continued the struggle with the Golf Club Council to have the first tee and fairway altered to overcome the problem and only after professional advice was taken from different quarters that they carried out the work. Only a limited number of balls come in now, probably one every few weeks and the risks are minimal.

It was us who introduced the sale of that house to Andrew and Sarah when they bought it about two years previous. Unbeknown to either of us at that time both Marjory and I had a fancy to live in it but never mentioned it to one another, so we decided immediately to buy it by doing a private deal. It was now time to put the two other properties on the market so I invited a friend of Jean's, William Jackson an estate agent from Perth, who I got to know quite well to come and value them. Because of its sporting value he marketed Ruie an Taoir as a mini estate. Property then was selling well and and both properties went very quickly.

Marjory, over and above her golfing, WRI, the family and other things she is involved in, is a very keen gardener. She grew her own vegetables at Gruinard, designed and planted out the garden at Ruie an Taoir with shrubs and trees with a keen eye for colour all year round and easy maintenance. She has put her own stamp on this one at Dalriada. She has not yet been able to slow down the grass from growing and I have to cut it two or three times a week. I take no credit for the many compliments we have had throughout the years about our gardens and readily admit it is all down to Marjory. I do the lazy bit and sit on the ride on mower. We spend a lot of our time each doing our own thing and one not knowing where the other is. We are usually home for supper together but when friends ring up to speak to either of us they think it is a big joke when they cannot be told where we are or when we will be home.

Catriona is following her footsteps as regards the gardening and undertook a course on Horticulture and Garden Design and passed with distinction. When in Berkshire over and above the garden at home she had an allotment where, helped by Hannah and Holly, she grew her own vegetables and flowers. Now that she is living at Cawder with a large garden she has set about planting it out with trees, shrubs and hedging. A section has been marked off for flowers, herbs and another for vegetables. Hens and ducks ducks have arrived for Hannah and Holly respectively to look after. Surplus eggs find their way into Inverness and up to Bonar or out at the gate under a "For Sale" sign. Bird feeders loaded with various seeds and pea nuts have been hung out attracting a large variety of songbirds including the woodpeckers. A pair of Red Leg Partridges have taken up residency as well and have got so tame that one of them entered the house the other day. The fences have had to be rabbit proofed and heightened to keep the roe deer out because any existing trees were stripped of bark. Red squirrels have been spotted in the trees adjacent to the garden and a proper wildcat was seen stalking along the fence side as well.

CHAPTER 49

A WAY OF LIFE HARD TO BEAT

In spite of all the ups and downs I had to begin with, I enjoyed my work and stay at Gruinard. Marjory did as well when she was not scraping me off the ceiling and getting my feet firmly planted on the ground again. It was a way of life and one not easily to put a price on. We met many interesting people from all parts of society. The public are too often given the wrong impression that salmon fishing, shooting and deer stalking is only for the rich but this is far from the truth. It is within the reach of many ordinary people. The majority of the lodges can sleep several couples and when the cost is divided up amongst them it comes to a few hundred pounds only and sometimes less than what some people pay to lay on a sunny beach abroad. Deer stalking can be even better value. Ordinary may be the wrong word to use because in my opinion we are all equal and one is no better than the other. At the end of the day what have we got? A narrow plot six feet long and six feet deep, often having a neighbour who you did not care for in the first place.

Yes, many wealthy and titled people came to Gruinard to fish the Carron but they got no more than Mr or Mrs from me and as often or not nothing at all. Sir was not in my vocabulary and taking my cap off was taboo as well. In fact I was more inclined to use it to fellow keepers or friends. On arrival some of them would ask, "What do we call you." My reply was, "Hugh, what else?" The ex army officers, Majors, Colonels, Brigadiers and Generals or a mixture of those ranks were the worst. On leaving the forces they should not be allowed to use their ranks. On more than one occasion I can recall telling them that as far as I was concerned their ranks went out at the window the day they arrived. Mostly I would be addressed by my surname, another military trend, but they were soon put right on that score as well. A retired Major was getting a ticking off from me one day for continually addressing me as Matheson, but I really had to laugh at him for in his apology he still kept referring to me by my surname only.

A party of five young army officers came to Gruinard for a week and they asked if I could take them ferreting rabbits. The burrows in the open fields were alive with them so good sport was assured. There was plenty of shooting from all of them but nothing in the bag to show for it. At one stage a young foreign girl came from the lodge to join us. She was intrigued by the goings on but asked if it was possible to hit the rabbits. I have to admit they were bolting well and running like stink. She then insisted that one of the officers should pass his gun to me to prove it. After shooting a couple she started to tease the men even more to the point that they packed up with the excuse they wanted to go back to the fishing.

The ferret I was using was a young one I got from Tom Ferguson at Ellon not long after I got the job at Gruinard. I wanted an albino Jill but he only had pole cat hobs and none of them had been handled. I picked the smallest one and Tom snatched it by the tail and dropped it into a sack I was holding. It screeched all the way home until I dropped it out of the bag into its box or cage as some people would call it. How do you start training a fully grown ferret that has never been handled? Well I tied a leather glove on to the end of a stick and tried to stroke him with it but each time he got it between his teeth and worried away at it like a terrier would do with a rat. I continued with this for several days until I was forced to gently hit him in the face with it. At first he was not put off by this until I got a bit harder on him and then he would back away from the glove. Then I put the glove on my hand and progressed from there until he became quite tame and eventually I could handle him bare handed. I was always cautious about getting a bite from him because he had powerful jaws that he used to crunch up rabbit bones and eat the lot with.

Ferrets have a habit when they do bite to hang on and not let go. I was going up the river bank one evening when Tara my Labrador bitch tried to pick up a very large ferrel hob which sunk his teeth into her nose and she could not shake it off. D J, an exceptionally large Labrador dog I was given by Colin and Loraine Donald, on hearing Tara scream ran over to her and sunk his teeth into the ferret at the same time leaping down the bank into the river and kept submersing it in the water until he was sure it was dead. He then brought it back up to me on to the path. I know George Anderson had two very large dog ferrets and I wondered if it could have been one of them. I never did know what he did with them and they certainly never went on the removal van. I borrowed them a couple of times and when they got into cover like bracken or scrub they would work it like terriers.

Tom's ferret turned out to be an excellent worker for several years, when all of a sudden, he started behaving strangely. He would not go down the burrows even although there were lots of rabbits in them. When I put my foot over the hole he just came back out at the nearest one and pranced about chittering and making weird noises as he looked at me. I had a problem getting hold of him and had to resort to snatching his tail. Next day when I opened the lid of his box to feed him he immediately leapt up on to my chest, something he had not done or even tried before. I brushed him off and he fell back in the box and he started the weird noises again and as Mr Lewis, a previous owner of Gruinard Estate said about his gamekeeper Harry Munro, "He would have to go." And in the records it was shown that a few weeks later he was dismissed.

Days later I was talking to the crofter George Ross or Geordie "Buidhe" as he was often referred to because of Gaelic for the fairness of his hair or from the yellow bloom on the whins where his forefathers grew up above Gruinard Farm, when he asked who the party at the rabbits were. When I told him they were army officers his response was, "Heaven help us if that is what is protecting our country." George and his wife Elsie were excellent neighbours. George, who can have some very strong views at times, is good for a story or two. Good craik as the saying goes. Not only was it one of the tidiest crofts in the area but I reckoned it was the most efficiently run one as well. No thistle, bracken or rushes survived for very long on that croft. George worked for the Forestry Commision full time and Elsie did a lot of the work herself. Up on the hillside above the house that part of a croft is normally called The Brae and most of the tenants have re seeded and ditched that piece of their land to improve the grazings. Elsie went a big step further, digging out and gathering all the stones that she could find and making piles of them. They are quite visible at the moment but I can imagine in years to come, people will wonder how they got there. Most of the time it was a team effort but very often Elsie would be out there on her own clipping sheep, harvesting the silage and even doing the ploughing and now since their retirement they are never seen without the other. If you happen to call by chance on George and Elsie you are always assured of a cup of tea with home baking. I'm sure she has a ready supply in the freezer but never the less it is second to none.

George loves to talk about his poaching exploits along with my brother Arthur, how they cycled up to Croick , stayed overnight in a disused shepherds house until daylight and then set off out the hill towards the top of Gormloch, a mountain above the loch of that name, but at first did not see any beasts near to hand. For something to eat they raided the greenhouses at Gruinard Lodge the night before and took a supply of grapes and other fruit with them for sustenance. The greenhouse doors were always kept locked but a key was made in preparation. Spying from the top they saw a stag down in Glen Alladale. Not wanting to go home empty handed there was nothing else for it but to go down and shoot it, which they did, but in their enthusiasm they shot a second one.

The first stag was gralloched and dragged to the top when they saw Donald Clark the Alladale stalker along with a shooting party complete with pony, making their way out the path from the lodge. Not wanting to be seen by Donald, they lay low until the time was right to carry on again to the old house at Glaschoille where they stayed until darkness fell before cycling home. The last shepherd to live in that house drowned himself in the Blackwater just below the house and it has remained empty ever sinse. I understand the new owner of Forrest Farm has partially restored it. Both of them were very fit and strong men, boxing and throwing the hammer were regular past times. It was nothing for them on similar missions to walk over Carn Bhren into Gledfield and Glencalvie estates to shoot deer. George's father, Davie restricted them in the number of bullets he would let them take to the hill to prevent them from shooting more than they could handle. Two bullets they had this day when they wounded the second beast and George followed it until it stood up in the side of a burn. No doubt if it was left long enough it would have died but George took a good sized stone and hit it hard on the forehead knocking it out. The knife completed the job.

In those days there was a tar macadam road that came across the hills from Ardross, down through Diebidale and Glencalvie to Gruinard and beyond. Carcases were often taken to the nearest point beside that road and the same night after dark, they would return in Ally Matheson's hire car driven by Willie Coul. One night Willie took the wrong fork in the road and ended up at the front door of David Macleod, the keeper's house at Diebidale. I remember Willie coming up to our house one wintry evening to collect deer carcases and on leaving he could not get up the icy brae to the main road. He kept reversing back and trying several times but in the end went over the bank and a lorry had to come next day to pull him out.

George and Arthur were equally proficient at salmon poaching. A gaff and a roll of chicken wire across a ford was all they required for that. Local butchers and hotels were not averse to buying their ill-gotten gains. Something George told me about salmon I noted with interest and that was they often ran the river in pairs. When fishing, legally I may add, if you caught one salmon you very often caught a second one straight away from the same pool. It was not unknown, whilst playing a salmon, to have a second one swimming alongside it just like my Labradors did, performing every movement together to the point that you could almost net both of them at the same time.

A night on the ford at the Bend Pool George recalled when two salmon came up to the netting. They got one but the other went off back downstream. When they got back to the house George's father told them that the two fish would be a pair, running the river together and to go back to the ford as the second salmon would return within half an hour. Sure enough it did and met the same fate. This theory was also confirmed when a salmon leapt over the netting. It came back downstream looking for its mate. I can relate another story to that Ford when the pair of them was fencing for my father on the Braelangwell side. A salmon came up the ford and not having a gaff or a net, one armed with a spade and the other with a fence post took off after it. Arthur connected with the spade slicing the fish in two, cruel in one sense but unique in another.

I came home from leave from the Air Force and George suggested that we should go out to the hill for a haunch of venison. I did not need asking twice and next day, George with his rifle, flasks of tea and sandwiches, we set off up over Carn Sallachy and then dropped down on to the Glencalvie/Gledfield march where a bunch of hinds were feeding. I wanted to get on with the job but George in his experienced way decided we would have our tea first and at the same time pick out a couple of yield beasts. After a short crawl George got us into a good position and after finding a suitable rest on his piece bag he shot the two hinds. It sounds a long way to go for a piece of venison but when you are young and fit you never think anything about it and from that part of the hill you are sure of getting a good carcase and as one gamekeeper said to me if you are prepaired to travel that far you are entitled to one.

If you were not taking home the whole carcase George showed me how to prepare the haunches and saddle for carrying. The carcase was gralloched in the normal way then skinned back from just behind the shoulder to the start of the saddle. The carcase was cut in two at that part and the loose skin folded back and securely tied. This way the meat was kept clean and not too much blood got on to your clothing. With the feet left on and the haunches still attached to each other and with one leg over each shoulder it was a comfortable journey home. George knew the hill like the back of his hand and instead of climbing back over the cairn we went round about it at that level and came home via Gledfield and Dounie Estates for easy walking. That was the first of many visits to the cairn for a beast.

CHAPTER 50

THE ESSEX "POACHER"

Not long after my posting to Upminster I got friendly with Eric Kite, one of the Home Beat Officers there. He also dealt with all the firearm applications and was very familiar with the countryside of the beat. He already had one duck flight pond near his home which I was invited to shoot at but soon afterwards we leased the shooting rights on a nine hundred acre farm owned by Arthur Mee at North Ockenden, Essex. This turned out to be a great success with several more ponds which we cleaned out and fed regularly. We counted the ducks in at night and when the numbers went up over a hundred and twenty we would shoot it. There was also a small wood on it and after cutting rides through the brambles and scrub we had some nice days shooting pheasants and partridges. Arthur and his wife were very pleased with what we had done to enhance the shooting side of it but also the increase of song birds to the extent that he left strips of wheat round the edges of his fields to improve things even better. We never went short of grain to feed the game. Other farmers would ring Eric up asking him to come and clean out grain stores ready for the new crop and in return they were more than happy with a brace of birds now and again.

Eric and Brenda

As our friendship developed Eric came up on regular shooting holidays with me to Scotland and with the blessing of the gamekepers we always went to the hill for a beast each. There was heavy snow on the ground at the time of one of our excursions and we did not expect to go very far to find deer but on the way we found the back end of a sheep sticking out of the snow. With our bare hands we dug it out to find more and more in front of it. We took twelve in total out of that snow drift and felt we had duly earned our piece of venison. The same day we watched a peregrine falcon take a grouse in mid flight but on seeing us it dropped it. I walked over to the hole in the snow where it fell and picked it up but it slipped out of my hands like a bar of soap. Further on we came across another grouse that had been killed. If that was not bad enough a half eaten mallard lay on the stones at the edge of a burn but we were not able to identify the bird of prey that flew away from it. About twenty yards upstream and round a bend in the burn about eight or more mallards were gibbering away with no hurry to fly away. From that I assume it was a peregrine.

On another holiday we went out again for a beast and before leaving, George Anderson said to avoid the path on our way home as the owner often went for a walk up that way. We shot two yield hinds at the back of the cairn and discarding the head and shoulders as George showed me and set off for home. When we started to climb out of a deep burn I realized that I did not have the rifle on my back and had to go all the way back to look for it, the strap having broken and I was not aware of it. Eric was to carry both hindquarters and saddles up to the top. On catching up with him I asked where he had left them. He said, "By a grey stone." Everywhere we looked in the failing light there were loads of grey stones or rocks sticking out of the heather, resulting in a long search and a weary trek home in the dark.

I think it was our next mission we decided to drag both the hinds home whole from one of the aportionments. Again it was after dark and my back was killing me. The first thing I did was to take several pain killers and on top of that Noel poured out a very large whisky or two to each of us before sitting down to dinner that Margaret kindly kept hot for us. Between a mixture of alcohol, medicine and exhaustion I crashed out and did not wake up until near midnight, with Noel and Eric in the meantime, dealing with the carcases and no doubt having a few more drams.

I cannot recall just how many times Eric came up to Scotland with me but on each occasion it usually took the same pattern. We would travel up overnight arriving at a transport cafe at Strathcathro in Angus just before daylight. I would have it prearranged with Bert Burnett who by this time was keeper at the Burn Estate for us do some ferreting. From there we would go on to Hill of Minnes to stay for a few days shooting mallard at the Minnes Dam or geese on Esslemont Estate with Tom Ferguson. From there we would travel up to Gruinard to stay with Noel and Margaret and on the return journey go to some of the keepers shoots for the cock pheasants etc. Eric had a lovely Irish Red Setter called Sophy. She would work and point at the rabbits very close to you and was fun to shoot over. I was concerned though when we went to the keeper shoots that she would be mistaken for a fox and get shot.

One of the trips Eric took his four bore shotgun with him and Tom was anxious to have a crack at the geese with it. We arranged to meet him before daylight and when we got to the field we took cover in a big ditch with a hedgerow in front of us knowing that the geese would land in the field behind us. Tom's instructions were that Eric would fire the four bore first and on no account would him or I fire our twelve bores. The first skein came low beating their wings into the wind as Eric fired and missed. If the hearts of the other two were like mine they too would have been beating just as fast. Tom took the next shot with the four bore and being unprepared for the kick back and the boom it let off ended up on his backside in the water, surrounded by a cloud of black powder smoke. We were still laughing when the next skein came towards us but they swung wide. They wanted me to take the next shot with it but I declined and just as well I did for I was the only one to get a goose that morning. The pair of them decided that the geese were too near to them for a four bore but enjoyed the experience just the same.

A few of the summers Eric came up to our holiday cottages with his wife Brenda and Emma their daughter. Most of their time was spent walking up the hills or the glens. They got to know many of the local people and were made very welcome to call for a blether or for a cup of tea. Willie once said to Noel, "He would be an interesting person to speak to if you understood what he was saying." Like ourselves they enjoyed a good party and were well into Scottish dancing. Marjory and I were pleased that they made the long journey to our Golden Wedding celebration and they have promised to come back again this summer but we will not be going back to our old pursuits.

CHAPTER 51

AT THE RIVER OR ON THE HILL

When I came up from London to fish in the very early spring it coincided with Fred Walker's week on the South Esk and I used to get a day each year from Bert Burnett at my old haunts on the North Esk. One morning he came down to try the river himself and to see how I was getting on. When asked, I said he could either have a fiver or a fish and after thinking about it for a second or so he chose the salmon which he was very pleased about. Later on he returned with the same interest and I asked if it had to be a tenner or a fish. Again he chose the fish. At the end of the day Bert still got his tenner and I got my fish. Another year I was fishing the gorge just below the Gannochy Bridge and had caught two salmon when Bert came down to see me. When he asked if it was not time I was away home I thought I had overstayed my welcome. He then told me that out of the shelter of the gorge a blizzard was blowing and that many of the roads were blocked by the drifting snow.

I set off, again with a salmon in the boot, for Hill of Minnes but immediately got stuck in a snow drift just short of Fettercairn. I managed to back the car out of it and get it off the road into an old quarry hole. A tractor driver who I knew gave me a lift into Fettercairn where I was hoping to stay the night in the Ramsay Arms but it was packed out with stranded motorists so I had no chance. I rung Frank Low and he came down in the Landrover for me and I stayed the night with them. Whilst Frank and I tippled away at a bottle of Grouse, Agnes his wife rustled up some supper for me and their daughter Alison phoned around to let people know where I was. Good hearted people. It was lunch time the next day before the road was opened again.

George's sheep had a habit of wandering over the hills on to Gledfield, Strathusdale and Glencalvie Estates and most of the crofters would go out on the same day to gather them in for clipping, compulsory dipping, lambing or whatever was current at the time. When they got home after one of those outings Geordie Heatherlea realised that he had lost a set of new false teeth which he had previously removed, and after wrapping them in a hankerchief put them in his jacket pocket. Apparently George and him met in with each other somewhere at the back of Carn Bhren at least a couple of miles from home and whilst they were talking Geordie pulled his hankerchief from his pocket to blow his nose on. It was a very strong possibility that the teeth were lost at that point so both of them returned to search for them. I would have thought it was like looking for a needle in a haystack as the saying goes. However, on reaching the area one said to other I think it was about here we stood talking and on looking down in the heather, the teeth were lying at their feet. Geordie lost his pipe in the hill another time whilst crossing a burn. He tried to retrieve it but it got washed away. Some considerable time later Ronnie was fishing the Gruinard beat on the river and hooked on to something other than a fish. On reeling in his line there was Geordie's pipe, two remarkable recoveries.

I was home on holiday when Noel and I went out for a beast just at the end of the rutting season. We stalked a herd on the Gruinard/Glencalvie march. Although not in season we had made up our minds to take a yield hind instead of a smelly old stag and there were several of them in a small corry down below, with umpteen stags roaring their heads off all round about us. Like George, Noel was in no hurry until a massive stag, still roaring, appeared about twenty five yards behind us. It was more frightening than my very first outing at Diebidale. He was so close and staring at us. Noel had plenty of stalking experience but was taking no chances with this fearsome monster. I suppose his size was probably quite normal but the fact that we were lying down and he was silhouetted against the skyline and sort of towering over us made him look all the bigger. I had the rifle and Noel said, "If that b...... comes any closer put a bullet in him." However, I took a quick shot at a hind and off every beast went including our friend or foe.

On reaching home whose car was sitting at the door? David McLeod, who was now the keeper on Amat Estate and him and his wife used to visit my Mam and Dad regularly. Both Mam and Mrs McLeod used to write poetry and items for a magazine. Noel was not bothered about them being there but my mother was. She did not know what to say when they kept asking where we were and how long we were likely to be. We came directly into the kitchen and tried to scrub up as best we could but David did not need any guesses what we had been up to. He probably got the smell of deer from our clothing. I later asked Noel if anything was said about it but apparently the McLeods' enjoyed a piece of the venison just as much as we did.

One of the many yarns I had with Willie MacDonald he told me about a moonlight night when he went along to Jamima and Lizzie's croft. They were two of Willie's aunts and lived in the cottage almost directly across from the lodge. Willie had the gun to shoot a beast coming into the turnips, when in the darkness he saw the movement of what at first appeared to be a stag but suddenly realised that what he was aiming at, was David the keeper who was stalking the same beast. Who was the luckier of the two? Willie crawled away and made for home concerned about the accident that might have happened.

Willie was always troubled with both red and sika deer coming into his turnips and other crops. The sika had a habit of digging up the potatoes with their feet and antlers. Often the problem was the damage they did and not the amount they ate. They were regarded as marauding deer and it was quite legal for Willie to shoot them but not us. Noel regularly shot them, not only on his crofts, but on Willie's as well. Brian McLeay set up a game dealers business at Shinnes near Lairg and that went from strength to strength and is run now in conjunction with a very successful shell fish business exporting to Europe. He paid good money for the carcases and I know Noel was as good a customer as any. Many, many crofters were at it provided it did not interfere with their day jobs. Often when I was up on holiday from London Eric and I would join him.

The keepers did not like this going on because some of their best stags, feeders as they were referred to, fell to the bullet. The quality of the heads was never a consideration, only the weight when reckoned in pound shillings and pence. Venison from such out of season tough old brutes finding its way into the food chain did nothing to promote the sale of this meat in this country. Noel, like many crofters had a pickup truck and powerful light plugged into the cigarette lighter holder. A sweep over the fields with that to locate the deer, bang, bang, throw the carcases in to the pickup and off down the road to gralloch them in the byre. Next day they would be off to Brian's. No hygiene regulations in those days and it would have been rather impolite or an insult to leave the heads and feet etc behind for all to see.

Jack McNicol was keeper in Amat at the time. Willie as he thought was shrewd enough to know that Jack always listened to the news at nine or ten and that was the optimum time to strike. What he did not know would not bother him as they say, but Jack was too long in the tooth for that. He knew fine what was going on but because it was sort of legal in one sense, there was nothing he or any of the other keepers could do about it, and the law remains like that to this day provided the documentation with the Red Deer Commision for Scotland is in order. We never gave any of that red tape a single thought. As often as not a .22 rifle was used and then I got a .303 and latterly a .222. For night shooting we were supposed to have the correct calibre of rifle and let the police know that we were out. Sometimes on hearing rifle shots, Jack in his Landrover would make a token effort by driving down the glen to show the flag so to speak. Jack was a great salmon fisher and a master of the art in dibbling. He had a very unusual acquired accent, one not easy to imitate. He was very much from the old school of keepers and addressed everyone as Sir or Madam but overdoing it to the point where some of the guests would behind his back mock his style of raising the cap and attempting to get the accent on "Good Morning" right. He was a nice man and so was his cousin Dick. Dick, until his recent sudden death, was in his nineties and still fishing as much as ever but up north on the Borgie.

Dick's son Richard who is a lecturer at Thurso College for students attending the game keeping and estate management courses has been involved with breeding and training pointer and setter dogs just about all his life. Not only does he work them on the grouse moors for shooting parties but runs them in the Field Trials up and down the country and over in Ireland as well. There are not many awards or trophies he has not won and is a popular judge as well. He has taught rugby in the north schools and because of his position at the college has been highly credited by the students for finding them placements for their practical training leading to full time work later. All of this was being discussed by my self and two of my friends and we decided to nominate him for a national award. It was left for me to compile the report and to get references from a number of people who knew Richard and his selflessness. It was submitted with the full backing of the Lord Lieutenant, a

Member of the House of Lords and a Member of Parliament but was unsuccessful. The head of the college got it that year instead.

Like most experiences some are remembered better than others. Noel told me of one instance when Margaret, my sister in law, and him were driving down the road with a sika in the back of the pickup when it came to life again and how he wrestled with it until reaching home. Willie was complaining about a very large stag with thirteen points doing damage and that it was so bold it came into the fields even in daylight. Marjory and I went up this night to do the business and I shot the stag near to the barn. It was so heavy that Marjory and I could not drag or lift it into the estate car I had. Even when Willie came to help us we really were struggling and each of us thought that the others were not pulling their weight. Later in daylight, we found that we were trying to drag it across stones on old ruck founds.

Sometimes we would check with Willie by telephone to make sure he did not have visitors, particularly on nights if we were to have a cup of tea and a dram and spend some time with him. Willie had a sister in Lairg and he would sometimes say, "I'll 'phone you back Alice." That was the code to tell us that he already had visitors. If he told you he had visitors in the field that meant the stags were in and to come along. One night I was up there with my brother in law, also Eric. I briefed Eric on what the procedure was to be. He was to operate the light and as soon as he picked up beasts in the field he was to hold the light on one until I fired a shot at it and then immediately to swing on to another and so on. This night there were three Sika. I shot the first one and in the shadows of the light I could just see the second one and downed it whilst Eric was still looking to see if I had hit the first one. I got a glimpse of the third one and fired at it. We drove into the field and picked up the first two but could not find the third one. Eric was making apologies for not being quick enough with the light but that did not bother me as we had two to take home. Next morning Willie rung to say we had left one of his visitors behind. I was curious to see where it fell because the only light we had away from the vehicle was a hand torch otherwise we would have found it at the time. It was across a ditch and beside an old ruin. It was not uncommon for deer to run fifty yards or so and then drop down dead.

During a snowfall Eric Kite and I went up from Culrain knowing that deer were in on the turnips. We shot four and on our way down past Braelangwell we shot another three. My Escort Estate car had front wheel drive and was an excellent motor in snow when empty because of the weight of the engine over the front wheels. When the back was loaded it was completely useless. During our time up at Amat quite a bit of drifting snow had fallen at Culrain and to get up to Lower Hilton we had to take the deer out of the vehicle half way up the hill. After dragging the first ones up to the shed we used the barrow for the others with one of us pulling with a rope tied to the axle and Marjory doing her bit as well. All of this left trails of blood on the snow covered road and next morning we were out with shovels trying to cover it up but the biggest mess came when a thaw set in.

Back at Amat Willie had an easier method of disguising the mess by driving the sheep over it several times. Severe frost set in at the same time and the carcases lay frozen for near a fortnight before we were able to process them.

Mr Fowler of Glecalvie Estate, because of the huge losses of mature stags shot as marauding deer, fenced off his estate from Amat and most of the other estates down the glen. Fairly quickly deer numbers started to rise and Gruinard became a nice little hind forest as they are referred to, carrying about a hundred and sixty hinds and calves. During the rut about fifteen to twenty stags came in on the ground and we would shoot about four of them. As time went on the heads got better and now it is not unusual to see a couple of Royals.

After Noel had his accident I continued the arrangement with Willie until I took the job at Gruinard. I could not then be seen to have a foot in each camp. A new keeper arrive at Amat and him and I set out to manage the deer in a more responsible way and according to the current numbers at the time we disciplined ourselves to shoot a limited cull each season, at the same time struggled with the other estate owners to fence the hill off from croft land. Jean Matterson and I disagreed over the Glencalvie fence. She thought the deer should have freedom to roam. My theory was that it would make the other estates including Gruinard, look after their own herds more responsibly, at the same time Glencalvie ground outside the fence, known as Sallachy, would act as a sanctuary and prevent over shooting. This turned out to be the case and the deer did well on it, heavier carcases and very little warble on them, unlike the beasts lower down nearer the woods. A limited number of stags with good heads are now consistently coming off it annually.

Jean thought the money she set aside for the lodge renovations would leave sufficient left over to fence off her section of hill but enough said about that. Later, she did fence off about a mile or so to stop leakage down to the farm and across the river. It was a few years later when she completed her section and now the whole hill is fenced off right across all the estates and over the Struie and a proper Deer Management Group formed, something that I advocated in the first place but because of the way things turned out I was not to be part of it.

CHAPTER 52

THE GILMOUR FAMILY

Jim and Fiona Gilmour got the job at Gruinard when Marjory and I left. Jim, a Kilmarnock man, had completed his keeper/land management course at Thurso College and had worked as a ghillie for Lord Thurso on the river of that name. He had a spell on a salmon netting station at the mouth of the Halladale and was a river bailiff and at the end of the season helped out with the hind stalking. I saw him as a good all rounder and well qualified for the job. Fiona was in hotel work and although young and not so experienced also qualified for her side of the work. I first met Jim at Pointer and Setter trials up at Bighouse near Forsinard, where he was staying and working. At the trials I just happened to mention to a friend of mine, Johnie Cruickshank, that I was thinking of giving up the job at Gruinard. Minutes later Jim was tapping me on the shoulder asking if it was true. We agreed to keep in touch and that I would let him know when the time came. The job would be advertised anyway.

I mentioned to Jean that we would be leaving her employment in the not too distant future. This, understandably put her on the spot because she did not know when to expect it. Marjory had some reservations about leaving but she was looking at it from a financial point of view more than I was. I promised Jean I would give her plenty of warning and I discussed it with Mr Milligan, the factor, as well. Between them they decided who ever came would first work with us for six months and that they would be on trial to see if they were suitable or not.

There were a colossal number of applicants for the job but ninety per cent of them lost their way in a paper sift. The better ones were whittled down until it was Jim and Fiona and two other couples. One couple withdrew because the pay was less than what they were already getting. When the applicants arrived they were directed to the lodge to be seen by Jean and Mr Milligan. They would then be sent over to us on the pretext of seeing the house and for me to show the husband the river etc. This way we would be able to interview them a second time and separately. After they had gone all four of us would have a discussion to see who we each thought was best suited. Mr Milligan and I thought Jim and Fiona were, while Marjory thought the other couple were more suited. Jean did not express a preference for either, saying they would sleep on it, not together I may add, and decide between them the next day.

Jim beat Mr Milligan into telling me that they were given the job. He was ecstatic about it. Mr Milligan was to tell me later that Jim could not hold back his joyful feelings when he told him. I was one hundred per cent sure they chose the right couple and I still do. When I knew who was in the short leet I took it upon myself to go up to Forsinard and make some enquiries from keeper friends I knew up there. They all spoke well of Jim and Fiona and I am sure they helped me in making my mind up about them.

Jim, Fiona and young Kevin lived up at the old schoolhouse when they first arrived at Gruinard. They did not have their own transport to begin with so I gave them the use of the estate van that I was using. I bought another one for myself as I knew I was going to need one anyway. Jim and I got on very well together. At the very start I said to Jim, "Whilst you are working with me we will do things my way. When you work here on your own you can do things any way you like I will not be bothered." Fiona found the lodge work more testing than the hotel work she had been used to. Marjory had set very high standards for herself and expected everyone else to be like minded.

After a couple of years Conner Gilmour was born and is now attending Tain Royal Academy. Like Kevin, Jim taught him to fish for trout and salmon and shoot both feathered game and deer. They both have become very competent in both arts and help Jim with many of the estate tasks. Kevin caught his first salmon when he was ten years old and shot his first stag when he was eleven. I remember when Jim and Fiona first arrived and Jim would be asking Kevin what he had been doing while he was at work. Invariably it was an imaginary number of pheasants, woodcock or rabbits he had shot. Conner caught his first salmon when he was eight and shot his first stag when only ten. Both of them had plenty practice on the target before hand and Jim has never held back in allowing them to further their skills ever since. To take it a stage further, "If dad eats it so do I."

Marjory and I tendered our official resignations to coincide with the end of the fishing season and moved to Ruie an Taoir. Jim and I have remained very good friends ever since. I often go up to the estate to see what is going on and for a blether with both of them. If he needs help with any work I lend a hand, at the same time teasing him that he cannot do without me. We regularly lamp for foxes both at Gruinard and at Bonar Bridge where I had vermin to kill. We also do the fox dens together and a host of other things. Like the salmon I caught I never kept a record as such for the foxes and cubs we killed but Willie Ross, one of the Bonar Crofters, who was always keeping tabs on numbers said to me a few years ago, "You must be over four hundred now." Having said that it has made little or no difference to the overall population in the district but lamb killing on the crofts has almost been eliminated completely and I would like to add that in appreciation of this the Bonar crofters were very good to me when I retired. I thought it was uncalled for but seemingly they knew best.

More recently Jim offered me a part time job three days a week as ghillie on the river for the Glencalvie guests but I gave that a miss. I often rib him about how he managed to burn a whole year's supply of logs in a greedy stove during his first three months at the schoolhouse. I was privileged to be asked, as was Marjory, to be witness at their registrar's wedding in Lairg. He rung me the other morning to borrow something and asked what I was up to. When I said I was up on Carn Bhren with Noel stalking a hind he thought I was going round the twist until I said, "The book Jim, material for the book." Then the penny dropped. Many of the fishing guests that Marjory and I knew, still come to Gruinard and it is good to hear from Jim and Fiona about the parties we knew.

I would not like to single out any one party in particular who came to Gruinard because they were all good in one way or another. When they stayed in the schoolhouse there was only sleeping arrangement for four people and most of the time men took up the four rods. Some weeks two couples came if the wives fished as well. The men on their own tended to live mostly on boiled ham for the week and of course, washed down with plenty of refreshment.

When the lodge was ready for the guests it could sleep fifteen and the number of rods went up to five. A cook was employed directly by the party or through an agent. Marjory's work load increased considerably and had to employ extra cleaners at the weekends for the big change over on a Sunday. Because of fire regulations things were far stricter, but fortunately we had only one small incident in that respect when the lounge chimney went on fire. No damage was done and the local fire brigade was on the scene very quickly. The laughable side to this story was a lone fireman standing on the top of the chimney stack of this huge building spraying water from a garden watering can down the chimney. It is a proven way to deal with a chimney fire instead of lots of water gushing from a hose and creating a horrible mess in the room below.

The first party I am going to mention is Admiral and Mrs Mason and their lifelong friends, Captain and Mrs Lloyd, who can only be described as real gems. Marjory used to say you would never know they were in the lodge, so clean and tidy in every respect. They brought their own silver and maintained the same standards in the dining room as if they were still aboard ship. For their week, I regarded it as one of my week's holidays and over and above looking after them at the river, I fished for them as well. At the end of my first week with them, both men tipped me very generously. With the money, I bought two terriers, Jake and Twiggy, for use in connection with my work. They looked like long legged smooth coated Jack Russels but were out and out mongrels. When they arrived for their second weeks fishing I told them they were the proud owners of a dog each and that was how their money was spent. Before leaving at the end of that week they wanted to give me more money but I told them it was not necessary, having tipped me so well the first time. Captain Lloyd said, "The dogs have to be fed." From my conversations with them I gathered they were all very keen gardeners and one morning when Admiral Mason was parking his car on the grass in front of the kennels he said, "Hugh, I don't think much of your lawn." I replied, "There is one good thing about it." The Admiral then said, "I don't see anything good about. What do you mean?" My reply to that was, "If it was any better than this you would not be parking on it." The Captain then said, "Well done Hugh, you tell him."

The majority of guests coming to Gruinard were very generous to Marjory and I. Keepers and ghillies depend on tips to make up their wages for a better standard of living. At the river it was not just the time you spend with them and the advice you gave them but all of the work throughout the year looking after the river banks, cutting back scrub, bracken and pruning trees. Repairing paths, steps, styles and gates that can be easily opened and shut is very important to the guests as well, all of which was done out with the fishing season. Cutting a year's supply of dry firewood and kindling was a big task in itself by the time you got it home, split and stacked. Grass cutting almost on a daily basis had to go on when you could snatch an hour or so, even at lunch time or in the evenings. When I look back in my youth you seldom came across a gate on a path that could be easily opened or shut. Very often it was an old bed end or bed spring with reams of barbed wire to negotiate. I could safely say now that you could walk the entire length of most salmon beats and not encounter the same difficulties.

Saturday we regarded as a day off but unless you were away for the day there was always something to be done or someone knocking on your door for one reason or another. Jean often came into the house and one day when Marjory and I were having a cup of tea I said to her she could always smell the tea-pot. In reply she said, "That's only because you are always in here drinking tea." Sunday was a full working day with one party leaving and another arriving. It took the same pattern, bag up any fish for going away, fill up the log boxes in the lounge and an emergency supply kept in the courtyard. Get rid of a week's waste and as I said, cut the grass. The new arrivals had to be met and shown the river and a general run-down on what to expect for the week. Some of them who were new to fishing would also want a bit of instruction even before going to the water. However, this may sound a bit contradictory to the time I took off for doing the house building but because of my pension and tips I could afford to pay Geordie Bruce for his help.

For me personally tipping was always a time of embarrassment and I would have been more than happy for the same amount to be added to my wages. I know on some estates a set amount is stipulated so the guests know before they arrive what is expected of them. Without offending the average to the generous ones I'm going to relate one or two instances from those at the very bottom of the scale. Firstly are the guests who do not tip at all and I respect that but when you get a little brown envelope with two pounds in it I would much have preferred if that same person just said thank you. When ten people sharing the week's fishing gives you the same little envelope with eighteen pounds in it, not even two pounds each, after having one of the best week's fishing for the season it becomes an insult. I have seen the little brown envelope go smartly back in a guests pocket at the very first signs of my hesitation to accept it. Another large party between them handed me a twenty pound note as two of them were about to drive off in their car. I threw it back in the drivers lap and said, "That will get you a coffee going down the road." They were the most disrespectful party that I know of whoever came to fish the Gruinard beat. Fortunately there were not very many of their kind.

Jake and Twiggy were about the best terriers you could have and many a happy day I had working them. When they were just puppies under training I would point to rabbit holes, road culverts or any other place for them to enter and say to them, "What's in there?" When they understood this they automatically checked out the likely places and sometimes I would have planted a fox tail for them to find. They got into the habit of taking the tails out to play with and the two of them would then have a sort of tug of war with them and all of this stood them in good stead for the real thing in the spring time at fox dens. The two of them did not always agree with each other and to begin with they often had some ferocious fights until one particular day Jake had Twiggy by the throat and I thought he was going to kill her. I had to take drastic measures to stop him and when he came round Twiggy was tanking into him and she got blamed for everything. After that day they never fought again and they happily shared the same kennel. As the saying goes you have sometimes to be cruel to be kind.

On rabbit shoots or walked up rough days they were fantastic at flushing out game and any rabbit that made good his escape would be chased to the nearest burrow but they soon returned to the line where all the action was. If other dogs were about Jake would carry the odd rabbit back to me. On one of those days a hen pheasant was shot at and wounded. A number of the guns saw where it came down in a small cluster of whins so we went back to look for it. Several Labradors including my own spent ages trying to find it but in the end we had to leave it. We had only gone a couple of hundred yards along the road when someone shouted, "Look what's coming." This was Jake with the pheasant. I never said it at the time but I think he must have dug it out from a rabbit hole under the whins where the Labradors could not get at it. That same day I saw Marcus Munroe's Labrador climb a bushy willow tree to recover a pheasant.

Jake would not allow anyone other than myself to pick up or even touch shot game. After the rabbits were laid out for a "photo shoot" by two Italians and we were in the process of putting them in the larder Jake did his usual guard duty by standing over the rabbit nearest to him when one of the Italians made to pick it up. Jake snarled at him in his usual threatening manner to the extent that both men ran for cover in their car and would not come out until Jake was put in his kennel. My brother in law, Eric and a friend took him with them when they went rabbit shooting but he would not allow them to pick up the dead ones. They had to walk on and then one of them would slip back when Jake was not looking. He was the same at the river bank and would stand guard over any salmon caught.

I think the funniest story I can tell about him was when Kim Sawyer, myself and Sandy Fraser a police dog handler from Inverness were out at a fox den waiting for the vixen to come in at night fall. The vixen was not particularly lamp shy but would not come near enough for a shot so the plan was for me to stay at the den with Jake and for the other two to walk forward to a more advantageous point. This went according to plan and Kim shot the vixen at which point I let Jake go and he was at the carcase first. Kim suggested taking the carcase back for me to see and bent down to pick it up. Jake was not having any of that and sprung at Kim's shoulder. Sandy said, "That's not the way to take anything from a dog." He turned his backside towards Jake and made to pick up the vixen when Jake saw him off as well by biting him through the seat of his pants. Needless to say the carcase was left where it was with Kim saying, "If Hugh wants to see it he can come here and look at it."

Earlier that day when Sandy and I were at the den Jake took seven cubs out of it. After numerous failed attempts to reach them in the den he pinpointed from above where they were and started to dig down on to them. I made a small hole with the spade and this was enough to move them to where Jake got at them. Jake adopted the same pattern at each den you went to, one sniff and he was on his way to the next one if there was nothing in it. If the den was occupied he would cock his leg at the entrance and then sniff around the surrounding area again cocking his leg several times. You would almost say he was getting psyched up before entering the den because all of a sudden he would race for the main entrance and in he would go to do the business and the last place you wanted to be when he came out was down on your knees looking into the hole for as sure as hell he would have bitten you in the face. So often in this situation I had to draw back quickly from him snapping at me. The den was his territory and he took charge.

Sunday was change-over day for the guests in the lodge and the cook before leaving gave Jake a bone which he lay under a bush chewing. I was cutting the lawn with the tractor and gang mowers when to my surprise I saw Jake coming down the drive from the direction of the main gates with what appeared to be a cat in his mouth. When he came to me it was a fox cub I was presented with. He immediately took off again towards the gates so I followed him in the van taking Cora my Labrador with me. Jake was flushing more cubs from a patch of rhododendrons and when two of them ran on to the road Cora picked them up and brought them back to me still alive. I chucked them into the back of the van and went to join Jake who by this time had killed another four. There was a den a short distance away and I think when the cubs got too big for it the vixen moved them into a bed she made in the leaf mould below bushes. With any amount of food lying about for them I think they could have been there for a couple of weeks at least although no one had seen them until that day. One of the cubs in the van met its fate by getting under the clutch pedal. The other I caged up to entice the vixen in for getting a shot at her.

Marjory came out of the house one morning to see Jake with something along the track near the Dutch barn. She went to see what he had but as she got near to him she could see it was one of the many feral cats that frequented the place. Jake just put a paw on the carcase, bared his teeth and snarled at her not to come any nearer. Marjory like my self was very fond of the dogs and was somewhat hurt when Jake was struck by a car at our back door and the vet had to put him down because of internal injuries. He was a great character in many ways, loved the children and would not go into his kennel unless you picked him up. When I said bed to him he would just roll over and wait there. For the children's benefit I would change the word to dead and he would roll over just the same.

Marjory was not so fond of another dog I took for training. It was a Weimaraner that belonged to my niece, Katherine and because it was a house dog at home we took it into the house as well but if Marjory went upstairs this dog would not let her down again or in and out of various rooms. His bark was quite frightening but I just ignored him and walked past him. At home he would chase after the deer and one night before bedtime I took him out on the lead for a walk. He must have heard, smelled or seen deer across the road in the wood because all of a sudden he lunged forward and almost pulled my arm out of its socket. Katherine was very understanding when she was asked to take him home. Marjory had another encounter with aggressive dogs at Gruinard Lodge. She was cleaning the lounge one morning when two Pit Bull terrier type dogs would not let her out. Fortunately she was able to climb through a window and get away from them. That party was not invited back.

Tony Pardoe and party are also worthy of a mention, or at least Tony himself who always came to my house on a Saturday evening to say thank you and for a farewell drink. To put it in other words, just to get drunk, with me on one occasion going to bed with my Barbour jacket and waders still on. Another time I arranged for a car salesman and friend, George Campbell, to bring up an ex-demonstration Rover car for me to look at with a view to buying. I was sitting on a bench seat having a drink with Andrew Cunningham the ex colleague from our London Police days, when Tony arrived in his battered old Range Rover. I got another glass and he started dramming along with Andrew, but Andrew could see where it was leading to, and as Tony poured him more drink, it was slyly tipped on to the grass. George then arrived and Tony jumped to his feet and started banging his fists on the roof of the Rover and telling me the car was a load of rubbish, and that I could have his rust bucket of a Range Rover instead. Tony kept trying to get George out of the car and saying he would test drive it instead. Poor George never got the chance to get out of the car or to say a word. He kept squinting up at the roof expecting it to cave in. I got into the car and George managed to drive away from him and when George was going over the good points about the car he ended up by saying, "And it has a good roof as well."

Tony was gone by the time we got back which I think was just as well. Next morning I was jokingly accused of pouring the stuff over his throat. Apparently he was adamant that he would go for a last cast in spite of the wishes of his fellow fishers. They in the end had to go looking for him and found him asleep behind a rock. It may not have been the same week but I was fishing with them one evening when the river was in spate. I hooked what was thought to be a very large salmon at the head of the Little Rock Pool. I was fighting to get it into the edge of the bank but the heavy water kept taking it away from me. This performance went on for at least half an hour and although everyone gathered round about me none of them would take the rod in case they lost the fish. Eventually all was revealed when an old ex-army blanket came to the surface to roars of laughter.

CHAPTER 53

OTHER GOINGS ON

I have seen the Carron in all its moods but a week when Eric McGee, an arms dealer from London, and his wife were up fishing it was in flood after a dry spell and all the rubbish of the day was floating down, branches, twigs, leaves and quite dirty as well. I went up to meet them at the Craigs. Mrs McGee was sitting on the bank and as I approached her she asked what I thought of it. Thinking it was the river she was talking about I said, "A waste of time." "No" she said, "The fish." "What fish?" I asked and she pointed to one on the bank. Her husband had caught it a few minutes earlier and I would have put money on it that no fish would have been caught that morning. The fly could have been the only thing fighting against the flow that attracted the salmon to it.

Richard Buckley and family who still come to fish the Carron was always good for a laugh and when he arrived for an extra week at the Schoolhouse after the fishing season had ended we decided that he would ring Ronnie up and ask if he knew where I was and did he know where the key to the house would be. He was also to tell Ronnie that he was up for an extra week's salmon fishing. Ronnie bit straight away and pointed out to Richard that the closing date was past but it was alright by him. Both of them knew each other well and after a chat and a laugh about it, it was then Ronnie's turn to get one on me. The following spring the McGees took the Braelangwell fishing for a week and were staying in that lodge. They wanted to stay on for a further week so they rented one of our holiday cottages and came to fish at Gruinard because we had no guests in and the proper lets had not begun. During that week Ronnie rung for his usual chat about things and asked how the McGees were getting on. He went on to describe the mess they made of the lodge at Braelangwell and how they had been firing an airgun at a target on the back of one of the internal doors. If that was not enough Margaret was furious at them for allowing their cat to scratch the upholstery on the armrest of the lounge chairs. All the time he was laying off about this I was wondering what damage was being done in our cottage. The answer was none he made it all up to get his own back on me.

I know scientists say animals and fish see colours different to humans but one day John Shepherd Barren, the inventor of the hole in the wall cash machine and the pin number, arrived to fish the Moral. I could not believe it when I saw the colour of the nylon he put on. It was one of the brightest blues you could imagine unless for a hair rinse and far from the more sober and standard colour of nylon I was used to. I never said anything to him but thought he would be lucky to get a fish with that on. Half way down the pool he hooked and landed a nice six pound salmon. I was wrong again but now look at all the different colours of lines that are used.

Mr and Mrs Shepherd-Barron, for a number of years took the Braelangwell fishing and I would often see them on the opposite bank. One evening I went along to feed the ducks on the pond when I heard the scream of a fishing reel coming from the direction of the Rock Pool. Being inquisitive I went over to see who was fishing to find that it was one of their sons' who had hooked a salmon. I know there are three of them so I'm not going to make a guess at the name. This young man immediately told me it was his first salmon and asked for advice on what he should do. The only reminder he needed when playing the salmon was to keep his rod up, otherwise he made an excellent job of it. He had no net or gaff with him but there was a nice sand spit where ne could beach it. I gave him full marks for that as well. I then told him to carry the fish well away from the water edge and kill it with a stone. I'm sorry young man but you were not meant to throw the stone at the fish's head unless of course you felt very accurate in hitting the target.

Because the Carron was very much a spate river the banks were in constant need of repair. It was eating into the bank behind the old kennels so a machine was taken in to shore it up with material from the riverbed. In the process a new low water pool was created and the question then for Jean was to name it. She decided that the name of the first person to catch a salmon in it would be used. However, the first person do that had a double barrelled handle so she opted against that one. The next person was Lord Griffiths, a circuit judge from the London area. Hence the name Judges it has today. It does not sound right but Lord Griffiths said it was his first salmon after fishing for eleven years but he went on to catch his second salmon from that pool the same week.

Yes I have seen the River Carron in many of its different moods from practically a trickle to some violent flooding. If there was torrential rain or worse still a cloud burst up on the hills of Glencalvie, Alladale or Croick the river could rise two feet or more in minutes if not seconds. If I heard thunder in that parts I made sure that the fishers were warned about the dangers of a sudden rise and to avoid wading. I can talk from my own experience when I waded out to the middle of the Kennel Run to fish towards the far bank when this wave of rising water lifted me off my feet and started to wash me downstream. Before I quite realised what was going on I was on my back but had the presence of mind to steer myself by whacking the water with my rod to reach the far off bank which was nearer and to grab the bracken and pull myself out. I walked up to Braelangwell Lodge and Ronnie gave me lift home. At the time I had two guests fishing the Moral which was just above me and they witnessed the same wave going down the pool. They tried shouting to warn me of the dangers but because of the noise of the river I did not hear them. It was a huge relief for them to see me on dry land again even if it was the opposite bank.

Special permission has now to be got from SEPA before remedial or improvement work can be carried out in any river. It was often said that the machines caused pollution and disturbance to the fish. From experience I would say that is wrong on both counts. I took Jochan with his JCB into The Moral to fill in behind trees that were placed to shore up the bank. I said to Jochan if he found large boulders to throw them back into the pool to create places for salmon or trout to rest behind in high water. Had I been asked what the fish would do whilst this went on I would have said they would move up stream into deeper water to get away from the noise and disturbance. That day salmon kept rising about thirty feet across the pool from the JCB and did not appear to be bothered in any way by the activity. As for pollution there was virtually none. A small amount of oil colouring appeared on the water surface but disappeared after a few minutes when the machine reached its working depth.

Geordie Ross from the Dornoch area is a marvel with an excavator. He came to place armoured rock along part of the bank at The Washerwoman and he could pick up pieces of rock that weighed about six tons or more with the bucket of his digger, as if they were in his bare hands, and turn them around or upside down until he was satisfied that they were in the right position. Because of the size of the machine and the rock the noise was considerable and no doubt a good deal of vibration as well. After about an hour of this a fisherman came down to the opposite bank to fish for salmon. Geordie stopped his machine and I apologised to the gentleman for the disturbance and that we would wait until he had fished the pool before starting again. He insisted that we should carry on and that he was not bothered whether he caught a fish or not. Reluctantly we did, and after a few casts the gentleman hooked and landed a nice salmon. I am convinced that canoes or boats passing downstream cause no disturbance to the fish either. This can be substantiated by fish numbers caught when trolling for trout or salmon on lochs, also fishing from a boat on rivers like the Tay or the Tweed.

Then there were the geriatrics as they called themselves who came in the month of March each year and what a hardy bunch they were. Some of them were into their eighties and in spite of the atrocious weather they often had they were not put off by it and stuck at it to catch that elusive "springer". Marjory had them in the kitchen where they could partake of their lunch in some comfort and get circulation back into their veins . I think they were all pretty heavy smokers , mainly the pipe with various tobaccos and with a mixture of steam from their wet clothing it was almost possible to cut the air with a knife. The most remarkable member of them all was Joe Gozzett from Rogart. He suffered from muscular atrophy which causes a weakness and degeneration of the muscles. Joe undeterred by this illness was just as determined as the others to enjoy his week's fishing and to put something on the table at the end of it.

I was more than happy to have ghillied for Joe the entire week but on no account would he have me or any of his fellow fishers anywhere near him. Watching from a distance, sometimes with binoculars, to make sure he was alright and had not fallen into the river I could see him throw the rod over a fence or style and then struggle to clamber over it the best way he could. When fishing the Pool Moral which he enjoyed I watched him several times go up and down the banks on his hands and knees and in between casts throwing the rod a yard or two forward in front of himself. Whether he enjoyed his independence I will never know but unquestionably that was the way he wanted it. When speaking to his Son in Law, Don Kenniston, also a salmon fisher, I was told that there was another possible reason for wanting to be on his own. Apparently he was not averse to putting on a "Toby" instead of the fly he should have been fishing with, a man after my own heart.

One very warm sunny day I was with a titled lady fishing the Washerwoman. I am not sure but I think she worked for the Royal Family. I helped her out on to a ridge of rocks to try and reach salmon showing close to the opposite bank when the treble got stuck in her jumper. I thought it would be a simple job to remove it but the hook went through into her bra which made things a bit embarassing. I often wondered what people would have thought had they seen what was going on with my hands. Was I taking advantage of the lady's precarious position on the rock and having a good grope? No but we were having a hell of a good laugh about it.

The guests always arrived on Sunday afternoon's and I would go and meet them, particularly if it was their first time. Again it was a titled lady and her husband and as usual I was trying to picture in my mind what they would be like. My first thoughts were that she was a bit of a snob but he would be fine to ghillie for. It turned out to be the complete opposite with him thinking he had the right to fish down every pool first and only go to the best places. If he did not get his own way he took the huff and with a face like thunder he just stood there looking at the toes of his boots and stamping the ground. I tried to get him to let his wife play one of the several fish he caught, but no, as far as he was concerned she could catch her own.

She turned out to be a very jovial person, a pleasure to be on the bank with and would often comment about her husband's behaviour. She had two problems, well three if you counted the husband. The first one, in spite of being a good fisher she was not lucky enough to catch a salmon, but then she never got the chance to fish a pool first. Secondly she was forever needing a piddle. At first she would ask where to go so as not to be seen but after a few times trailing off some distance she would say, "I'm sorry, turn your back I need to do it again." Down the chest waders would come each time. After a couple of days or so I would take her fishing rod and have a few casts with it in the hope of getting a fish on for her but never managed to do so. It just was not her week.

There was a lovely gentleman by the name of Westmacott, a retired estate agent who had his own grouse moor in the north Durham area who unfortunately had a heart attack and thought there was no point in coming to Scotland with friends to fish. What was equally depressing, disease had wiped out large numbers of grouse and his moor was not going to be shot that season. He owned a golden Labrador which went with him everywhere. This dog did something that I saw no other dog do and that was to stand for ages poised over a mole hill and when the time was right would dig furiously and for most bring the dead mole back to you. Now I have watched moles putting up earth and dried to jab them with a fork, dig them out with a spade or shoot them, all to no avail. On one such attempt I dug every run from where the mole was last seen working to every dead end. Looking at the area afterwards you would have thought I had dug over a vegetable plot but I never found the mole. Next morning there was a mole hill right in the middle of it and not far from where I last saw it. Just recently I was told that if you pour Jeyes Fluid into the run it will not kill them but scare them off. Catriona has bought the fluid but has not yet tried it. One morning when I first went to work at Gruinard I set some mole traps on the lawn. When I came home later in the day some of them were sprung but on checking them all that was in them were potato crisp papers. I didn't need two guesses who the prankster was. A couple of days later Ronnie said to me, "I see you are at the moles."

Mr Westmacott did come and I made a point of spending as much time as possible to give him the chance of at least fishing the easier pools and to which I could drive my van to. I even arranged with Ronnie that he could fish the odd pool on the beat his guests were on. We had just finished fishing the March Pool and he suggested returning to the house for a coffee. Whilst he was making the coffee I nipped down to put a fly over the School Run. In the first few casts I hooked a salmon. I played it for a minute or so until it settled down. I then climbed up the steep bank and stuck the rod firmly in the branches of a fir tree. I went back to the schoolhouse, had quick cup of coffee and then asked Mr Westmacott if he could come and help me get my Willie Gun freed. At first he did not want to because of his condition but I assured him all he had to do was to hold on to the rod and that he would not have to climb down the steep bank to the water edge. On arrival at the tree I told him to take the rod and reel up any slack line while I went down below. As you can imagine the surprise he got when the fish went a bit frantic. Standing by the tree he played it and took it into the bank for me to net. He thought I was mad, I could have lost it and all sorts of other things like him having another heart attack. To me it was just another fish and so what, if it did break free in my absence.

The best part of the fun to me was the initial strike. It had that good feel factor, excitement and stimulation from a rush of adrenalin, with everything else that followed was a kind of secondary pleasure. I got the same sort of feeling when my Labrador would come out from cover with a missing bird on a shoot day, grouse springing from the heather at your feet when taking the pointer or setter in on a point. The satisfaction that you were doing things right was there as well. If children were with me when I hooked a fish, in spite of concern by the parents, I often handed the rod over to one of them even when they sometimes were barely fit to keep the point of a big rod up in the air. To see the different expressions on their faces made it all the worthwhile and to hell with it if the fish got away as I my self have lost so many in my lifetime.

The youngest person to hook a salmon during my time at Gruinard was six year old Robert Dewdney from Surrey. On the Sunday evening his father asked me if it was alright for Robert to dangle a worm in the water whilst he fished beside him. The next question was where could he get some worms? That was left to me and in the morning the two of them went up to the Lower Craigs. It was not very long before they were back with a six pound salmon. Robert's dad told me how he sat him down on the rocks beside him and told him what to do which basically was very little. At the most he thought Robert, if he was lucky may catch a brown trout or a salmon par. But as soon as the worm was in the water the salmon took it and almost pulled Robert in. His dad was near enough to grab Robert and the rod. When the salmon was landed he was then not sure if he should put it back or what. I was delighted for Robert, a proud little boy, and the smile on his face said it all as it was prepared for going home. I made sure he got his name in the Trout and Salmon magazine but a lot of guests after that would not believe it. A local paper at his home in Surrey took up the story and printed an article in it. At school Robert had to stand up in class and tell all the other children about it. For the records I showed it as having been caught on a "Watnot" for some people to say it must have been a name given to a home tied fly.

I went to the Washerwoman with Richard Cave who promised his mates that he would buy them a bottle of champagne to celebrate the salmon he was going to catch. We had to be off that pool at 1pm and not having caught anything I asked Richard for the rod to have five minutes of Braelangwell time. My very first cast I felt a salmon take the fly and quickly tried to hand the rod back to Richard. Whilst both of us had our hands on the rod the fish took off with Richard successfully landing it. Back at the schoolhouse Richard tried to riggle out of buying the champagne by saying I caught the fish. Just to keep the argument going I was adamant that he caught the fish and not me. In the end Richard had to stump up with the bottle.

One of the best weeks fishing any party had during my time as ghillie at Gruinard was one in early May when Robert Cowe and his friends, Francis Kinloch, David Briggs and David MacKenzie were fishing. They were up in the schoolhouse at that time and they told me that they would go straight to Pool Moral in the morning and catch up with me later. They knew the river well and did not require me to be with them. The river was in great order and at a perfect height for the big Moral Pool, having got its name because of its majestic appearance. Balmoral Castle got its name in the same way. Bal in gaelic meaning home and together with moral, majestic home or house.

I was splitting logs in the stick shed when all four of them arrived back from the river. I fully expected them to have caught several fish and asked them, "How many then?" "None" was the reply. I honestly did not believe them because the river conditions were so right, and on record, it was one of the best weeks of the season. I thought they were just "pulling my leg" and persisted in asking how many they caught. Robert, very abruptly said, "Go and see if you can do better. We are off for breakfast."

I grabbed the rod which was always propped up at the back door of our house and off to Moral. I started to fish at the best known lie and on my second cast I was into a fish, which I landed. In those days all fish caught were kept and any salmon I caught before 6 pm the guests could claim them. I did the same with a second salmon and was playing a third one when the guests appeared above me on the top of the bank. I heard one of them say, "The b......d has one on," and in a friendly way began to give me a load of stick. Worse was to come when they saw the other two on the bank. I told them, "Less of the abuse, they're on the take now, get fishing." If they were not on the take earlier that morning they certainly were in the mood by this time. All four started fishing with a 2 inch Willie Gun brass tube fly, the same as I had caught mine on.

Robert was into a salmon immediately followed by Francis and David Briggs. To make space for the guests I moved downstream to some rough water below Moral and hooked and landed a fourth fish. David MacKenzie netted it for me and he then started fishing where I had been but he had no luck there either. I carried on fishing until supper time and had landed eight salmon in total. By Thursday night my total was up to sixteen but by no means a record, only a few good days fishing. By then everyone had a share but some luckier than others.

Hugh, Robert, Francis and David McKenzie

There was no question about the fact that David MacKenzie was just as good a fisher as any of us. The only difference that day he was using a floating line whilst the rest of us had on fast sinkers. By Thursday evening we had caught 33 salmon, and not another fish was caught that week until 9pm on Saturday evening when a friend of mine, Willie Nicholson, caught his very first salmon, a seven pounder from the Keeper's Pool. I was not there to see it but apparently he was fishing with a trout rod with an old fashioned brass reel and about twenty five feet of line. Whilst playing the fish he had to run up and down the rocks to keep abreast with it. To reel in he had to twist the handle of the reel as if using a tin opener. However the fish was securely netted and left on my doorstep for my return. He was there as a guest of Robert, so on Monday morning I took the fish down to him at his place of work, to find that his mates were giving him a hard time because he did not have the fish to prove his story. It was a different story when I told Willie to collect the fish from my vehicle and show it to them.

That was a remarkable week for us on the Gruinard beat but the opposite bank did equally well with 27salmon. Another good day I had or should I say an hour, was when I caught six salmon between noon and 1pm from the Washerwoman pool and all on the Willie Gun brass tube fly. The name speaks for itself. Apparently in years gone by a woman living on the Braelangwell side of the river, took in washing for payment and that was where it was done. The couple who rented the fishing that week invited a local resident to join them for the day and I was asked to direct him to the Washerwoman Pool but when he did not turn up I decided to go down and fish it myself. I then met in with the guests who told me that they had already fished it but to carry on. I believe a run of salmon came into the pool at that crucial moment and I just happened to be the lucky one. When I got home I rung Ronnie Ross and told him. He immediately went over to the lodge to tell his guests and one of them got up from the lunch table and went to the Washerwoman where he caught another four salmon. I also rung the Schoolhouse and asked my guests to come down to my house after they had their lunch. I did not give them a reason and they thought there was something wrong until they saw the salmon laid out on the grass by the kennels. Days like those are long gone and no one knows the reason why and whether or not they will return in the same numbers in the future is any one's guess.

I was really pleased for, and proud of Jean Matterson with her achievement from the Washerwoman. She always kept a week's fishing in May for herself and friends. She was on her own and hooked a very large salmon. After playing it for a considerable time she, still on her own, managed to land it and then struggled to carry it home the half mile to the larder where it weighed in at a massive 30 pounds, the second heaviest fish recorded as having been caught on the Gruinard Beat of the Carron. She also was fishing with a 2 inch Willie Gun tube fly, and to my mind the best salmon fly ever made, so much so, that to this day you will find very few other flies in my tackle box. Guests coming to Gruinard often said to me that there was no need to ask me what fly I recommended. Not quite true because I had a liking for a teal blue and silver tube when the sea trout and grilse were on the go.

My nephew Scott Shepherd fished the Willie Gun any time he was up at Gruinard and told me it was not a fly commonly use at that time on the Dee or the Don where he normally fished . After his Carron experience he used it successfully to the point that other anglers were curious to know what he was catching salmon on when they were not. Scott brought a friend we called Brucie up with him. He was a very likable young lad and fitted in with everything that went on, both in the house and at the river but he was not that keen on fishing himself. He preferred to run up and down the river bank checking on everyone to see what salmon were caught. He took it upon himself to run back to the larder and weigh the fish and report back to me and the other fishers. One day I was down in the village for fuel for my van and Brucie was in the passenger seat while Scott sat in the rear. I was coming out from the pumps at an angle and because I could not see back along the main road I said, "Anything coming Brucie? He replied, "Not a lot." I just had to laugh but Scott was not amused. I had the fishing for myself and family that week and as I did each year invited a few friends as well.

Fiona playing a salmon   *This cast maybe*

I have heard many people argue that the Willie Gun was designed and first made by a man of that name who was a gamekeeper from the Brora area. Apparently this is not true and that the credit goes to another man, Dusty Miller, a fly dresser from the same locality. He first tied it as a hair-wing on a brass tube for early spring fishing when the fly has to get down deep. Many variations came later. Willie Gun was the first man to try out this tube fly on the River Brora and caught ten salmon with it in two consecutive days. So from then on the Willie Gun fly rose to fame and so much pleasure has been got from it.

With a lot of persuasion from Jean's mother and my self she agreed to have the salmon mounted by Willie Forbes, a first class taxidermist from Braemar in Royal Deeside. He made a beautiful and so life like casting of it. Until she sold Gruinard, Jean had it displayed in a glass case above the entrance to the lounge in the lodge for everyone to see and dream of catching a bigger one or at least matching it. Incidentally, but no less important, Ronnie Ross whilst employed by Jean's grandfather at Gruinard caught the heaviest recorded salmon at 31 pound from that beat albeit down at the Whirl Pool near Invercarron Bridge. He was fishing with a salmon fly on the tail and had a Durham Ranger number eight or ten with a gut loop fly on the dropper. The salmon took this fly and whilst he was playing it a seatrout which later weighed two pounds took the salmon fly. Ronnie described the salmon as a very red September fish with a head that made it look more like a cod. From its snout to the back of the gills it measured fourteen and a half inches and had it been caught and weighed when it first came into the river its total weight would have been a good deal more. Because of its ugliness it was used for baiting vermin traps.

In the mid fifties when Mr and Mrs Lucas owned Gledfield Estate their Gamekeeper, Laurie MacDonald caught a salmon of 42 pounds from the pool under Carron Bridge. Several people I know either saw the fish at the time it was caught or saw pictures of it later, including cuttings from a newspaper. In 1945/46 Mr Lambert from Braelangwell Lodge caught a 44 pound salmon from the Bulwark Pool down below Balnabruich which at that time was owned by Balnagown Estate. In the early nineteen forties Sandy Henderson who was gardener for Mr Lambert had permission to fish for salmon, mostly in the evenings but sometimes he would have a cast in the morning before going to work. On one such occasion he hooked a very large salmon in what was known as the New Pool but was unable to land it for several hours. This pool came about as a result of a tree falling into the river a few hundred yards upstream from the Bulwark and when spate water gouged out the river bed around it. Once the tree had gone the river bed returned to normal and the pool no longer exists. Struggling with it for a very long time, which was described to me as the best part of the day, the salmon having got under the roots of the tree and only with the help of his neighbour Willie Munro from Balnabruich, was the fish landed. The most talked about weight of this salmon was 54 pounds but I have heard it said it was only fifty two pounds. In either case it must be the heaviest one caught on the Carron.

The smallest salmon I know of was caught in the month of March by a Mr Craig from the very small pool if you could call it that between the Gardiners Run and the Gardiners Pool. When he brought it back to the larder he was not sure if he had done the right thing. I assured him it was a freshly run salmon weighing almost on three pounds. Ronnie arrived at the same time and Mr Craig was pleased to hear him say, "What a lovely little salmon." Many grilse come in weights a lot less but I guess that this was a first for a Carron salmon. A winter salmon I caught in February from the Boat Pool had me puzzled because I had never seen one before. It is difficult to describe the colour but it was obviously not a kelt and not an early fish that had lost its silvery sheen. I thought of holding it in a pool in the rocks for Ronnie to have a look at it. Then I thought if I am in that much doubt I may as well just put it back in the river, but later when describing it to Ronnie he assured me that it had been a winter fish having come into the river in November or December and because of its excellent condition it would have been good to eat.

I could only boast of one at 24 pounds but what a fascinating story to it. I went up one evening to fish the Moral. Ronnie was on the opposite bank with a guest who was already fishing. This pool is so wide that it can be fished at the same time from opposite banks but when a fish is hooked others reel in to give the lucky one space to play the fish. In the first few casts I hooked a salmon in the middle of the pool and immediately it went dormant in deeper water. I tried for ages to move the fish without success and the guest went back to the lodge. Getting impatient, I asked Ronnie to hook on to my line as I feared it had snagged on something. Reluctantly, Ronnie agreed but in the process he hooked a salmon. No sooner had he done so when the tip of his rod came off. In his usual calm way he walked down stream, dropping the rod to water level and waited for the tip to float towards him. Back in business, fish landed, and eventually hooked on to my line we took it in turns trying to free the line and get the fish on the move. Six feet either way was our maximum. Getting desperate I asked Ronnie to slacken off and I would hand line and break off if necessary. The fish was hauled to my bank and after a lot of Mickey taking from Ronnie I managed to get the salmon into the landing net, only for the handle to break and everything to fall back into the water. Nothing else for it I jumped into the river almost waist deep, and threw the net and salmon on to the bank, to find that it was trussed up with both lines and Ronnie's fly embedded in the top of its head. Ronnie, for the part he played in all of it, tried to claim it for the Braelangwell records. For a number of years now, because of the catch and return system operating on most if not all rivers, salmon are measured rather than weighed and in my mind very much guess work when estimating the weights. This particular salmon measured fory two inches long and its girth was well in proportion to that length but still only weighed 24 pounds. Today fishermen using whatever chart they look at would claim it to be around thirty pounds but how wrong they would be. So for me two or three salmon making up that weight would please me a lot more.

CHAPTER 54

THEY DON'T COME MUCH BETTER.

One of the pleasures of working at Gruinard Estate, 1984 to 1997, was to have Ronnie, Margaret and family on the opposite bank. Although not that long ago I regard those years as the good old times when salmon fishing was still good and memories were filled with good hearted rivalry, banter and leg pulling.

Ronnie and I were fishing opposite banks of that great pool again when Ronnie's pipe yet again required firing up. I'm sure he burned more matches than tobacco. He made a cast, tucked the rod up under his arm pit whilst proceeding to light his pipe when a salmon took the fly. Getting his priorities right he just leaned backwards, further and further, 'til almost on his backside, to keep the tip of the rod up. Continuing to strike matches and only after a good plume of smoke surrounded him did he get on with the job of landing the salmon. How cool!

When the river was frozen over you could be sure that Ronnie and the children would appear at our house. It scared me and I told him off about it on more than one occasion. I'm sure he was infatuated by the ice in some way. When deer stalking he took the Argocat on to a hill loch for a bit of fun, spinning round and round and other manoeuvres by operating the steering brakes. The argocat went through the ice but fortunately did not sink. They were designed for use on water but the underbelly had to be watertight. Ronnie had no option but to walk off the hill and get assistance from Marcus Munroe, the head keeper at Alladale. They had an ex-army tracked personnel carrier that would just about go anywhere, and from my own experiences in it, I would say some pretty scary places. For it to rescue the Argocat was not a problem.

At one time, Braelangwell had the stalking of the deer at Forrest Farm and it was an experience in itself to travel in the argocat with Ronnie down the long twisting icy road from Loubconich

Often it was after dark, with limited lighting and Ronnie's only speed, flat out and with the Argocat slewing everywhere you fully expected to go over the bank at any moment. We always made it though. Following a deer drive one day there were a lot of deer carcases to come off the top of Gormloch. Ronnie's Argocat broke down and he and I went next day in mine for it and also the dear. We soon had the repair done and we each tied on seven hinds on our machines and set off for home, but knew there were another five carcases to pick up on the way. Because Ronnie had a newer machine than mine we lashed them on to his with the intention of taking some off again before climbing up a steep part of the hill. However, on reaching it, we decided to carry on up as we were, and if we got stuck we could unload some at that point. We chugged over the top and the only mishap we had was after everything was loaded on to the trailers and heading for the larder at Braelangwell. I missed a gear in my van, let the clutch out too quickly and the

Argocat and load broke the ropes, shooting off the back of the trailer. Ronnie was away down the road without noticing.

Another hairy experience with Ronnie and Argocat in tow was when he was out hind stalking on Gormloch with David Cowe from Helmsdale. First of all I shot a hind down by the water edge of the loch itself and went down to pick it up but because I was so low in fuel the engine kept cutting out, even when I tried reversing out of where I got myself into. There was only one other option and that was to try and drive the Argocat through the water around the edge of the loch keeping as near as possible to the bank. My Argo, as they are more often referred to was far from watertight and as it was beginning to fill up around my feet I was glad to see a place where I could beach it. That done, I was then off to Ronnie's rescue. This time, he had to be towed down to the road from the face of Gormloch. There were no proper fixings for the rope which had to be tied round about the cab on each machine. We thought it would be wise to leave the rope long so that Ronnie had a better chance of stopping it from crashing into the back of mine. In theory it should have worked but Ronnie's Argocat had little or no brakes, resulting in his machine going past me several times until the rope tightened up to stop him. That was fine but every so often my Argocat was slung round sideways almost to the point of capsizing. I think David was glad to be firmly seated in the pickup for the remainder of the journey home.

During a deer drive at Forrest Farm I witnessed a very unusual incident which no one could explain the reasons for it. It was well past the rutting season, probably January or February, and only hinds were being shot. Several hundred yards below me in the line somebody fired a rifle shot at a hind but did not kill her instantly. She just stood there swaying slightly and as I watched expecting her to fall, a young stag little more than a nobber raced up to her, jumped on her back and mated her. I had watched many hinds being mated so it was unquestionable as to what I saw. It ended with the usual thrust from the stag and the hind going down head first. When I got to her she was quite dead. In that few moments she must have given off an aroma, the same as she would have done had it been at the height of her season or did something come over the stag to take advantage of the situation and commit rape.

Whilst on the subject of rape and when I had a kennel full of dogs one of them was a randy old English Setter. He was always jumping on the back of bitches but one day I put a young Irish Setter dog, and I repeat dog, into the same kennel. In a flash they tied. I could not believe my eyes and later when I spoke to my vet he said, "I suppose it happens." It was however the first he had heard of it.

The same day and at the end of the drive we were coming down off the hill at a very rough part in my Argocat. Stephen Mackenzie was walking in front to pick a safe route for me but he inadvertently led me into an exceptionally steep spot which was far too chancy for me to drive down, so we tied a rope to the back, and Steven, Sandy Fraser, Kim Sawyer and Alan Dean, like a tug of war team held me back as I edged my way down over it. On reaching the Blackwater River we found it to be partly in flood. At the crossing place, knowing the Argocat would get washed down-stream, I decided to enter the water higher up and aim for getting up the opposite bank at the crossing. The current was stronger than we all estimated and I floated down beyond the ramped bit. Kim, without hesitation jumped into the river, got on to the bank and with a rope thrown to him saved the day. There was no other crossing place for miles downstream and because there were no bungs in the floor to stop the water getting into the Argocat it inevitably would have sunk.

It was supposed to be a secret at the time between Stephen and I but I know he won't mind me telling this story. We were at a den this night trying to shoot a scary vixen that kept her distance travelling in an arc some way off but always lay for a while at a particular view point. "Shimmy" an apprentice joiner who was with us was asked to stay at the den and keep the light on the fox whilst we walked out in the beam of the light to get near to her. When we got to within shooting distance of her we crawled up on to the top of a knoll with the rifle at the ready. I was to put our light on the fox and for Stephen to fire immediately. The eye continued to glow after the first shot and I thought Stephen had missed. Reluctantly he fired a second shot and then a third but still we could see the eye. When we got up to it we found a dead stag that had been shot in the head three times. Its body was out of sight in a hollow and the head stretched forward on a bank with the antlers lying back over the neck and shoulder, none of which was visible to us at the time. When we got back to the den "Shimmy" told us the fox had ran off at the sound of the first shot but what a coincidence that the two of them should be lying so near to one another. Sorry Stephen.

Ronnie and Margaret will always be remembered by Marjory and I with fondness. Ronnie was a great colleague to work alongside and as a fisher he had more experience and knowledge of the river Carron than the rest of us put together. Margaret is a lovely person. In spite of her long and hard work in the lodge she was devoted to her family but still found time helping others and at activities in the locality. She is renowned far and wide for her catering and culinary skills and also for the fabulous parties she held at Braelangwell. She has recently given up her position as a Justice of the Peace and now, I have to find someone else to sign my firearm applications.

Ronnie and Margaret have retired from their full time job at Braelangwell but are both as busy as ever. Ronnie still ghillie's part time on different rivers roundabout and in his spare time can always find something to tinker about with. One of his hobbies has always been making walking sticks and I know he will not thank me for this little insight I'm about to tell. The usual way of softening tups horns for shaping into stick handles is to heat them with steam or boiling water. Ronnie thought he had a better method and put one into Margaret's microwave oven to do the job. Whilst this process was going on Ronnie will tell you how he ran out to the garage to get a vice grip or similar tool to hold the hot horn with but by the time he got back to the kitchen he could barely see himself for smoke and the obnoxious smell was overpowering. Margaret could undoubtedly describe the aftermath of this better than I can but the microwave and much more from the kitchen found its way to the Council tip. Ronnie never said whether or not he was able to salvage the horn.

Ronnie at Moral

A book in its own right could be written about Ronnie but I am going to mention one more little story. Many years ago, he got into a bit of bother over some young eagles. Neil Graesser from Rosehall was up at Braelangwell fishing and during a break for lunch Neil asked Ronnie if he was going down to the village hall that night to hear the talk on golden eagles. Ronnie replied, "No, the sheriff told me all I need to know about eagles."

Another gentleman and fisher I was privileged to meet at Gruinard was Mr Owen Lawrence- Jones from Essex. With his family and friends he took two weeks fishing at Gruinard and two weeks grouse shooting and fishing at Ben Armine. He invited me up to Ben Armine to join them for a day at the grouse. It was arranged that he would pick me up at my house at 7am but my friend Eric Kite was up on holiday. With him, Marjory and I and armed with a bottle of whisky and a bottle of Drambuie we went to visit Noel and Margaret. The rusty nails went down so well that I slept in and had to keep Mr Jones waiting while I got the gun and other essentials to take with me.

I stuck a few chocolate biscuits in my pocket but on arrival at Ben Armine it was made known to Andy Aiken and his wife Liz that I had come unprepared food wise. Mr Lawrence-Jones asked if she could make up a lunch for me and, "Yes, do him some breakfast as well." He said. I was not too sure about having the bacon and egg etc but then, I was a guest and had to be polite. The party going to the hill was Owen Lawrence-Jones with his curly coated retriever, John his son, and a restaurant owner from Chelmsford. We were to shoot over a lovely English Pointer bitch, trained and run by Andy.

We were not far on to the hill with the pointer quartering the ground beautifully when she got her first point. Owen called to John and I to go in on the point to shoot. I declined the offer but Owen said, "When we are on the river Hugh you are in charge, but today I am in charge. On you go." I did but at the same time I was praying the birds would fly out to John's side. They did the complete opposite and I missed with both barrels. Mr Lawrence- Jones kindly said, "They are not as easy to hit as you think Hugh." Owen did not shoot but was an excellent host for the day. I soon relaxed and ended up shooting an equal share of the bag. Andy's dog performed her duties with perfection. She had great style, fantastic nose and one hundred per cent steady to shot and flush, a delight to watch.

My only other experience of shooting grouse, or should I say at them, was in 1954 when I came home to Gruinard on leave from the air force. It was a Saturday evening when I sneaked the gun out of the house and armed with a box of 12 bore cartridges set off up Bain's burn keeping out of sight until I reached the open hill where the grouse were. There were literally hundreds of them. I meandered along putting up one covey after another and each time nothing to show for two empty barrels. This went on until the last cartridge was fired. On the Monday I met in with Geordie Heatherley and he said, "That was a fine evening the Commander had at the grouse. I wonder how many he shot?" Well you already know who the Commander was.

A random records check for the years between 1903 and 1929 for Gruinard Estate shows, that 12,421 brace of grouse were shot, averaging 443 brace per year. Evidence of one line of old grouse butts on the lower ground indicate that some driven days took place but most of the ground was shot over English pointers and setters. On 12th August, 1908, 100 brace were shot. Scent was bad and the birds weak. I wonder how many of them were "cheapers". During my time at Gruinard we shot only 12 brace or under for one day per season. The first couple of years or so we walked them up but then hired in dogs. I'm sure having seen Andy Aiken's pointer working influenced me in that decision. Nancy Reed was first to come with her English setters, followed by Stephen Franks with his English Pointers. Most people going to the hill wear boots of one kind or another but guests were intrigued by Stephen who always wore gym shoes. He said he could run after the dogs faster in them. Stephen is a dedicated falconer and was probably more interested in that than going out with shooting parties. He is licensed to breed birds of prey and often when I have been in his house I've watched them on close circuit television. Although his favourite falcon is the Sparrow Hawk over the years he has had Goshawks, Harris Hawks and Peregrines as well. Stephen is a very kind man and there is always a welcome to the many friends who call on him. You can be assured that he will always have interesting stories to tell you and the offer of help in any way he can is never very far away as he did when he loaned me a pointer dog when I was short of them during the grouse season.

Stephen or "Tweets" as he is known to older friends first got interested in falcons in 1945 when along with a friend he took a young Sparrow Hawk out of a nest and decided to rear it himself in spite of being at Boarding School and the added difficulties that that entailed. Because of War Time rationing food was not easily come by and trapping mice did not go down well with some fellow students. He often had to rely on parcels of meat sent to him by post from his mother. Plastic bags were not invented by then so it was not unusual for the parcels to arrive with the blood oozing out through the brown paper. A couple of years later he acquired his second Sparrow Hawk and came up on holiday from Devon to fly it on the Scottish grouse moors, particularly Birichen Estate which at that time was rented by James Robertson Justice the film actor and who had a house at Spinningdale. With both of them having a common interest in flying falcons a long term friendship developed. Stephen also flew falcons for Balnagown Estate which lead him to being asked to personally deliver a Harris Hawk to the Sultan of Brunei.

With a suitable Harris Hawk and seated in a chair strapped to the floor behind the cockpit of a very large chartered transport plane flew out from Stanstead Airport for and overnight stop in Singapore. It was crewed by three ex- RAF Airmen and also on Board was a Gurka security guard and a chauffeur to drive a Rolls Royce which was part of the cargo. Stephen was supposed not to let the falcon out of his sight and care for it at all times but because of all the other valuables and antique furniture on board, the plane had to be locked up over night. Concerned about the drop in temperature, generators were brought out to the plane to overcome this problem and maintain the right conditions for the hawk. On completion of his responsibilities at Brunei part of the deal was that his fare home would be paid via Tokio and Vancouver giving him the opportunity to visit a friend in Canada.

CHAPTER 55

A PRESENT FROM WILL AND
FIRST TASTE OF EARL GREY

After an unusual meeting with Will Sloan, an Irishman, but living in the Isle of Man, he later came to dog for us for several years. Marjory and I arrived home one Saturday afternoon to find my Labrador and two terriers had been put into one kennel and the other three kennels were packed with a variety of English and Irish Setters, their vocal chords stretched to the limit. No explanation was left by the owner(s) and when the evening had passed without anyone returning for them I set about to feed them. An abundance of fresh water had been given to them earlier.

The following morning Jean Matterson came knocking on our door. She was just as gobsmacked as I was. I think at first she thought I had taken leave of my senses, but I assured her someone would be back for them. That evening yours truly Will Sloan and another Irishman, John Kerr from Aberdeenshire arrived to stake a claim for the dogs. They had decided to go up north to do a bit of socialising and perhaps felt the dogs would be safer with a stranger in his kennels. "Sure it'll be alright." said Will to John."

That meeting with Will was to be the first of many yarns over a cup of tea and drams, dogging and rough shooting days. Because I had been working in London I was not aware that Will and John had been coming north for so many years and had dogged on so many Highland Estates. I was also unaware how popular and well known Will was. On a spare day he had, he invited me to travel up to Thurso where he had some doggy business to do with Claira Campbell, who ran boarding kennels, and who in earlier years had hired out pointers and setters to estates for the grouse season. "Dash The Wonder Dog" went with Will everywhere and took pride and place on the front passenger seat of his vehicle but reluctantly had to take second place that day. Every fifteen miles or so Will would ask if I knew so and so. More often than not the answer was no, but not for much longer. There was an open door for him wherever we went.

Major John Whitelaw and Corrie doing his stuff at full speed

It was not long after that when Will was invited to dog at Gruinard and by that time my fascination and interest in the breeds grew greater and greater. After many attempts Will talked me into having my own and very first Irish Setter. He told me to go up to Claira's where a bitch of his had a litter of pups and to have the pick of the litter. She was the one and only puppy allowed into our house. She did not like the cold and would stand with her face close up to the log fire and when that got too hot for her she would turn around and warm the other end. When she was taken outside to do her business, a yard or two from the door was far enough and then bolt back in to the fireside again. The training that followed was great fun and satisfaction. I had her pointing grouse at four months and before 12 months she had won second place at a trial at Kintradwell. When she eventually went out to live in the kennel with my other dogs she learned how to turn the knob on the gate to get out. My only regret was not having done it sooner.

When I was about to retire from Gruinard Estate and go to live at Ruie an Taoir I thought there was no hill ground for me to run Sophie so I decided to sell her to the Game Conservancy at Crubenmore. Will then got me into training Irish Setters for him and another Irishman, Declan O'rourke from Dublin, but I soon found that they were not all as easy as the first one and a rather expensive hobby to take up. He also encouraged me into Field Trials. With time on my hands I was able to join Will on his dogging days, each running dogs time about, but with Will taking the responsibility, even when my dogs did their own thing.

The bags were never that high but it was a pleasure to be on the hill with so many nice people, some not bothering to raise a gun, preferring to just watch the dogs. Then there was the social side of it when the shooting parties came off the hill and retired to the lodges. One in particular, Invercharron House owned by Claire and Rory Macnamara, where everyone sat down to drinks, some stronger than others, and a fantastic spread for creamed teas, freshly baked scones, home-made jams, fruit and sponge cakes. I must not forget to mention Rory's mother Mrs Avril Macnamara who played a large part in this hospitality and never failed to be ready for pouring out the tea as we walked through the dining room door. I am sure it was a tradition that went back as far as Rory's grandfather's time, Admiral MacNamara. It certainly did when his father Carol was alive. It was there that I was first introduced to Earl Grey tea. However, I was assured by Will that the only way to drink it was with a good drop of the hard stuff in it. I'm sure he only took that blend of tea just to get another dram.

Ben Loyal is another estate foremost in my mind. The kindness shown to Will and I there extended from the hospitality in the house to being invited to shoot woodcock with Count Kanute and his friends. At the end of one of the days at Ben Loyal the Count asked Ian Smart his keepr to prepare six of the fourteen birds we shot ready for cooking. When Will Sloan told him that Eppie Buist maintained that they should not be drawn but cooked with the gut still in and to have that on toast, he replied. "Ian, do it my way. Send the inners to Eppie for her toast." As a little thank you for our day I sent him a cookery book with how to cook woodcock in it. I got a note back from him to say that he was not going to change his mind.

I could go on but not without first mentioning Major John and Lesley Whitelaw from Strathpeffer who had a shooting lease for deer and grouse on the Garve side of Ben Wyvis. Most of the days were spent on pretty steep faces where the grouse were, but the going was far from easy. My problem, for obvious reasons, was keeping the dogs from quartering too far down hill. No matter which moor you went to, at the end of the day a post mortem was held, to analyse the course of events. Strathpeffer was no exception and one evening whilst having our usual tea, fruitcake, biscuits etc or whatever refreshment you preferred, one of the guests who had been out on the hill in crutches was thanking me for being so patient with him. Major Whitelaw interrupted by saying, "It's not Hugh you should be thanking. It's the dogs for having to stand on point for so long."

CHAPTER 56

FOXES AND HOODIES

Rory Macnamara very kindly allowed me to train my dogs on his hill ground at Airdens, Sleastry and Garvery. Ted and Eve Watts from Balblair Estate did the same and for which I am also very grateful to both of them. Rory had a part time keeper killing foxes and other vermin on his ground but for some reason he moved down south. Rory and I came to an agreement for me to take on this role in return for getting the use of the hill for training. He also gave me the full use of a Landrover Discovery and had a lamp on the roof fitted on it for me. I saw this as an extension of my hobby with the dogs and it was good to keep me active and to remain in touch with neighbouring gamekeepers and crofters. I started several years ago in the spring of the year when the crofters were losing a lot of lambs to foxes. Al and Elaine Munro from West Airdens were the first to get in touch with me, and him and I went to search a patch of whins on the bank of the public road where we found a den with carcases strewn about it.

Al and I spent about three or four hours with a power saw cutting the whins to get proper access to the den, after which the cubs were gassed and the vixen shot by colleagues, David Campbell and Andrew MacKay. Within days of finding that den, Elaine found another and I asked all the keepers from various estates to come at night to lamp for foxes. The plan was to swamp the area and it paid off. I was never one to keep a tally on paper of anything but that spring I ended up dealing with no less than six dens, five of which were within a mile of each other and not far off the same public road. I think the total for young and old was thirty six head. I was lucky to have had so many keeper friends willing to turn out at night to help me and a lot of the credit for the initial cull goes to them. On one night alone there were as many as nine of us targeting the dogs and vixens, leaving the cubs to be dealt with in the daytime.

I'm going to digress here but still on the crofts at the back of Bonar as it is generally referred to and because of my interest in the area I was given copies of a Missive of Let for lands on the Estate of Ardens (Airdens) , dated Whitsunday, 1880, and extracts from a report to Edinburgh for Ardens Rental, 1784. Some of the clauses in the first documents I think are worthy of mention:-

- Power to resume possession in case of bankruptcy or death of a tenant.
- Reservation of minerals and power to make roads.
- Power to straighten marches and charge extra rent for extra arable land added.

- Proprietor has power to stipulate the number of animals allowed to graze the hill pastures. Penalty of five pounds per head for over stocking.
- The tenants shall be bound each year when called upon to give two days free labour or one day with a horse and cart or pay the proprietor three shillings for each day in lieu.
- The tenants shall be bound to the rules of good husbandry in the management of the land.
- The tenants shall be bound to protect the game and hares on the Estate and shall warn off poachers and other trespasser; and they shall not keep more than one dog each.

The second was a hand written document written by Eachan Calder, born 1923, himself a tenant and his forefathers before him. In the course of my work for Rory I got to know him to some extent but would have enjoyed the pleasure of more of his time.

> Alexander Forbes, pays £3-10 for miln – also for land £1-10 rent, 5/- for Custom peats, two wedders, twelve custom hens, half a wintering for a colt and four shearers for one day. (Peat stacks had to be a certain size and if over that you paid extra)
>
> William Leith, joint tenant with his father John Leith, pays £2 rent, with a wedder, six fowls, 6/- for custom peats. He is also bound to winter a colt and to furnish six shearers yearly and perform services as the other tenants.
>
> Andrew Calder (Eachan's Great Grandfather), pays £1-15 money, also a wedder, six fowls, 5/3 for custom peats, and six shearers in harvest. He is also bound to perform some other services and to winter a colt yearly.
>
> Finlay Logan, pays £1-15 money rent, also a wedder, six fowls, 3/9 for Custom peats. He and John Munro tenant in Rhinamain are bound to winter a colt between them and to perform some other services.
>
> John Munro alias Roy, pays £2 money rent – also a custom wedder, six fowls, six shearers, 6/- for custom peats and some other services.
>
> Alexander McKay, pays same as John Munro.
>
> Andrew Ross, pays same as John Munro
>
> Donald Murray alias Bain, pays same as John Munro.
>
> John Ross, pays £1-15 money rent, also a custom wedder, six fowls and six shearers, 4/6 for Custom peats, also bound to winter a colt and to perform other services.

Eachan passed on to me a third document to me on the history of Ardens collected 1913. It reads as follows:-

Ardens was granted to John Grey of Skibo by Earl John of Sutherland fifth of that name this was previous to 1573. Kenneth Macalister being then tenant of Ardens he was left in possession by John Gray and on his death Angus Mackenneth succeeded him as tenant. Angus Murray, Bailie of Dornoch, having acquired a morgage over Ardens endeavoured to raise the rent but Angus Mackenneth refusing to pay more was turned out and the land was let to his cousin. This so angered Angus that he murdered his cousin, wife and two sons and nine other people who successively endeavoured to occupy the farm. After the ninth murder no more tenants could be found for Ardens and Angus Murray being tired of the property assigned his right to the property to Gilbert Gray of Skibo who conveyed it to Robert Gray of Ospisdale his second son. Meantime Angus Mackenneth had again obtained possession so Robert Gray dispossessed him and took one Finlay Logan in as tenant who was murdered by the same Mackenneth being eventually killed by the Greys in 1605.

I do not wish to bore readers with writing another list of tenants who back in 1745 who had decrees against them for arrears in rents varying from 8/- to £6-15/- I have not troubled myself to work out a comparison to the value of money to day but to me the rents and other services demanded in those years look pretty steep to me and it is not surprising that so many of them were in arrears. How times have changed with proprietors and tenants living today in perfect harmony and it is a joy to be associated with them. One retired crofter told me that he had suggested to the present Landlord that rents should be increased but I was assured it fell on deaf ears.

A lady at Gruinard Lodge asked me for a set of stag antlers but I did not have any at home but knew of a set about two miles out on the hill. The stag had had died almost a year earlier so I explained to her that they would have lost their colouring even if they were still there. I drove my van up as far as I could on a hill track and then walk the remainder of the way. I took Sophie my red setter with me. As I got near to where the carcase was a shepherd passed by above me calling and whistling to his collie as he gather up sheep. Whilst I was whacking the head and neck bones against a rock to break them off I noticed a fox asleep about fifty yards from me. At first I thought it must be dead when it did not run away from the noise. I decided then to go home for my rifle. On my way back on a quad bike I decided to stop and check the accuracy of the rifle because I had not fired it for some time. When I opened the box I found that I had only three bullets in it. However, I fired at a small stone about a hundred yards from me and it was spot on.

When I got up to the same rock the fox was still there with its belly heaving from deep breathing. It was obvious that it had eaten a huge meal and that it was sleeping it off. I had no knife with me to do a post mortem so I took the carcase home with me to find that a whole lamb had been eaten. The same night a crofter rung me to say he had lambs killed so we assumed we already had the culprit. But no, the killing went on until another dog fox was shot not far from the first one. So there were two dog foxes working together and travelling at least two miles to the field where they got the lambs from even although having to pass through other fields with lambs in them.

One night I was flitting back and fore between two dens and shot a number of cubs with my .17, a fantastic rifle for vermin and more, and left the remainder for Jim and I that night. It was daylight by the time I set off for home and there was a hooded crow sitting on a fence post at the right distance for a shot. I knew I had to be quick in getting it before it flew off. I had a board across from the passenger seat of my Discovery to the dashboard with a firm cushion that I could slide along it for resting my rifle on to get the right angle for any target. With the rifle ready I up and fired at the hoody and at first I was momentarily surprised at what looked like a plume of feathers that flew out of it. To my horror I overlooked the fact that the side window was still up and that I had fire the shot through it. What looked like the feathers was the glass shattering, leaving a tiny hole through it. I have to admit I laughed out loud but always the same question arose when I told anyone the story. Did you get the hoody? The answer was no and a replacement window, a second hand one at that which I had to go all the way to Banchory for, cost me forty pounds plus fuel. I did not have the heart to charge Rory for it. Some you win, some you lose.

What remained of that spring and into the summer I tramped the hills with Patch, an orange at white English pointer dog and a borrowed terrier, looking for dens. Patch was not only an excellent grouse dog but he had a thing about fox smells as well. If he got the scent of one he would stop briefly, go to where it was concentrated most, and cock his leg where the fox had done his business the night before, buried food for later, or urinated at a den mouth. Patch made my job easier for the years that followed, but I was always on the lookout for new dens being opened up. Sometimes I would be out on the hill at daylight with my binoculars spying for sightings of foxes. Dog foxes have a habit of visiting the den at that time of day, either with food for the vixen or her cubs. You can get another indication from afar of cubs present at a den when you see the hooded crows scavenging about it for remains of rabbits, birds and for anything else the cubs have been feeding on such as a roe deer calf I once saw dragged in. I loved walking the hills and this gave me a sence of purpose to it.

One annoying fact that I came across on several occasions, and it did not matter which estate you were on, was local people like shepherds or crofters, who got to know where dens were situated, and could not resist the temptation to have a look. One crofter I know tried to get his Corgie dog down a den when it was obvious that cubs were in it. Needless to say the vixen and the cubs were well gone by the time I got to it. The human scent at a den or any other disturbance is more than enough to make a vixen move her cubs, thus making the keeper's job all the more difficult. Sometimes she will hide them in different places and not always in dens. It can be in deep heather, under whins or any other sheltered location. I have seen me going to a den and there would be absolutely no scent or any sign of any evidence of foxes present. It was only when the terriers went down that hole did you know for certain if she or her cubs were at home.

I do not believe in digging out foxes unless the terrier is in trouble, and this can happen if you come across an old vixen hell bent on protecting her cubs and you have a dog that is so hard headed and does not have the sense for his own good to back off. The disturbance, no matter how well you repair a den, will put vixens off from using it for years. I know other keepers will dfispute this. The same applies when burning heather. I found it advisable not to burn over a den for the same reason. I never tried it myself but I was told by older keepers who did not enjoy modern facilities like high powered lights, modern rifles with powerful scopes, to light a fire at the den to bring the vixen in closer to be killed with a shotgun. A fear I had was inadvertently letting my terriers go into dens where badgers may have been present. I can assure anyone reading this that badgers, foxes, including cubs, and rabbits can cohabit happily together in the same holes, and the only legal way of dealing with this situation is to sit out day or night and shoot the foxes as they appear.

I was always sceptical about sightings of big cats whatever they were thought to be. A crofter's wife was out one morning about five thirty checking the ewes at lambing time when she saw a big cat run off towards a fir wood. Later in the day I was told about this but told that under no circumstances was I to make this public. Jim was not available to go out lamping that night so I went on my own. About eleven o'clock I saw the cat not far from where it was seen in the morning. I put the light on it several times and it was quite happy to stay there. At first there were no lights on in the crofter's house and I was unhappy about holding the lamp and shooting as well. To do it I would have had to stand outside the vehicle and use the door as a rest. It would have been no problem had the light been a fixed one on the roof. Then a light appeared in the house but before going for assistance I would check once more that the cat was still there. This time the cat after raising its head high bolted for cover among whins and trees and although we scoured the area we never saw it again. The killing of fully grown sheep and lambs continue to go on throughout the Highlands and evidence shows that big cats like Pumas are to blame but so far as I know only one has been cage trapped in the Beauly area.

CHAPTER 57

THE FAMOUS RIPPLES

While all of this keeper work was going on Declan came over from Dublin with a young Irish setter bitch called Ripples for me to train. I don't think she had ever been out of a kennel and I can only describe her as wild. The first day I opened the kennel gate she ran flat out and none stop for about half a mile until she hit the tidal water and went straight into it. She came back but I had great difficulty catching her, to put her back in the kennel. I sat in the large shed I had with a rope attached to the door. When she was bold enough to creep in, I pulled the door shut behind her. It was then a case of making friends with her to gain confidence in me but it took a long time. I thought if I got her into the house things might improve but the difficulty with that was, house doors have to be pushed shut. However, I rigged up a contraption to overcome that, and when I got her in, I would rub gravy on my hands for her to lick and give her other treats. If I lay on the grass with my face down she would come right to me to the point of stepping over me but if I lifted my head she was off like a rocket.

Once I got her humanised I started her training and she came on very quickly. Will was the first to see her working and was the first to shoot a grouse over her. Declan then drove over to see her progress with a view to entering her for the novice stakes in the field trials. He was very impressed and said she was not only good enough for the novice stakes but open stakes as well. Declan made entries for her in Scottish novice stakes and I was to be the handler. She was a very skinny dog no matter how much you fed her and because of this she was very fast on the hill, so much so that on wet days water came off the heather behind her like spray from the back wheel of bike with no mudguard. Will watching her run one day said, "She's got some engine that dog."

I won two of the novice stakes with Ripples and this qualified for her to run in any of the open stakes there on. After that Declan took her back to Ireland and over a couple years or so he made her up to a Field Trial Champion. Her bloodlines have been sought after ever since. Will then brought me two Irish Setter dogs from the same blood lines, Pat and Corrie by name, for training. Half way through their training Will rung to see how they were getting on and to ask if they looked differently in appearance. They were from the same litter but Pat had a white blasé down his chest. Will chose him and I was to have Corrie in lieu of payment. Declan as before came to see if Pat was suitable for the trials and took him home with him that day. Not only did Declan make him up to Field Trial Champion but he went on to win the All Ireland Championships as well. Another Irish Setter bitch Declan took over for me to train was Emma who also went on to become a Field Trial Winner or Champion. I would say the most expensive hobbies I ever had but it was all worthwhile.

Corrie turned out to be a great shooting dog and he and Patch were the stalwarts of my team when I took over all of Will's dogging days following him having to retire from hill work, after being taken to Wick Hospital where it became apparent that a leg would have to be amputated. He was transferred to Raigmore in Inverness for this to be done and it was at the airport when I first met his wife Janet, when she came over to be with him. Janet was a good looking lady and I had no difficulty in recognising her from a photograph that Will had shown me a year or so previous. We were walking down the road after a day at the woodcock together when he suddenly produced the 'photo from his pocket. Jokingly, I said to him, "How did an ugly bugger like you get such a nice looking wife as that?" The 'photo was quickly snatched from my hand and at the same time Will said, "You have not done too badly yourself."

Will had previously tried Marjory and I to go over to the Isle of Man for a holiday but I kept putting it off. Eventually Andy Cunningham and I went for a few days and had a marvellous time with them. They very much wined and dined us, showed us just about every inch of the Island and before coming home Will, even with his artificial leg, took a setter dog that he was in the process of training, on to a piece of hill ground for me to see going through its paces. The whole Island is a beautiful place but I would single out Port St Mary where they lived in a flat overlooking the harbour where the Guy Ritchie lifeboat was berthed and also the picturesque village of Port Errin.

We always kept in touch by telephone and then one evening he gave me the shocking news that he had terminal cancer. Worse was soon to come when Declan 'phoned to say that Will had died. This was met with great sadness by all who knew him. Declan, Steve Robinson, Jean Brown and my self arranged to meet at Isle of Man Airport before going to the house. Others arrived from Yorkshire and all over Ireland. It was to be a celebration of Will's life and Janet and family made sure of that, the way Will would have wanted it to be. The name and reputation of this great character will live on for many years to come. A web site, Ardoon Dogs, is almost devoted to him entirely. A facial picture of him appears on one of the editions of Isle of Man postage stamps and Janet and his daughter Ann have donated two lovely trophies in his memory, to be competed for in the dog trials.

Working pointers and setters were never taught to walk to heel as other gun dogs do. When they go on point they lead you into where the birds are and not you leading them. I always took about three or four dogs with me and it was easier if you had an extra pair of hands to look after some of them. Ian Bruce, a retired fireman from Birmingham, who sadly is no longer with us, and his wife Doreen lived near to us so, when I needed help with anything Ian was always first choice. He looked after my dogs when I was on holiday and did a lot of heavier tasks about our home and garden which I was limited in doing because of my back problem.

Doreen is an accomplished artist, exhibiting her paintings at local art shows and judging at competitions. Beauty is in the eye of the beholder as they say, and for me, her best is that of woodcock. She is currently President of the Culrain and

Invershin W.R.I. Both of them did well with their exhibits at the local fruit and vegetable shows. I must say that Ian also was a canny lad with the paintbrush and I don't just mean at the house decorating. By talking to Ian I got the impression that they spent just about all their holidays in Scotland. No matter what area you mentioned they had been there, and had an intimate knowledge of the places. He had a fantastic memory for the names and could describe things in great detail. The happy days we had together will live on.

I called on Ian and Doreen about once a week or fortnight for a cup of tea and a good chinwag. My excuse, not that I needed one, was to deliver the latest copy of the Shooting Times after I had read it. Doreen for most was out walking their two lovely Labradors or riding her pony. Ian kindly allowed me on two occasions to use each of his dogs as a stud dog, and what smashers the pups turned out to be. Some of them went to homes down through Scotland and England as far as Berkshire. I still hear from their delighted owners. My granddaughters, Holly and Hannah, each got a pup and now that they are living at Cawder in Inverness-shire I see lots of them.

On the hill Ian and I, depending on whether Patch or Corrie was performing better than the other, would argue which dog was best. Ian favoured Patch and he was quite serious about that, but just to be different I would say Corrie was the better dog. I used to accuse Ian of being prejudiced, preferring Patch just because both of them were from England. Because I was ten years older than Ian he would tease me by calling me Dad. In return I would tell him he was just the Doggy or Kennel Boy depending where we were at the time. The guests got into discussions about the dogs as well, stating their preferences. To me it depended entirely on where there were grouse and which dog was running at that time. At the end of day before coming off the Invercarron hills Ian's pace tended to quicken and one elderly gentleman found it difficult to keep up. Several times I had to tell Ian to slow down and accused him of getting the whiff of whisky in his nostrils better than the dogs were scenting the grouse.

Corrie was different in as much that he would retrieve shot birds and if he got a point some distance away from you he would lie down or set as they say and wait until myself and the guns arrived. The problem with this was if he got the point out of sight of you, the difficulty then arose in finding him. His colour blended in with the heather so well that on more than one occasion I walked on to him and accidentally flushed the covey. He is now over in Lewis and the owner there puts an orange jacket on him for the same reasons. Patch I gave to a falconer from the Huddersfield area and adapted to that very well.

Odd dogging days took Ian and I to many different estates as far south as Glen Lyon and Forsinard in the north. South of Inverness there were plenty of birds but north of that it was the norm to get only three or four brace per day and the dogs had to work really hard to find them. On one visit to an estate near Tomintoul I asked the head keeper on arrival what bag was expected. He told me it was twenty brace and that we would be off the hill by 2pm. In spite of the dogs getting points every few hundred yards or so, the shooting was the worst I had seen. At 5pm the keeper told the guns to unload and pointed out where the vehicles were parked. We headed down the hill with only 15 brace in the bag and on reaching the lodge we were not even offered a cup of tea. This kind of hospitality was not what we were accustomed to and there were no tips either. Ian and I often compared this day with one at Kylachy Lodge near Tomatin. Like the salmon fishing it was pleasing for me to see young boys or girls shoot their first grouse. It normally happened on family outings to the hill where the parents would give priority to the children. Ledgowan was one good example where four teenagers shot their first grouse within an hour. Another was at Pate Estate at the head of Loch Monar, accessed by boat only. Dougie Lippe the keeper, at his best seamanship, came down to Monar in a motor launch to pick Ian, the dogs and myself up, and return us again in the evening. It was of special interest for Ian and me to go to Pate Estate, both of us having read the fantastic book "Isolation Shepherd" written by Iain R. Thomson. After that visit you could somewhat relive some of the experiences he had there.

I was asked by Eppie Buist if I would do a day's dogging for a friend of hers, Mrs Mann. It was to be at Kyllachy Lodge and the party of guns were aged from twelve to sixteen years old. Ian and I had a very enjoyable day there. The boys, with an air of professionalism, shot extremely well and we had no problem getting our bag of 12 brace. The 12 year old even had a right and left with his double barrelled four ten. I know there are a lot of ifs and buts to everything, but had those boys been at Tomintoul with no bag limit, I could only make a wild guess at the number of grouse they were capable of shooting. I still maintain that a good day's dogging is hard to beat and that the size of the bag is of little importance.

When I started working for Rory the hill was sadly needing a lot of the heather burnt. It was pretty rank and in need of breaking up with much younger stuff suitable for a grouse diet. There was a lack of grit for the grouse as well so Ian and I set about putting that right. Each season, weather permitting, we were out there burning. We did not have the modern equipment available to us that keepers have today. Unfortunately, the last fire we had it took off out of control on us and ended up on a neighbouring estate with Rory being presented with a very large bill for the damage done. We were always so careful and burned breaks to stop fires getting away from us and that morning was not an exception. I know the wind changed at the moment it took off but it had all the appearance of a secondary fire burning in the air about a meter above it. I often wonder if there was some kind of methane gas at that spot.

I knew there was no chance of Ian and I putting it out so I told him not to knock his pan in and to just put out the back burning. My mobile phone had no reception so I set off for help. Two fire brigade units and about twenty to thirty helpers, mostly keepers came out but by this time it had crossed the march and was raging through a plantation of pine trees on Auchenduich Estate. I tried to get a helicopter out but they wanted a signature from the land owner on the form first. That was not possible and eventually when the fire was heading for some houses at the side of the Bonar Bridge to Lairg Road did they come, but not before getting lost on the way. Imagine not seeing a heather fire raging across the hillside only a couple of miles from them. Before the fire was completely out the helicopter ran short of fuel and had to go back to base, not a very efficient system.

After dark and after everyone went home Ian and I got split up, each of us putting odd little bits of burning out. When Ian was finished in the area he was in, he came looking for me but could not find me so he walked home. At that time I was down at the burn next to Lairg Estate when I saw the light of a hand torch approaching me. This would have been about 1am and I thought it was an odd time for somebody to come and help. When I switched the headlights of the Argocat on, that was the last I saw of this person although he was only about a hundred yards from me. He had crossed the burn to the fire because I could distinctly see his footprints the next day in the powdery ash. We can only assume he was there for an ulterior motive.

Late in the evening Marjory and Doreen drove up to Auchenduich with sandwiches and drinks for the firemen and helpers. She met the owner's daughter, Kythie, who was laying off about the damage the fire had done and that if she got her hands on the person who lit it she would wring his bloody neck. Later on she asked Marjory what her interest in the fire was anyway and when Marjory told her it was her husband who had lit it Kythie said, "I'll still ring his bloody neck". The following morning Mr Rory Macnamara and I walked over the hill to see how much damage had been done and after that out of courtesy we went to see the owner of the neighbouring estate but the person to answer the door was Kythie. I introduced myself as the person whose bloody neck she wished to ring and I said I would look forward to that.

When I was still at Gruinard Ronnie raised the alarm to say that a hill fire had got away on him. It was a Saturday afternoon and fortunately most people were at home including fishing guests in the lodges. I think it was roughly thirty five men and women who turned up and successfully put out the fire before it did serious damage in a plantation of small conifers. Everyone just grabbed what they could to beat out the flames including paddles from a canoe, shovels and clothing. Noel told me of a story when he set fire to the Gruinard hill and it spread on to Amat Estate. When speaking to Willie Macdonald the same evening and asking him what he was up to Willie replied, "I'm sitting out at the end of the house in the brightness of a fire reading the paper."

CHAPTER 58

A REMARKABLE OLD LADY

Eppie Buist, who I was privileged to know, lived to the ripe old age of 98 years. She was the daughter of Sir John and Lady Brooke of Mid Fearn Estate, Ardgay. Her first job I could safely say was kennel maid to her father's large team of pointers and setters. It was big business in those early years with plenty of grouse, to hire out dogs to other estates or to sell on puppies or trained dogs to them. Eppie was very much involved in all of this until war broke out. She told me that because of the drop in demand for dogs drastic measures had to be taken. They had a total of sixty at the time and after selecting twenty of the best the others were all put down. "Gone to Australia" as she called it.

Throughout her life Eppie never lost her love for pointers and set up her own kennels at Katewell, Evanton, in partnership with Jim Howden and appropriately named them "Fearn Pointers". It was during the time I ran Ripples in the trials when I first got to know her. I was asked to give her a lift to and from the dog trials at Amulree in Perthshire. I was a bit apprehensive about this lady in her eighties who I had never met and did not know very much about. What would she be like? What would we talk about? Would we have anything at all in common? Need I have worried? It was a joy to be in her company and on arrival at the hotel she introduced me to everyone as her new driver, secretary and nanny.

I liked her sense of humour. When we came off the hill that day we were having a cup of tea in the cocktail bar. A waitress came in and gave us each a menu for dinner that evening to look at. It was a bit early for that but we had a look at it anyway. In a loud voice Eppie said, "I'm not having steak for sure." She was indirectly referring to the enormous backside on a woman who came in and stood up in front of her. As the lady turned round Eppie, with a quisical grin on her face looked at me and slipped from view behind the menu.

That was the first of many outings with her. She often came up to Bonar to watch me training my dogs or for me to take her to visit mutual friends including Claira Campbell near Thurso whose dad kept kennels and hired out pointers and setters at the same time as her father. They had so much in common and both of them could reel off pedigrees for any dog mentioned. My knowledge of pedigrees was very much limited so I would slip away to see Flora, Claira's daughter. She at one time was a game keeper and rented land at Bower where Will, Declan, myself and others spent some days rough shooting. I think we all went there for nothing other than Flora's hospitality.

A typical day was to get up at 6am, have tea and toast and off for an early morning goose flight, home for a full cooked breakfast about 9am and start our rough shoot about 10am. Flora put down pheasants and partridges and had some good cover for woodcock. There was plenty boggy ground for lots of snipe and a few ducks got up off a stream that ran through it. We came back to the house in time to have a cup of tea, a hot pie or sausage roll, before going for an evening duck or woodcock flight. One or two would sometimes go for a shot at roe. Then it was home to bath, change and down to the local bar for a beer. Dinner was something else. Flora was an excellent cook and better than could be found in many a five star hotel. Five courses and as much wine as anyone wanted to drink, not to mention the spirits that was on tap at any time of the day. Yes Flora you did us proud.

Every so often I would call on Eppie on my way to Inverness, have a coffee with her and a catch up with the doggy news. If I took too long in calling she would be on the 'phone to ask why. Although latterly she shuffled about with the aid of two sticks, it did not stop her from going out to the hills in an argocat, across the fields on the back of a quad bike or from going up with a friend in a glider. I would ask her how she was and it would be passed off with one amusing description or another, such as a creaky gate, a car with no chance of passing an MOT, and so on. If my memory was as good as hers was, I could tell you more of them. Top of the list of her pet hates were politicians and officials from the Kennel Club in London. Having said that, many of them came to Dornoch Cathedral to pay their respects and join about six hundred other people to celebrate the life of "Eppie Buist".

Another couple I was introduced to by Eppie Buist was Tony and Caroline Fenwick from Langwell Estate in Wester Ross They had a problem English Setter dog as they called it. When they took it on to the hill in the grouse season it always ran off on them sometimes for half an hour to as much as half a day. They were convinced that the dog, Ben as he was called, did it deliberately but after I took him home I found that he had a poor sense of direction. This coincided with what David Campbell the Langwell Estate keeper had to say about him. When he went over the top of a knoll or ridge he seldom came back.

I worked on this by hiding on Ben. When he was running away from me and when he was not looking I would dive into deep heather or behind a rock and then whistle to him to come back. One minute as far as he was concerned I was there and the next nowhere to be seen. You could see a sense of panic in him not knowing where to look first. When he did come back he would go straight past me until he got my scent and you could see how pleased he was to see me. He reached a stage where he kept looking back to see if I was still there and after about a month you could rely on him to return from where ever he was.

I jokingly said to David I was going to run him in the trials. He was good in every other respect and I seriously thought he had the potential Again I was down at Amulree but this time to run Ben. Mr and Mrs Fenwick drove up from Lincolnshire to see him running. When it came to Ben's turn to run I cast him off to my left and he went a good distance downhill. Mr Fenwick said to his wife, "There he goes, off again." On one pip of the whistle and much to the owner's surprise he turned immediately and came straight back to be cast off again in the opposite direction. We did not win anything that day but was very near to it in later trials. He went home to Langwell with a certificate of merit which they were all proud of.

They had two other dogs, Corrie and Blaze. Corrie is a good looking dog, fantastic worker and as reliable as you could wish for. The biggest problem we all have had with him is the fact he climbs out of every kennel he is put into in spite of any barrier you put in his way His blood lines go back as far as the famous Altnaharra strain. On the sale of Langwell Estate I was asked to find a good home for him, and he is now with Jim up at Gruinard. Last season Jim asked me to come up and run him for few of their days and I enjoyed them very much with Mr and Mrs Cluff, family and friends.

Through Steven McKenzie, Head Ghillie on the famous River Oykel, I was introduced to Mrs Lilian Rowecliffe from Surrey who wished to purchase a Labrador puppy. She and I went to look at a litter and we both chose the same one. She wanted me to train this pup to a very high standard as a pet come companion. Mrs Rowcliffe new exactly what she expected of this dog and gave me one list as long as my arm of the things the dog must not do, and an equally long list of things it had to do. Because she was out of the country a lot, on fishing trips I may add, I was to have the dog for fifteen to eighteen months, but we agreed that she could take the dog out for walks when she was up in Scotland. She was delighted with the outcome and still thinks the world of him to this day.

Since then and on her recommendation, I have sold puppies and trained dogs to just about every member of her family, and the requests for puppies keep coming. Recently I had a 'phone call from a lady in the south to say that she had met in with Mrs Rowcliffe in an airport lounge. In the course of conversation she mentioned that she was looking to buy a flat-coat retriever and a cocker spaniel. According to this lady, Mrs Rowcliffe told her she knew of only one person who could find the right dogs. What better a reference could you get than that. I fixed the lady up with the flat coat but suggested buying a cocker nearer to her home because of the tail docking legislation in Scotland.

Mrs Rowcliffe has a cousin living in Paris and her husband wanted to buy a fully trained black Labrador dog to go shooting with on his estate in the south of France. A bit like Mrs Rowcliffe he also knew exactly what he wanted. He said there was no hurry, to go anywhere I wanted to as long as I came up with the right dog, and that expense was not a consideration. Mrs Rowcliffe confirmed all of this and I travelled all over Scotland, England and even went over to Northern Ireland to look at dogs.

I bought this fantastic dog in Fife to go to France. I had narrowed my searches to five dogs which I thought would be suitable, the one in Fife, one each in Cheshire, South Wales, Newmarket and near Edinburgh. My plan, which I rung and told the owners about, was to travel south, see the dogs working, and on my way home buy the one I liked most. When I rung the owner in Fife he was so cock sure of himself and was adamant that I would go no further than him. I changed my plan and went to see him first and as it turned out he was right. He gave me an excellent demonstration of the dog's ability and I was more than happy in my own mind that I was buying the right dog. The only thing I had to satisfy myself with was if he was good with children and I would not know that for certain until I got him home.

Before going to Fife I said to the owner I wanted to see the dog retrieving freshly shot game. It was out of season for pheasants, partridges etc but I was assured there would be plenty of rabbits on an estate where he rented the shooting. We set off working a Springer spaniel with the Labrador walking at heel. The rabbits were popping down burrows out of shot but in desperation the owner fired two shots at a mallard drake that got up from some rushes. A little further on he missed another one and did likewise with partridges. Heading back to our vehicles some cock pheasants ran into a mixture of long stalky grass and small trees. He was a bit wary of being seen from the windows of the big house where the owner of the estate lived. As I said he was desperate so he shot one of them and after some excellent retrieving there was only one more thing for me to find out and that was the bottom line, the price of the dog.

I had him for two months and found him to be perfect in every respect. I felt lucky to have been able to purchase one of such good calibre. An extra ordinary thing about him was he could scent out golf balls wherever they were. I just could not work it out as he dug up some of them from several inches into the ground where they had been chewed by mice and lay there for years. The buyer flew into Inverness airport in his private jet to pick up the dog and about two years later did the same for a friend who bought a fully trained bitch.

In my travels I bought two bitches for myself one in Kent and one in Northern Ireland near Belfast. Neither of them was suitable for going to France but when I got back to Stranraer I crossed over to Durham where I saw the perfect bitch. She was equally as good as the dog from Fife and both the gentlemen were delighted with their purchases. When I first rung a seller in Northern Ireland I got such a genuine and honest description from him that I decided to do a deal over the 'phone. He was reluctant to go through with it because a person known to him over there was coming to see the bitch the following night. After a lot of persuasion and a promise to put a cheque in the post that afternoon he agreed on the deal but it was going to be a few days before I could get over there. When he asked what happens if you don't like the dog when you see her will you want your money back? "No" I said. "By then she will be mine anyway even if she only has three legs." He did not see a funny side to this and went off on a tirade about his honesty, which I never doubted in the first place.

The very first dealings I had for dogs going abroad was for two black Labrador bitch pups I sold to a serving Squadron Leader in the German Air Force at Oldenburg. It was arranged that he would fly into R.A.F. Kinloss in Morayshire with an Alpha jet and that I would meet him there. I think he must have arranged things with the ground staff about security because none of them were in sight when I got to the hanger. A couple of friends went with me and we carried the pups out to the jet which was sitting a little distance away on the hard standing. Karl, as he was called, produced two oxygen bags and a pup was put into each of them and then put into separate cubicles on the side of the plane. Karl bade us goodbye and took off. By the time we arrived back at Gruinard he had already rung to say how long it had taken him, and that the dogs were in his garden having just finished a good meal. We communicated for several years and the dogs had been trained for finding and tracking wounded deer and probably wild boar as well. They did well in trials for this type of work.

CHAPTER 59

CAMBUSMORE AND OTHER SHOOTS

Over the last few winters I went with my Labrador to pick up at the pheasant and partridge shoots at Novar and Skibo Castle. I was also at Tressady Estate but the shoots there ended last year in failure. Previously I went regularly to Cambusmore Estate when the driven pheasant shoots there were run by Head Keeper, Martin Livings and his "side kick" Jamie Neal. Over and above the syndicate days of which I think there were about twelve, under the auspices of a very eminent gentleman John Roberson from Spinningdale, there were many rough days and I don't just mean the weather, although that was bad enough on many of them, when we had to plough through the scrub, whins and bracken for a mixed bag of ground and feathered game.

Unless it was a shoot day where you knew Martin would be, one place at Cambusmore you did not want to be, was driving up the narrow Loch Buidhe Road for as sure as a cat has got whiskers you would meet Martin driving his landrover down by The Ladder or round some bend as if he owned the road, drinking coffee from a flask top in one hand and often rolling a fag at the same time with the other. The Ladder by the way is a bypass for salmon and sea trout to get up the River Carnock where otherwise the steep waterfall would prohibit them from going any further. They were I understand built from natural stone in Victorian times and each step forms what I can only describe as a rectangular box measuring ten feet wide and several feet deep. Water diverted from the river some four hundred yards above the falls comes down into them at one corner and goes out at the other end. There is a whole series of them and when the water is at the right height the fish have no difficulty in negotiating the steepness. I have looked at them many times and I could safely say that they are as good today as the day they were built and far more in keeping with the surroundings than the concrete ones I have seen elsewhere.

Prior to going to Cambusmore to pick-up, I took out of pity, a very large black Labrador dog called DJ from Colin and Loraine whose son was taking it to the vet to be put down because he could not cope with it. It came on the understanding that I would keep it for three months but if I could not make a working dog of it I would find another home for it. I was picking-up at Gledfield Estate at the time for a very good friend Stan Allum the head keeper. My bitch cut the pad of her foot soon into the day and Stan asked what I would I would do? I said, "I will try DJ , I have him in the van." DJ performed as if he had been doing it for years and surprised everyone when he leapt over a deer fence about seven feet high and brought back a hen pheasant the same way. That leap was to be one of many involving retrieves over high fences. On the keepers day at Gledfield I went into the old kitchen garden to find shot birds and when my dog was looking for them she brought back Stan and Sylvia's pet goose. It was none the worse of its ordeal but within a short space of time the dog brought it back again but this time Sylvia was out to see what the commotion was about. She was not a happy lady having had the goose for twenty odd years and that night she was putting on a dinner for everyone taking part in the shoot. I have never been into buying flowers for anyone but that night I decided to make an exception and say my apologies with a bunch of flowers. I was forgiven and the goose went on to live for a few more years.

When I first got DJ he could not swim. He would remain stationary and thrash the water until it was almost into a froth but once he got the hang of it he would take on the roughest and strongest of rivers if he thought there was something to retrieve from the opposite bank. If he saw a salmon rising in a pool he would swim out to where he last saw it and dive under to look for it. He would do the same if you threw a stone in the water. It was at Cambusmore standing behind the guns when he came into his own. Without being told he would gather up every bird that fell and was fantastic on runners. He could tell when a bird was hit even if it flew on. He would take off like hell after it and invariably after a while he would come back with it and leave it with the rest of them by my feet. A couple of times he chased one out into Loch Fleet and brought the bird back. On one particular drive before lunch, and as I always did, I would leave him on his own to look for pricked birds in a small wood nearby. When he was coming back across the field with a cock pheasant Martin said, "How often do you have to shoe that beast." He really was a big but gentle dog

He had a great temperament towards other dogs unless they pushed him to the limit like Jake often did. At Glen Rossal shoots there was a black Labrador there that would fight with its shadow but one day he met his match. This dog raced up to DJ and fixed him by the side of the neck. I guessed what was going to happen and did nothing but watch. DJ gave this dog a terrible flogging which it badly deserved until it ran off with tail between his legs. In his own way he had a friendly habit at home of greeting people walking towards him by going out to meet them and taking their hand in his mouth and walking along side them. I tried my best to stop him from doing this and I had every opportunity because he did it regularly with me but people who did not know him thought he was biting them and would try and pull their hand away. Fortunately he never did it with children.

Like every other estate I went to, Martin organised a day for the keepers and beaters and at the end of it all his wife Sharon provided us with a scrumptious sit down meal with all the booze to go with it. It never failed to be anything other than a very jolly night even if you did find yourself on the floor having sat on the "dicky" chair to catch the unsuspecting. Then there was Melanie the young hair stylist who tried to make the best of a bad job, her problem being the shortage of material to work with. Jamie was an excellent cartoonist and decorated the walls with many caricatures. Each of us was reminded of unusual happenings that we were responsible for throughout the season and was taken to task about them and given a small but funny gift. One relative to my self was a mini first aid kit complete with an artificial thumb. It just so happened that my gun went faulty and each time I pushed off the safety catch both barrels fired off with the top lever splitting the end of my thumb. It had twice been to a gunsmith in London for repair but in the finish I surrendered it to the police for scrapping but unlike the car scrappage scheme I got nothing for it.

A full time forest ranger was a regular beater on Saturdays, a very nice person but a man of few words. So that he could have a drink afterwards I gave him a lift to one of the end of season keeper's shoots and during the meal he was tippling away at the whisky. He was presented with a microphone as his gift and by the end of the night he was up singing and telling Sharon how he fancied her. When it came for me to take him home he was well sloshed and after a mile down the road he could not find his gift and wanted to go back for it. However, we found it in the car and I give him credit for feeding his dogs before heading into the house. On reaching the back door he thought it was locked so he then tried the front door. Kenny's wife was supposed to be out at another party. I was having to hold him up most of the time until he told me to stand aside whilst he put his shoulder to the door and force it open. When the door burst open he landed spread-eagled on the hallway floor. His wife came out of the sitting room to see what all the commotion was. I got him to his feet and he said, "Just make out you're sober." I left him on the settee and although I tried to talk to him weeks later he had nothing to say about it, whether he remembered or not I do not know.

When the second injury happened to my thumb I was a paying guest on a rough day at Cambusmore with some local people including Gregor McLeod. At lunch time we went indoors for our lunch and Gregor took in a litre bottle with a small amount of Sloe Gin in it and thimble size glasses to give us all a drink. He left himself open for some ribbing when he said the bottle had lasted him for a couple of years. I said, "Not surprising seeing the size of the glasses." I also took in a bottle of Sloe Gin and gave everyone a drink. Gregor, getting his own back on me said in his toast to us all, "And Hugh I hope your thumb aches for ever more." The injury ocurred the first shot I fired that day but I carried on with the party working my Springer spaniel next to Gregor. For all of that day including a woodcock flight in the evening I cannot recall seeing more consistently good shooting. I have been at night time duck flights with him when he has shot equally as good.

I am a strong believer that no one should go shooting for game unless they have a suitable dog fit for the purpose. Of course the exception to this is if you are in the company of other people with dogs. The dog need not be the most obedient or well trained animal as long as it does the job. Does it really matter if it runs into shot or as soon as a bird hits the deck. To me it does not matter a hoot. Having said that I admire the dog that will walk to heel all day without being on a lead or sit at a peg without being shackled to a chunk of iron screwed into the ground until the drive is over. As often as not they are not the best of game finders when it comes to "runners", or difficult birds over a river or such like unless they are in the charge of experienced handlers who do a lot of picking –up.

"Peg dogs" for most of the year are family pets and yes it is the privilege of the owners who have paid for their days shooting to bring them along and many of them are quite happy to be left with a couple or so birds for their dogs to retrieve. Then you get others who want all birds left for their dogs and as often as not they only succeed in finding a few easy ones, leaving the remainder for the picker-up with experienced dogs to find. By this time "runners" are well gone and birds that fell in flooded water are usually in the next parish. Whilst all of this is going on, wounded birds are left lying on the ground albeit sometimes tucked into the nearest piece of cover to eventually die but not before going through a considerable amount of stress and suffering. Some drives takes longer than others and I say quite categorically that it is totally wrong and unjustified to leave bird to the end of a drive before being picked up and dispatched immediately.

I do not wish to single out one shoot more than others because there are plenty of them up and down the country where I have been either beating or picking up so I talk with plenty of experience but one lady I know thinks it is more up-market to leave the picking up until the drive is finished and not have dogs running about distracting the guns. Snobbery I call this. I happened to be at the same shoot as her one day when she was picking-up near to me. I left to go and find a partridge that fell a little distance away and when I got back the head keeper quite rightly pointed out to me that he had found another eight birds where she had been as if I was to blame. The lady had gone by this time and he was obviously not happy about it. He would have preferred it if she had not been there at all and left the regular pickers-up to get on with what they were being paid to do. All birds were picked up in the end and it proved the point he and others often made. It pleased me to see the beaters coming in at the end of a drive no matter where you were with birds that their dogs had picked up but you could rest assure that in the bothy at lunch time you heard about it. All good banter especially from the Cocker men who rubbished the Labradors.

I also looked after Italians who came over for the woodcock shooting. They stayed in a lovely property built by the new owners of Cambusmore Estate. Normally eight guns, a driver and one helper came for a few weeks each season and my job was to act as their agent and organise enough suitable ground for them to shoot over, collect all monies, pay the estates, keepers and help generally on a day to day basis. They brought over their own pointers and setters and unlike my dogging days they had a bleeper on them that sounded when standing still on point to birds to indicate to the owner where they were. Other dogs running at the same time on recognising the sound would make their way to the point and back the first dog. This was necessary because of the thick scrubby woodland they worked in. Most if not all of them would retrieve the dead birds. I never came across another party so enthusiastic about woodcock shooting as them. Twice I witnessed a right and left and when I said they qualified for becoming members of the

Woodcock Club they were not interested. One of them said it was not his first right and left at woodcock.

I could not fault the Italians I went out with but other parties including French ones did not have a very good safety record. Woodcock shooting, because of the way the birds behave when flushed requires the greatest of care to avoid shooting fellow guns or dogs. Several accidents have taken place recently but fortunately no one got fatally injured although one agent lost an eye. With any firearm it is imperative that the user is qualified and competent in its use and not just out in the field but at all times. Roe shoots were equally risky when the animals broke back through the line of guns and some careless person would fire at them without making certain a fellow gun was not it the line of fire.

I am going to quote a few local instances of pure carelessness and yes I know that can be attributed to my self as well where simple safety precautions were not taken. The first relates to a wild fowler who was cleaning his semi automatic shotgun in a local hotel bedroom. The gun which should never have been loaded went off, the discharge went down through the floor and hit a member of staff in the room below. Fortunately she was not seriously injured. A game keeper and his friend before leaving the house to go hind stalking had a bullet go off from their rifle, again going down through the floor boards and bursting a water pipe below. Another game keeper arriving home from a day's stalking taking the loaded rifle into his house and whatever he was doing or thinking about the rifle went off. The bullet went through the living room wall to a bedroom, through the clothing in his wardrobe and continued into a cupboard housing the copper hot water tank. It only stopped after gouging the side of the cylinder. Taking a new suit from the wardrobe to a tailor to be invisibly mended he thought that was all he needed to do to keep quiet about what happened. The tailor said to him, "I hope you were not wearing this at the time?" He thought, "What's the point of trying to keep quiet about it."

Two crofters from the Rogart area some years ago went out in their old Ford Thames van to try and get a stag for the pot. The passenger was armed with a shotgun loaded with cartridges containing heavy slugs. On spotting a beast near to the roadside he hurriedly requested the driver to stop who did rather abruptly causing the passenger to get thrown forward and then backwards in his seat causing the gun to go off and blasted a large hole in the roof. The van had seen better days anyway and lay in a quarry hole until it was subsequently buried by a local contractor. Needless to say the stag lived for a little longer.

Ronnie cannot be blamed for this but had a narrow shave when coming home with a foreigner from a day's stalking. A fox was seen not far from the road and the foreigner asked could he shoot it. Ronnie stopped the pick-up, the guy got out and resting the rifle on the roof took a shot at the fox. Not looking where the end of the barrel was pointing, the bullet ripped a hole in the top of the cab and the shrapnel hit Ronnie on the top of the head. Although not seriously injured, the cap he was wearing had seen better days. A nephew of mine did a similar thing with little or no damage when shooting rabbits with a .22 from the bonnet of my van.

He also did not allow for the fact that the scope he was looking through was that few inches above the barrel.

If anyone is lucky to be alive today it is Ronnie. He was zeroing his big rifle one day when the charge backfired blowing the cocking mechanism from the bolt back past the side of his head to end up in oblivion. The right side of his face was scorched and his ear was bleeding. The top of his jacket at the shoulder had a hole ripped in it. One of his forefingers caught a blast out from the side of the breach, squashing the middle joint and leaving the finger burned to the bone and half closed for months. He still suffers from deafness in his left ear and had a couple of flash backs nearer to the time it happened. His finger, although still tender has healed well. The shock of all of this made him reluctant to fire a rifle again but when my friend Eric Kite came up from London with a new rifle needing zeroing and the barrel floated he went to see Ronnie knowing that the job would be done to perfection. This got Ronnie back on target and has been grateful to Eric ever since. Another friend of mine made good recovery from a shooting accident where a bullet entered his tail end and after breaking up ended up in his chest cavity. He also is lucky to be alive. I don't know if it is true Robert but I was told at the time of arriving at the hospital you were more concerned about the nurses going to cut your new tweeds off.

CHAPTER 60

LOVE AT FIRST SIGHT - WELL NOT QUITE

While I was stationed at Stonehaven Alan McConachie was at Lodge Walk in Aberdeen and was in digs with a Mrs Murray in Albert Street. He contacted me with a view to meeting up for a drink so I drove up to Aberdeen and we went to the Caledonian Hotel which was to become our regular watering hole before going to the dances at the Palace Hotel or the Beach Ballroom.

This particular night the dance at the Beach Ballroom was rubbish so we decided to go elsewhere. Alan suggested Kintore but I was sure I had seen an advertisement for a marquee dance that night somewhere about Aberdeen's outskirts. However, we set off for Kintore but after passing through Bucksburn a Policeman was in the middle of the road directing traffic. We thought there had been an accident or something and followed his directions to turn into Forrit Brae.

The cars in front of us then turned into a field where a good going dance was in progress in a marquee. We decided to go in and soon afterwards Alan met a neice of Mrs Murray's, Grace Munroe from Rogie Hill Farm, Skene, now married and living in Australia. Along with her were her two brothers, Harold and Roy, and this very attractive looking girl who we were introduced to as Marjory Shepherd. So, when I am now asked where I met Marjory I say, "In a field". We danced together quite a bit throughout the night and when I offered to escort her home at the end of the dance she accepted. I would not say it was love at first sight nor did I imagine then that one day she would become my wife. From leaving school she worked in the cash room at Marischal College in Aberdeen.

Marjory lived with her parents Charlie and Edith Shepherd at Hill of Minnes Farm, Foveran. Her two younger brothers, Eric and Ian, were still at school, whilst Kenneth was out in the Persian Gulf at RAF Sharjaw and Bob was nursing at Kingseat Mental Hospital before enlisting in the Army. Kenneth on his return from the Gulf got posted to North Luffingham during which time he met and married Mary a lovely girl in every way from Bourne, Lincolnshire. Soon afterwards Kenneth bought his first lorry and now with two of their sons, Craig and Andrew he has several on the road. Ian started work with a blacksmith near to his home at Hill of Minnes before going on to work in Aberdeen for various oil companies. He is at the moment Area Manager for one of them and looking after their interests in Europe and Africa.

Edith was born and brought up at Craiglash, Torphins with her Granny and Grandad, Elspeth and James Smith. Her dad, also James Smith was killed during the Second World War. About the age of twelve for a very short time she went to live and work for her Aunt Nellie Smith and her Uncle Sandy Tough a bobby at Cairnbulg. She then returned to Craiglash until she was sixteen when she moved to Greenden, Balmedie to be reunited with her mother who we have always known as

Granny Hutcheon and to join her half brother Johnie and half sisters Madgie and Eileen for the first time. George and Charlie were born later. As far as relatives go her claim to fame is being related through the Smiths' to Donald Dinnie the famous Scottish Athlete who carried two stones (The Dinnie Stones) with a combined weight of 775 pounds across the width of the Potarch Bridge near Kincardine O'Neil.

By coincidence I worked with Kenny Tough, a son, in the police at Bucksburn and because I was catching a lot of salmon on the River Don he approached me to see if it was possible for him to take up the sport. I told him that there was no reason why he could not catch a salmon and offered to loan him my rod. "No, if I am going to do it I will go and buy my own." He said. He then went in to Aberdeen and bought everything they told him he would require. Soon afterwards he joined me at the river and after a quick lesson on how to cast with a spinning rod he had two beautiful salmon on the bank without any further assistance from me. The River Don at Grandholm was one of the filthiest stretches of water that I ever had occasion to fish. It was below the discharges from the paper and woollen mills and other industrial premises. One could not see the lure or a salmon until it came to the surface. Each time before making a cast you had to clean the hooks of all the unpleasantries and I can assure you there were many. In spite of the conditions beautiful fresh salmon could be caught.

Granny and Grandad Shepherd

Charlie was born on 18th June, 1916 at Rhynie, Aberdeenshire and went to school at Tullynestle where in his latter years was not the flavour of the month with his teacher. At this time his father James Shepherd was at Balquharn Farm and spent most of his time as a cattle drover between the Cabrach, Portsoy, Aboyne and Alford Mart and possibly many more places in between, with Charlie bunking off school to join him. After leaving school at the age of thirteen or fourteen he worked a pair of horses at Corsindae, Bog of Fintry and Rhinds Home Farm, Balmedie where his father worked as cattleman on the neighbouring Eigie Farm. During this time Charlie met Edith Shepherd from Greenden and after he went to Castle Fraser Home Farm to work, he told me how he cycled the twenty miles or more back and fore to Balmedie to keep up this relationship until they got married and settled down at Castle Fraser. Marjory was born on 12th December 1937 at Castle Fraser and six months later they all moved to Hill of Minnes.

Charlie with his loyal pair

The horse drawn mower and binder

Charlie was the farm grieve to a Mr Wishart who had a number of farms and under him were two tractor men, and two cattlemen or bailies as they were called, the latter two living in the chalmer or bothy but getting their food from Edith in the farmhouse. The bailies never stayed much more than a year or so but one who was called "Auld Johnie" stuck it out for much longer. At the table he had this habit of pulling his cup away when he did not want any more tea poured into it. This used to infuriate Edith because of the mess he caused and because she told him off so many times about it but took no notice of her.

Hoeing turnips

Cattle at that time were tied up in stalls and after feeding in the morning they had to be mucked out by barrow. It was much later before the byres were converted to courts which made the work easier. In the summer time the cattle were out in the fields and if the bailies had nothing to do indoors they had to help with jobs like hoeing turnips, haymaking, harvesting or other "orra" work. At harvest time the crops were cut with a binder and when dry enough in the stooks the sheaves were brought in to be built into stacks or rucks in the cornyard. Marjory would sometimes drive the tractors from stook to stook and was more popular at that than I was. Whoever was building the load thought I was too jerky but I got my own back on them if I was forking by putting several sheaves up at the same time and making them work for their money. In the winter time when the cattle were inside, a ruck would be brought in as and when required and put through the threshing mill and the grain bruised for feeding, both pieces of equipment belt driven by a stationary engine. The one for the mill was a massive thing and also powered the generator for charging the batteries for the lighting system. It started up when the first light went on and stopped when the last light went out and Marjory used to say that if she or any of the others came home late at night they could not put a light on for fear of their father hearing the engine start up.

Two dairy cows were kept on the farm, which Charlie looked after and Edith, like my mother was just as adept at making butter, crowdy and cheese. The only difference was that in the dairy she had a mechanical separator and when cranked separated the cream from the milk. Mam had to let the milk settle in large basins and after a few days skim off the cream from the top with a special ladle. For making the butter her churn was different to the one we had at home. It was of the tall plumper type and could cope with larger quantities of cream at any one time. They both had clappers for moulding the butter into rectactangular shapes like you buy butter in today or in rounds which my mother had a wooden mould with the imprint of a cow's head on it to stamp the top of it with.

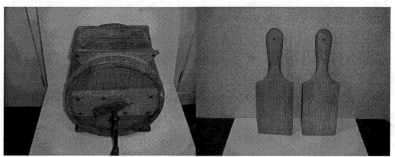

Like the Churn Mam used (Timespan, Helmsdale)   *Butter pats*

In the early sixties farming in Aberdeenshire was going through a bit of a revolution with most jobs being done mechanically. The two remaining Clydesdale horses at Hill of Minnes were more or less redundant with tractors and other machinery taking over, but still very far from the sophisticated electronics and remote controls of today. The first tractor I saw there was a David Brown Crop Master but before that they had a Marshall with a single cyclinder two stroke engine that give off a distinct sound every time it fired resulting in it being nicknamed the "Pom Pom" tractor. Hill of Minnes, because of its fertility and heavy cropping, was known as the Garden of Foveran and Charlie said it used to be worked with three pairs of horses. One or two younger horses came unbroken after being bought cheaply by the farmer at the sales. Their cattle at that time were nearly all black, probably Aberdeen Angus bought in for fattening. Many of them were bought at sales in Grantown on Spey or from up in Orkney.

The only sheep on the farm was during the winter months when a flock master rented the grazings. The sheep, usually ewes, would stay for only a few weeks at a time before moving on to other rented farms. It was only after a change of ownership that lambs were bought in for fattening. Charlie looked after them and took an interest in training collie dogs in the process. One of them was a pup I bought for him from Alan McLean a shepherd at Loubconich. It was on a Hogmanay night and a good going party was taking place at the MacGregor's home in Amat. What I remember most about the party was Ali MacGregor standing on a kitchen chair singing and shouting, jumping up and down and banging his head on the low rafters. In his own way he was conducting the music and keeping the dancers at it. When I took the pup down to Hill of Minnes Edith said it had rickets. Rickets or no it turned out to be one of the best dogs he trained and when sold it went on to win at the sheepdog trials. What I remember most about it was the continual sickness in the car.

Bringing in the harvest

When Mr Wishart put Hill of Minnes on the market a lot of interest was shown in the sale. Everything was got ready and laid out in a field for a farm sale or a roup as it is more commonly called down Aberdeen way. Several prospective buyers came to view the farm and I remember Charlie saying that one farmer gave him half a crown or two shillings and six-pence for showing him around which took the best part of a forenoon. A bit grippy he thought and did he want him to be the successful buyer or not?

However, it was bought by William Donald Senior, owner of William Donald and Son, a meat processing factory at Portlethan. Mr Donald already owned a farm at Kemnay and more in Kincardineshire and like the others Hill of Minnes was to be used as a self supporting cattle bank. Huge numbers of prime cattle were required for processing and a ready supply had to be available at short notice.

Lorry loads came and went almost on a weekly basis and it was Charlie's job to make sure they were finished off for the required grades.

Charlie and Edith spent forty three years, 1938 to 1981, at Hill of Minnes. Both of them saw many changes throughout those years not just the way farming itself progressed, but ownership changing hands, workers that came and went and their own lifestyle changing for which I would say very much for the better. Edith as long as I remember her, has always said she did not like the place but sticking it out for forty three years she didn't do too bad. When I asked her if she ever had the case packed to leave she said, "Only when Mr Wishart put the farm up for sale." Mr Donald, one of the prospective buyers, told Charlie that if he did not get Minnes there would be a job for him at Cockley one of his other farms and Edith was looking foward so much for this move. When twelve o'clock arrived on the day the sealed offers were opened to see who the successful buyer was Mr Donald rang to say, "He was." Charlie was heard to reply by saying, "I will just stay on at Minnes then." Edith was really disappointed because she wanted to get away.

Charlie's retirement coincided with him contracting "farmer's lung disease" and was unable to continue with the heavier tasks on the farm. Eric, who had worked under him from almost the time he left school, took over from him but still under the supervision of his father who continued on a part-time supervisory role for a few years. By this time Charlie and Edith had moved to a pensioner's house at Newmachar and spent a successful retirement on the bowling greens' both in-door and out. Charlie had another hobby but a more profitable one making stag horn thumb sticks and shepherd crooks. He had various shop outlets and Gruinard Lodge for their sales making a tidy little sum in the process. He was grateful to Neil Ross near Kingussie for a ready supply of tup horns. Charlie lived on until reaching the age of 88 years but sadly he died on 27th January, 2005, and was interred in the cemetery at Newmachar. Edith, at 95 years young, is still going strong, keeping good health, looking after herself and getting about by free 'bus trips to wherever she can.

When William Donald sold Hill of Minnes Eric and family moved to Tillbouries one of his other farms. He was still there when his marriage broke up but not long after that he met and married Sheila who was to be his soul mate for the next fifteen years. Eric always fancied to go lorry driving but was unsure about making the change but with Sheila's encouragement he took the plunge and went to work for the Council Roads Department driving his pride and joy, a six wheeled Foden. The work covered many aspects of road maintenance but I would be safe in saying he was at his best when working on his own clearing the roads of snow or out gritting at all hours. Together they bought a house at Culter but later moved to Westhills. They lived life to the full and unlike Marjory and I did most things together, bowling, caravanning or just visiting, including trips to Bonar.

I was privileged to know Eric from his time in short trousers stretching to his untimely death fifty years later as a result of an aggressive form of leukaemia. As a Brother in Law I could not have wished for a better one. I would like to think we had a lot in common and I enjoyed the many stories and encounters he had to relate. He did not take to fools gladly and was never slow to express his views on them. He was very much a family man, and like Sheila, kind and caring even when the young ones were not always thought to be up to their very high standards. He has left a huge gap in the family but happy memories will live on not only by those closest to him but also with the four hundred or so who came to Skene Parish Church for a celebration of his life.

My courtship with Marjory continued through the summer of 1959 and in the spring of 1960 we got engaged to get married. Marjory came up with me to meet my parents at Gruinard and on our way through Inverness we bought the ring. At that time when you went up the strath at Dounie you could see Whale Cottage in the distance high up on the hillside and I kidded her on that was where Mam and Dad lived. I would describe it as a low key event with no special celebrations. When we announced the 12th of November of that year for our wedding day both Charlie and Edith were taken by surprise and, "Why the hurry?" they asked. Did they think a bun was in the oven?

To me Hill of Minnes was a home from home and I spent many of my days off duty at the farm. I keep getting reminded by Edith of the very first night in their home how I told her off about standing at my back whilst I was having tea with others at the kitchen table. I cannot remember it myself but I do believe her because it is one of my pet hates. I will stand aside to let people through a door first and it is the same when I'm driving. I prefer to follow rather than be followed. In a restaurant or similar I like to sit with my back to a wall and face everyone. Where I get it from I do not know but maybe it comes from my early time in the police.

When out at Hill of Minnes a good deal of my time was spent ferreting or shooting rabbits down the big ditch or up on the hill on a neighbours land. The Minnes mill dam was a great source for Mallard ducks and many a good hour or two I spent at it. There was plenty of barley to feed them with and for most there was a good evening flight came in. Before coming up from London Eric, my brother in law, made sure the dam was well fed to ensure good sport. Early morning could be just as good and if the sea was stormy along the coast they would fly in during the daytime for shelter. Grebes, Water Hens and Coots frequented it as well. Some biggish trout were caught but the only success I had was with eels. Water from the dam passed through the wheelhouse where there was an antiquated ram pump that pushed spring water up to a tank at the top of the hill park from where it back fed to the house, steading and the farm.

Punchy, the farm collie could always be seen in the fields with Charlie unless my car was at the door when she got out in the morning. She would then wait for me to appear knowing that for most I would be going out with the gun and she just loved that. She was fantastic at retrieving ducks from the water and on one occasion she brought two out at the same time. Most of her retrieves were from the dam and luckily not from a river. She always made for the nearest bank where she dropped them. I only saw her carry on land once and that was a brown hare I shot in the field where the Clydesdales were. When they galloped over to her she picked it up and headed straight for me with it.

Charlie shot five wild geese at the dam one morning and Punchy took them out as well. One of the geese Edith plucked and prepared it for supper one night. We all thoroughly enjoyed it but a surprise was to come later after I sent away the ring that was on one of the legs to find that it had been ringed in Iceland twelve years previous. It must have been in the cooking for it to be such a tender old brute. At home we did not have the opportunity to have roasted wild duck and Edith gave me plenty of it. Pot roasted until the meat is coming away from the bone with chips, peas, onions and gravy and I just love it. No orange sauce, wine or other additives. Marjory got too much of it then and now she has gone right off it. I have had venison cooked in red wine and with walnuts but it does nothing for me. I have always preferred the true taste of any game.

My shooting at Hill of Minnes came to an abrupt halt, albeit temporarily, one wintry snowy night when George Fullerton the farmer from Milton of Minnes gave me permission to shoot wild duck coming into his snow-covered corn rucks. While I was waiting for the ducks to come in I laid my gun against one of the stacks to have a piddle. Unexpectedly about a dozen to twenty ducks started to drop in above me and in the excitement I picked up the gun and fired off two shots. I could not understand why I had not killed at least one but then when I went to reload I found that I had blown four inches of the end of one barrel and six inches of the other. Unbeknown to me snow had got into the barrels and the build up of pressure caused them to burst in the way they did. The remaining twenty four and a quarter inches of good barrels were still legal and came in handy in later years when out ferreting in the woods.

Hill of Minnes was a house where Edith and Charlie made visitors, and there were many of them, most welcome. They were both keen card players and young and old were encouraged to join in. The noisy but friendly arguments and all the hilarity was unbelievable and when late into the night Charlie who would be trying to get to sleep would be out of bed stamping on the floor of the bedroom up above for everyone to be quiet. The big room at the front of the house was the scene of many a good party with live music to dance to. When Eric Kite and I came up on holiday there was usually a big get-together that included Johnie Hutcheon and his wife Irene from Greenden, their good friends Jock and his wife "Dosh" Dorothy Kemp from Cairntack, Belhelvie, Geordie Bruce and his wife Madgie, a sister of Edith's, Granny Hutcheon and many more as well. I arrived at Granny Hutcheon's one night after a day's fishing at Fettercairn and the usual crowd were having a get together with plenty of alcohol being consumed.   At one point and I cannot remember what started it but Irene had me down on the floor rubbing cream cakes into my face. The carpet was not a pretty sight but the new jumper I was wearing was worse. Apparently I kept saying, "What will Marjory say about it."

Irene, Bill, Eileen, Johnie, Marjory, myself, Geordie, Dosh and Jock
At a Bobby's ball

Irene and Dosh were great fun and one night after a party we found stag antlers, feet and thorns in our beds. A trick if you could call it was for either Eric or I to sit on a kitchen chair and the pair of them by placing two fingers under our thighs could lift us up off the seat and holds us there. Neither of us are light weights so I don't know how they did it. Another thing they did was to get one of us stooges to stretch out on our back over three chairs and without touching us they could remove the middle chair without us dropping to the floor. Another night I was under threat from them and it ended up with me running from the house as I thought they were going to have the trousers off me.

A surprised party, none of it planned by Marjory or I was the "Feet Washing" just before our wedding. It was customary then for close friends and family to take the intended couple by surprise, strip them down to underwear and sometimes more and give them a good blackening with boot polish. We did not escape this ritual either when one evening the usual gang arrived at Minnes and did the business after which we adjourned to the Whitecairns Hotel to celebrate the occasion with drinks. Afterwards we returned to Minnes for more refreshments and help to scoff the food that was previously prepared. Because we were out in the country perhaps we got off lightly and did not go through the ritual of being tarred and feathered, carted through the streets and end up tied to a lamp post somewhere.

When we went to London we spent a lot of our holidays at Hill of Minnes and Catriona and Fiona loved it. Edith, from morning to night would dote on them hand and foot and they could do nothing wrong. She had a very large and strong whirly jig for drying the washing on and nothing pleased her more than to lift them up to hang on while she spun it round and round. Better than any swing or roundabout in a public park. It was not just our girls she loved having but all her grandchildren. At ninety five years of age she still loves the company of other people especially ones she can have a laugh and a bit of fun with.

Every Wednesday Marjory stayed overnight with her Auntie Madgie, Geordie her Uncle and family at Caperstone Crescent in Aberdeen. A sleep over you would call it today and we would meet early evening and go for a meal. I would on the odd occasion stop over myself as it was another house where everyone was welcome. In fact it was a trait in all of that family. On a Sunday we often went up Royal Deeside for a picnic and a game of rounders after going to Crathes Church to see the Royal family. Another Aunt and Uncle, Bill and Eileen Shearer had various pubs over the years and some good nights we had with them. Greenden or Greeny's as it is more often than not referred to was another place where we gathered if only for a game of croquet on the lawn or to spend an evening with George and Eileen or Charlie and Isobel although we saw more of them up at Hill of Minnes or at weddings or other functions.

CHAPTER 61

BACK TO ABERDEEN

When my tour of duty ended at Stonehaven and came up to Lodge Walk I also got digs with Mrs Murray and her husband William who had his own taxi hire business. Alan McConnachie and I more or less became members of the family and often ate with them in the kitchen. They took in holiday makers during the summer and it was not unusual to come home to find that our beds for the week or more would be up in an attic room. She looked after all of us very well and nothing was too much for her. The perfect landlady.

Willie Murray, their son, and I were to get married more or less at the same time and ministers preferred to marry you if the couple were both members of the church. Willie was courting Helen Wilson from Corsindae Farm at Sauchen and we both arranged to see the minister near to our digs with a view to becoming members of his church. On the night of our first meeting with him we parked our car round the corner from his house and took a shortcut over some grass to his door. Willie was first to go upstairs to his study. When I went up, the stair carpet every second step was stained with dog "poo." The minister apologised for the unusual smell and asked if I was getting it. Being polite I said, "No, not really." But I knew perfectly well what had happened. Willie had picked up the dog dirt on one of his shoes as he crossed the lawn. We had a few more meetings with him as well as attending some church services but he never mentioned anything more about it.

One Sunday afternoon Willie arrived at our flat with a very big salmon, I think about sixteen pounds, asking where I sold my fish. Early that morning along with friends he had been fishing without permission on the River Don up near Castle Fraser. It was the first I knew about it but the early Sunday mornings I could relate to and apparently it was a common occurrence.

Marjory and I got married on the planned date at Foveran Church and had our reception in the New Inn Hotel at Ellon at a cost of ten shillings and sixpence per head. It had a fantastic reputation for weddings, dinner dances or just a place to go for a meal. Leading up to our wedding date foot and mouth disease broke out amongst the cattle on many of the farms in Aberdeenshire. Although Hill of Minnes was not directly affected there were restrictions on the movement of cattle and every road end had to have facilities for disinfecting peoples foot wear and car wheels. You were never sure where the next outbreak would occur and one could not help thinking it might affect our wedding arrangements. Luckily it did not but Bill and Martha Burnett who were at Longside Police Station were unable to attend because of it. Having gone to the New Inn recently with Edith and other members of the family I would say nothing has changed after fifty years or so. The reception went well until after the meal and the band we had booked did not arrive on time. One of them was a lorry driver that Geordie Bruce knew from work and he was able to say that the driver had been diverted on his way back to Aberdeen to go to Glasgow for a return load. It did cross my mind that there was another reason because I had occasion to report him for speeding. However, although a bit late when they did arrive they certainly made up for lost time and gave us good music for the rest of the night, before going on to Hill of Minnes to continue the party and help to eat the Sunday dinner. I should have asked the hotel to get a special licence to open the bar before normal opening times but this was not done. Like the band, I think everyone made up for lost time with that as well. I know I did.

The bride and groom

About the only thing I was left to arrange was to where we would go to spend our first night of married life. I never did anything about it and stopped after midnight at a roadside telephone kiosk and rung the Bay View Hotel at Stonehaven and got in there. We went on to Perth, Edinburgh and St Andrews after that before coming back to Hill of Minnes to set up home in a flat in Rosemount Viaduct, Aberdeen. All our worldly possessions were carted in several trips with a hired Ford Anglia from Minnes to the flat. The only down side to the flat was the seventy steps up to it and the shared toilet on the landing. I had previously arranged to rent a ground floor one but the owner let us down by changing his mind at the last minute. We were grateful to Geordie Bruce for getting the one we did but when we knew Catriona was on the way we moved to Broomhill Road and stayed there until being allocated our first police house at Fettercairn.

Fifty years later at the Lochardil house hotel, Inverness (it's only water)

We could only have been married a month or two when my wandering lust set in again. An advert appeared in the local paper requesting people from the north east to go out to Illinois in America to work on a mink farm. Marjory and I discussed this and decided to have a go at it. I wrote off for more details, particularly what sort of accommodation they had for married couples, which turned out to be a hostel with everyone sharing. We did not fancy this so we abandoned the idea. Perhaps it was just as well from what I now know. I could not visualise Marjory handling mink or the smell in any shape or form. Having lived in eleven different houses Marjory said to me the other day that she would decide when and where our next move would be, adding that she had spent most of her life following me around.

I cannot see a move in the near future but the inevitable will come when things get too much for us at "Dalriada". At the moment Marjory is so engrossed with her golf and W.R.I. that I do not envisage her giving that up or even scaling back for one minute. For the Ross-shire W.R.I. Federation she has just completed twelve years on the Housewifes and Handicraft Committee, Bulb and Baking Convener, a Central Council member at Headquarters in Edinburgh for six years. Being a member of the Culrain W.R.I. Institute since we moved back to Scotland she has held all the senior committee posts and has been a regular winner in the competitions including the Bulb and Baking trophy thirteen times.

I forget when she first joined Bonar Bridge and Ardgay Golf Club but over the last ten years or so she has excelled in that as well getting her handicap down to eighteen. With this past time she has held all the senior committee posts in the Ladies Section including Secretary twice, Vice Captain, Captain and is shortly to take over as Ladies Captain for a second time. She has won most trophies in that section including the Club Championship twice and at the open days with Jackie Clarke won both the Handicap and Scratch trophies. Marjory takes part in competitions throughout the Highlands and has just returned from a week's golf at Ballater and Balmoral. Bonar Bridge and Ardgay Golf Club has a very strong and popular Ladies Section with members from other clubs coming long distances to play regularly. I would stick my neck out and say that when it comes to organisation and fund raising they are the backbone of the club.

CHAPTER 62

CATRIONA, ALAN, HANNAH AND HOLLY

Catriona graduated from the University College, Cardiff with a BSC (Econ) in European Studies in French and Italian. From there she went to study at the West London College of Higher Education obtaining a Bi-Lingual Secreterial Diploma in French, Italian and Spanish.

She first worked as a Personal Assistant to the Managing Director of Sunquest Holidays, London, specialising in holidays to Turkey, Romania and Bulgaria, moving on to International Vacationer, London as Account Executive organising conferences and incentive travel world wide. Still in London she then took on the role of Account Manager with Bahamasair the Official Airline of the Bahamas, also as Account Manager for Airline Associations, Richmond, Surrey in charge of The Nassau, Cable Beach Paradise Island Promotion Board responsible for the sales and marketing of 28 hotels in the Bahamas. This was followed in sales and marketing for a chain of hotels in Maritius and the Seycheles.

Moving on from accounts manager, sales and marketing she worked as a consultant to the Bahamas Ministry of Tourism. She set up a European wide training programme for travel agents to assist them sell holidays in the Bahamas and in the course of this produced a training manuel and video, organising training sessions and yearly trips for five hundred European Travel Agents to visit the Bahamas for a week.

By this time she had met Alan Rawlinson who was Managing Director for operation at the London Office of RPMC (UK), a company that specialises in the key disciplines of event management, entertainment marketing, hospitality, travel incentives and much more in the world of sport. In May, 1980 they both went out to the company's office in Los Angelos where Alan continued within his field of expertise and Catriona worked as Product and Development Manager for research and costing for events and escorted incentive travel world wide.

On 18th, March, 2000 they got married in Las Vegas but soon afterwards returned to England where on 1st April at All Saints, Church, West Sussex a service was held for the reaffirmation of their vows followed by a reception for all the family and friends.

Hannah was born on 4th September, 2000 and their second daughter, Holly was born 11th December, 2001 with Mum taking time out from work to look after them but studied and gained her City and Guilds in Horticulture. On moving home to Burghfield Common in Berkshire both girls attended the Mrs Bland Infant School and Catriona took on the role as teacher assistant and secretary of the Parents Teachers Association. For the school she set up and ran the Gardening Club for which the children won numerous awards and competitions.

Outwith their day to day school activities Hannah has been a member of the Rainbows, Brownies and is now a Guide. Holly joined the Beavers, was a Cub and a Brownie but will shortly be enrolling as a Guide. Now that the family have moved to Cawder near Nairn, they both are members of the Nairn Area Amatuer Athletics Club and the Scottish Athletic Association. They both represented Cawder School in the Orienteering Championships. Hannah also represented the school in the Northern Scottish School Athletic Championships and was a bronze medal winner in the relay team. Hannah is a representative of Cawder School Council and is now a House Captain. Holly is a member of the Whale and Dolphin Conservation Society and also the R.S.P.B. Both are members of the Bonar Bridge Ardgay Golf Club and Hannah and her Mum competed in the 5K Race For Life Marathon.

Today Hannah and Holly are off up to Thurso to take part in inter-schools cross country running.

CHAPTER 63

FIONA, TIM, ISHBEL, ROSANNA AND GIDEON

Fiona after getting her Foundation Certificate with Distinction in Art and Design at Kingston Polytechnic went on to Winchester to obtain BA (Hons) Degree in Textiles and later to be chosen for The Young Designer of the Year into Industry Award for the year 1986 to 1987. For a short spell she worked for a carpet company during which time she stayed in a hotel in Jackson Bridge near to the "Last of the Summer Wine" country. We visited her there for a few days staying in the same hotel and on the first night I met a man at the bar who said he and two of his friends had been up to the North of Scotland on holiday to make a wild life video and putting the emphasis on filming an eagle. When I asked him, "Was it on the top of a telegraph pole?" He said, "Yes but why did you know that?" I then said to him, "That was a bussard you saw and not and eagle." I then went on to explain to him that the bussard was nick named the "Telegraph Pole Eagle" where I came from because of so many holiday makers making that mistake. When asked where they saw it, for most it would be on the top of telephone pole. This guy then 'phoned his friend who thought he was an authority on birds and told him to get to the bar and hear what I had to say. There was quite a laugh in the bar that evening because they had told so many people about the trip and having filmed an eagle.

However, "What Goes Round Comes Round" as the saying goes and the last laugh was to be on me that night. I was drinking "Rusty Nails", half whisky and half Drambuie. None of them in the bar had heard of them including the publican who asked what they were like. I suggested he should try one but he would only do so if I tried a "Jackson Bridge Special". We both agreed but I had no idea what I was letting myself in for. He drunk his "Rusty Nail" and enjoyed it. When it came to my turn he took a half pint size glass and put something from each optic into it along with a bottle of Babysham. I thought to myself I can cope with that but then he broke a hen's egg into the glass and handed it to me. I asked for a fork or a spoon to whisk it up but that was not allowed. I had to drink it as it was. Only one thing for it was to down it in one but no the egg remained on its own in the bottom of the glass. I was not into eating raw eggs but I did manage to swallow it without it breaking.

For her next job Fiona worked at Mansfield Knitwear designing men's jumpers and between 1990 and 1995 was Senior Menswear Designer for Courtaulds who was a major supplier to Marks and Spencer. During this time she was elected as a member of the Design Committee travelling to New York, Italy, Germany and France.

Tired of driving up and down the motorway to London to meet buyers she opted for a year at De Montfort University to take a Post Graduate Certificate in

Education where she passed with Distinction in Art and Design. The following three years she taught Art and Design at Chellaston Technical College. By this time she had bought her own house in Nottingham and met her husband Tim Dyke from Chorley who was studying for a degree in surveying. They jointly bought a house at Kinoulten before getting married at Croick Church on 1st August, 1998 and in April the following year our first Grandchild, Ishbel Diamond Dyke was born. Whilst Ishbel was still a little baby they bought a house in Inverness and moved north.

Tim had no difficulty in getting work in Inverness and first worked on the East Gate Centre before moving on to other contractors connected mainly with road construction. He has since set up his own company and works successfully as a freelance surveyor. Fiona took a part time job as an art teacher at the Moray Firth Middle School near Ardersier but decided to give that up to spend more time at home to develop her flare for painting and to do a bit of tutoring. She exhibits under the name Fiona Matheson at many of the Art Shows in the Highlands and in 2010 won an award as "Best Visual Artist". Her work can be viewed on her Website, www.fionamatheson.com.

On 7th August, 2000 their second daughter Rosanna was born and six years later on 6th March our first Grandson, Gideon Stanley Dyke was born. Both Ishbel and Roseanna got a place at Crown School and Gideon followed them this year. I am pleased to say that all three of them are doing well with their education and taking part in many other school activities. Rosanna represents the school at cross country running and at Gymnastics travelling to Aberdeen and Perth winning trophies in individual and team competions. Both girls represented Crown School at the Highland Council Musical Festival at Edin Court Theatre. They are also members of the Inverness Ice Skating Club winning medals locally and nationally. Gideon, only five years old has not been shy to take to the stage at the school nativity play and is coming on with his swimming lessons and his football training. At home when it comes to play he has a fantastic imagination, an eye for detail and has no problem reading instructions when it comes to creating models of one thing or another. To know that Ishbel started secondary school this autumn makes me think, "Is she really that age already." Let's hope all the grand children continue to do well.

CHAPTER 64

TO ROUND OFF THIS STORY

It is a common saying that "age does not come alone" and it is no exception in my own case now that I have crept up to my seventy sixth birthday. Crept is the wrong word to describe it because the years have flown past. Every day seems to go faster than the one before. In my childhood and younger years when I heard my parents and older people talking about this very same thing I could never understand what they meant. There was I and others of my age longing for the weekend or other special times like the school holidays to arrive. Thankfully I am in remarkably good health and have fared well in that respect without too many days off work or visits to a hospital. My back injury during my time in the Police gives me constant pain but I have learned to live with that and I'm lucky to be able to pursue the things I like doing best, but slower and in a less fit fashion of the past.

My cross country performance today comes with a warning to watch my step, more stumbles and falls. Ditches I would once have skipped across are that half a yard or more wider and instead of landing firmly on the opposite bank I am more often or not over the wellies in the water. Fairly recently I went to cross a rather boggy type ditch to collect a deer that I had shot and not only did I get wet feet but I could not help myself from sitting down in the quagmire. With my knees up to my chin and my rear end well and truely bogged down I had no option but to roll over on to my side and crawl out. Most of my tweed jacket including the sleeves up to the armpits took on a blood coloured look from the rusty coloured water. When I took it to the dry cleaners the lady said, "Sorry we cannot accept blood stained clothing." After explaining my misfortune she took it in and what a wonderful job they made of it.

To put one hand on top of a fence post and jump over or at least climb up and spring off the top wire are also just memories. The knee joints are no longer supple and unable to withstand such thumps anymore and how good it would be if it was feasibly possible to fit grease nipples but not just to the knees. Fortunately on the odd foray I go out on today, friends like Jim Gilmore and Garry McLennan are patient and understanding, hold down the wires, slow the pace down or position me where I do not have much walking and in a discreet way looking after the "Old Git" as Martin always called me.

Kenny Campbell the "Strongman" from Bonar who carried out an endless number of charity events to raise money for cancer research and who will be remembered by people up and down the country for carrying all sorts of heavy objects including an organ to the top of Ben Nevis has helped me over the last year or so with heavy work I did for Tim and Fiona at their new house in Inverness and also for Cartriona and Allan's one at Cawder, not to mention the ones here at home. There are not many tasks that Kenny hasn't done. He can turn his hand to anything and is always willing to help. With the endless list of stories he has told me if ever I was to write another book it would be about him. Only this weekend to raise money for cancer charities sponsored by www.iconic-balance.com he single handedly carried and manhandled a boat to the summit of the Ben Nevis. Because of the weather and his age he said it was one of the hardest challenges he had undertaken and was sure he would not have made the last few hundred metres if it was not for the wrist band he was wearing. The following weekend he completed his fiftieth trip to the summit to take the boat home again to avoid leaving litter on the ben.

Only this week I was up on a set of step ladders taking boards down from the rafters in my garage when I had a nasty fall banging my head on the concrete floor leaving me unconscious for about half an hour. I still cannot remember the fall but between Marjory and my self we have worked out that after getting up off the floor I put my glasses into my jacket pocket and with the aid of a sweeping brush walked into the house where I took off my wellies and put on my slippers. Marjory saw me loiter about in the kitchen and in the hallway outside the dining room door at the same time watching her on the computer. She thought I wanted on to it but never said a word to her.

The first I remember about all of this was coming too and sitting in my favourite chair in the sitting room and finding blood on the back of my head. At that point I called to Marjory, "I think I've had an accident." When she came through I could not tell her what had happened or what I had been doing previously so I asked her to go out to the garage to have a look. When she told me that the steps were on the floor and broken in two alongside pieces of timber I remembered what they were for but it did not jog my memory regarding the accident itself. There was one long length of boarding still to come down so I assume I was tugging at it when I over balanced. Plenty of friends and family have jokingly suggested to Marjory that she pushed me. We laugh about this and also the fact that I would not part with the sweeping brush when Marjory said she would take it and get a walking stick for me instead. Robert my builder friend called to ask if I needed an estimate to repair the concrete floor and Hamish when he came home from offshore said, "I saw the ambulance but I just thought you were being taken off to an Old Folks Home."

When the ambulance arrived from Lairg to take me to Raigmore Hospital I was still in a bit of shock and was still not keen to hand over the brush. The CT Scan showed that I had no fractures only some bruising to the brain and as you can guess some wise cracks followed that as well. For now I have to put up with dizziness and some other after effects which I regard as a nuisance and not letting me get on with jobs in hand but people keep telling me to count my lucky stars that the fall did not have more serious consequences.

I was fortunate to have enjoyed a very happy childhood. We had a loving, caring and hard working Mam and many a son did not get on working for their Dad as I did. Married for fifty years speaks for itself. Two daughters, their husbands and grand children have brought us nothing but joy and contentment. My time in the Royal Air Force was a bit of an adventure and although at the bottom end of the Police Profession I had no wish for it to be any different. Back to country pursuits put the icing on the cake so to speak. If I had to single out any period in the twenty six years in the force it would by far be my time at Fettercairn. Yes I've had a charmed life, luck has been on my side in many ways, met so many good people, always being able to do the things I wanted to do and never without a shilling in my pocket. Where I go from here is anyone's guess.

Annex 1

Picture of the old grate at Wester Gruinards

Wester Gruinards with Sgodachail burn and Fanks in background

Aftermath of a frozen Carron at the boat pool

Sgodachail Burn where I learned to fish with bent pin and worm

The rock we played on

A relic

The Whales Eye with Cottage in the Background.

Otter damage

The view from my armchair at Dalriada

New Zealand relatives

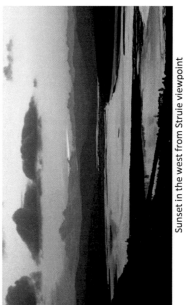

Sunset in the west from Struie viewpoint

Early morning sunrise from Dalriada

Ladies in Portugal

On holiday at Kilarney

The electrician harrowing the oat seed

The gentlemen in Portugal

The end result (Lower Hilton)

Hand wringer at the ready

Robert getting the demolition started.

Ruie an Taoir before we started

Ruie an Taoir – The finished article

Irvine, Sarah, Andy and Helen Checking Out the Buffet

Charlie Povey, Geordie Bruce, Robert and the Cashier with hands in her pockets

Before the Guests Arrived For the Party

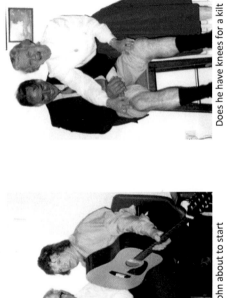

Willie and John about to start

Does he have knees for a kilt

Margaret Ross, Elsie, Kate Matheson, George, Jack Campbell , Brenda, Willie, Alistair McRae

A morning at the rabbits

A present from Fiona

A Minnes shoot

Jake and Twiggy after a training session

Jean Matterson and her 30 pounder

The Willie Gun and my fly box

Jake, Twiggy, Cora and the six beauties from the Washerwoman

Serious business for John Mortimer (Cumbernauld)

Weather conditions did not deter George Campbell   Jim and Tim after landing a nice one from Moral

Ronnie and Margaret at Martha's Vineyard   A day out with Stephen

Pat, Corrie and Patch waiting their turn

Will, Declan and Ripples

Dash the wonder dog

Home from a den and five more the following night

Ronnie at the centre of it

Doctor Graham Stuart and Marjory getting stuck in

Counting grouse with Ian and Sandy Fraser

Kenneth, Ian, Bob and Eric

Doreen Bruce and Eppie enjoying a dog trial

Happier times

Hill of Minnes

Catriona and Alan and extended family

Bride and bridesmaid

Catriona and Alan after the church blessing

Fiona and Tim

Speech time

Alan and Catriona

Wedding Guests – Colin, Lorraine, Irvine, Sarah, Andy and Helen

Easter egg time at Dalriada

Ishbel, Rosanna, Holly, Hannah and Gideon (Hannah's 11th birthday)

At the top of Ben Nevis

Kenny on his way up the Ben